FROM ORGANISATION TO DECORATION

From Organisation to Decoration: An Interiors Reader is a reader for students, scholars and practitioners interested in the theories, processes and principles of the aspects of the theory and practice of interior architecture, interior design and interior decoration.

The book is divided into three parts, which reflects the focus of the different strands. It aims to contextualise, explore and clarify past and present debates in all three areas of the field of interiors. Each section is concerned with the processes, histories and ideas that shape the interior and includes discussions about development, identity, organisation, conservation, material and surface concerns and attitudes towards the host building. A broad range of writings are included – cultural theory, historical essays, scholarly papers, commissioned texts, extracts from books, interview transcripts, and magazine and newspaper articles. A case study and an annotated guide to further reading concludes each section, thus offering a succinct overview of the theories and ideas underpinning the interior for the beginner, as well as providing stimulation for students and practitioners in the field.

Graeme Brooker is a Principal Lecturer in Interior Architecture at the University of Brighton, UK. He is the co-founder of Interior Educators (IE). Between 1997 and 2004 he taught Interior Architecture at Cardiff before moving to Manchester where, between 2004 and 2010, he was the Programme Leader of both the BA and MA Interior programmes.

Sally Stone is the Director of the college of Continuity in Architecture, a postgraduate studio for teaching and research at the Manchester School of Architecture, where she is also the leader of the MA Architecture and Heritage course. Sally lectured in Cardiff before moving to Manchester. She still practices as an Interior Designer with Francis Roberts Architects.

From Organisation to Decoration

An Interiors Reader

Edited by Graeme Brooker and Sally Stone

Routledge
Taylor & Francis Group

LONDON AND NEW YORK

First edition published 2013
by Routledge
2 Park Square, Milton Park, Abingdon, Oxon OX14 4RN

Simultaneously published in the USA and Canada
by Routledge
711 Third Avenue, New York, NY 10017

Routledge is an imprint of the Taylor & Francis Group, an informa business

British Library Cataloguing in Publication Data
A catalogue record for this book is available from the British Library

Library of Congress Cataloging in Publication Data
From organisation to decoration : an interior design reader /
Edited by Graeme Brooker and Sally Stone. – First edition.
    pages cm
Includes bibliographical references and index.
1. Interior decoration.   2. Interior architecture.   I. Brooker, Graeme, editor of compilation.
II. Stone, Sally, editor of compilation.
NK2110.F76 2012
729–dc23

2011051035

ISBN: 978-0-415-43619-9 (hbk)
ISBN: 978-0-415-43620-5 (pbk)

Typeset in Frutiger
by RefineCatch Limited, Bungay, Suffolk

MIX
Paper from
responsible sources
FSC® C004839
www.fsc.org

Printed and bound in Great Britain by
TJ International Ltd, Padstow, Cornwall

Contents

List of Sources and Acknowledgements

The authors and publishers gratefully acknowledge the following for permission to reproduce material in the book. Every effort has been made to contact and acknowledge copyright owners. The publishers would be grateful to hear from any copyright holder who is not acknowledged here and will undertake to rectify any errors or omissions in future printings or editions of the book.

Penny Sparke. (2004) 'The Domestic Interior and the Construction of Self: The New York Homes of Elsie De Wolfe' in S. McKellar and P. Sparke (eds.) *Interior Design and Identity*, Manchester University Press, pp. 72–91. Published with permission of the author.

Viviana Narotzky. (2006) 'Dream Homes and DIY: TV, New Media and the Domestic Makeover' in J. Aynsley and C. Grant (eds.) *Imagined Interiors: Representing the Domestic Interior Since the Renaissance,* V & A Publishing, pp. 258–267. Published with permission from ©The Board of Trustees of the Victoria and Albert Museum, 2010.

Joel Sanders. (2002) *Curtain Wars – Architects, Decorators and the Twentieth Century Domestic Interior,* Harvard Design Magazine Winter/Spring 2002. Published with permission of the author.

Manolo De Giurgiu and Marco Romanelli. (1994) 'Figures of Living' from Rassegna 58, *Statement of Interior: Italian Apartments 1947–1993,* pp. 4–7.

Shigeru Uchida. (1994) 'The Bounds of Privacy: Boundary and Domain in Japanese Culture', edited from a lecture delivered at the 11 November 1994 symposium *3rd Yokohama Big Design.* Published with permission of Shigeru Uchida and Uchida Design Inc.

Jean Baudrillard. (2005) 'The System of Objects', translated by J. Benedict in *Volume 3: Radical Thinkers*, London: Verso, pp. 15–28, and pp. 30–47. Published with permission of Verso.

George Ranalli. (1999) *Carlo Scarpa Architect: Intervening with History,* The Monacelli Press, pp. 39–43. Published with permission of author.

Vittorio Gregotti. (1983) *The Exercise of Detailing,* Casabella, no. 492, June 1983, p.11. Published with permission of Casabella and the author.

Mario Praz. (2008) 'Sir John Soane' from *An Illustrated History of Interior Decoration* by Mario Praz and translated by William Weaver. © 1964 Longanesi & C., Milan. English translation reprinted by kind permission of Thames & Hudson Ltd., London.

Edith Wharton and Ogden Codman. (1898) 'The Historical Tradition' in B.T. Batsford *The Decoration of Houses,* pp. 1-16.

Witold Rybczynski. (1987) *Home: A Short History of an Idea*, London: Penguin, pp. 217-232. Published with permission of Penguin.

Anne Massey. (1990) 'The Emergence of Interior Decoration as a Profession' from "Interior Design Since 1900" by Anne Massey. © 1990, 2001 and 2008 Thames & Hudson Ltd, London. Reproduced by kind permission of Thames & Hudson.

Jean Baudrillard. (2005) 'The System of Objects', translated by J. Benedict in *Volume 3: Radical Thinkers*, London: Verso, pp. 30–47. Published with permission of Verso.

Charles Rice. (2004) 'Rethinking Histories of the Interior' in *Journal of Architecture*, 9:3, Autumn 2004, London: Taylor and Francis. Published with permission of Taylor and Francis.

Hugh Casson. (1968) *Inscape: The Design of Interiors*, London: Architectural Press. Published with permission of the publisher and *The Architectural Review* .

Fred Scott. (1991) 'Towards a New Agenda' in *The Inside Edge,* The Designers Journal, September 1991. Published with permission of the author.

Patrick Hannay and Oliver Lewis. (1991) 'Towards a New Equilibrium' in *The Inside Edge,* The Designers Journal, September 1991. Published with permission of the author.

Drew Plunkett. (1991) 'Towards a New Aesthetic' in *The Inside Edge,* The Designers Journal, September 1991. © Drew Plunkett . Published with permission of the author.

Robert Venturi. (1988) Extract from *Complexity and Contradiction in Architecture,* New York: Museum of Modern Art. Published with permission of the MoMA.

Robin Evans. (1997) 'Figures, Doors, Passages' from *Translations from Drawing to Building and Other Essays,* AA Documents 2, London: AA Publications. Published with permission of AA Publications.

Jun'ichirō Tanizaki. (1977) Extract from *In Praise of Shadows,* New Haven: Leetes Island Books.

Graeme Brooker and Sally Stone. (2008) 'Off-The-Peg: The Bespoke Interiors of Ben Kelly' in *Interior Atmospheres,* Architectural Design, May/June 2008. Published with permission of the authors.

Frank Duffy. (1997) Extract from *The New Office,* London: Conran Octopus Ltd. 'The New Office' text copyright © Francis Duffy 1997. Published with permission by Conran Octopus Ltd.

Andrea Branzi. (2002) *Exhibition Design as Metaphor of a New Modernity* from Lotus International 115, Exhibitions, 2002/4, pp. 99–101. Published with permission of Lotus International.

Siegfried Kracauer. (1995) 'The Hotel Lobby' translated by Thomas Y. Levin in *The Mass Ornament: Weimar* Essays, Harvard University Press.

Johan Van De Beek. (1988) 'Pattern of Town Houses' in Max Risselda (ed.) *Raumplan Versus Plan Libre, Adolf Loos and Le Corbusier 1919–1930,* Rizzoli International.

Sébastien Marot. (2003) 'Memory' from *Sub-Urbanism and the Art of Memory,* London: AA Publications, pp. 6–16. Published with permission of AA Publications.

Denise Scott Brown. (2010) *Interior Space,* AA Files 56, London: AA Publications, pp. 64–73. Published with permission of AA Publications.

Robert Irwin. (1985) Extract from *Being and Circumstance: Notes Toward a Conditional Art,* Lapis Press, pp. 9–29. Published with permission of the author.

Beatriz Colomina. (1994) *Privacy and Publicity: Modern Architecture As Mass Media,* TEXT only from pages 233–281, © 1994 Massachusetts Institute of Technology, by permission of The MIT Press.

Dora Crouch. (1985) 'Early Christian Architecture Adaptive Re-use' in *History of Architecture: Stonehenge to Skyscrapers,* McGraw-Hill, pp. 114–124. Published with permission of the author.

Crimson. (2002) 'Re-Arch' Extract from *1994–2002 Crimson Architectural Historians, Too Blessed to be Depressed,* 010 Publishers, pp. 65–76. Published with permission of 010 Publishers.

Rodolfo Machado**.** 'Old Buildings as Palimpsest: Towards a Theory of Remodelling' in *Progressive Architecture,* 11: 76, pp. 46–49. Published with permission of Architect/Hanley Wood LLC.

Ignasi de Sola-Morales Rubió. (1985) From Contrast to Analogy: Developments in the Concept of Architectural Intervention from Lotus International 46, Interpretation of the past, 1985/2, pp. 37–45. Published with permission of Lotus International.

Graeme Brooker and Sally Stone. (2004) Extract from *Rereadings: Interior Architecture and the Design Principles of Remodelling Existing Buildings,* RIBA Enterprises. Published with permission of the authors.

Philippe Robert. (1989) 'Adaptations: Architecture as a Palimpsest' extract from *Adaptations: New Uses for Old Buildings,* Princeton Architectural Press, pp. 6–11.

Fred Scott. (2008) *On Altering Architecture,* London: Routledge, pp. 167–183. Published with permission of Routledge .

John Ruskin. (1880) *The Seven Lamps of Architecture,* Dover, 1989, pp. 353–360. Published with permission of Dover Publications Inc.

The SPAB Manifesto,www.spab.org.uk. Public Domain, courtesy of The Society for the Protection of Ancient Buildings.

The Athens Charter for the Restoration of Historic Monuments, public domain, www.icomos.org/en/component/content/article/179-articles-en-francais/ressources/charters-and-standards/167-the-athens-charter-for-the-restoration-of-historicmonuments

The Venice Charter: International Charter for the Conservation andRestoration of Monuments and Sites, public domain, www.icomos.org/en/component/content/article/179-articles-en-francais/ressources/charters-and-standards/157-the-venice-charter

Alberto Grimoldi. (1985) *Architecture as Reparation Notes on Restoration in Architecture* from Lotus International 46, Interpretation of the past, 1985/2, pp.116-122. Published with permission of Lotus International.

James Strike. (1994) Extract from *Architecture in Conservation: Managing Development at Historic Sites,* London: Routledge, pp. 7–18.

Introduction

The interior is a subject that is fascinating. It has connotations of depth, profundity and strength while, conversely, it also suggests an ephemeral and fleeting or imprecise position. The word itself has actually gone through several changes in meaning, which may go some way towards an understanding of the disparity in its perception and also add to its somewhat oblique qualities. It came into use in the fifteenth century and meant the basic division between inside and outside and was also used to describe spiritual and inner nature of the soul. By the early eighteenth century, it had also come to mean the inner character of an individual and the non-coastal territory belonging to a country. It was only at the beginning of the nineteenth century that interior came to designate the inside of a building. The concept of interior decoration as a creative entity is essentially a product of the twentieth century; before this time, the design of the interior was an outcome of a close collaboration between the architect and craftsmen. The upholsterer was responsible for the soft furnishings, and the architect for the hard finishes. The profession is equally young; it emerged at the end of the nineteenth century to become a respectable occupation, and it wasn't until the 1970s that it required an associated university based education. In the twenty-first century interiors is a flourishing and prosperous field, with a multitude of designers, educators and students, happy to refer to themselves as 'interiorists'.

The design and study of the interior is a practice that has always had close associations with surface pattern and texture, soft furnishings and the adornment of space. The Modernist search for transparency and the direct connection between the inside and outside, led to the diminished role of the interior designer. It was a movement that eschewed ornamentation and applied embellishment, and it is possibly because of this that the subject has wrestled with the image of an ephemeral, non-consequential subject.

The connection between interior design and gender is one that is much debated. Industrialisation and the need of the man to leave the home to go to work each day, meant that the domestic interior became the preserve of the woman, and thus the first professional interior designers were female. The tendency for the subject to sometimes be somewhat theatrical, combined with possibilities of the non-threatening relationship that could develop between the residents of the house and the decorator, meant that it was also a viable occupation for gay men. Perhaps in the Twenty-First century it is something that will no longer be seen as having any importance, and designers will be valued only for their ability.

The complicated question of the difference between interior architecture, interior design and interior decoration is one that is always open to interpretation. Interior design is a term that has traditionally been used to describe all types of interior projects. This would have included everything from decoration to remodelling; however, in view of the fact that building reuse has become such a highly regarded practice it has clearly become necessary to divide the main subject and define more clearly the individual specialisms. This would be a good point to clarify the exact nature of each area; the exact disciplines inevitably overlap, but by and large the differences seem to concern the magnitude of change to the occupied space.

Interior decoration is the art of decorating interior spaces or rooms to impart a particular character and to function well with the existing architecture. Interior decoration is concerned with such issues as surface pattern, ornament, furniture, soft furnishings, lighting and materials. It generally deals only with minor structural changes to the existing building. Typical examples of this practice are the design of domestic, hotel and restaurant interiors

Interior design is an interdisciplinary practice that is concerned with the creation of a range of interior environments that articulate identity and atmosphere, through the manipulation of spatial volume, placement of specific elements and furniture and treatment of surfaces. It generally describes projects that

Figure 1 Sigurd Lewerentz, Chapel of Resurrection, Woodland Cemetery, Stockholm, Sweden. This very atmospheric and axial interior is lit by a single large window that throws natural light over the catafalque. [Credit: ©Sally Stone]

require little or no structural changes to the existing building. The original space is very much retained in its original state and the new interior inserted within it. It often has an ephemeral quality and typically would encompass such projects as retail, exhibition and domestic interiors.

Interior architecture is concerned with the remodelling of existing buildings and attitudes towards existing spaces and structures, reuse and organisational principles. It bridges the practices of interior design and architecture, often dealing with complex structural, environmental and servicing problems. This practice encompasses a huge range of project types from museums, galleries and other public buildings, through office and other commercial buildings to domestic developments.

Although the three professions can all be classified differently, the element that unites them is the fact they are all working within a given context; the design of all interiors is ultimately site-specific. It is this factor that makes the design of every interior so individual, even the design of a branded retail interior is dependent upon the available space that it has to occupy. Typically, when working with an existing space and building, or the proposal for a project drawn upon the screen or page, the architect, designer or decorator will use the analysis and understanding of the qualities of that container to provide the impetus for change. This process of investigation and examination is a matter of acceptance of what is already on or around the site, and the willingness to accentuate these found elements or narratives. This method of comprehension encourages a responsiveness and a sensibility that is described by Rodolfo Machado in his essay "Old Buildings as Palimpsest":

> . . . in remodelling, the past takes on a value far different from that in the usual design process, where form is generated "from scratch."[1]

Interiors is a field that is often deemed as being intellectually undernourished, a factor that has led to a paucity of publications that underpin this area of study and practice. The teaching and understanding of interiors has always had to rely on architectural and art theory, therefore using ideas that never really quite fit. This has created a lack of identity or distinction from architecture, and a lack of a particular relevant body of knowledge that fits the subject matter. Books about interior decoration generally fall into two categories: coffee table picture books that have little room for theoretical argument or design discussion and self-help manuals that give instruction about the practical aspects of domestic decoration. But recently, the study of interiors is beginning to be seen as a serious academic subject, an area of interest in its own right rather than an adjunct of architecture or an expansion of surface decoration. To study the nature of the interior of a building is to study the culture of the people who occupy those inside spaces. The manner in which we occupy space defines who we are, how we act, how we interact and how we live. The room provides the stage for nearly all of human interaction, as Shakespeare put it: "All the world's a stage, And all the men and women merely players; They have their exits and their entrances . . ."[2]

The redesign and reuse of an existing building is a sustainable approach to creating the built environment. The construction of new buildings uses large amounts of energy; the procurement and manufacture of materials both uses energy and imbues these new elements with embodied energy. The reuse of an existing building to accommodate new use is a very sustainable approach to creating new space, by adapting the existing building stock, the amount of natural resources required to construct a building is greatly reduced. The structure is already in place and quite often many of the services may already be on the site. Therefore the embodied energy in these elements can be saved through upgrade and reuse.

This book is designed to serve as a reader for students, scholars, and practitioners who have an interest in interior design, interior architecture and interior decoration. Interiors is a subject that encompasses the analysis and understanding of existing or yet to be built buildings, the nature and qualities of interior space, and an intimate examination of the characteristics of the decoration. This reader aims to contextualise, explore and clarify past and present debates in all three areas of the field of interiors. The reader consists of a mixture of important popular and rare existing essays and it aims to contextualise current debates regarding interior design, interior architecture and interior decoration. It endeavours to introduce readers to a number of seminal, yet relatively unknown works, placing them alongside writings and interviews from more prominent sources and a series of texts written by prominent designers and theorists working with existing buildings. The book aims to make clear ideas already prominent in the field of Interiors and clarify the interdisciplinary aspects of this specific area of design practice and theory.

The book is divided into three parts, reflecting the three strands of interior theory and practice. Each chapter is then further divided to three separate sections, each of which examines a different aspect of the individual subject.

Figure 2 Carlo Scarpa, Querini Stampalia Foundation, Venice, Italy. The foyer area acts as a transitional point between the exterior and the interior. The canal water is allowed to rise into the building thus providing the users with a direct connect with the city. [Credit: ©Sally Stone]

Part 1, Interior Decoration, contextualises the role of decoration and ornament, furniture and materials. Identity looks at both the personality of the decorator and how nationality can influence the design of the room. Process examines the actual practice of the decorator and History analyses the evolution of the subject.

Part 2, Interior Design, examines the nature and philosophy of the subject. Identity investigates the character of the subject, Organisation looks at the manner in which designers approach the creation of interior space and Function analyses particular programmatic requirements of interior design.

Part 3, Interior Architecture, explores the robust reuse of existing buildings and the processes and principles of interior architecture, adaptation and the appropriation and remodelling of a building. Context examines the manner in which the situation or surroundings can influence the remodelling of the individual structure, Process looks at the approach that the interior architect will take and Conservation analyses the various issues involved with the preservation of a building.

Sally Stone and Graeme Brooker

References

1. Machado, Rodolfo. 'Old Buildings as Palimpsest'. Progressive Architecture, 1976.
2. Shakespeare, William. As You Like it.

PART 1

INTERIOR DECORATION

Introduction

The twenty-first century has brought a renewed interest in ornamentation. Decoration, which in the modernist world of pure white walls was for so long frowned upon, is enjoying a renaissance. Ornament was seen as unnecessary; it was perceived as obstructing the appreciation of the pure form, it contaminated the cleanliness of the pristine lines; it was a crime.

Texture or even perceived texture had become the prevalent technique, from beautifully woven Scandinavian rugs, to woefully rag-rolled walls. As long as there was no discernible pattern, then the unadulterated emptiness of the spaces could be truly understood. Internal decoration and in particular wallpaper had become such a symbol of derision, that by the mid-1990s, the patterns had become so uninteresting, so boring and so innocuous that Laurence Llewelyn-Bowen described the manufacturers as ". . . having delusions of blandeur". Wallpaper itself was considered to be such a contentious and contemptuous material that again, by the mid-1990s, it became the ironic title of a fashion and design magazine. Adolf Loos had a lot to answer for!

Actual decoration in the purest sense was something that had almost disappeared by the end of the twentieth century. Texture and artefacts ornamented the domestic space. But at the beginning of the twenty-first century, architects and designers have rediscovered the joy of pattern, of motifs, of ornamentation. This revival of internal decoration seems to have been a natural progression, from the small point of focus within the room; a picture or soft furnishings perhaps. This has led to larger and larger decorated areas and ultimately to the patterning of whole walls and even buildings. Decoration has once again become a respectable and well-used language of international architecture and design. New methods of digital manufacturing have exposed economically viable possibilities. Techniques, which at the end of the twentieth-century were both time-consuming and costly, are now easily accessible.

Interior decoration originally exclusively referred to a domestic space, and popular conception of the profession is that it is still specifically concerned with colour and fabric within the home, but the subject is much larger. Public spaces including churches, hospitals, libraries, hotels, tourist centres and restaurants all need the services of the interior decorator. It is his or her responsibility to generate a particular character for the spaces. The decorator also has to work with other industries including plumbers, painters, upholsterers, electricians and furniture suppliers. So successful interior decoration is created out of collaboration, sensitivity and an understanding of history, culture, technology and materials, all combined with a knowledge of the needs of the users.

This part of the book is divided into three sections and each will focus on a different aspect of the discipline of decoration. The **identity** of interior decoration is one which is also open to interpretation. Whether it is the subject itself, the profession or the individual, the subject is always fighting social preconceptions of the status of the subject. The study of interior decoration is the study of a culture. The manner in which we occupy interior space has a direct link to the identity of a society. Whether it is the mediaeval great communal hall or the present day huge number of single occupant dwellings, the interior provides a valuable insight into the cultural conditions and practices. Walter Benjamin famously said, "To live is to leave traces" and this evidence portrays the identity of the society that left them. The essays in this section discuss the national, individual and cultural personality of interior decoration.

Interior decoration is the practice of providing a distinct layer to the inside of a building. It is generally a fairly non-structural subject and is concerned with decoration, ornament, artefacts, soft and hard furnishings, colour, texture, textiles, heating, plumbing. This is a complex **process** that involves a great deal of interaction and knowledge on the part of decorator. This selection of essays concentrates upon the manner in which the designer will develop an approach to the design problem.

The **history** of interior decoration is a subject that is always open to interpretation. Although buildings and monuments can often stand the test of time, the ephemeral quality that the interior possesses means that it is often lost or altered. It is not often that an interior will survive intact. Changes in the manner in which we live will inevitably mean that the interior of the building is altered to accommodate these advances. For example, mediaeval houses have been divided to provide privacy, or Victorian homes are supplied with updated technology to serve today's occupants. This is combined with the difficulty that the contemporary viewer has of placing himself or herself in the position of the original occupant. Because, of course, our perception of the past is determined by our present. That is, the manner in which the past is perceived is not solely dependent upon the available information about the past, but it is also influenced by the interpretation of that information by the contemporary individual or society. Historians generally have to rely upon second-hand information, such as paintings, etchings and written descriptions. The artist or writer, who had his or her own agenda when creating the piece, has already subjected these to interpretation. The three essays and the building study show how the historic interior can be analysed and interpreted.

Interior decoration has entered an age where it is much more accepted and therefore respected as a profession. Decoration has a distinct history and theory as this small selection of texts proves.

Sally Stone

Eileen Gray (1878–1976)

Eileen Gray's strength and personality allowed her to work in the design profession at a time when few women were permitted to achieve design independence. She started her career as a lacquer-worker, studying under the Japanese master Seizo Sugawara, making screens, decorative panels, bookcases and beds. The modernist movement proved to be an inspiration and she designed houses and furniture in the clean spare style that was so characteristic of this era. The E1027 house or "Maison en Bord de Mer" is probably the most well known. This was a "total work of art" and contained such famous pieces of furniture as the E1027 circular glass occasional table. In later life she worked extensively with le Corbusier, although much of her designs are still uncredited.

SECTION 1.1
IDENTITY AND LANGUAGE

Introduction

Interior decoration is a discipline with a mixed history; it is often regarded as silly and inconsequential and is treated with prejudice and distain. It is inevitably an ephemeral subject; because it is so easy to update and is therefore closely connected with fashion and fads. The identity and status of the interior decorator has always been open to ridicule and, for many years, interior decoration was seen as the preserve of women and gay men. Indeed, the decorator when featured in the media is normally portrayed as a flamboyant, colourfully dressed effette man.

The profession is relatively young; historically the upholsterer would take charge of the soft furnishings, while the architect would supervise the decoration of the walls and so some sort of agreement was contrived between them. It wasn't until the late nineteenth century that the professional interior designer emerged from this confusion. It was, as Penny Sparke discusses, a respectable occupation for women, as the domestic interior was seen as their domain. This has possibly contributed to the notion that the subject lacks substance. And so the identity of the subject, the profession and the individual designers is open to speculation. Two of the essays in this section discuss the causes of this cultural perception. Penny Sparke outlines the beginnings of the profession, while Joel Sanders deliberates upon the present-day status of the decorator.

The national identity of both the users and the decorators also contributes to the manner in which interior space is occupied. Two of the essays discuss the particular attitude of their own country towards the interior. Manolo De Giorgi and Marco Romanelli examine the nature of the Italian apartment while Shigeru Uchida considers the manner in which Japanese interior space is delineated or bounded.

At the end of the twentieth century, the status of the interior decorator began to change. TV make-over shows, combined with greater income and more leisure time, have created a great interest in the subject. Viviana Narotzky examines this phenomenon.

Successful interior decoration is created out of collaboration, sensitivity and an understanding of history, culture, technology and materials, combined with a knowledge of the needs of those who will occupy the space. The decorator needs to be sufficiently strong to blend these factors in a convincing and erudite manner; flamboyance is something else.

The practice of the man leaving the house during the day to go to work meant that the home became a female domain; this was something that really began at the end of the eighteenth century. This separation of living and working for the man ensured that the woman spent the majority of her time within the domestic environment, and thus it became a space over which she had control; the home became a feminine space. A special relationship developed between the woman and the private interior; it had in effect become an extension of her personality. The manner in which it was decorated and the taste that was displayed became the material manifestation of the woman's personal identity, and so by the end of the nineteenth century, interior decoration emerged as one of the few acceptable occupations, along with teaching and nursing, that a woman could follow.

Penny Sparke discusses this phenomenon, with particular emphasis upon the work of Elsie de Wolfe, who emerged as one of the first female professional interior decorators. De Wolfe, who abandoned a career on the stage to become a designer, was an independent, unmarried North American, all of which contributed to the formation of her own approach, but also created a style that epitomised this particular time and place. This was a country in which social aspirations, femininity, and an ambivalence towards sexuality and about nationality allowed her to create interiors that provided a break with the past and a shift towards a specifically American view of the future.

De Wolfe also regarded herself as an educator, and Sparke describes how the houses that she designed were regarded as inspirational models for other women. De Wolfe felt the need to escape the claustrophobic clutter of the Victorian home and look forward to a light and clean future. She had an obsession with the most modern technology, from electric lighting to steam heating, and also began to bring elements of the garden into the interior; a thoroughly modern woman.

Penny Sparke is an eminent academic who has written extensively about the twentieth century interior. In this essay, "The Domestic Interior and the Constructs of Self: The New York Homes of Elsie de Wolfe", she discusses a favourite subject with thoroughness and clarity.

Spanish born **Viviana Narotzky** in her essay, "Dream Homes and DIY: TV, New Media and the Domestic Makeover", charts the rise and fall of these types of programmes. She documents how the rise in popularity of DIY, combined with extended leisure time and the increase in "reality" television programmes contributed to the mass appeal of the shows. Narotzky is well placed to tell this story: she qualified as a product designer then obtained a doctorate in History of Design from the Royal College of Art and has written and lectured extensively on design and contemporary material culture, and curated shows on contemporary and twentieth century design. Within this essay, she laments the lack of integrity that was inevitably created within the house; the visual character of the themed spaces was based upon whimsy. Traditionally nature or qualities of the rooms were formed by or related to the function, "What emerges here . . . fragmented spaces separated from their entire domestic system".

TV home makeover shows were extremely popular in the late 1990s and early 2000s. They were based upon the idea that over a weekend, a domestic room could be provided with a new image. It was almost a game-show format, and was portrayed as a relatively easy and fun activity. Competitive decorating: even Mark Twain didn't go that far! The British-made *Changing Rooms* was probably the most popular show of the genre. Although much ridiculed at the time, it tapped into the western psyche; home ownership was at its highest level and the manner in which the house was decorated was an extension of the owner's personality. Thus, interior design and decoration became a mainstream subject, albeit a very narrow version of it.

The programmes made massive stars of the interior decorators who had been recruited to advise the homeowners upon the best approach. Laurence Llewelyn-Bowen emerged as both the most well regarded of the designers, and also as the most ridiculed. His flamboyant style of dress was matched with an equally exuberant personality, but this was underpinned by a genuine passion for and knowledge of the subject.

Joel Sanders is a New York based architect and academic. He published *STUD: Architectures of Masculinity* in 1995, and is committed to exploring how issues of gender and sexuality might impact the discipline of architecture. This essay, "Curtain Wars", which was published in 2002, explores how the rivalries between architects and interior designers stem from entrenched cultural stereotypes about gender and sexuality.

Sanders identifies the contested territory of the treatment of the window as the moment of transition between the architect and the interior decorator. It is at this point that the hard walls of the architecture meet the soft furnishings of the decoration, and it is the curtains that are the element that has divided architects and decorators since the emergence of the profession of interior decorators in the late nineteenth century. He suggests that this deep-rooted rivalry has less to do with the control of the material finish and is more concerned with profound social anxieties about gender and sexuality, particularly the social construct of the heterosexual architect verses the homosexual interior designer.

Sexual orientation is a very important element in the identity of the interior designer. Sanders suggests that many women and gay men are aware of the performative nature of life and thus better positioned to appreciate the innate links between fashion and interior design. Decoration is an ephemeral subject, and therefore more subject to the whims and fancies of fashion than the permanence of architecture could ever be. Crucially, Sanders argues that the low esteem with which the field of interiors is held is a direct consequence of its main protagonists being either female or gay men. Architects have in the past strengthened this view, and thus reinforced their own masculinity, by defending themselves against the unspoken accusation that within every architect is a closet decorator. Sanders celebrates the manner in which decoration is now becoming a more acceptable and respectable activity, and in a move of great sympathy for the architect, he describes how they have become disempowered by the client, consultants and colleagues; all of whom combine to give the impression that the architect is an unaffordable luxury.

As architects begin to embrace the design of the interior and the exterior of the building, where does that leave the decorator? Interestingly, Sanders doesn't take the argument to the conclusion, that given that it has become completely acceptable for the architect to embrace their femininity, it is fine for them to consider the interior decoration as well as the architecture, the ephemeral is as important as the permanent; what is the future for the interior decorator?

Manolo De Giorgi and **Marco Romanelli** in their essay "Figures of Living" present a discussion of the qualities of the post-war Italian apartment, and celebrate the return of the consideration of an interior tradition within the design process. The design of the Italian apartment is a practice with a long and complex history. It is a subject that is steeped in custom and tradition. Modernism, De Giorgi and Romanelli argue, neglected the interior. The architecture of the building was concerned only with the form of the exterior of the building; the interior space was little more than a plan and section problem.

De Giorgi and Romanelli celebrate this move away from the modern movement to a more contextual approach, as epitomised by the work of such designers as Carlo Scarpa and Franco Albini. The design of the apartment is much greater than an adjunct to the exterior; it is a three-dimensional interconnected complex matrix of relationships. It is difficult to successfully design such spaces; the designer needs to be able to work at a variety of scales from 1:200 to 1:1 and to develop an understanding of the quality and nature of materials. They have to be able to communicate with craftsmen, understand the nature of the existing space and also interpret the needs of those who will live in the space.

The authors are designers, writers and journalists; they have written extensively, individually and together, especially for such important publications as *Domus* and *Abitare* and thus are well placed to discuss the position of Italian interior design and decoration. This essay, which was published in 1994, begins with the philosophical musings of the nature of the history of the immediate past, and how does the designer come to any conclusions without the benefit of distance? It is the responsibility of the journalist to arrive at these conclusions and this essay goes some way towards supporting that argument.

Shigeru Uchida was born in Yokohama, Japan in 1943, and is one of the country's leading designers. He established his own practice in 1970 and then Studio 80 with Toru Nishioka in 1981. His products and furnishings all seek to blend and harmonize cultural legacies with design. "I'm interested in something beyond the visible or touchable, that is, the existence within the invisible. Throughout the 20th century, we have placed too much emphasis on the visible, considering that they are only concrete things."

Within this essay, "The Bounds of Privacy: Boundary and Domain in Japanese Culture", he examines the "kekkai constructs" or bounded domains. The piece begins with the assertion that there is a direct link between privacy and the "self", and then says that "self" doesn't exist in Japan, which by association, means that neither does privacy. The Japanese cultural notion of boundary differs greatly from the western idea, as does Japanese spatial awareness. The boundary encloses the order within the interior and separates it from the chaos of the exterior, but it is the nature of the boundary, the very element that provides the division, that confines and limits the physical space where the cultural differences are most apparent.

There are three different classes of kekkai constructs in Japan. The physical kekkai or brute kekkai are things that are not easily moved. They provide a permanent barrier between one side and the other. A perfect example of this is the Great Wall of China. Kekkai devices are temporary or movable elements such as fences or sliding doors. This classification also includes extremely ephemeral barriers such as the straw ropes around a shrine. The third category of kekkai is hardly a barrier at all; they are spaces that do not definitely belong to anywhere. They are intermediate spaces, spaces of transition and marginal zones, all of which are very important in Japanese culture

Shigeru Ushida stresses the importance of cultural memory and a return to the traditional way of thinking. These philosophical musings upon the notion of self, space and boundary provide an insight into this heritage.

Sally Stone

Building Study: Court Essington

The Cotswolds, UK
2006
David Archer Architects

Court Essington is a seven-bedroom arts and crafts property, which sits within two acres of grounds and commands impressive views across the Cotswold countryside. The approach by the architect to the restoration was to retain as many of the original features as possible, thus invoking the character of the original house. This was complemented by a new garden conservatory, around which the activity in the house focused.

The original Edwardian features of the house have been restored to their original condition, an approach that Viollet-le-Duc would have approved of; he advocated a reconstruction to a pristine condition. This of course denies the aging process, but does give a fairly good idea of what the original interior would have been like. This restoration was combined with the need to update all of the technology within the property, so that it was suitable for the twenty-first century occupant.

The architect used the garden room as the starting point for the decorative scheme. This was painted white and is flooded with natural light. The palette of colours gradually intensifies as the spaces move away from this moment of brightness. Rooms on the south side of the property are decorated in a light palette of warm whites, reflecting the sunshine from the south-facing conservatory. But deeper into the plan the palette strengthens, with gold decorative wallpaper along the corridor, ochre yellow in the pantry, card room green in the bathrooms and a polka dot wallpaper in the guest room.

The architect has decorated the house in a style that is totally in keeping with the architecture, but pastiche has not been resorted to; it is unquestionably part of the twenty-first century.

Laurence Llewelyn-Bowen (1965–)

Laurence Llewelyn-Bowen made his name in the 1990s as the flamboyant designer on the TV makeover show, *Changing Rooms*. This was a DIY home improvement show, the object of which was for couples to swap houses with friends or neighbours, with each pair doing up one room in each other's homes. They were always assisted/directed by a designer and Laurence Llewelyn-Bowen emerged as the most charismatic and controversial character on the programme. His somewhat contentious attitude was always underpinned with a sound knowledge and an instinct for good design. He now has his own design company and is a regular broadcaster on more serious design matters.

1

The Domestic Interior and the Construction of Self

The New York Homes of Elsie de Wolfe

Penny Sparke

Source: *Interior Design and Identity.* S. McKellar and P. Sparke. Manchester University Press, 2004, Ch. 4, pp. 72–91

So it is, looking backward, that I see my own career in the terms of the houses I have made for myself. They were the cradle in which my desire for beauty was nurtured. They were the laboratory in which its principles were given full and free expression.

(Elsie de Wolfe, *After All*[1])

The meaning of the domestic interior is not fixed. Rather history has pulled it and pushed it in response to the ideological headlines of the moment. From the mid-nineteenth century until well into the twentieth century, for example, it became the repository, for the most part, of meanings generated by and for women. While men continued to inhabit the domestic arena, and certain rooms in the house were identified as 'masculine' in nature, the belief that the home was nonetheless a predominantly feminine sphere became widely accepted.[2] This belief in the existence of a special relationship between women and the domestic interior resulted not only in their strong presence in that physical space but more fundamentally in their creative efforts to elaborate it and thereby imbue it with meanings. Through the consumption of goods with which to construct a home, through choices regarding its decoration and through direct productive work resulting in ornamentation and display, women increasingly became the key progenitors of the meanings that came to be embedded within the domestic interior. In that process of elaboration women found a means not only of representing the dominant cultural themes of the day – family, class, nation, etc. – but of externalising 'themselves'. As a result, their homes became material manifestations of their personal identities.[3] As economic, social, cultural, technological and political circumstances made women's identities undergo a process of permanent transformation, the domestic interior became an increasingly articulate representation of that process of change.

Women's ability to see their homes as mirrors not only of broad cultural themes but of their individual selves coincided with their growing professionalisation in a number of distinct spheres, especially in areas which were seen as 'natural' extensions of their accepted gendered roles, such as education, nursing and interior decoration. The idea that decorating the domestic interior could be seen as a viable form of paid work for women emerged first in Britain in the last two decades of the nineteenth century as a natural extension of women taking the responsibility for home decoration on an amateur basis and of increasing numbers of women being trained as architects but ending up working on the interiors rather than the exteriors of buildings.[4]

Professionalised interior decorating by women also took off in the USA at the end of the nineteenth century and, by the outbreak of the First World War, the female interior decorating profession was well established, with a number of individuals having set up highly successful decorating businesses.[5] In this period American society was marked by a high degree of mobility and the home took on a key role as a marker of acquired social status. 'In a shifting society', the literary critic Lionel Trilling, has explained, 'great emphasis is put on appearance.'[6] Certainly at this time the aesthetic of the domestic interior came to play an increasingly important role in status formation, and most clients invited a reading of their homes which prioritised their positions in society.

Increasingly, also, in those years of growing female emancipation and independence, the notion of 'gender' became uppermost in many women's definitions of 'self'. Through the manipulation of 'taste' values female interior decorators took on the role of representing women's identities through the creation of a visual language for the home. Arguably, however, the identities they created most effectively were their own.

The work of the American interior decorator Elsie de Wolfe is a case in point. Indeed, her creations were so overtly expressions of herself that her clients had to sign up to a de Wolfe identity. While this undoubtedly suited many of her newly arrived clients, who had little confidence in their own tastes and who sought confirmation of their new positions in society through the ownership of an interior decor which had proved its social acceptability, for her more self-confident and creative clients it was less appropriate. The wife of the painter Walter Gay, for example, was unhappy about such an imposition of taste. Commenting on a house that de Wolfe had decorated for herself, she explained: 'I would rather furnish my own place, and express my own personality. This house, exquisite as it is, expresses Elsie de Wolfe.'[7]

Although de Wolfe created a considerable number of interiors in the decade 1905–15, some for the public sphere but mostly for private clients, it was in the interior schemes she created for herself that she developed her language of identity representation most effectively. As it was primarily her own identity she was intent on representing, it was a process which involved a close knowledge of self as well as an acute understanding of the cultural forces which had defined her and which continued to reinforce her own self-image. Her success as a professional decorator undoubtedly stemmed from her ability to focus on those aspects of her own persona with which other women could identify. Indeed the aspects of herself which came to the fore – her enhanced characterisation of her own 'femininity', her social aspirations and her ambivalent sense of her own nationality – proved to be those with which many of the female members of the emergent elite of American society were also preoccupied and which they sought to express through their domestic interiors.

Although de Wolfe quickly became a leading figure in the decorating profession in the first decade of the twentieth century she derived many of her ideas from others. Many of her decorating strategies, for example, were borrowed from the writer Edith Wharton and the architect Ogden Codman who, together, had published the influential book *The Decoration of Houses* in 1897. Unlike Wharton, however, de Wolfe became a prolific practitioner. She turned professional in 1905 in the wake of statements by Candace Wheeler about the possibility of women moving into a career in interior decoration, following the model of Wheeler herself.[8] However she ignored Wheeler's advocation of an extensive training prior to becoming a professional. From the outset she was committed to reaching a wide audience and to taking the private arena of the domestic interior into the public sphere.[9] Indeed she saw the two spheres as being fundamentally interdependent and interchangeable, and she moved freely between them apparently unaware of the barriers that existed for others. She also sought self-expression for others on a significant scale. In her book *The House in Good Taste*, published in 1913 – a compilation of articles which had already appeared in the women's magazines *Good Housekeeping* and *The Delineator*, ghost-written by Ruby Ross Goodnow but with de Wolfe's name attached to them – the decorator was forthright in her view of the importance of the interior as a form of self-expression for women: 'It is the personality of the mistress that the home expresses', she explained. 'Men are forever guests in our homes, however much happiness they may find there.'[10]

The homes de Wolfe created for herself, it can be argued, played a key role in the decorator's construction of herself. She was a highly fashion-conscious woman and perceived the interior as being, following after dress, a layer around the body. Indeed, to a significant extent, for de Wolfe, the domestic interior could be seen, essentially, as a form of identity construction in the manner of dress, created either through disguise or through revelation of what it was covering. Fresh from a career in the theatre, which she abandoned in 1905 to become a decorator, de Wolfe knew all too well the importance of the physical stage set for the drama that is enacted against it.

The interiors de Wolfe created to act as important backcloths for her own life in New York in the years leading up to the First World War were situated in two houses, one of them located on the corner of Irving Place and East 17th Street, where she resided between 1892 and 1910, and the second at 123 East 55th Street, where she lived from 1910 to 1915. While she decorated the interiors of these houses in the capacity of an 'amateur' she also devoted her efforts to professional work from 1905 onwards. In the latter capacity her projects included numerous commissions for private houses across the USA, a woman's club, a school dormitory, an automobile interior, an opera box, theatre sets and a model apartment for an exhibition.[11] The taste values which informed the decoration of her own homes were highly personal ones, informed to a significant degree by her own strong social aspirations, her overt and fine-tuned sense of her own 'femininity' – and of her 'Americanness' which was defined by its juxtaposition with her acquired 'Europeanness'. When she worked for others the same values were frequently in evidence.

THE WASHINGTON IRVING HOUSE

Elsie de Wolfe's life as an interior decorator began in 1905 when she was commissioned to design the interior of New York's Colony Club on Madison Avenue, the city's first all-women's club. It was a remarkable commission, coming as it did to someone who was untrained and who had up to that point worked as an amateur. The building was designed by Stanford White, the creator of many of New York's best-known men's clubs.[12] De Wolfe was selected for two reasons. The first was personal. The ex-actress lived with Elizabeth Marbury, a member of an 'old moneyed' New York family and her theatrical agent. Marbury was on the board of the Colony Club and undoubtedly exerted some influence in acquiring this commission for her friend.[13] In addition Stanford White was a neighbour of the two ladies in Gramercy Park and a visitor to the Sunday afternoon gatherings that they hosted for the cultural elite of New York.[14] Like Marbury he also recommended de Wolfe to the board of the Colony Club. His confidence in her ability to undertake the project was rooted in his close knowledge of what she had managed to achieve in her own home.

Marbury had long been a resident of Irving Place, the site of her family home. The couple had first met in 1887, when de Wolfe was still an amateur actress, and their close relationship was to last for the next quarter of a century. They moved into the little Irving Place house in 1892, a year after de Wolfe had become a professional actress and, five years later, in the publication year of Wharton and Codman's book, de Wolfe undertook a major refurbishment of its interior. In essence she transformed it from a dark, gloomy, cluttered, typically Victorian space filled with potted plants and knick-knacks into a brighter, more roomy, set of spaces in which light and air were much more in evidence. As she explained later, her plan at that time had been to 'devote all

my leisure to making over this tiny old dwelling into a home which would fit into our plan for life'.[15] She clearly used the gaps between her theatre performances to good effect and took the opportunity to experiment with interior decorating strategies which would give the couple a more comfortable and elegant life-style.

The strategies that de Wolfe developed in the Irving Place refurbishment stayed with her for years. Primary among them was a dependence on French eighteenth-century decorating style and on antique and reproduction French furniture. In the dining room at Irving Place, for example, she painted all the woodwork and the furniture white. She felt quite justified in looking to France for inspiration, explaining later: 'Miss Marbury and I have a perfect right to French things in our drawing-room, you see, for we are French residents half the year. And besides this gracious old house welcomed a fine old Louis XIV sofa as serenely as you please.'[16] From the early 1890s onwards de Wolfe and Marbury went annually to France, and in 1905 they bought a house in Versailles – the Villa Trianon – which was to play an important part in their lives – in de Wolfe's case, until her death in 1950.

The decorator's appropriation of eighteenth-century French taste provided a means of bypassing the Victorian interior. Her personal dislike of what she felt to be the claustrophobia of that idiom was rooted in her childhood which had been spent in a New York brownstone house. Her father had been a doctor of Nova Scotian origin who died penniless, and de Wolfe led an unremarkable middle-class childhood in typically nineteenth-century surroundings. 'I was an ugly child', she was to explain in her autobiography. 'I lived in an ugly age. From the moment I was conscious of ugliness and its relationship to myself and my surroundings, my one preoccupation was to find a way out of it. In my escape I came to the meaning of beauty'.[17]

On one level, therefore, it is possible to see de Wolfe's interest in the interior as social aspiration expressed in aesthetic terms. The gloom could, she felt, be replaced by light and air, qualities she had observed, as a young girl on a visit to England, in eighteenth-century country houses of the aristocracy and in the interior styles and furnishings of the same era, and of the same social group, that she saw in France during her visits with Marbury. From an early date she began to buy French furniture and have it shipped back to the USA. As she became increasingly known as a decorator her knowledge of the French antique furniture trade and her links with key dealers put her in a strong position, and she made as much money from supplying such goods to clients as she did by embellishing clients' interior spaces. The remembered emotional impact of the lightness of those old pieces, compared with their heavy Victorian counterparts, inspired an evocative description of a room she had seen in Europe – 'a room where the windows diffused and undulated the light, where space enveloped one like a silken mantle, where the colors were blended in a gentle camaraderie and where graceful furniture invited repose and comfort, created a kind of peace in me and made me feel at home.'[18] De Wolfe was clearly trying to create something of that sort of ambiance in Irving Place. The result represented a form of personal liberation, a release from both the physical constraints and the melancholia created by the environment in which she had been brought up. The link with Marbury freed her from the limitations of what she had felt to be a suffocating middle-class upbringing and the restrictive taste that had accompanied it. Along with the inclusion of items of French furniture, colour was used strategically to bring light into the house. Her chosen colour scheme – grey-green, rose, dull yellow, white and cream – consisted of eighteenth-century-inspired soft pastels which she was to use in many interiors to come. 'One colour', she explained, 'faded into another so subtly that one did not realise that there was a definite colour scheme.'[19] As was to become a common strategy in many of her later interiors, she took her colours for Irving Place from individual items which were to go into that space, in this instance a Persian rug and a Chinese carpet. The narrow hall was embellished with a green-and-white-striped ribbongrass wallpaper, a feature she was to use again in the foyer of the Colony Club. Many times over in later years the epithet 'spring' was used to describe the tone of the green in question, revealing the regenerative power that decorating held for de Wolfe.[20]

In Irving Place de Wolfe removed a late nineteenth-century 'cosy corner' from the bay window, replacing it with a tiny conservatory, complete with a white marble floor, climbing ivy and a small fountain. This provided a prototype for what was to become a defining feature of her mature decorating language: the indoor garden. It re-emerged in the famous 'trellis' restaurant in the Colony Club and in the many winter gardens that she went on to add to the large houses of members of the 'nouveau riche' across the USA in the first decade of the century. Clients whose interior schemes included winter gardens included Mr and Mrs Ogden Armour in Chicago and Mr and Mrs Ormond Smith on Long Island. She also added one to the New York town house of Mr and Mrs Benjamin Guinness.[21] The idea of 'outdoor-indoor' ambiguity was to reach its zenith in the work of the European modernist architects of the 1930s who took it much further than de Wolfe.[22]

Although the work of this late nineteenth-century amateur interior decorator was both eclectic and historicist in nature it demonstrated, nonetheless, a nascent modern sensibility. From one perspective de Wolfe can be seen to have been working in a transitional mode, rejecting the past in favour of the new, although using models from a deeper past with which to locate that sense of novelty and modernity. Indeed in a number of ways de Wolfe displayed an affinity with what could be seen as a prevailing shift in the USA at that time towards a more rational 'modern' attitude to life, an approach which found an important outlet in another face of contemporary American feminine culture, the 'rational household movement', which took its ideas from scientific management.[23] De Wolfe's often reiterated use of the term 'light and airy' bore witness to the fact that she aligned herself with the idea of modernity to a significant extent and that her vision looked backwards and forwards simultaneously. However stylistically dependent the decorator's work was on eighteenth-century European taste, in the context of turn-of-the-century USA it represented a break with the past and a shift towards a specifically American view of the future. Her commitment to that future was particularly apparent in the practical – non-decorative – faces of her interiors where, in line with the general American confidence in and enthusiasm for technology, de Wolfe incorporated into her interiors all that technology could offer, from electric lighting to steam heating. Even through her evocation of the past, however, de Wolfe's work can be understood as providing a framework for a modern definition of both womanhood and nation, both for herself and for her clients.

The personal tension felt by de Wolfe around the subject of her own nationality – between, that is, her indigenous American and acquired European identities – was a recurrent theme throughout her life and influenced her interiors from an early date. From the 1890s onwards she spent her summers in France, and after the First World War she moved to Paris only to return to the USA when she was forced to do so by the advent of the Second World War. She remained first and foremost an American during her absence, however (in spite of the fact that she married an English peer in 1926), and provided a point of focus for other wealthy Americans travelling in Europe, relying on them as clients and supporters. Paradoxically she needed to embrace French taste in order to be able to define herself as an American while at the same time her only way of defining herself as a modern American was to spend a large proportion of her life in Europe.

If themes arising from her class aspirations and nationality tensions underpinned the interior decor of the Irving Place house, so did those relating to de Wolfe's understanding of her own gender identity. Her transformation of Irving Place represented an opportunity to leave the past behind and to define her new lifestyle as that of an unmarried independent woman living closely alongside another woman in a same-sex relationship.[24] She gave away little about her sexuality in her interiors but they were very revealing constructions of her gendered identity. Her fundamental decision to use the domestic interior, which was understood in this period as a primarily 'feminine' space, as her 'canvas' was in itself a mark of her preoccupation with gender.[25] In her refurbishment of Irving Place de Wolfe has told us that she was setting out to create a home. More than that she wanted to construct an interior space in which she would feel 'at home'.[26] For her, this clearly meant being at one with the cultural trappings of femininity. As an actress she had been better known for her couturier gowns – made by well-known names such as Worth, Paquin and Doucet – than for her performances and she saw the acquisition of 'beauty' as a necessary requirement to keep the 'ugliness' of her childhood at bay. Beauty, for de Wolfe, was synonymous with 'feminine beauty' and she dedicated her life to a pursuit of this ideal using her own face and body as a kind of experimental laboratory. In her later years she underwent extensive cosmetic surgery, and throughout her life she paid great attention to her appearance through careful diet and daily exercise. Her career as an actress had represented one means of moving from the world of reality into one of fantasy where an 'alternative world', provided by costume, make-up and stage sets, facilitated a reconstruction of 'self' in which beauty could be made to play a part even if it was not naturally present. As a decorator de Wolfe came to depend on the domestic interior as a substitute for the stage as a site of identity construction.

The interior decor of the Washington Irving House, as de Wolfe liked to call it, after the writer who was thought to have lived there, was unequivocally feminine. The pastel colours and light decorative touches were offset by a rigorous practicality

and a sense of comfort representative of the other face of femininity. The inclusion of many tiny details were witness to the decorator's practical approach. The presence of a little bowl, for example, in Miss Marbury's bedroom, described as being of 'just the proper color' and intended 'to hold pens and clips and odds and ends' was a sign of her commitment to providing a place for everything.[27] She also positioned mirrors, which she used extensively in her interiors to create an illusion of space, to allow her to see the back of her head. The couple's belongings were stored in a highly organised manner in large closets, yet another example of the practical side of the domestic femininity that dominated the interior they inhabited.

A level of domestic comfort was also deemed central to de Wolfe's formula for the successful interior. This was expressed primarily through the soft furnishings that she utilised. Irving Place saw her first use of chintz, a fabric she had seen in English country houses some years earlier. It was used, for example, complete with a bird of paradise print – one of de Wolfe's favourite patterns – as a bedcovering fabric in Miss Marbury's bedroom, and again in the same room as an upholstery fabric on the sofa, on a little side chair and on what de Wolfe herself described as 'an adorable little screen of white enamel, paneled with chintz below and glass above'.[28] The bedroom of each woman boasted a daybed, an item considered by the decorator as an essential component of any woman's bedroom, enabling her to take a necessary daytime nap. Each room also contained a writing table and a variety of lamps positioned conveniently next to the writing and reading areas, which included the bed.

The final manifestation of conventional femininity in de Wolfe's interiors which found its way into Irving Place was a commitment to decorative objects – not the bric-a-brac of the Victorian home but a more selective display of significant items. In her 1897 refurbishment of the house she threw out many of the theatrical mementos which had previously filled her display cases and adorned the mantelpiece in the drawing room, replacing them with paintings and prints which she fixed to the (by then) plain-panelled walls. The hall, for instance, featured a series of fashion plates discovered in France, while a Nattier painting took pride of place over the mantelpiece. (It was to appear again, as did de Wolfe's Breton bed, in the East 55th Street house.) Flowers blossomed in vases on mantelpieces and pattern adorned many of the fabrics. The decorator was restrained in her use of patterned surfaces, however, tending to prefer walls painted in a single colour to wallpaper.

The Washing Irving house played a seminal part in de Wolfe's oeuvre. It was her first attempt at a whole interior and it brought together all the formative influences on her life up to that point, among them the negative memories of her childhood and the positive effects of living in foreign countries and exposure to different cultures. It enabled her to experiment with a new interior language which was at the same time both backward- and forward-looking; it allowed her to align her personal aspirations with her spatial environment; and it provided her with a means of representing 'herself', defined through the cultural filters of class, gender and nationality. More importantly it gave de Wolfe the means of externalising her aesthetic preoccupations and of creating an identity for herself which was in keeping with her new-found freedom and lifestyle. Perhaps most importantly it became her 'home' for a significant period of time, and as such gave her a stable emotional base from which she could move forward with confidence.

123 EAST 55TH STREET

If the re-decoration of Irving Place performed an important aspirational role for de Wolfe, that of 123 East 55th Street was the full-blooded realisation of that aspiration. She decorated it while at the height of her success as an interior decorator. By 1910, when she purchased the house, she had already decorated the Colony Club in New York as well as a range of private residences in, among other places, Chicago, San Francisco, New Jersey, Long Island and upstate New York.[29] However, East 55th Street never acquired the same level of personal meaning for the decorator as did Irving Place, and she did not look back at it later in life with the same level of nostalgia. This was partly because East 55th Street, although created for them, was never fully occupied by the two women together, and it remained a 'model' house for others to emulate rather than becoming a real home for de Wolfe. It represented her professional skills at their peak but it did not have the same personal resonance for her as the little Washington Irving house.

In 1901 the architect Ogden Codman, co-author of *The Decoration of Houses* and a frequent visitor at de Wolfe and Marbury's Sunday gatherings when he was in New York visiting from Boston, was commissioned to undertake some work at Irving Place. The historian, Pauline Metcalf, has documented the fact that Marbury and de Wolfe hired Codman to make alterations to the Irving

Place drawing room. The brief was to create a 'salon' with the 'mellowed atmosphere of French society'.[30] He achieved it by installing panel mouldings and painting the walls ivory. Mirrors covered the doors and a niche for a statue was built into one end of the room. De Wolfe later claimed authorship of the niche herself, but it is clear that by 1901 she had learned to collaborate closely with architects. This was reinforced four years later through her work with Stanford White on the Colony Club (although White had died before the completion of the project). Indeed, during the first decade of the twentieth century de Wolfe worked with a wide range of Beaux Arts architects, among them Arthur Heun in Chicago and Hoppin and Koen in New York.

De Wolfe's work with Codman on East 55th Street was highly dependent on the project, undertaken by the two, which had immediately preceded it. Earlier in 1910 she had asked him to work with her on what was to become a 'show house' – 131 East 71st Street – in New York. With her new-found wealth the decorator was able to enter into entrepreneurial activity, and the idea of renovating an ordinary New York terraced brownstone, and demonstrating to others what it was possible to achieve, provided her with a perfect opportunity for some publicity. De Wolfe described the East 71st Street house as a 'plain, ugly house like tens of others'.[31] Indeed it undoubtedly closely resembled the house she herself had been brought up in, and the project's appeal was clearly the personal challenge of being able to replace ugliness with beauty, as if by a flick of a fairy wand. The project also served another important purpose: it was a way of demonstrating to that sector of the public which inhabited similar houses all over the USA that they also could transform their interior spaces and bring 'modernity' into their lives. As the decorator herself explained: 'My object in taking this house was twofold: I wanted to prove to my friends that it was possible to take one of the darkest and grimiest of city houses and make it an abode of sunshine and light, and I wanted to furnish a whole house exactly as I pleased – for once!'[32] The implications of those words were, perhaps, that at Irving Place she had not been able to entirely align 'self' with the interior schemes, as Marbury's taste had also had to be accommodated. Seen from one perspective, she was using East 71st Street to show that what she had set out to achieve at Irving Place, for personal reasons, could be emulated by anyone who wished to do so. In other words her work in the private sphere was being exposed in the public arena as an encouragement to others to make interventions within their own private environments. The potential commercial spin-off, of course, was that they might employ an interior decorator, hopefully Miss de Wolfe, to help them undertake that transformation. The project served, therefore, to blur the edges between the public and the private sphere, as well as to reinforce the process of the commodification of the domestic interior, an inevitable result of the professionalisation of interior decoration.

Codman's role in the revitalisation of East 71st Street lay in the significant restructuring that was undertaken on the house.[33] It included taking the entrance from the first floor down to ground level so that a little courtyard with an iron railing and box trees could be added (the only means by which to include the 'outside', which was so important to de Wolfe); replacing the existing stairway with a spiral staircase half way down the house to facilitate the removal of the narrow hallway and allow the rooms at the front to extend fully across the 17-foot breadth of the house; and adding a five-storey servants' quarters to the rear of the house in what had been the backyard.

Most of the decorating strategies employed by de Wolfe at Irving Place were repeated at East 71st Street, though to rather more dramatic effect. Her favourite tactic of applying to the interior scheme as a whole colours deriving from artefacts chosen for the decor was employed again: in the first-floor bedroom, for example, a pair of Chinese jugs, coloured turquoise, mauve, mulberry, black and cream, inspired an intense colour scheme for the interior, which included mauve chintz curtains. A number of items of furniture were specially made for the room. In all her schemes de Wolfe was as happy to have reproduction furniture made for her as she was to use 'genuine' antiques. At other times she had no qualms about painting old pieces of furniture to give them a new lease of life. Her approach revealed her social background: she did not come from a world where fine pieces of furniture were inherited and where it was sacrilegious to talk about 'reproduced' pieces. Marbury, who came from an upper-class family, was committed to her inherited pieces, and this could well have caused friction between the two women at Irving Place. At East 71st Street de Wolfe had a free hand and was able to construct new interiors which, rather like the stage sets she had been so familiar with, could create an illusion of the past but which did not themselves belong to that past. Nothing could be more 'modern' than her commitment to sunshine and light, and the freedom with which she blended together disparate pieces of furniture. Describing the drawing room that covered the full width of the first floor she wrote:

I am growing tired of the plain, white walls and white woodwork, and of the carefully 'matched' furniture of the over-cautious decorator who goes warily. Somehow the feeling of homeyness is lost in such an arrangement. In the drawing room there is furniture of half a dozen styles, but all in harmony. There is a long sofa of gray-painted wood covered with a needlework tapestry in soft gray and rose and creamy tan. There are several chairs of the same wood and tapestry, and still others covered with a dull-rose brocade.[34]

The house at East 71st Street allowed the decorator to exploit her skills to the full and to consolidate an aesthetic which, while still dependent on eighteenth-century French taste, was also very much 'of the moment' in early twentieth-century New York. As in Irving Place, however, practicality also determined many of the decorating decisions. Every possible opportunity to use space effectively was exploited and a storage cupboard was added in every little niche that permitted one. De Wolfe herself coined the slogan 'Suitability, Simplicity and Proportion', and she followed it so ruthlessly that while an elegant loggia with a black-and-white chequerboard marble floor and a highly decorative porcelain stove were considered 'suitable' for the dramatic entrance space, the servants' quarters at the back were much more utilitarian in appearance.[35] The decorator emphasised her commitment to this area of the house, explaining: 'I firmly believe that the whole question of household comfort evolves from the careful planning of the service portion of the house.'[36]

Rapidly following the completion of East 71st Street, which was opened with a grand reception, de Wolfe purchased a very similar house on East 55th Street. This time the intention was to use it as a new home for Marbury and herself. Once again Codman was employed to undertake the necessary architectural work, and exactly the same restructuring programme was implemented. A marble floor was installed; a statue rather than a stove was set into a niche in the entrance hall; and the room arrangement was almost identical to that of the show-house. The multiple mirrors used in the hallway to create a sense of space resulted in the property being christened 'the little house of many mirrors'.[37] Attention to practical detail was in evidence once again, this time through the presence in the hallway of a writing table complete with paper and writing implements which de Wolfe justified with the following words: 'How often I have been in other people's houses when it was necessary to send a message, or to record an address, when the whole household began scurrying around trying to find a pencil and paper!'[38]

De Wolfe's bedroom was on the second floor at the front, with Marbury's immediately above it. They had direct buzzer communication with each other from their bedrooms. She dedicated enormous energy to the interior decoration of this house, conscious that it was to become their home. The distinction between East 55th Street and the show-house became somewhat eroded, however, as the shift from amateur decorating to professional work undertaken in the commercial arena meant that de Wolfe's private world was becoming indistinguishable from her public sphere.

The drawing room at East 55th Street was a result of what were by then characteristic de Wolfe decorating strategies, tried and tested in a number of projects. Mixed furniture pieces were clustered in groups; rugs covered the floors; the walls were covered with wood panelling; and metal candle sconces (fitted with electric lights) flanked a marble mantelpiece which was topped by a mirror. Light decoration, provided by fabrics, paintings and vases of flowers, contrasted with the plainness of the panelled walls. The interior gave the impression, above all, of having been created over a period of time. This evolved look was something de Wolfe prized and she had commented on how happy she had been with the reading room in the Colony Club because it had the same feel to it. The East 55th Street drawing-room scheme was rooted in a quest for 'homeliness' pointing to the conceptual heart of de Wolfe's decorating philosophy.

The contradictions, tensions and complexities of class, gender and nationality that were Elsie de Wolfe were the essence of her work. She moved from one class to another. She combined an ambivalent sexuality with an exaggerated femininity. She refused to commit herself to life within one country or culture. The only unambivalent thing about her was that she was an interior decorator, though even in that capacity she refused to draw a hard-and-fast line between amateur and professional work and between the public and the private spheres. In the year leading up to the First World War she used interior decoration to represent and constitute 'herself and, in turn, offered that representation to others. In so doing she helped create a new profession for women, assisted in moving the interior away from the stamp of Victorianism

and influenced the tastes of a vast number of women, across a range of social classes, for several decades. In the process she also pushed forward by several stages the domestic interior's potential to represent and constitute personal identity.

NOTES

1 E. de Wolfe, *The House in Good Taste* (New York: Harpers & Brothers, 1935), p. 52.

2 For a discussion of the gendering of rooms in the nineteenth-century domestic interior, see J. Kinchin, 'Interiors: nineteenth-century essays on the "masculine" and "feminine" room', in P. Kirkham (ed.), *The Gendered Object* (Manchester: Manchester University Press, 1996).

3 See L. Auslander, 'The gender of consumer practices in nineteenth-century France', in V. de Grazia and E. Furlough (eds), *The Sex of Things: Gender and Consumption in Historical Perspective* (Berkeley: University of California Press, 1996), p. 79, who argues that the domestic interior moved from a representation of class, family and nation to one of women's individual gendered identities.

4 For information relating to professional interior decorators working in Britain in the late nineteenth and early twentieth centuries, see L. Walker, 'Women architects and the arts and crafts alternative', in J. Attfield and P. Kirkham (eds), *A View from the Interior: Feminism, Women and Design* (London: Women's Press, 1989), pp. 90–105. The work of Agnes and Rhoda Garrett is especially interesting in this context. A number of British books, by women, on the subject of the domestic interior appeared in the 1870s, notable among them L. Orrinsmith, *The Drawing Room, its Decoration and Furniture* (London: Macmillan & Co., 1878) and Mrs H. R. Haweis, *The Art of Beauty* (London: Chatto & Windus, 1878).

5 In addition to that of de Wolfe, the businesses (and the names) of Ruby Ross Goodnow (later Wood), Nancy McClelland, Elsie Cobb Wilson and Rose Cumming emerged in these years.

6 L. Trilling, *The Liberal Imagination* (New York: Garden City, 1950), p. 210.

7 W. Rieder, *A Charmed Couple: The Art and Life of Walter and Matilda Gay* (New York: Abrams, 2000), p. 119.

8 In 1897 Scribner of New York published Edith Wharton and Ogden Codman's hugely

influential *The Decoration of Houses* (new edn, New York: W.W. Norton, 1978). Two years earlier Candace Wheeler had published a two-part article entitled 'Interior decoration as a profession for women' in *The Outlook*, 6 April 1895, 559–60, and 20 April 1895, 649.

9 De Wolfe undertook a number of projects outside the private sphere of the home, though she continued to work in the domestic idiom in those projects. They included the interior of the Colony Club (1905–7), a dormitory for Barnard College (1907), and the interior of the Vacation Savings Club Headquarters (1913), all in New York.

10 De Wolfe published a series of articles in *The Delineator* (October 1911–May 1912) and *Good Housekeeping* (May 1912–June 1913). They formed the basis of her ghost-written book *The House in Good Taste* (New York: Century, 1913), from p. 5 of which this statement is extracted.

11 Jane S. Smith's biography of Elsie de Wolfe, entitled *Elsie de Wolfe, A Life in the High Style: The Elegant Life and Remarkable Career of Elsie de Wolfe, Lady Mendl* (New York: Atheneum, 1982), gives a brief account of some of these designs. Most remain unresearched in any detail.

12 Stanford White was known for a number of men's clubs in New York, among them the Players' Club (1889), the Century Club (1891) and the Lambs' Club (1904).

13 For Marbury's account of her relationship with de Wolfe, see E. Marbury, *My Crystal Ball* (New York: Boni & Liveright, 1923).

14 Accounts of Marbury and de Wolfe's entertaining and of the Colony Club commission can be found in Smith, *Elsie de Wolfe*, and in A. Lewis, *Ladies and Not-So-Gentle Women: Elizabeth Marbury, Anne Morgan, Elsie de Wolfe, Anne Vanderbilt and Their Times* (New York: Viking, 2000).

15 De Wolfe, *After All* (New York: Harper & Brothers, 1935), p. 51.

16 De Wolfe, *The House in Good Taste*, p. 32.

17 De Wolfe, *After All*, p. 3.

18 *Ibid.*, p. 48.

19 De Wolfe, *The House in Good Taste*, p. 11.

20 De Wolfe, 'The story of the Colony Club', in *The Delineator* (New York), November 1911, p. 370.

21 Of the many winter gardens she created in this period, those for Mrs Ogden Armour's house 'Mellody Farm', built in Lake Forest, just outside Chicago, and for Mrs Ormond G. Smith's 'Shoremond', built on Center Island, New York, were two of the more dramatic.

22 Le Corbusier's 'Pavillion de l'esprit nouveau', created for the Paris Exhibition of Decorative Arts in 1925, for example, eliminated the distinction between 'inside' and 'outside', to the extent of leaving a tree on site which penetrated the roof of the pavilion.

23 Scientific management was a form of Taylorism which aimed to rationalise the work process. Applied to the home, it aimed to streamline the housewife's work by reducing the number of her steps and re-organising her tasks. Christine Frederick's publication *Household Engineering* (Chicago, IL: American School of Home Economics, 1913) outlined these ideas most clearly.

24 For a more extended discussion of de Wolfe and Marbury's relationship, see R.A. Schanke and K. Marra (eds), *Passing Performances: Queer Readings of Leading Players in American Theatre History* (Michigan: University of Michigan Press, 2000).

25 For an elaboration of the notion of 'separate spheres', see J. Wolff, 'The culture of separate spheres: the role of culture in nineteenth-century public and private life', in J. Wolff, *Feminine Sentences: Essays on Women and Culture* (Cambridge: Polity Press, 1990).

26 Smith, *Elsie de Wolfe*, p. 51.

27 De Wolfe, *The House in Good Taste*, p. 41.

28 *Ibid.*, p. 38.

29 Many of the private commissions de Wolfe undertook between 1907 and 1915 resulted from her work on the Colony Club and were for women who were members of the club.

30 P. Metcalf, *Ogden Codman and the Decoration of Houses* (Boston, MA: Boston Atheneum, 1988), 21.

31 De Wolfe, 'Transforming a small city house', in *The Delineator* (New York): February 1912, 132.

32 *Ibid.*

33 Plans of Codman's structural changes to the house can be seen in the Codman Archive, Avery Library, Columbia University, New York.

34 De Wolfe, 'Transforming a small city house', 132.

35 Codman Archive, Columbia University, New York.

36 De Wolfe, *The House in Good Taste*, p. 50.

37 *Ibid.*, p. 42.

38 *Ibid.*, p. 44.

2
Dream Homes and DIY
TV, New Media and the Domestic Makeover

Viviana Narotzky

Source: *Imagined Interiors: Representing the Domestic Interior Since the Renaissance.* J. Aynsley and C. Grant. V & A Publishing, 2006, pp. 258–267

There's not a house in Britain left untouched by the *Changing Rooms* attitude.

Laurence Llewelyn-Bowen
Changing Rooms designer
(The Mirror, August 7th 2004)

Running from 1996 until its last season in 2005, the TV reality show *Changing Rooms* has without a doubt been a fundamental contributor to current representations of the home. The programme features two neighbouring couples, who exchange their homes for two days, redecorating each other's space under the guidance of an interior designer and with a fixed, limited budget. By 1998, *Changing Rooms* was regularly attracting 12 million viewers to its prime-time slot on BBC1 and was soon to generate numerous international spin-offs.

While interior designer Llewelyn-Bowen's claim that it has left no house untouched might seem at first to be far-fetched, its profound impact on mainstream ideas of the home, domesticity and the design of interiors can hardly be denied. Through programmes such as *Changing Rooms*, and other interior design series such as *Design Rules* or *Home Front*, reality TV domestic makeover shows have developed and established an over-arching discourse of design in the home that seamlessly merges traditional perceptions with the latest lifestyle and cultural trends.

The long-standing Victorian premise of the home as a safe haven, a retreat from the cares and worries of public life that provides the stage for the most intimate expressions of individual identity through design and decoration, is given a post-modern twist in an attitude that refuses to engage with notions of good or bad taste. The New Age's design gurus no longer tell one what to like. Rather, they aim to help us find ourselves, announcing that 'there is no right way, no wrong way, but only your way.'[1]

But this domestic ideal of the home as a personal sanctuary, constructed by means of regulated aesthetic practices and individual expression, is a composite picture in more than just its relation to aesthetic form. If the medium is the message, as Marshall MacLuhan proposed almost half a century ago, then this message is a very fragmented one. Following the economic logic of contemporary merchandising and product tie-ins, programmes like *Changing Rooms* and *Home Front* have spawned their own microcosm of multi-media incarnations, offering branded products across a diverse range of technological and media platforms, from books, to computer software, to the internet. Each one of them elaborates its particular variation on this narrative of home, giving rise to a unique phenomenon in which these discourses are adapted to suit varying modes of representation and mediation.

The TV programmes favour dramatic tension, drawing the viewers into a private space where the ultimate success or failure of the makeover is above all an expression of the home as a site of emotional investment. At the same time, working with the flexibility inherent to new media, the BBC's *Changing Rooms* website presents the home as a blank canvas made of pre-defined colour-in areas, the discrete receptacles of a seemingly endless choice of possible dreamworlds. The books, on the other hand, engage comfortably with a long tradition of advice literature, providing know-how, inspiration and practical tips from the experts. But more importantly, they offer to position our relationship with domestic interior design as a natural outcome of our personal engagement with the zeitgeist. They tell us, in other words, that 'home' is the ultimate expression of who we are right now: diverse, creative, expressive, changeable, unique, and in control.

Essentially an evolution of DIY and design advice, contemporary domestic makeover TV shows are part of a culturally and historically framed discourse on the home, design and interiors. Drawing on the mass appeal of reality TV and celebrity culture, they have popularised a vicarious, shifting and essentially 'spectacular' experience of the contemporary domestic interior.

THE GOOD HOME

There is an absence at the heart of domestic makeover shows, as has historically been the case with other attempts to help homedwellers improve their domestic environment. Put bluntly, a perceived absence of taste. But it is the presupposed absence of a very particular kind of taste that drives design advice, the ever-elusive *good taste*, as well as the lack of a certain type of skill in the general public: the specialist know-how that underpins *good design*. Interior decorating has long been a 'middle-class ritual',[2] largely officiated by women. If the 19th century saw them mostly as the sensitive agents that shaped the private sphere, by the turn of the century the emphasis of an emerging modernist discourse was on the interior as the manifestation of an artistic individuality, an outlet for every woman's creative drive.[3] In that sense, while remaining somewhat distant from the lofty realms of High Art, amateur home decorating was seen as a practice strongly linked both to aesthetic skills and to individual expression. Expert advice on such matters, therefore, can be seen as a constant endeavor not just to educate an easily misled public, but also as an attempt to police the formal boundaries of this creative drive, circumscribing its expression to the limits set by the professionals.

Throughout the 19th and 20th centuries, an ever-increasing abundance of books, specialized magazines, exhibitions, commercial fairs, trade manuals, museum displays, offered encouragement and inspiration on how best to be an artist of the domestic sphere. Home makeover shows therefore participate in a now well-established historical lineage of multi-media design advice, mediating design ideas and representing an ideal dwelling space. Before the advent of television, and in this particular case reality television, trade shows and model homes were the main sites where prospective homemakers could come as close as possible to 'real' interior design solutions. *The Ideal Home Shows*, for instance, established in 1908 and still a yearly event today, would have supported their quest for inspiration and advice, offering a commodified palette of fashionable trends, new materials, emerging domestic technologies and shifting cultural priorities.

In America, the Idea House project, which took place in 1941 and 1947 under the auspices of the Walker Art Center of Minneapolis, Minnesota, was a striking if little-known example of the merging of art and commerce in the construction of the domestic sphere.[4] Idea House was a Modernist exercise in design promotion, developed in the context of economic recession and American postwar reconstruction. It offered fully-fitted, architect designed display houses as a source of ideas for the visiting public to choose from. The two houses were constructed with the support of manufacturers who contributed materials, furnishings and fittings. While none of these were listed in the show houses themselves, information leaflets were made available to the public with full details of items, prices and suppliers. In the words of Daniel Defenbacher, the project's instigator, 'As a consumer, every man uses art … His medium he obtains from stores, manufacturers and builders. His composition is his environment'.[5] An unprecedented combination of cultural and commercial aims, Idea House offered the home artist a catalogue of tools. It has been suggested that 'the discourse around the modern house is fundamentally linked to the commercialisation of domestic life'.[6] While these various settings of ideal interiors were undoubtedly a direct manifestation of this trend, they nevertheless upheld the enduring rhetoric of the homeowners as artists, inspired creators of the everyday.

From the mid-1940s, television offered an even easier way of consuming the art of homemaking, as well as what seemed to be a perfect platform for the dissemination of notions of good design. An early attempt to do the latter joined in an increasingly uneasy partnership the newly established Council of Industrial Design and the BBC. The *Britain Can Make It* exhibition held at the Victoria and Albert Museum in 1946 provided the perfect occasion for a joint effort between the two institutions to raise public awareness through programmes such as *What Is Good Design?*, *What's in a Chair?* and *The Designer Looks Ahead*. These extremely didactic offerings soon gave way to a slightly more consumer oriented approach, in which the BBC left behind the CoID's concerns with reaching out to designers, retailers and manufacturers, shifting instead towards productions that tried to address the needs of the average homeowner and provide a modicum of televisual entertainment. Thus in 1951, *Rooms to*

Let Unfurnished followed a family of four in its upwardly-mobile relocation from a basement in Bermondsey to a larger, three-bedroom modern council flat in Streatham. With the help of a designer and a budget of £150, contemporary furnishings were carefully chosen to enhance their new environment, while considering how best to adapt the family's existing possessions to fit in with the modern style.[7]

Given the rather tenuous links between contemporary domestic makeover programmes such as *Changing Rooms* and the established canon of high design, however, it is tempting to place them more squarely in the DIY camp. The rise of self-built home improvement in 1930s and 1940s America coincided with the launch of government-sponsored loans aimed at creating better quality housing, by encouraging home ownership and facilitating projects such as electrification and the installation of new technologies and appliances in the home. It was therefore closely linked to the structural modernisation of households, driven by a social agenda that sought to promote a better standard of living through the shared effort of federal funding and individual labour. DIY was presented as a patriotic activity, first in the context of a make do and mend war-time ethos, and later as a practice that enabled returning war veterans to settle down into a well-deserved, comfortable suburban life. The remodelling of homes was also intensely pushed by manufacturers, who engaged both with the government's economic plans and with the domestic dreams of a whole generation that was accessing home ownership for the first time. By the 1950s, DIY had become a huge industry and a mass culture phenomenon. Ambiguously positioned between work and leisure, it was associated with a cult of suburban family life that presented the home not just as an essentially feminine space, but also as a space protected from the alienating drudgery of corporate life, where men could engage in the construction of domesticity through suitably gendered practices. DIY therefore, posited the home as a space of empowering self-regulated male work, creative freedom, and constructive leisure.

In Britain, the 1950s had also seen the appearance of televised home improvement programmes, most famously Barry Bucknell's *Do-It-Yourself* BBC series, which attracted over seven million viewers, and what was possibly the first ever home makeover show, Bucknell's 1962 *House*. Through the course of 39 weekly episodes, Bucknell transformed a derelict Victorian house in Ealing into a sleek and modern home. Gone were the quaint fireplaces, moulded doors, picture rails and other period features. Walls came down to make way for more up to date open plan layouts, while modular functional furniture and the latest appliances completed a breath-taking transformation, dragging British interiors into the future and leaving behind a cloud of paint fumes and particle-board sawdust. As had been the case in America, the post-war government supported home improvements through the Housing Act of 1949, and the Rent Act of 1954, which enabled Local Authorities to provide generous loans to that effect. By the late 1950s, ideas about how to transform the home, and how best to do it oneself, had been made accessible to the public in a staggering variety of venues. These included the *Britain Can Make It* exhibition of 1946/47, the successive *British Industries Fairs* after the war, the *Festival of Britain* in 1951, the annual national *Handicrafts and Do-It-Yourself* exhibitions in the Empire Hall at Olympia from 1953, the *Do-It-Yourself Theatre* at the *Ideal Home Exhibitions* from 1955, and the *DIY* exhibitions at the Empress Hall, Earl's Court, from 1958. The first British DIY magazine, *The Practical Householder*, appeared in October 1955. By March 1957, it had become the biggest selling technical journal ever, with a circulation of one million.

As with other forms of making, DIY involved the development of specific skills and was an expression of personal aesthetic judgement. It also celebrated thrift, being in part a result of economic necessity:

> From the large number of letters we receive from both men and women readers it is apparent that the Do-It-Yourself movement is here to stay and not, as some thought, a passing phase. It is also evident from those letters that two reasons are responsible for it. The first is the enormous charges now being made for repairs and decorations [. . .] and the second is the deterioration in the quality of the work, notwithstanding the heavy prices asked . . .[8]

For the average home owner in 1950s Britain, DIY represented a manageable way of negotiating the rather daunting, if appealing, post-war modernity that Bucknell and the Design Council were so earnestly promoting through the BBC.[9] Self-built home improvements offered scope for the customisation of the modern, both in terms of cost and of formal appearance, providing the know-how to construct a domesticated and affordable version of contemporary 'good design'.

The emphasis on design-led 'making' that is part and parcel of domestic makeover TV shows might lead one to locate them within a historical narrative that stretches back to the emergence of DIY and the popularisation of 'good design', as a modernist project of self-constructed material progress. However, it is the ways in which makeover shows diverge from that story that define the particular nature of this all-pervading contemporary mode of representing the home and our relationship to it.

Throughout the twentieth century, the idea of the home as a site of social reform, the 'good' home as Utopian project, has been contending with the idea of domestic space as an expression of middle-class taste, and an emotional sanctuary. This tension can be easily mapped onto the contrasting narrative styles that structured the early DIY programmes, on the one hand, and home makeover shows on the other. While the former's educational vocation focused on the clear, step by step presentation of a process and on skill acquisition, makeovers prioritise narrative, appearance, outcome and drama. They lay bare a shift from function to representation in terms of the media's contribution to the self-made domestic interior.

These programmes are not about improving standards of living, or incorporating new domestic technologies in order to make positive structural changes to dwellings. They certainly don't have a background ideology linking them to a social agenda promoted by government institutions or current public policies. If anything, they are one of many extremely successful manifestations of the priorities of contemporary consumer culture, a site for the mediation of versions of middle-class taste and their relation to lifestyle as a vague, and vaguely life-enhancing, thing. Crucially, however, the way in which they present the transformation of the home, or rather, the transformation of rooms within the home, subjects the conceptualisation of the domestic interior to the overarching demands of the medium itself. As a consequence, television is no longer only a channel through which pre-existing ideas about the home and its appearance can be conveyed, but the very process through which they are constructed.

DOMESTIC INTRUSION

Through its constant and banal presence at the heart of the everyday experience of domesticity,

television as a medium is by its very nature linked with the spaces of the home – and not just the home as a physical space, but as a space of the mind as well:

> Once one takes seriously the fact that television is a domestic medium (and is characterised by programme forms specifically designed for that purpose), it becomes clear that the domestic context of television viewing is not some secondary factor, which can be subsequently sketched in. Rather, the domestic context of TV viewing, it becomes clear, is constitutive of its meaning.[10]

These meanings arise out of the sharing of televisual experiences, the interpersonal dynamics involved in what is watched when, how, and by whom, or the transformation of TV programmes and topics into a common currency that can be exchanged in the cultural economy of everyday life.

Home makeover shows have been described as a hybrid between two separate television formats, talk shows and reality TV.[11] On the one hand, the hosts engage in conversation with the home-owners whose rooms are being redecorated, encouraging them to share their ideas and concerns about the process that they are participating in. On the other, these programmes transgress the boundaries of the home, perverting the intimacy of the domestic environment by subjecting it to the gaze of millions of viewers, who watch them from the privacy of their own living rooms. This is the paradox that underpins the voyeur's pleasure, which reality television has made safely available to all.

In breaching the boundaries between public and private, domestic makeover shows embody one of the main tenets of modernist architecture's Utopian vision, that which sought to erase the visual limits between the inside and the outside. Television itself was from its earliest inception presented as a technology that would erase physical distance and conquer space, as an open window through which 'the outside world [could] be brought into the home, and thus one of mankind's long-standing ambitions [could] be achieved'.[12] It is the home that is now being brought to the outside world. Whether we really want an open window into our bedrooms is debatable, but the phenomenal success of domestic makeover shows seems to suggest that we do. It would appear that we have become comfortable with the notion that our homes might be subject to surveillance, that reality TV can do on the inside what CCTV cameras do on the outside, that Big Brother is not just a necessary evil, but actually good fun.

However, this suggestion of a relaxed domesticity, at ease with the idea of a foreign gaze accessing the intimate sphere of the home, is belied by the dynamics that are responsible for the fascination that programmes like *Changing Rooms* exert on their audiences. The high narrative point of home makeover shows, the final moment of truth known as 'the reveal', is in fact the dramatic representation of domesticity under threat. As the veil is lifted on the changes made over the course of the programme, the audience holds its collective breath and watches the participants' reaction to their revamped Swahili-themed living-room – secretly hoping that they will hate it. Subjected to the often eccentric creative whims of the designers, themselves bound by the producer's need to generate a televisual spectacle out of watching paint dry, homeowners are caught between the contradictory demands of show business, aesthetic judgement and an improved domestic environment. While design can help provide a more impressive dining room or a more sensual bedroom it can also be threatening to a placid, simple and enjoyable domestic life. Style is one of the ways in which the home can be put at risk: 'Maybe it's too arty for them' says a concerned neighbour about the scheme that is being suggested for her friends' bedroom. 'We could do it safe [. . .] but we won't' counters Laurence Llewelyn-Bowen. 'Come on, be brave. Trust me, I'm a designer'.[13]

The disruptions caused by the intrusion of a stranger into the safe haven of the home are a longstanding theme which has provided literature and cinema with some of their most dramatic narratives. The anxieties so often expressed by makeover show participants, about the emotional havoc that might be caused by an inappropriate assessment of the owners' taste – or by TV designers blatantly disregarding the owners' aesthetic preferences – speak of a deep-seated perception of the home as an emotionally vulnerable site. This very personal, carefully calibrated emotional balance, constructed in part through home possessions and visual form, can be easily threatened and destroyed by professionals. It is precisely this aspect that shows like *Changing Rooms* or *Home Front* exploit to the full. Every lime green brushstroke, every MDF folly, is the potential harbinger of a breakdown in the owners' pre-established sense of what is, for them, an appropriate visual expression of domesticity, leading to live televised distress and a surge in ratings. In 2000, the *Changing*

Rooms team gave an 18th century vicarage an 'outlandish and funky' makeover. On returning to her home the following day, the owner was furious:

> I think it's absolute crap, I really do. I think it's a traditional house and you've put a modern design in. The sooner we get it out, the better. I mean, breeze blocks in a house of this age? It's appalling.[14]

At the same time, the design of the makeovers recognises the primacy of our emotional attachment to domestic objects in the configuration of a pleasurable experience of the home. Cherished possessions are frequently singled out as focal points for the reorganisation of a room, or given pride of place in especially designed display features. Unfortunately, this doesn't necessarily diminish the risk involved in letting a designer manipulate those objects, as the owner of a valued collection of antique china teapots discovered when some hastily put together hanging shelves collapsed halfway through the makeover process.[15]

Although they pay their dues to the logic of commercial television in their quest for dramatic confrontations, TV makeover shows are the popular expression of an evolving and tense relationship between high-cultural or design-led discourses about the aesthetics of domestic interiors and mainstream taste. It is a conflict that has been with us throughout the 20th century, and which has seen the home as the main battleground between highbrow and lowbrow taste, experts and neophytes, professionals and amateurs. It is taken to its extreme in these reality shows where the conflict sometimes ends in tears, in front of the nation's eyes. But television has also provided a platform for equally intense, if more high-cultural, confrontations, such as Nicholas Barker and photographer Martin Parr's *Signs of the Times* documentary series, shown on BBC2 in 1991. Constructed as a series of interviews about the way in which people decorate their homes, *Signs of the Times* (with its apparently candid subtitle: 'A Portrait of the Nation's Tastes') extended Parr's interests in class and consumerism into the interior. It preceded the onslaught of reality TV makeover shows by just a few years, and in its producer's words, it set out, 'film narrative permitting, [. . .] to record as objectively as possible a wide range of contemporary tastes, and to present them so that viewers could judge them for themselves.'[16] Nevertheless, the result was a subtle but damning critique of middle-class tastes in home decoration and the discourses of social aspirations and personal identity that surrounded them.

MULTIMEDIA

While the concept of the makeover, which is essentially about highly visible and spectacular transformation, has a natural affinity with the medium of television, domestic makeover shows have found their way (as have others) into a whole range of different media. The rise of this type of programme from the mid-1990s coincided with the consolidation and expansion of the World Wide Web and of internet access as something that was no longer restricted to the workplace. As the numbers in PC ownership and personal internet accounts grew, the domestication of new technologies established a more organic connection between watching home improvement programmes, using makeover software and browsing related internet sites in a domestic context.

Essentially driven by commercial interests rather than by the intention to disseminate a particular idea through a variety of communication channels, this cross-media expansion adapted the televisual model to a variety of platforms. As a result, their discourses about the home, interior design and visual form, were often contradictory. They responded to the internal logic of the media without always presenting a cohesive approach.

This is particularly evident in relation to the role of both designers and owners in the process of home improvement. The TV programmes, by the nature of their format, emphasise the agency of the designers, while paying lip service to homeowners' requests or suggestions as to what they would like their interior to look and feel like. Ultimately, the owners' degree of control over the decisions taken and the final result is extremely limited. They are asked by the show's designers to perform certain tasks, ranging from painting walls to others that might involve a greater degree of personal contribution, such as making drawings, for instance. In most cases, however, not only have they not 'designed' what they're making, they also have no information as to how their work relates to the greater scheme under construction, and no choice as to where particular objects will be placed. TV domestic makeover shows are the celebrity designers' playground, an expression of their, not the owners', tastes. By being eccentric, demanding, stubborn or inspired, they reconfigure the home as a locus of dramatic narrative, presenting the practice of home improvement as a fun and exciting experience. The owners become a cast of secondary characters supporting the stars, in a script that involves celebrity design snobbery and populist entertainment.

In contrast, the spin-off books that accompany the series tend to reinforce more established notions of home improvement, that engage both with traditional approaches to design advice and contemporary discourses of individual control over the interior as an expression of personal identity. They graciously hand over the baton of taste to the amateur designer, reassuringly stating that 'your design should be down to your own personal taste – the concept of good and bad taste no longer has any credibility.'[17] Indeed, much of the advice and suggestions contained in these books, often proposing highly ornamental schemes, a mixture of period styles, homecraft practices like stencilling, textile dyeing or goldleaf application, would make any follower of 'good design' and 'good taste' shudder. But these are combined with more general information about colour, composition, the use of light and the effect and manipulation of materials. With the judicious application of all this, the amateur home improvers should be able, in contrast to their televised peers, to truly experience the home as a site of individual expression and creativity. 'Somewhere,' as the books suggest, 'where you, and you alone, have total personal control'.[18] Here, the populism of the TV shows, built around crowd-pleasing drama and celebrity appeal, turns into a populism that seeks to pacify middle-class taste anxiety:

> . . . change in design was led by the dictates of powerful taste gurus who pronounced . . . that rococo was out and neo-classical was in. Design [has] moved seamlessly overnight from an autocracy to a democracy and the bloodless revolution was effected by us, the people.[19]

Yes, the books seem to imply, by your home you shall be judged. Our living rooms are us, our kitchens an expression of 'what [we] want to say about [ourselves]'.[20] But we have now postmodernly moved beyond taste. There are no more taste gurus, is the earnest message of the domestic makeover gurus themselves. We are all creative, taste is a democratic commodity, we can all do it ourselves, and we will always get it right.

The BBC's website presents yet another vision of domestic space. *Changing Rooms* nestles under 'Design', as part of a hierarchy that structures, tellingly, the 'Lifestyle' section of the site. There, the

'Home' subsite is an umbrella for areas such as 'DIY', 'Design', 'Property' and 'TV and Radio'. This is the place to find 'design inspiration' online, and that particular menu takes the browser to a page where the BBC's design celebrities offer expert solutions for transforming and redesigning interiors. The home is shown as made up of a series of separate spaces: the bedroom, the kitchen, the dining room, the lounge, the attic, the playroom, the study. It is a traditional, essentially middle-class organisation of domestic activities, and offers no radical re-configuration of space. While colour or a favourite designer can be selected as the guiding source of inspiration, it is style, or better still, styles, that are offered as the main building blocks of the self-designed interior, the alphabet of the domestic makeover. They come neatly packaged, in a hybrid DIY reinterpretation of period features, design movements and ethnic influences.

The website forcefully presents domestic space as a themed environment, an Aladdin's Cave of available styles to suit a variety of tastes. Or even, as the online test linking attitudes and individual behaviour patterns to styles ultimately suggests, to a range of personalities. And if style and taste reflect our personality, then who could doubt that the alchemy of the domestic makeover will always be successful: as intimated by the gurus, it's not good or bad, it's 'me'.

Finally, the CD-ROM software, with three levels of 'design guidance', a range of layouts and styles, customisable inspiration boards, colour palettes, furniture selectors, and photo-realistic mock-ups, is perhaps the ultimate tool for the DIY representation of the domestic interior. Coming full circle, it provides the instant means not so much to physically alter our home, but to endlessly indulge in constructing changing representations of what it could be.

In its dizzying and ever-accelerating journey through the television screen, the home has undergone some fundamental transformations. While some of these have been for the most part a mediated reflection of various preestablished perceptions, the medium itself has increasingly become the crucible in which ideas of domesticity have been formed. Over the course of more than half a century, television has shifted from representing the spaces of the modern home as the site of rational, progress-informed agency, to offering a vision of domesticity that foregrounds drama, vulnerability, emotional attachments and scenographic display. This move from making to feeling mirrors a wider cultural transfer from post-war civic priorities to the more spectacular, and often self-indulgent, dynamics of our post-industrial consumer culture, and from a moral dimension to a fundamentally visual one. Certainly, the home has not been the only site where these changes have taken place, or even where they might be traced most accurately. Nevertheless, it does offer an exquisite setting for doing so, and has proved to be particularly responsive to the impact of mass-media representations of the domestic space.

In their recent request for advice to the interior design magazine *Living Etc*, a couple explained their dilemma in the following words:

'We have been slowly converting each room of our house with a theme. Cocktail Kitchen and Two-Tone Living Room were the first couple, and now we're moving onto the bathroom. We want it to be rock inspired . . .'[21]

Enhanced by the do-it-yourself capabilities of computer software and interactive websites, the 'themed' home seems to have struck the mainstream. Proactive home-makers experiment with styles as they would with colour or patterned wallpaper, cutting up their home into neat, discrete boxes and painting by numbers. Historically, the different rooms in a house have often had a particular visual character, generally derived from or related to their use. The modernist home resisted such discrimination, insisting on a clear overarching discourse of interior space. What emerges here, however, is not just a return to interior 'decoration', but the notion of fragmented spaces separated from their entire domestic system. Defined through form at least as much as through function, indifferent to 'good taste' as much as to 'good design', eclectic, playful and descriptive, they painstakingly construct a themed narrative of domesticity that courts spectacle, acknowledges ephemerality, and celebrates representation itself.

NOTES

1 Llewelyn-Bowen, Laurence, and Diarmuid Gavin. *Home Front Inside Out*. London: BBC Worldwide, 2002, p. 25.
2 Tiersten, Lisa. "The Chic Interior and the Feminine Modern: Home Decorating as High Art in Turn-of-the-century Paris." In *Not at Home: The Suppression of Domesticity in Modern Art and Architecture*, edited by C. Reed: Thames and Hudson, 1996, p. 20.
3 Tiersten, p. 28.
4 Griffith Winton, Alexandra. " 'A Man's House is his Art': the Walker Art Center's Idea House

Project and the Marketing of Domestic Design 1941–1947." *Journal of Design History* 17, no. 4 (2004): 377–396.

5 Griffith Winton, Alexandra. " 'A Man's House is his Art': the Walker Art Center's Idea House Project and the Marketing of Domestic Design 1941–1947." *Journal of Design History* 17, no. 4 (2004): 380.

6 Colomina, Beatriz. Quoted in: Griffith Winton, Alexandra. " 'A Man's House is his Art': the Walker Art Center's Idea House Project and the Marketing of Domestic Design 1941–1947." *Journal of Design History* 17, no. 4 (2004): 379.

7 Jones, Michelle. "Design and the Domestic Persuader: Television and the BBC's Promotion of Post-War 'Good Design'." *Journal of Design History* 16, no. 4 (2003): 307–318.

8 Camm, F. J. "The Practical Householder", Vol. 1 no. 9, August 1956, p. 671.

9 Oram, Scott. " 'Constructing Contemporary': Common-sense Approaches to 'Going Modern' in the 1950s." In *Interior Design and Identity*, edited by Susie McKellar and Penny Sparke. Manchester: Manchester University Press, 2004.

10 Morley, David. "Theories of Consumption in Media Studies", in Daniel Miller (ed.) *Acknowledging Consumption*. London: Routledge, 1995, p. 321.

11 Everett, Anna. "Trading Private and Public Spaces @ HGTV and TLC: On New Genre Formations in Transformation TV." *Journal of Visual Culture* 3, no. 2 (2004): 157–181.

12 Hutchinson, Thomas H. Quoted in Spigel, Lynn. "Installing the Television Set." In *The Everyday Life Reader*, edited by Ben Highmore. London: Routledge, 2002.

13 *Changing Rooms. Trust Me, I'm A Designer*. DVD, BBC 2002.

14 *Changing Rooms. Trust Me, I'm A Designer*. DVD, BBC 2002.

15 *Changing Rooms. Trust Me, I'm A Designer*. DVD, BBC 2002.

16 Barker, Nicholas. *Signs of the Times. A portrait of the Nation's Tastes*. Manchester: Cornerhouse Publications, 1992, n/p.

17 Llewelyn-Bowen, Laurence, and Diarmuid Gavin. *Home Front Inside Out*. London: BBC Worldwide, 2002, p. 9.

18 Llewelyn-Bowen, Laurence, and Diarmuid Gavin. *Home Front Inside Out*. London: BBC Worldwide, 2002, p. 17.

19 Llewelyn-Bowen, Laurence, and Diarmuid Gavin. *Home Front Inside Out*. London: BBC Worldwide, 2002, p. 16.

20 Llewelyn-Bowen, Laurence, and Diarmuid Gavin. *Home Front Inside Out*. London: BBC Worldwide, 2002, p. 25.

21 T&S. *Livingetc*, March 2005, p. 121.

3
Curtain Wars

Architects, Decorators, and the 20th-Century Domestic Interior[1]

Joel Sanders

Source: *Harvard Design Magazine*, Winter/Spring, 2002, pp. 14–20

Curtains, that element of the domestic interior on which the hands of the decorator and of the architect come directly into contact, embody many of the tensions and prejudices that have divided interior designers and architects since the emergence of the professional decorator in the late 19th century.[2] Here the hard walls designed by the architect meet the soft fabric that is the decorator's trademark, in a juxtaposition that confirms the common perception that architects work conceptually, using durable materials to shape space, while decorators work intuitively, adorning rooms with ephemeral materials and movable objects. Window treatments underscore the divergent design approaches of architects and decorators. Architects typically repudiate curtains, believing that this element that modulates vision compromises the architect's conception, obscuring and softening the precise geometry of architectural forms.[3] Decorators, for their part, consider curtains essential; veiling sunlight and views, curtains make domestic privacy possible and offer relief from the austere spaces created by architects often obsessed with form at the expense of comfort. Ironically, the "curtain wall," the iconic modernist glass facade that has come to embody so many key values of modern architecture—logic, structural integrity, and stripped-down form—takes its name from the curtain, the signature element of the interior decorator. But are architecture and interior decoration really oppositional practices, or are they, as the term "curtain wall" suggests, more interdependent than we think? Here I would like to argue that the supposed incompatibility between these two rival but nevertheless overlapping design practices evokes deeper cultural conflicts that are themselves bolstered and sustained by profound social anxieties about gender and sexuality.

CONTESTED TERRITORIES

"Curtain Wars," the professional rivalries that cleave the interior community, are not new; they date back at least to the 18th century. More often than not, the interiors of upper-class dwellings were then outfitted not by the architects who designed them but rather by upholsterers—tradesmen who supervised the activities of skilled craftsmen including furniture makers and rug manufacturers. Referring to the friction that often resulted from this division of labor, many writers, including Nicolas le Camus de Meézières (in 1780) and William Mitford (in 1827), levied the same complaint: upholsterers corrupt the spatial integrity of buildings.[4] Such tensions came to a head in the late 19th century when a new figure, the professional "decorator," arrived on the scene, usurping the upholsterer's role. Hired to coordinate and assemble the elements of residential interiors, the first decorators were often amateurs, self-taught society women from prominent families, who, like novelist Edith Wharton and designer Elsie de Wolfe, shared their good taste with their affluent friends and peers. In *The Decoration of Houses* (1897), considered by many the first handbook for the modern interior decorator, Wharton observed the battle that pits architects against decorators. "As a result of this division of labor, house-decoration has ceased to be a branch of architecture," she wrote. "The upholsterer cannot be expected to have the preliminary training necessary for architectural work, and it is inevitable that in his hands form should be sacrificed to color and composition to detail. . . . The confusion resulting from these unscientific methods has reflected itself in the lay mind, and house-decoration has come to be regarded as a black art by those who have seen their rooms subjected to the manipulations of the modern upholsterer."[5]

By educating a new breed of design professionals "to understand the fundamental principles of their art," *The Decoration of Houses* would, Wharton hoped, bridge the already entrenched architect/decorator divide. Interestingly enough, the novelist collaborated on this guide with an architect, Ogden Codman, Jr., who had helped her refurbish the interiors of her home in Newport, Rhode Island, and who later drafted the preliminary plans for The Mount, her villa in the Berkshires. But despite the cross-disciplinary intentions of the co-authors, in the end the text subordinates decoration to architecture. Wharton and Codman insist that "good decoration (which it must never be forgotten, is only interior architecture)" must obey the strictly architectural principles of logic, proportion, and decorum.[6] In many ways their description of the ideal relationship between architect and decorator mirrors the relationship between turn-of-the-century affluent women and domestic space: while houses were presumed to be a female domain, housewives were ultimately subject to the authority of their home-owning husbands.[7]

Since Wharton's era, not only have professional battle lines been drawn, but also architecture, whether viewed from the vantage of high or popular culture, seems always to emerge as the victor, commanding greater respect and prestige than does interior decoration. While the profession of interior decoration is scarcely a century old, the practice of furnishing the interiors of buildings is as old as the buildings themselves. Nevertheless, architecture has a long-studied history in the West (of monuments from the Parthenon to the Guggenheim, of architects from Ictinus to Frank Gehry), while interior decoration, conceived in this broader sense, has only recently been considered worth serious scholarship. And even when art historians and museum curators acknowledge interior design's legacy, they accord it a subordinate status. The very phrases "fine arts" and "decorative arts," used by art historians and museum curators to distinguish architecture from interior design, betray institutionalized prejudices. Such ostensibly innocent labels subtly but forcefully uphold the apparent superiority of architecture over interior design. Moreover, the structure of contemporary design education and professional licensing reinforces the disciplinary segregation authorized by scholars, dividing architecture and interior design into separate schools and departments, each with its own curriculum leading to different degrees and licenses.[8]

Bridging high and popular culture, design journalism perpetuates what I am calling Curtain Wars. Mainstream "shelter" magazines and professional architectural journals reinforce the architect/decorator divide through the different ways interiors are written about, photographed, propped, and graphically presented. Shelter magazines shy away from describing the designer's overall spatial conception, preferring instead to concentrate on furniture and objects, while architecture magazines tend to present interiors eradicated of all traces of the decorator. These journalistic conventions confirm each profession's mutual suspicion of the other—the architect's belief that furniture compromises the integrity of the spatial concept, and the decorator's conviction that the architectural shell is a backdrop for displaying valuable objects and furniture.

Yet despite the prejudices of educators, historians, and journalists, architecture and interior design inevitably intersect. The impulse to erect disciplinary hierarchies is a vain attempt to mask the overlapping, fluid nature of these two occupations. In practice, if not in theory, architecture and interior design do not so much oppose as presuppose each other.

How else do we explain architects like Richard Meier and Robert Stern picking fabrics and designing china, while interior designers like Thierry Despont and Steven Sills erect walls and install plumbing? Especially in cities like New York, where interiors comprise a major share of available work, architects and decorators are often in direct competition. Articles in popular magazines counseling readers on whether to hire an architect or a decorator highlight the interchangeability and confused identities of the two professions in the eyes of the public. For example, does an apartment renovation require the skills of an architect or a decorator? Common wisdom suggests (and some building regulations require) that if the project calls for relocating partitions, plumbing, and electrical wiring, then you need an architect; but if the job demands simply specifying freestanding furniture, fabrics, and finishes, you hire a decorator. But these distinct job descriptions break down during actual practice. Experienced architects understand that to maintain the integrity of their vision, they must select the furniture, fabrics, and objects. And savvy decorators, regularly called on to locate plumbing and wiring, routinely make architectural adjustments.

Perhaps the best evidence of the porous boundaries between architecture and decoration can be found in the work of those most responsible for erecting the borders in the first place—the first generation of modernist architects. As the literal separation between inside and outside breaks down with the development of the transparent curtain wall, so too does the boundary between architect and interior decorator. And that quintessential invention of modern architecture, "built-in" furniture (a hybrid between architecture and freestanding furniture), underscores the difficulty of determining where one practice ends and the other begins.

The advent of the "built-in" reflects modernism's advocacy of the totally designed architectural interior, a notion that ironically coincides with the birth of the professional decorator at the turn of the century. Avant-garde architects like Charles Rennie Mackintosh, Frank Lloyd Wright, and Ludwig Mies van der Rohe insisted on the integration of architecture and interior design, and their domestic work comprised custom-designed furniture and accessories. The Belgian Art Nouveau architect Henry van de Velde even designed dresses for his clients, so they would harmonize with his decorative schemes. As modern architects claimed to distance themselves from what they considered the superficial excesses of decorators, they assumed many of their roles and responsibilities, a practice that persists today. Nevertheless, to recognize such masters of modern architecture as Frank Lloyd Wright and Le Corbusier as important "interior decorators" who contributed significantly to the history of interior design would, in some circles, be tantamount to denigrating their legacy. How can we account for this contradiction at the heart of modern architecture, a practice that regards interior design either as entirely external or entirely internal to itself?

Should the boundaries codified by practitioners and scholars be understood as the architecture profession's defensive response to the rise of the decorating profession? Does the marketplace require both architects and decorators to differentiate their identities so that they can vie for the same clients? While professional competition is surely an important factor, I believe that the roots of these professional rivalries run much deeper. Institutional prejudices and interdisciplinary disputes not only perpetuate Curtain Wars, they are also symptomatic of our deepest and most ingrained anxieties about the nature of masculinity, femininity, and homosexuality—mirroring the broad cultural assumptions that shape our impressions of both disciplines, as well as our ideas about the identities of the professionals who practice them.

ENGENDERING RESPECT

By identifying manliness with the "authenticity" and womanliness with "artifice," the Western architectural tradition has for two millennia associated the ornamented surface with femininity. Discussing the origins of Doric and Ionic columns, Vitruvius famously wrote: "In the invention of two types of columns, they borrowed manly beauty, naked and unadorned for the one, and for the other the delicacy, adornment, and proportions characteristic of women."[9] For classical architects ornament was acceptable, provided it was properly subordinated to the tectonic logic of buildings, in much the same way women were taught to be subservient to men.

Of course, the status of ornament changed dramatically with the advent of modernism. Justifying their claim for an authentic, rational, and timeless architecture, architects like Adolf Loos and Le Corbusier enlisted gender prejudices in their quest to repudiate ornament, which they considered extraneous additions to buildings potentially corrupting their formal integrity. Evoking ornament's longstanding and pejorative association with femininity, these architects preferred stripped-down buildings, which they compared with "naked men," over ornamented structures, which they likened to over-dressed women. They found their archetypal model in the image of the male nude ("naked and unadorned"), the very antithesis of the female masquerader, embellished with clothes and makeup.[10]

The modernist argument against exterior ornament, based on its metaphorical resemblance to fashion, becomes even more extreme when brought to bear on the interior, where decoration becomes conflated with clothing.[11] Another term for curtains, "window dressing," with its allusion to apparel, underscores the intimate association of interior decoration with fashion and femininity. Like drapery on mannequins, drapes on windows "outfit" the domestic interior. While ornament, designed by architects, is at least materially and conceptually consistent with a building's skin, the fabrics and curtains selected by decorators are independent elements detachable from architectural surfaces. Draped with fabrics and finery, the decorated room calls to mind the decorated woman whose allure derives from superficial adornment—"womanliness as masquerade."[12] In *Women as Decoration*, published in 1917, Emily Burbank makes explicit this analogy between interior design and female costume, counseling women on how to dress in harmony with their surroundings. "Woman," she observed, "is an important factor in the decorative scheme of any setting—the vital spark to animate the interior decoration, private or public."[13]

Burbank's equation of women with decoration coincides with another historical development: the promotion of decorating as a woman's vocation. While architecture has, until recently, been considered an occupation of men and for men, interior design has, since its inception, been viewed as a practice, if not always of women, then certainly for women. "We take it for granted," Elsie de Wolfe wrote in 1914, "that this American home is always the woman's home. . . . It is the personality of the mistress that the home expresses. Men are forever guests in our homes, no matter how much happiness they may find there."[14]

It took a confluence of new historical forces—industrialization and the rise of the bourgeois family—to consolidate ancient prejudices and to transform interior design into a women's field. The notion of the domestic interior as predominantly a female domain, a concept often taken for granted, is, in fact, of recent origin, for historically the domestic household was associated with patriarchy. Aristocratic estates and their contents were passed down through generations of male heirs; they were the tangible signs of family wealth, power, and prestige. Throughout the 19th century, two linked factors profoundly altered this centuries-old tradition. The rise of industrialism made possible the manufacture of furniture. And the decline of the aristocracy and the rise of a socially mobile bourgeoisie created a new consumer, the housewife, whose role it was to purchase and arrange the commodities her husband no longer inherited.[15]

Feminist historians have exhaustively examined the impact of the gendered division of labor on domestic space. They have shown how, as the workplace became separated from the home in the 19th century and the domestic interior became the precinct of the housewife, a popular literature devoted to interior decorating emerged, geared to the female homemaker. Decorating, a practice once conducted by male architects and upholsterers, was thus appropriated by women—either "do-it-yourself" housewives or decorators, many of whom, like Elsie de Wolfe and Edith Wharton, were from wealthy, prominent families.

Professional status mirrors gender status: the subordinate relationship of interior decoration can be historically linked to its reputation as a woman's pastime. Not surprisingly, at the same time that 19th-century economic developments transformed both women and the domestic spaces

they presided over into signifiers of male wealth, financial forces finally gave interior decoration its due. Widespread affluence in the early 20th century fueled a burgeoning new market for home furnishings, a market encouraged by the popular press and geared to female consumers, one that continues to expand today.

Given that curtains and other interior accouterments have recently become bigger business, it could be argued that popular journalism now champions decoration over architecture, regularly showcasing domestic design in such venues as the *New York Times* "House & Home" section and *Martha Stewart Living*. And given also the strong affinities between fashion and interior design, it is no wonder that decorating has become a staple feature of the fashion press. Often produced by the same publishing house (for instance, Condé Nast or Hearst) and sold side by side on the newsstands, fashion and shelter magazines not only sometimes feature the same stories, but magazines like *Vogue* and *House & Garden* mirror each other graphically as well.

Disciplinary boundaries have become blurred not only on the pages of women's magazines. Stylists scout hip interiors as locations for fashion shoots, while top designers like Calvin Klein, Donna Karan, and Tom Ford (not to mention mass market companies like Banana Republic) have begun to produce lines of home furnishings to complement the "lifestyle" cued by their clothes. Fashion designers have thus shrewdly colonized a branch of design more closely affiliated with architecture. Have architects ceded a lucrative market to clothing designers because decorating is still tainted by its associations with fashion and femininity? Perhaps. But there is no doubt that over the past decade, the cultural currency of fashion has risen dramatically. The recent alliance between Prada and the Pritzker Prize winners Rem Koolhaas and Herzog and de Meuron suggests that, on the contrary, architects may finally be ready to relinquish their longstanding suspicions of fashion and decoration.

ENTER THE GAY DECORATOR

Curtain Wars implicate more than sex and gender; they also participate in the cultural construction of sexuality. Consider, for a moment, scenes from two Hollywood films, the 1949 adaptation of Ayn Rand's *The Fountainhead* and *Any Wednesday*, made in 1966. Both movies reinforce the image of the "macho" male architect; simultaneously, they fine-tune a newer cultural cliché—the gay interior decorator.

In *The Fountainhead*, Howard Roark, as played by Gary Cooper, personifies the architect as the epitome of masculinity. In the climactic trial scene, Roark defends himself for dynamiting his own project rather than seeing it disfigured by collaborating designers; the concept of masculinity is at the heart of his self-defense. A real man, says Roark, refuses to compromise his integrity and independence; the architect must follow his own vision rather than capitulate to the client's whim. In the final moments of the movie, Roark's adoring wife is conveyed upward by a construction elevator to the top of the architect's latest project—a highrise, of course—where he awaits her. Throughout the scene the camera's mobile eye is fixed worshipfully on Roark, who stands atop and indeed seems to surmount the skyscraper—an image that literally conflates the architect with manhood.

In *The Fountainhead*, professional identity is reinforced too by sartorial style. The clean lines of Howard Roark's dark suits, echoing the simple geometry of his buildings, indicate his heterosexual manliness. Similarly, in *Any Wednesday*, in a scene in which the male decorator consults with the newly wed played by Jane Fonda, the silk handkerchief that accessorizes the decorator's blazer betrays not only his design sensibility but also his sexual identity. And his flamboyant speech and gestures (which match the outrageous fees he freely admits to charging) call up the ubiquitous but suspect stereotype of the gay interior decorator.

If the history of the professional decorator has been neglected, the subject of homosexuality and interior decoration has been largely ignored.[16] Interestingly enough, two of the field's earliest and most influential members—Edith Wharton's collaborator Ogden Codman, Jr. and his notorious contemporary Elsie de Wolfe—were both homosexuals. A review of Codman's work in *Architectural Record* criticizes his interior designs for gaining "variety at the expense of virility."[17] While historians have described how decorating came to be considered a woman's pastime, they have yet to account for its emergence as a gay profession. One likely explanation is that interior design—like two allied design fields, fashion and theater—attracts a disproportionate number of gay men because gay men, already marginalized for their apparent femininity, are less reluctant to assume occupations that have traditionally been deemed feminine. But it is hardly coincidental that interior design, much like fashion and theater, is a discipline invested in

the notion of self-fashioning through artifice. Borrowing the useful concept developed by feminist and queer theorists of sexual identity as "performance," I have argued elsewhere that architecture participates in the staging of individual identity.[18] According to this view, masculinity and femininity are constructed through the repetition of culturally prescribed norms, including gestures, mannerisms, and clothing. Daily life resembles theater, a stage where men and women learn to act culturally sanctioned roles. Extending this analogy, we can compare interiors to stage sets that, along with costumes and props, help actors create convincing portrayals. Because of their outsider status, many gay men, like women, are acutely aware of the performative nature of human subjectivity. Could it be that this awareness, which some consider a survival instinct, allows gay men to be unusually well represented in decorating, a craft in which applied surfaces—fabrics, wallpapers, paint colors—are manipulated in order to fashion personality?

The idea that interiors express human and in particular feminine identity is a message reiterated in periodicals like *House Beautiful* and *Metropolitan Home*. Like apparel, décor is said to disclose the secrets of selfhood. Perhaps the most exaggerated and paradoxical examples of this staple of design journalism are photo spreads showcasing celebrity homes. Inviting us to identify with the camera's voyeuristic eye, magazines like *Architectural Digest, Vanity Fair*, and *In Style* urge us to peek into the homes of stars like Madonna and Cher. Suspending disbelief, we delude ourselves momentarily into believing that these contrived and often outré environments reliably mirror the authentic selves of their occupants.

Patrons have long looked to designers to outfit both themselves and their homes to communicate self-image to the outside world; but the rich and famous are not the only ones savvy enough to understand the importance of a well-appointed home. Since the 19th century, publications aimed largely at middle-class women have instructed amateurs on how to fashion themselves and their domestic environments to reflect who they are or aspire to be. With the feminization of the bourgeois home comes a new conception of the domestic interior: a unique abode that mirrors the temperament of its (female) homemaker. Taste, once considered an expression of class and breeding but now freed from its aristocratic associations, thus becomes understood as an expression of personality. Following a literary model established by architectural theorists from Vitruvius to Marc Antoine Laugier, two early and influential decorating texts—Wharton's *The Decoration of Houses* and de Wolfe's *The House in Good Taste*—counsel readers that decorating, much like architectural design, is essentially a rational process, based not upon whim or whimsy but rather upon objective principles. But as the genre of the decorating book evolved during the 20th-century, a contrary tendency emerged, one that sought to distance interior design from architectural precedent. Two popular books written by designers known for working with celebrity clients—Dorothy Draper and Billy Baldwin—illustrate this trend by upholding womanly taste, not manly reason, as a prerequisite for practice. Both counsel women on how to express themselves through décor.[19]

One might expect that this subjective design approach would make interior designers unnecessary: consult your inner decorator rather than hire a professional. However, as Draper's and Baldwin's texts both demonstrate, decorators quickly learned to take advantage of this union of décor and "womanly intuition," employing professional empathy as a strategy to distinguish themselves from "arrogant" male architects reputedly indifferent to client needs. Unlike stubborn architects who willfully impose their own ideas and values on patrons, the ideal decorator is a facilitator. According to Baldwin, "A decorator must first consider the kind of people for whom he works, how they lived, and their stated budget. Then, and only then, can he execute their wishes and requirements according to the best of his trained taste and experience."[20] Capitalizing on a seemingly innate ability to forge close and familiar client relationships, some decorators even came to resemble psychics, mediums who enable housewives to channel their inner selves through their domestic furnishings.

True to the genre of decorating literature, both Draper and Baldwin gloss over a fundamental contradiction posed by their endorsement of the intuitive creator: the attempt to teach skills that ultimately cannot be taught. Moreover, although both authors claim to disavow the "signature designer," the books ultimately validate this figure. Peppered with personal anecdotes, both volumes double as publicity memoirs. Ignoring the incontrovertible fact that people hire decorators precisely because they believe that "taste" can be purchased, Draper and Baldwin strive to convince the reader that hiring a famous designer will result in self-actualization.

Despite the sex of their authors, the subliminal portrait of the decorator painted in both these interior design books is of a female, thus playing into two of Western culture's long-standing associations with femininity: artifice, fabricated through the application of adornment, and subterfuge (while apparently submissive, women ultimately get their way by creating the illusion that others are in control). Not necessarily oppressive and limiting, these stereotypes have sometimes proved professionally beneficial. Under the right circumstances, the reputation of the cooperative and feminized decorator, when opposed to the figure of the domineering and unsympathetic architect, can pay off. ("I don't build for clients," says Howard Roark. "I get clients in order to build.") The gay male decorator's intimacy with his female patrons—coupled with his first-hand understanding of the crucial role interiors play in human self-fashioning—permits him to be trusted, to become, in a sense, "just one of the girls."

ENTER THE EMASCULATED ARCHITECT

The popular perception of interior decorating as inherently feminine, conducted by either women or effeminate gay men not only accounts for the field's inferior status, it also effectively threatens the self-esteem of many architects. For some practitioners, the unstable borders separating architecture from interior design touch directly on the vulnerability that lies at the core of manhood. Whether seen from the vantage of psychoanalytic theory or cultural history, masculinity, while seemingly invincible, is fragile.[21] The biological penis can never live up to the mystique of the cultural phallus. Architects are inevitably asked to perform certain "decorating" activities—like picking furniture and fabrics—that call into question their manliness. Already insecure about their attraction to tasks that society deems "unmanly," for some practitioners the architectural profession represents a strange sort of closet, a refuge that allows them (albeit with some discomfort) to engage in practices considered otherwise unacceptable for "real" men. Still, many architects feel they must defend against the sneaking suspicion that inside every architect lurks a decorator. Ultimately, architects disavow interior design as a way of overcompensating for masculine vulnerability; they are compelled to draw emphatic limits between two professions whose contours inevitably overlap.

At this point in history, with interior design finally beginning to receive greater professional and cultural recognition, Curtain Wars underscore the low self-esteem in much of the architectural profession, exacerbating the male architect's doubts about his self-determination and empowerment. The cultural priority accorded to architecture over interior design was never all that secure. Despite the grand historical narratives promoted by art historians, architecture, although an ancient craft, is nevertheless a relatively new profession that has struggled for respect. To this day architects sometimes have to fight to overcome their image as aristocratic amateurs.[22] In the absence of public belief that architects provide indispensable skills, architecture is often viewed as an expendable luxury. Why hire an architect when many states allow clients to enlist professional engineers or contractors to do the job? Although they endure similarly lengthy training and demanding apprenticeships, architects typically command significantly lower fees than do other professionals such as doctors, lawyers, and yes, even interior designers. And while the public image of the architect is as a dashing and sometimes charismatic figure, rarely does this positive appeal translate into actual value in the marketplace.

To add personal insult to this economic injury, architects often find themselves, despite their reputation for machismo, disempowered by colleagues and clients alike. The architect's expertise is often challenged both by those for whom he works—clients, developers, institutions—and by those who work for him—structural engineers, contractors, construction workers, and even decorators. (An interesting example of the age-old feud between architect and decorator involved Richard Meier and Tierry Despont at the new Getty museum in Los Angeles. Perhaps what proved so humiliating for Meier was not just that he was forced to compromise the integrity of his pristine galleries with "bordello-red" damask wall coverings, retro tapestries, dentilated cornices, and plastic moldings, but also that the infringement of the "suave" society decorator signified Meier's ultimate loss of control. But the real battle took place not between decorator and architect but between Meier and his client, curator John Walsh, who hired Despont in the first place. Contrary to the myth of the commanding architect, it is still the client who holds the purse strings and ultimately, the power.) In recent years a crisis of confidence has overtaken the architectural profession. As buildings become more complicated and expensive, architects have been "relieved" of many of the technical responsibilities they once fulfilled: specialists now handle engineering, structural, and construction issues. Often, in the case of large-scale projects like high-rise buildings, developers retain signature architects like Michael Graves to function as glorified styling consultants, hired to create clothing—building facades and lobby décor—for structures designed by others. Some trace this development to Philip Johnson, who was hired by Donald Trump in 1995 to style the exterior of the former Gulf and Western Building, now rebuilt to become the Trump International Hotel and Tower.[23] But the architect as skin decorator dates back to Postmodernism in the early 1980s. Transferring the logic of retail to buildings, developers like Trump acknowledge the cachet, prestige, and media attention associated with celebrity designers. In today's global marketplace, high-profile architectural practices are rapidly dismantling the once-firm boundaries between architect, decorator, and fashion stylist.

Yet in a world in which noncelebrity architects are increasingly marginalized by the public and their peers, it is no wonder that many architects might find picking upholstery and curtains uncomfortable; this seemingly inconsequential activity is tainted by its deep-seated associations with women and homosexuality. Today, however, as restrictive gender roles have become more flexible and alternative modes of sexuality are more openly expressed, professional possibilities are emerging—possibilities that portend the transcendence of the architecture/decorator divide. Not only are women now encouraged to be both high-powered professionals and nurturing mothers, but men are also increasingly permitted to express themselves through activities once closed off to them—they are free to be both athletes and aesthetes, breadwinners and homemakers. And decorating is finally coming out of the closet. Not only are shelter magazines showcasing domestic interiors inhabited by same-sex couples (who are often decorators), but professional journals like *Interior Design* also run provocative homo-social advertisements directed at both female and gay designers. Interestingly, journalism's belated but nevertheless welcome acknowledgement of the significant role that gays play in the design community coincides with an even more striking development: mainstream media like the *New York Times* and *Wallpaper*, and even companies like Ikea are setting their sights on a new household consumer—straight men hip to the latest decorating trends. In "Pulls and Pillowcases: It's a Man's World," a recent *New York Times* article devoted to how this burgeoning tendency has created new tensions between co-habitating men and women, journalist Rick Marin writes, "There are two kinds of men. The kind that spend long hours lying on the couch in front of professional wrestling. And those of us who prefer to spend our spare time shopping for the perfect couch to lie on. You'd think women would prefer to cohabit with the shopping man. Not necessarily."[24]

Now that the mainstream culture is finally beginning to accept the fluidity of gender identities, both architects and decorators are able to embrace one of the best aspects of domestic design: its ability to align activities once conventionally designated as distinctly "masculine" or "feminine": science and art, logic and intuition, architecture and interior decoration. Professionals who can integrate such supposedly opposite skills are newly empowered to question conventional and restrictive notions of gender and to invent a new design vocabulary that will merge the best features of the divided worlds of architecture and decoration. Collapse various distinctions—between building scale and human scale, stable shell and freestanding furniture—and architecture will finally be understood as continuous practices. Whether rigid or malleable, found on the inside or the outside, the surfaces of our buildings work like the clothing that covers our bodies; both are coded to enable us to articulate the various identities that we assume every day. The time is ripe for a new generation of designers to move beyond Curtain Wars and invent a hybrid design vocabulary that will allow a range of human identities and activities to transpire in domestic space.

NOTES

1 Many of the themes and issues explored here were raised in the "Curtain Wars" conference that I organized at Parsons School of Design in 1996.
2 The term "decorator," which originally designated an individual who practiced what we today call interior design, is now considered both obsolete and pejorative: it evokes the image of "decoration," a culturally denigrated concept that I will call into question. In the same spirit in which the gay community has revived the once-reviled term "queer," I will use the labels "decorator" and "interior designer" interchangeably, to both politicize and historicize the activity of "decorating" domestic space.
3 Frank Lloyd Wright never used curtains and thought of them as "unhygienic." Charles Gwathmey is quoted in the October 2001 *Architectural Digest*: "Interior design 'is a reductive process,' he asserts. 'Decorators think of coming in and adding to "enrich," and I think of our work as the opposite. The interior does not want to be covered up; it does not want to be added to. . . . If I design a window wall, the details of that window wall—its materiality, its proportion, the fenestration, the way we control the light—are all integrated and thought about. The idea of coming in and saying, "Let's put a curtain over that!" is totally antipathetical and totally contradictory' " (p. 100).
4 Le Camus de Mézières insisted that the furniture of an important bedchamber should be designed by the architect "and not by the upholsterer who should confine himself to executing the design"; William Mitford claimed that "the upholsterer's interest . . . is in direct opposition to the architect's credit." Peter Thornton recounts these, as well as other attacks against the upholsterer, in *Authentic Décor: The Domestic Interior, 1620–1920* (New York: Viking, 1984).
5 Edith Wharton and Ogden Codman, Jr., *The Decoration of Houses* (New York: Classical America and Henry Hope Reed, 1997), xx.
6 Ibid., 13.
7 But Wharton represents an exception to the paradigm: Vanessa Chase argues that Wharton's intellectual and economic independence allowed her to successfully invert typical gendered power relationships in the design of her own home, The Mount. See "Edith Wharton, The Decoration of Houses, and Gender in Turn-of-the-Century America," in *Architecture and Feminism* (New York: Princeton Architectural Press, 1996).
8 I confront the professional rivalries and contradictions described here on a daily basis. As a licensed architect based in Manhattan, apartment renovations comprise much of my practice, work that has required me to augment my architectural training with decorating skills that I never learned in school. Intending to rectify this gap, I attempted, when I became director of the Graduate Program in Architecture at Parsons School of Design, to incorporate interior design classes into the curriculum. However, my efforts to merge disciplinary boundaries were frustrated by the school's institutional structure: Parsons had recently established a separate Department of Interior Design.
9 Vitruvius, *The Ten Books on Architecture*, trans. Morris Hicky Morgan (New York: Dover, 1960).
10 See Mary McLeod, "Undressing Architecture: Fashion, Gender, and Modernity," and Mark

Wigley, "White Out: Fashioning the Modern," in *Architecture in Fashion* (New York: Princeton Architectural Press, 1994). Mark Wigley's *White Walls, Designer Dresses: The Fashioning of Modern Architecture* (Cambridge: MIT Press, 1995) discusses in depth the ambivalent but nonetheless pivotal role fashion played in the discourse of modern architecture.

11 Here I am elaborating on the notion of "architectural dressing" discussed in the introduction to the collection of essays I edited, *Stud: Architectures of Masculinity* (New York: Princeton Architectural Press, 1986).

12 The phrase was coined by psychoanalyst Joan Riviere, herself a dressmaker before writing the famous 1929 essay, "Womanliness as a Masquerade." See *Formations of Fantasy*, eds. Victor Burgin, James Donald, and Cora Kaplan (London and New York: Methuen, 1986), 35–14.

13 Emily Burbank, *Women as Decoration* (New York: Dodd, Mead and Company, 1917).

14 Elsie de Wolfe, *The House in Good Taste* (New York: The Century Company, 1913).

15 Two books that survey premodern developments are Mario Praz, *An Illustrated History of Interior Decoration* (New York: Thames and Hudson, 1982) and Thornton, *Authentic Décor*. For a discussion of the invention of the modern professional decorator, see "The Emergence of Interior Decoration as a Profession" in Ann Massey, *Interior Design of the 20th Century* (London: Thames and Hudson, 1990).

16 One of the few authors to address the prominent role of gay and lesbian practitioners in interior design is Aaron Betsky, who takes up this topic in *Queer Space: Architecture and Same-Sex Desire* (New York: William Morrow and Co., 1997).

17 "Some Recent Works by Ogden Codman, Jr.," *Architectural Record*, July 1905, 51.

18 See *Stud*, 11–25.

19 Counseling female readers on how to express themselves through décor, Draper writes: "Your home is the backdrop of your life, whether it is a palace or a one-room apartment. It should be honestly your own—an expression of your personality. So many people stick timidly to the often-uninspired conventional ideas or follow some expert's methods slavishly. Either way they are more or less living in someone else's house." Dorothy Draper, *Decorating Is Fun! How to Be Your Own Decorator* (New York: Doubleday, Dovan, and Co., 1941), 4; Billy Baldwin, *Billy Baldwin Remembers* (New York: Harcourt Brace Jovanovich, 1974).

20 Baldwin, 73.

21 Although they offer different explanations, both cultural historians and psychoanalytical theorists argue that modern masculinity is in crisis. Historians attribute this to the aftermath of the Second World War that transformed traditional roles in both the workplace and the home. See Michael S. Kimmel, "Consuming Manhood: The Feminization of American Culture and the Recreation of the Male Body, 1832–1920," in *The Male Body: Features, Destinies, Exposures*, ed. Lawrence Goldstein (Ann Arbor: University of Michigan Press, 1994). For a psychoanalytic reading of masculinity as masquerade, see Kaja Silverman, *Male Subjectivity at the Margins* (New York: Routledge, 1992). Several recent books explore the crisis of masculinity in terms of the depriving yet felt-to-be-necessary distance boys create from their mothers in order to feel like independent, "manly" beings, a distance girls feel less need for (see, for instance, *The Reproduction of Mothering*, by Nancy Chodorow, *In a Time of Fallen Heros*, by William Betcher and William S. Pollock, and *I Don't Want to Talk About It*, by Terrence Real).

22 The professional standing of the architect is a relatively recent invention. During the Middle Ages, architects belonged to guilds and were considered artisans. While the names of some master builders have been recorded for posterity, it was not until the Renaissance that the status of architects, along with that of artists, was elevated from anonymous craftsmen to individual creators. Even then, professional recognition did not come quickly. From the Renaissance through the mid-19th century, architecture was still considered an "art" largely practiced by amateurs like Thomas Jefferson, who personified the self-taught "gentleman architect." Not until the establishment of academies like the Beaux-Arts in Paris in the 19th century do architects define themselves as experts who learn not on the job but in school, a change in status that leads to the licensing of professional architects in the early 20th-century.

23 Tracie Rozhon, "Condos on the Rise, by Architectural Stars," *New York Times*, July 19, 2001, "House and Home."

24 February 8, 2001, Section F, 1.

4
Figures of Living

Manolo De Giorgi and Marco Romanelli

Source: Rassegna 58, *Statement of Interior: Italian Apartments 1947–1993*. 1994, pp. 4–7

A history of the quasi-present, lacking the usual distance from the subject matter, is a history mainly built on the affective relationship between the author and his research subject. This "immediate" history in which the time separating the fact, its recording and its rationalization has been cut, indicts some of the subjective distortions of those who not only record an event but also have been responsible for its production.

"Statement of interior", is a story that is still in progress, continuously subject to verification, a story written by designers, rather than by historians in the narrower sense of the word.

1. To speak of interior architecture, or in other words to speak of the interior as an architectural problem, seems quite unusual today, even in a context such as the Italian, where that scale of design had been highly privileged and where extraordinary results had been reached as early as the late fifties. Theorizations on the urban dimension of design, the irrevocable deterioration of typological research and the easy exhibitionism of drawn architecture or of postmodern poetics have later caused many of us to lose sight of this "inner", and somehow founding, dimension of architecture. We often discover today that we are no longer able to either design or interpret a building on the basis of a correct inhabitability of its interior. On the other hand it is still possible to retrace, in our opinion, the foundations of the design attitude, focused precisely on inhabitability, which had made an Italian architectural tradition. According to a scheme characteristic of a nation like ours, where histories are made by a succession of exceptional events, occasions and personalities (without creating an average level or a widely diffused awareness), one can make a parallel history of architecture, that touches the official one at some points only. A history made by architects, with strong inclinations and skills for structuring the interior space. A history originating from the undeniable watershed represented by postwar reconstruction, continuing to this day, involving, at an indisputably high level, the young generations of architects.

2. Already in the years following World War II interior architecture took precociously heed of recording the problem of reading the historical data by shifting its meaning away from the idealistic concept of cultural asset to the modern and all-inclusive one of the "existing", in the new configurations of trace, clue, material residual. The theme of the reading of the existing has thus overridden the rigid value–non-value dualism of philologic-stylistic-chronological kind, making way for the more general theme of the interpretation. The path for a possible use of the existing heritage in a spatial-physical-anthropological sense, as the material condition and premise for design, has thus been traced. Albini's and Scarpa's readings in existing containers therefore represent guides as well as essays of historical interpretation, applicable also to major architecture, more ambiguously ensnared for long periods in the postwar years, either in the trap of historicism and other "isms" or paralyzed in its operations of reading by the poetics of the *tabula rasa* so dear to many representatives of the Modern Movement.

3. We can identify, in the succession of these interiors, the symptom of an "adjustment of the fire" for the architectural discipline. Today when we are finally in a position to analyze a history that has essentially been made "by and for" the upper middle classes, free from complexes, but above all lucid in recognizing relapses, at very different scales of design, of a large number of the buildings that have left their mark on that history. Relapses which, actually, are more important than those provoked by apparently aimed projects, demagogically attired in educational or demonstrative intents for the benefit of the poorer classes. Today, when such moralistic and pedagogical attitudes are a thing of the past, we finally

manage to recover a tradition that has been rejected by history, reconsidering the paradigmatic and fruitful design sequence of the Italian apartment.

4. The school from "the inside" is a tough one, a hard apprenticeship which presupposes great skills in controlling the builder's yard and working on a wide variety of scales, from the 1:200 of the configurations of the whole to the 1:1 of the details. It requires determination and skill in establishing a dialogue with the users. All this has generated a method that adopts the ground plan as its main instrument, continuously verifying in the cross-section that which is gradually defined on the plan, wholly independently of the elevation. Such condition, if based on the very definition of a discipline operating within a container, has over the decades become an unconscious sheet anchor for the following generations that tackle the subject. And it has recently been defended from mannerism and scenographic approach of an architecture solely aimed at the making of a façade image. At the same time the quick, and one could say inevitable, transition from the plan to the builder's yard, which characterizes the work on interior, has enabled these designers to concentrate on the making, the necessary verification and the implementation of the validity of the ideas drawn. A verification made concertedly with the most critical of judges, the dweller of the house. On the one hand, therefore, an extraordinary oscillation between the measurement in milli-meters and the direct planning, on the builder's yard, together with the workmen, and on the other an extraordinary oscillation between one's own experience of living, and that of others. But this is not all. There is a further balance which, by radicalizing, poses on the hand the necessity to consider the work of the architect "in interiors" as a "service job", thereby suggesting the figure of the technician, and on the other the possibility of a totalizing intervention and the consequent delineation of an artistic figure. These positions have for a long time been considered as alternative, if not even contrasting, while it must be underscored that both are, at the same time, part of the specific aspects considered by those who conscientiously operate with interiors. Then, in particular, the second argumentation, i.e. that of the artistic quality, leads to the deduction of another distinctive characteristic of architecture "in interiors", namely the ability to throw a real bridge between design disciplines and artistic disciplines. The hidden common denominator for those who operate in these two contexts is the greater proximity with the material as compared to those who are, on the contrary, interested in interventions on a larger scale. In fact the material, whether it is a work on semifinished building products and on assembly, or is completed in the artistic intervention of others, has a primary importance in the interior dimension. In this interpretation, and likewise in the founding planimetric attention we already mentioned, the work of interiors becomes an important and basic school for the entire operative range of the architect, providing sensibilities and knowledge that are otherwise not easily accumulated.

5. In the future perspective interior architecture acquires, especially as far as design is concerned, with which it has often been erroneously confused, an important moralizing function. In the face of the theme of the excessive, of the waste and the proliferation of the objects in the domestic space in reiterated and at times under-used types of furnishing, interior architecture can represent a bridgehead in the dismantling project, relaunching the theme of built-in furniture as equipment for the house rather than for its inhabitants. The result is a reconsideration of the dwelling in terms of volumetric encumbrance, recovering to the elements of interior architecture a modern-ancient centrality (user who adapts to the dwelling, to the niche). In this logic, with regard to the world of furnishing production, an additional contribution to interior architecture is given. In fact the interiors presented here were both matrix and verification for a great number of furnishings which later passed from the singularity of those places to the space without limits of mass production.

6. Even in the particular and decidedly experimental condition which has often assimilated it to a "work of art" or relegated it to the "one-off" sphere, Italian architecture has provoked, in anthropological and material-culture terms, a relapse on the theme of inhabiting that is more relevant than that caused by morpho-typological architecture itself in the last twenty years, incapable of seeing the dwelling as anything but a problem of elevation and planimetry. "Italian dwelling interiors" in other words managed to create a model which today identifies a very clear and "specific" aspect of design culture (a mixture of prothesis-architecture, of craftsmanship, of temporary installations, of object culture) while it is not possible to retrace an equally specific character in the typological models elaborated for residential architecture.

5
The Bounds of Privacy
Boundary and Domain in Japanese Culture

Shigeru Uchida

Edited from a lecture delivered at the 11 November 1994 symposium *3rd Yokohama Big Design*

My topic today is potentially a problematic and also very interesting subject. No doubt the word "privacy" conjures up an image of a "self" surrounded by an invisible barrier that cuts it off from all others, but such a scheme of "self" just does not seem to be found in Japan.

Rather, I would like to discuss the notion of "boundaries" in terms of the more succinct expression, *kekkai*. Originally a Buddhist concept, a *kekkai* was said to exist at the divide between the sacred and the profane, in which the profane was in essence an analogue – a continuum – through which crop up sacred times, places and persons. Such sacred "moments" are digital – that is, discrete isolates. It is within this structure, where cutting out demarcations in linear time-space allows transcendent elements to emerge, that I see the very source of the "self".

Ego, subject, "self". But what is this "self" that perceives a "world" here and now, that dwells within that "world"? Irrational as it seems, it is conceivable only as an in-bounded "non-world" set off from the "world".

Granted, the idea of carving a small, exclusive sub-area out of that continuous world-space bears an undeniably close relation to the idea of "self". And of course, the act of fencing something off relates closely to that of possessing. Yet surely the concepts of "sacred" and "profane", not to mention the very means of demarcating their boundaries, must vary greatly with their respective cultural contexts. No doubt such distinctions had their beginnings in erecting physical barriers between either side, so that what lay within these barriers or without stood as utterly disparate dimensions. Eventually, such spatial registers became less physical and more emblematic devices, that is, mere perceptual constructs. Fixed rigid barriers are not absolutely necessary where some

form of notational index will suffice. I will touch upon this point again later.

SPATIAL AWARENESS VIA VERBALISED DOMAINS

As I see it, notions of privacy and its bounds are deeply rooted in the cosmologies of particular cultures. Hence any Japanese scheme of demarcating boundaries based on Japan's native cosmological premises will differ vastly from that of Western societies. This is an important consideration to bear in mind.

In order to reflect upon typically Japanese spaces, I would like to examine "*kekkai* constructs" or "bounded domains". I should emphasize that I am not speaking of *kekkai* strictly in the Buddhist sense, but rather more generally as a small, circumscribed space.

As is frequently pointed out, human beings do not perceive the world as it is. The act of naming always enters into the picture, as do what I have termed *kekkai* constructs. We can only grasp the entirety of the world when it is divided up into more concrete spaces by various *kekkai* or demarcations.

That is to say, our living environment is full of boundaries, as well as the domains that these various boundaries establish. Furthermore, our spatial awareness depends upon verbalisation of such demarcated domains. Differences between the various human means of carving out spaces or their verbalisation are among the best indicators of cultural differences between peoples. At the very least, *kekkai* constructs or bounded domains are in no way universals common to all ethnicities the world over.

Let us consider myths of "inside" versus "outside". The act of making a boundary necessarily frames a duality composed of a closed "inner" realm and an excluded "outer" realm. Herein we see a *kekkai* or boundary formed at the dichotomy or contrast between the order (cosmos) within the community and the confusion (chaos) without. In most cases, the origins of boundary myths are to be found in a fear of the unknown, the foreignness of what lies outside the sedentary farming community. Such mythologized fears of the dark world outside serve to set up *kekkai*, which in turn cement the "sameness" of whatever lies inside while underscoring the "otherness" of all else outside.

Relationships between those within the community and those without, between the interior and exterior of the house, between one room and another, would all seem to manifest the distinct cultural values of a given people. Just as it is certainly true that our post-19th-century way of life has come about through the dissolution of such myths. Yet if we look carefully, we can often detect such cultural roots surfacing even in contemporary society.

Thus we can see why *kekkai* constructs are so closely linked to the cosmology of each culture. As long as human beings put names to things so as to make the world their own, cultures with different languages, cultures with divergent spatial percepts will necessarily differ in their versions of the world. Let us now turn to the subject of cosmology and privacy, mainly in Japanese architectural space, in terms of various schemes of spatial partitioning.

PHYSICAL *KEKKAI* AND *KEKKAI* DEVICES

I find three different classes of *kekkai* constructs here in Japan. The first is that of "physical *kekkai*". These are fixed and not easily moved – *kekkai* as obstacles. They are what we might also call "brute *kekkai*". The inside of the barrier is quite visibly cut off from the outside and any communication in-between is obstructed. The Great Wall of China is a prime example, but we might also cite the walled cities of Asia Minor, such as Troy, as well as Dubrovnik in former Yugoslavia.

Fortress walls were put up to protect the inhabitants from barbarian invasion. Physical structures completely surrounded the space. This is the most basic pattern of *kekkai* construct, the starting point from which humanity – we Japanese included – began to enclose space.

The second class is that of "*kekkai* devices". From this point we begin to see Japanese cultural

tendencies emerging. They may include temporary or moveable elements; or, if architectural in nature, they put up little resistance to physical force. *Ikegaki* (hedges), *magaki* (plaited-bamboo garden fencing), *mon* (gates), *shikimi* (crossbars), *koshi* (lattices), *shoji* (translucent paper sliding doors), *fusuma* (opaque paper sliding doors), *noren* (partition curtains), *shikii* (door-sills), *kutsunugi ishi* ("footware removal" entryway step stones), and *chozuhachi* (stone washbasins) are all typical examples of such devices. Likewise, most means of demarcating temporary ceremonial or festival grounds may by extension be considered *kekkai* devices. The Shinto *shimenawa* (sacred straw rope), which derives its name from *shimesu* "to show" – or possibly from *shimeru* "to occupy" or the homophonic *shimeru* "to tie" – thus carries the meaning of a "sign", a "hold", or a "close".

Sacred or holy precincts are often roped off with *shimenawa*. One can often see four bamboo posts set up by the roadside and strung with *shimenawa* to create an impromptu sanctuary, frequently for consecrating a building site. Even the act of joining hands at a celebration, or a sumo wrestler who ritually girds (*shimeiv*) himself with a loincloth, shows the same degree of signification.

This second class of *kekkai* device is much more subtle than physical *kekkai*. While equally visible, it simultaneously incorporates unseen or tacit demarcations. Let there be no mistake: though the examples I've cited are fairly unambiguous, not everything in this category is so straightforward. Frequently, we find a complex complementarity of interrelationships. Take, for instance, a latticework *koshi*, one of the more subtle spatial partitions. Physically, the lattice grid hints at the functions of a wall, yet visually it obstructs nothing at all. It is, in other words, a partitioning device that works on the level of conscious recognition. Here then, is a partitioning device that truly reflects the special character of Japanese spatial concepts. For in Japan, when separating space A from space B, instead of fixing a rigid barrier wall, it is also important for each side to know what is going on on the other. This is a connective analogue boundary that both segments and mediates between either side to allow some flow between the two. The *fusuma* door may be closed, but it still provides a hint of what might be going on in the next room. Even the decoration on *fusuma* panels often features some motif that it has in common with the decoration in the adjacent room. This design move clearly reflects an awareness that spaces A and B are always mutually engaged and interacting.

The cultural bases behind these subtle boundaries, as we will see later when we discuss "suppositional *kekkai*" and "taboo *kekkai*", are replete with complex complementarities.

DOMAINS AS RITES OF PASSAGE – MARGINAL ZONES

The third category of *kekkai* – which would hardly seem to constitute boundaries at all – are those special Japanese spaces which I will call "marginal zones". These are spaces that arise as passageways from A to B, which relate very closely to both A and B, yet really belong to neither. They are non-A, non-B spaces such as the under-eaves or the *engawa* exposed corridor areas that wrap around traditional Japanese houses.

By a passageway from A to B, I do not mean merely a momentary transition, but a whole intermediate realm that exists as a rite of passage partaking at once of time and space, that is, a site of initiation. We have seen how myths of inner versus outer, myths of order versus chaos, have their origins in the dichotomies that arise when a community posits a foreign world "out there". A boundary of distinction must be drawn for such myths to arise.

Yashiro (shrines) and smaller *hokora* (spirit houses), things that are imbued with magic significance and that serve as village boundary markers and furthermore keep out evil spirits, are all *kekkai*. They quite clearly indicate a line, an in-bounding articulation of closure, and it is for this reason that we tend to picture *kekkai* divisions as linear demarcations.

Nonetheless, a marginal zone is a non-A, non-B space that belongs neither to A nor B. It is, in other words, an unaffiliated "detached" space. And the significance of that "detached" space lies in the rite of passage that sets a non-worldly *hare* (pure) realm apart from the everyday *ke* (defiled) realm. In *chanoyu* – the tea ceremony – to cite one example, we find a ritualistic space that guides us to the tearoom. The *roji* (tea-garden) is just such a space; it is always found paired together with the tearoom. Tea-master Sen Rikyu taught that "it is essential to know *suki* (humility) in the *roji*", for the activities inside the tearoom constitute an "other world" apart from daily life. To be conducted into that "other world" means casting off worldly affairs and attaining the sphere of *mu* (nothingness) and *ku* (emptiness). And that entails passing

through a "detached" marginal zone. It is no coincidence that the ideal to which the rustic tea aesthetic aspired was a "mountain hermitage in the city's midst". That is, an otherworldly refuge imagined far off in the immortal hills yet right in the centre of town.

Or again, this marginal zone is given architecturally embellished expression in traditional Japanese houses at the under-eaves where the interior extends into the exterior. There most commonly we find the *engawa* and a place for the somewhat ritualised removal of shoes prior to entering the house as is the Japanese custom. In ancient Japan, however, this under-eaves space was more open and natural, while the removal of one's shoes was quite literally a ritual to exorcise the evil forces outside. This space is still strongly external in character, though strictly speaking it is "detached", belonging neither to the exterior nor interior.

This sense of marginal space has contributed greatly to Japanese culture and art. The interior that pushes out toward nature allows a deeper communion with the environment, a more lingering appreciation of beauty. Witness the *Manyoshu* and other ancient Japanese poetic classics abounding with expressions of the spiritual grace of living together with nature.

So much, very simply, for bounding constructs that divide spaces A and B; yet there are still other visible and invisible factors that further reinforce spatial interrelationships: "suppositional *kekkai*", "conventional *kekkai*" and "taboo *kekkai*".

Japanese spatial articulations, certainly most of the *kekkai* devices we have already discussed, are premised to a greater or lesser extent upon the act of "supposing". The sanctuary roped off by the *shimenawa* is without a doubt a "suppositional *kekkai*" underwritten by pre-agreed assumptions. Indeed, when we start looking for culturally distinct signifiers, *goza* (straw mats), *mosen* (wool runner carpets), *dohyo* (raised earth rings), almost any area bounded by lines or surfaces can be considered "suppositional *kekkai*". A garden may be likened to an island, viewed as the mythical Chinese paradise of Mt. Penglai, and so on, to enjoy a heightened sense of creativity. The rule of thumb being that "suppositional" constructs always scale up, with mere points perceived as lines, and lines seen as planes. More unique to Japan, however, is the cultural tendency to "suppose" structures upon what is not present. Let us consider this *waka* verse by the late-12th-century poet Fujiwara Teika: "Casting wide my gaze/Neither flowers nor crimson leaves/

From this bayside hovel of reeds/In the autumn twilight." One of the most famous selections from the Shinkokinshu anthology, it sings of sparseness and poverty, the "supposition" of what is not there giving rise to a contrast, the paradoxical absence of any substantial thing of beauty only adding more pathos to the scene.

CONVENTIONAL *KEKKAI* AND TABOO *KEKKAI*

Finally we come to "conventional *kekkai*" and "taboo *kekkai*". These are truly culturally specific. Even "*kekkai* devices" and "suppositional *kekkai*" such as we have examined are based upon systematised taboos and conventions. Nowhere are these formulaic systems ever clearly set forth. In this sense, "conventional *kekkai*" prove little more than hypothetical constructs founded upon tacit understandings, which might easily fall apart. Japanese culture must therefore incorporate an element of moderation lest it self-destruct as a cohesive entity. But since ancient times, moderation has prevailed over the social order directly through a pervasive status system, conversely elevated to an aesthetics of knowing one's place, the roots of which can be traced to the community, that is, to the "in-group out-group myths" held by the common people. Shared bonds within the community are a product of the socio-cultural mechanics of "exclusionism". By creating "others" a "we" comes into sharp relief. Deep down in the regenerating, replicating life of the community we find such hidden mechanisms in the form of taboos directed at some object to be avoided. Overlaying these taboos are stories, folktales, and mountain lore. A typical song about a villager spirited away to an "other world" may thus convey the terrors of estrangement from the community, the underlying message being that no matter how tiresome the daily routine within the community, the world outside is unimaginably worse. Community bonding involves laying down a large number of taboos.

Strangely enough then, at least by contemporary standards, peeping came to be fairly characteristic behaviour in Japan. Even so, people did not go stealing glances all the time; particular contexts governed when it was acceptable to peep. The issue here, as we have seen earlier, was that Japanese boundary markers such as *kekkai* devices can be physically ambiguous. Given the aim to compose a partition that interposes between spaces A and B yet allows them to communicate, it stands to reason that Japanese culture would be permissive about wandering eyes. Looking through such partitions ceased to be active peeking and became passive peeping – just happening to see. That much was permissible or unavoidable; anything else, of course, would be considered extremely rude. A very fine line draws both the spying party and the spied upon into a relationship of being permitted and permitting. It establishes certain mutual conventions of aesthetic: actually seeing what is "not seen", knowing what is "not there". Or perhaps "not knowing" what is there. Mutually exclusive propositions must be allowed to co-exist. This is a form of "suppositional *kekkai*". Such is the very complex character of the truly paradoxical relations, manners and other social constructs which have been codified into Japanese culture.

Consider, for instance, the ancient codes and customs surrounding *oshi-idashi-ginu* or *uchiide no kinu* ornamented kimono sleeves. Heian period noblewomen, when riding in an ox carriage, would let a sleeve trail out below the split-reed blinds that supposedly concealed their person, thereby hinting at whoever was inside. "Conventional *kekkai*" at times serve to give spatial qualities to social status, so as to confer a mutually accorded space within the status system. This is never an actual space; no actual divisions break the continuum between upper and lower classes, or between men and women. It is far more the case that these are psychologically defined and consciously affected conventions. Still, the idea of substituting an abstract concept with a tangible spatial corollary is typically Japanese.

NATIVE COSMOLOGY AND WESTERN CULTURE

For the sake of argument, I have categorised three different types of *kekkai* constructs, which however appropriate, do not necessarily cover the whole of Japanese spatial awareness. They are merely general parameters. Let me stress that these various constructs never interrelate in any simple manner, but overlap in truly strange and complex ways to create the polysemous character of Japanese architectural space.

The point of emphasising what I have called *kekkai* constructs is that native Japanese spatial concepts are still alive in Japanese society today. Thus I have explained something of Japan's culture of *kekkai* constructs, when actually they go back to a more fundamentally human level. Draw a line on the floor and there we have a partitioned or even an enclosed area. The same holds for surrounding an area with posts.

These means of establishing boundaries transcend the particular cultural properties of any one people. Or to take the discussion further, even those "conventional *kekkai*" seemingly already gone from contemporary life have not in fact disappeared, but only slipped down into the underlying Japanese cosmology.

Ever since the Meiji Restoration in 1868, we Japanese have striven to achieve a modern Westernised society, learning in the process that "culture is never lost". Many lament the loss of Japanese traditions. Indeed, in actual fact, modernisation has dismantled many different national cultures and cosmologies, not just Japan's. Yet when discussing culture, it is more useful to look at all that was "not lost" in spite of the Westernisation policies of the Meiji regime. Naturally, I do not mean to say that all aspects survived modernisation. The demise of traditional politics and community bring new changes to the social order. Yet even a political environment must draw upon native cosmological premises. The real issue here is whether, in our transition from pre-Meiji to modern life, we ever really prepared ourselves for the change or gave proper ceremony to that rebirth. Did we undergo any kind of initiation? The answer is no. And for that reason, our present lifestyle is in confusion.

We have now reached a point where we must judge things unemotionally. We are living in the modern world. Furthermore, we live in a world of electronic media. But it is also true that we still live in the same real space that is Japan. Modernisation may have been inevitable, but can one maintain that Westernisation ultimately suited Japan's own cultural cosmology? Was any attempt made to make it more suitable? As I see it, much of Japanese culture is an accumulation of elements either symbiotically acculturated or accepted as they are, without question, from abroad. In which case, the task at hand would now seem to be to check how this biomass of Western culture is being digested in the Japanese cultural tract.

Either way, even with the one-dimensionality that modern rationalism brought to maturity in today's information-oriented society, in which global social, cultural and political newsbites race around the world in real-time, I do not feel that the world will or can be dominated by a single reductionist logic. I sincerely believe that each different cultural sphere will eventually rediscover its own distinct time and space, while timely new methods will come to transcend this one-dimensionality.

What is important today, then, is whether or not timely methods can develop from here on. Here, in addressing the subject of *kekkai* constructs, my motive has been to consider whether these traditional Japanese spatial concepts might serve as bases for the creation of still newer, more timely methods. Naturally, I do not expect any sudden solutions. Nonetheless, when considering ideas for the future, I believe a "recycling of cultural memories" is a good place to start.

BIBLIOGRAPHY

AKASAKA, Norio/"Ijinronjosetsu"/1985/ Sunagoyashobo/Tokyo

AMINO, Yoshihiko/"Muen Kugai Raku"/1978/ Heibonsha/Tokyo

BOLLNOW, Otto Friedrich/"Mensch und Raum"/ 1994/Kohlhammer/Stuttgart

ELIADE, Mircea/"A History of Religious Ideas" /1978/The University of Chicago Press/ Chicago

ELIADE, Mircea/"Images and Symbols"/1991/ Princeton University Press/Princeton

HIDA, Norio/"Sakuteiki-kara-mita-Zoen" [SD sensho 193]/1985/Kajima Shuppankai/Tokyo

HORIGUCHI, Sutemi/"Rikyu-no-Chashitsu"/1977/ Kajima Kenkyujo Shuppankai/Tokyo

INOUE, Mitsuo/"Nihonkenchiku-no-Kukan" [SD sensho 37]/1969/Kajima Shuppankai/Tokyo

ITO, Teiji/"Nihon-Dezain-Ron" [SD sensho 5]/1966/Kajima Shuppankai/Tokyo

KUBOTA, Jun/"Yugen-to-Sonoshuhen" [Koza Nihon-Shiso Vol. 5]/1984/Tokyo Daigaku Shuppankai/Tokyo

MATSUOKA, Seigo/"Kachofugetsu-no-Kagaku"/ 1994/The Tanko-Shinsha Co./Kyoto

MORI, Osamu/"Teien"/1988/Tokyodo Shuppan/ Tokyo

MURAI, Yasuhiko/"Sennorikyu-Sonoshogai-to-Chanoyu-no-Imi"/1971/Nihon Hoso Shuppan Kyokai/Tokyo

NAKAMURA, Masao (Editorial Supervisor)/ "Chashitsu-to-Roji" [Sukiya-Kenchiku-Shusei]/ 1979/ Shogakukan/Tokyo

TARUMI, Minoru/"Kekkai-no-Kozo"/1990/Meicho Shuppan/Tokyo

SEN, Soshitsu/MURATA, Jiro/KITAMURA, Denbe/ "CHASHITSU The Original Drawings and Photographic Illustrations of Typical Japanese Tea Architectures and Gardens"/1959/The Tanko-Shinsha Co./Kyoto

"Girei-to-Seimeigenri" [Quarterly: Shizen-to-Bunka Summer #37]/1992/Nihon National Trust/Tokyo

"Shoshuraku-no-Chimei" [Quarterly: Shizen-to-Bunka Summer #41]/1993/Nihon National Trust/Tokyo

"Chashitsu-wo-Yomu" [Nagomi June]/1991/The Tanko-Shinsha Co./Kyoto

"Shikiri-no-Sign" [Nagomi May]/1992/The Tanko-Shinsha Co./Kyoto

SECTION 1.2
THE PROCESS OF DECORATION

Introduction

The process of interior decoration is considerably more complex that the simple selection of interior surface treatments. It is a subject that is often primarily considered to be concerned with the qualities of the domestic environment, but really this is just the starting point. The subject can refer to the decoration and furnishing of interior spaces in homes, offices, schools, and public spaces. It deals with all aspects of lighting, colour, texture, furniture, flooring, fabric, window treatments, and accessories. But how does the designer even begin to select these elements? The essays collected within this section consider the approach that the designer may take to the process of interior decoration. They don't discuss the viability of one surface finish over another, or the practicalities of how to select the perfect piece of furniture. These essays look beyond these hands-on considerations, to how a designer arrives at the underlying theoretical approach to the project. They examine the need to understand how the intimate details of an element will relate to the complete interior, and how a relationship between the detail and the whole is established. This is more complex than collecting a swatch of samples together, but is deeply rooted in the knowledge of the properties of the materials being used and the possibilities that these offer.

There are four essays within this section, and each deals slightly differently with this matter. Baudrillard discusses the status that is attached to every material, colour and object. This significance, he argues, is based upon cultural value. Both Gregotti and Ranalli discuss the importance of understanding how the detail is related to the whole: the nature and character of the complete interior should be made obvious through the understanding of just one small part. Enzo Mari, the Italian product designer, is credited with the saying "The spoon is like the city" and "My design for the small size has the dignity of a skyscraper".[1] These both epitomise the need to focus upon the detail, not to leave it until the final stage of a project, but to embrace it as part of the conceptual approach to the design problem. Brooker and Stone do discuss a practical approach to the design problem, but this is again far from the conventional conception of the decorative process. They discuss the consequences of the appropriation of foreign or incongruous objects to populate a redesigned interior.

The main focus of the book, *The System of Objects*, by **Jean Baudrillard**, which was published in 1968, is upon consumerism and the manner in which different objects are consumed in different ways. Baudrillard argues that all objects say something about their users and consequently are innately fetishistic. Although much of his early work was influenced by Marx, it is significant that within this publication Baudrillard concentrated upon consumption rather than production, arguing that the ideological origin of need precedes the production of goods to meet that need. In that meaning, not use, is primarily transferred through consumer objects and that the individual in effect buys a group identity with each over-determined purchase.

Baudrillard, in what is the opening section of the chapter "Structures of Atmosphere", begins with the declaration that the entire system of modern living is based upon the counterpoint between design and atmosphere. These, he explains, are two aspects of a single functioning system. He then proceeds to elaborate upon this theory through a series of short sections, each of which describes a different aspect of atmosphere within the interior. Atmospheric value, he claims, can be applied to colour, to materials and consequently to objects such as seats or beds. Each of these values is based upon the manner in which the particular society will read the particular element, so choice is based not upon individual free-will, but upon a complex system of acknowledgement and conformity.

George Ranalli is a Manhattan based architect with a reputation for the design of beautifully detailed, contemporary architectural solutions to the problems created by the conservation and reuse of existing buildings. He is obviously passionate about the work of Carlo Scarpa, and much of his work reflects the obsessive nature with which Scarpa approached detailed design and the understanding of material prop-erties of the interior. Much of his own aesthetic is obviously derived from this study, not so much with the language, but more the understanding of the relationship between the detail and whole.

He has also written fairly extensively about Carlo Scarpa and this essay, "History, Craft, Invention", examines the process of creating an intimate connection between the existing building and the contemporary users through the design of specific elements. Ranalli describes Scarpa as a "craftsman of the highest order" and this enabled him to establish intense relationships with those who were to construct his buildings.

Ranalli's essay opens with a poem about the work of Carlo Scarpa by non other than the great archi-tect, Louis Kahn. Of course, they held mutual admiration for each other's work and did actually work together. Scarpa exhibited with Kahn, Paul Rudolph and Franco Albini in an exhibition called "Lines of Research: From Abstraction to the New Structures", for the XXXIVth Venice Bienalle 1968.

Ranalli describes their relationship, which had its basis in a deep fundamental approach to architec-ture. By the late 1950s both Kahn and Scarpa had "begun to distance themselves decisively from the functionalist aesthetic and machine technology of the modern movement". Although both had their architectural basis within modernism, in what was the beginning of a fundamental shift away from that movement, they individually began to embrace history, craft and the vernacular. For Scarpa, like Kahn, there was no discontinuity between image and realised form. His work, which grew out of the craft tradi-tion, was rooted in a sense of regional and local culture and material workmanship. History, which was suspended so violently by modernism, was accepted within the work as an essential ingredient, allowing for the accumulation of meaning.

Interestingly Ranalli dwells upon Scarpa's ability to draw his intentions. His extreme ability to commu-nicate his thoughts to those that he was working with ensured that the architectural and decorative ideas that were evolving through the design of a series of projects were constructed to the highest possible standards.

Vittorio Gregotti is a practising architect and academic, whose work is often linked with the contex-tual movement, and is discussed with the same reverence as the great Italian architects Aldo Rossi and Giorgio Grassi. Within his work is a search for authentic differences and for their articulation on many levels at once. He strives to create a truth; to the building, to the situation and to the finest detail. He believes that all things have to have a form, and these automatically communicate a message.

This essay, "The Exercise of Detailing", muses upon the importance of tectonic expression, in that a building should be articulated and should be able to be read through the details. Within this text, Gregotti laments the lack of material truth evidenced within modernist buildings. He then explains how such Italian architects and designers as Scarpa, Albini and Ridolfi followed this in the 1950s and 60s, and describes the elegant manner in which overt constructional details are apparent in their work.

Within his essay, which was published in 1983, and therefore at the moment when post-modernism was beginning to become a recognised style of architecture, Gregotti bemoans the hurried reconciliation between tradition and history that led to a lack of articulation of the parts at different scales, and a general lack of tension in the translation from drawing to building. He urges the reader to study the works of classical architecture that can provide evidence and memory of the original links between orna-ment and construction. Even the mediaeval use of fragments or spolia, which could be thought of as exemplary architectural details, are a source of integrity.

Gregotti is apparently fond of quoting Auguste Perret, "Il n'y a pas de detail dans la construction", which translates loosely as: even the smallest detail is crucial to the realisation of the whole. Gregotti himself provides an even more ambiguous interpretation: "detail is certainly not just a matter of detail". It is this sense that the building is designed not as a series of separate individual projects, but as an organised and interrelated whole.

Brooker and **Stone**, in their essay "Spolia: Inappropriate Appropriations", discuss the strategy of reusing specific elements of a building or culture in a new or radical manner. Spolia is an archaic term that describes the reclamation of existing architectural elements to incorporate them into new buildings. It was once a well-acknowledged practice to remove individual elements from a disused building and reuse them elsewhere. This would have included complete sections of the building such as an ornate bay window, perhaps a magnificently carved doorway or even a mosaic floor. But Stone and Brooker argue that it is also a thoroughly post-modern tactic, in that contemporary architects and designers will take existing objects and elements and, with deliberate incongruity, place them within a new context.

This appropriation of fragments or details ensures that both the individual element and the context are considered with greater discernment. The nature of each is heightened and the juxtaposition between the two can accentuate both. One of the examples that is examined in some detail is the Bohen Foundation in New York. Three moveable shipping crates have been placed within the huge white warehouse type space of the gallery. These not only define the display spaces, but also act as the office, a meeting room and bookshop.

The ancient and contemporary manner in which spolia has been employed has been divided into three categories. This taxonomy is deliberately vague, but it does allow the authors to describe in more detail selected examples of the practice. The groupings are: Ready-mades, Persistent Meaning, and Continuity and Permanence.

Ready-mades catalogues those elements that are already complete and may even be new, which are then removed from their intended destination and placed within a new venue. Ready-made is a term that came into prominence when it was used to describe the conceptual art of Marcel Duchamp, who, somewhat controversially, elevated mundane everyday elements into works of art. Persistent Meaning describes projects that use fragments or parts of a much larger collection, which are reassembled in a new manner to create something original. The category of Continuity and Permanence covers elements that have lost their original meaning and been given a completely new purpose when they are reused.

Brooker and Stone describe a process that provides the interior decorator with a tactic to create contemporary spaces that have a direct link with a history or culture beyond the enclosing walls.

Sally Stone

Reference

1. Beppe Finessi. "Enzo Mari. The Small as Method". Rassegna 71: Small Objects, 1997.

Ettore Sottsass (1917–2007)

Ettore Sottsass was a prolific Italian designer. He began his career at Olivetti and was responsible for the revolutionary red Valentine typewriter. In 1981, with a collection of young designers, he established the "Memphis" design group. They fully embraced the post-modern concept of plurality, contradiction and change. Memphis was launched with a show of over 40 pieces of furniture, ceramics, lighting, glass and textiles. These were patterned, lopsided, vivid, and sometimes silly; a far cry from the modernist aesthetic which was prevalent at the time. Sottsass continued to work in the design profession for such illustrious clients as Alessi, Knoll International, Fiorucci and Esprit.

Building Study: St Mary of Furness

Lake District, UK
2006
Francis Roberts Architects

E. W. Pugin designed the church, which is large, ornate and Gothic. It opened in 1867, although the tower and steeple were not completed until 1888. Edward Welby Pugin (1834–1875) was the eldest son of Augustus Welby Northmore Pugin who is remembered for the Gothic interiors of the Palace of Westminster. After his death in 1852, Edward took up his successful practice and completed more than one hundred churches

Francis Roberts Architects are prominent conservationist architects who have a reputation for the sensitive approach to the preservation and remodelling of existing buildings. When they were commissioned to carry out the conservation work to the church, they found that the interior had been painted off-white, a popular colour in the mid-twentieth century. This they felt was an opportunity to not only restore the building to its former glory, but also a chance to embellish, with decoration, certain elements within the building. The architects took this as their cue for the redecoration from the capitals on the columns that formed the arcade. These were alternately either abstract or decorated with verdant foliage.

The complete interior was redecorated, but special emphasis was placed upon the polygonal east apse. This has been repainted in a rich and romantic manner, thus acknowledging the focus and importance that this area has. It is deliberately more dense and complex at the base, gradually becoming more simple, and lighter as it rises up the interior walls, thus encouraging the congregation to lift their eyes and turn their thoughts towards the heavens. The ornamentation is precious and opulent and it serves to emphasise the architectural language of the apse. The method that the architects used to ensure the quality and consistency of their design was to draw at full size the shapes and patterns; these were converted into stencils by the decorator, who then transferred these layers of ornamentation to the walls.

The language of the redecoration was based upon the style of architecture combined with a wish to create a rich and appropriate image. The architects have taken a particularly tactful and sympathetic approach to their successful conservation and redecoration of the St Mary of Furness Barrow church in Cumbria.

6
The System of Objects

Jean Baudrillard

Translated by James Benedict

Source: *Volume 3: Radical Thinkers*. Verso, 2005, pp. 30–47

II STRUCTURES OF ATMOSPHERE

The term 'interior design' sums up the organizational aspect of the domestic environment, but it does not cover the entire system of the modern living space, which is based on a counterpoint between design and atmosphere. In the discourse of advertising the technical need for design is always accompanied by the cultural need for atmosphere. The two structure a single practice; they are two aspects of a single *functional* system. And both mobilize the values of play and of calculation – calculation of function in the case of design, calculation of materials, forms and space in the case of atmosphere.[1]

Atmospheric Values: Colour

Traditional Colour

In the traditional system colours have psychological and moral overtones. A person will 'like' a particular colour, or have 'their' colour. Colour may be dictated by an event, a ceremony, or a social role; alternatively, it may be the characteristic of a particular material – wood, leather, canvas or paper. Above all it remains circumscribed by form; it does not seek contact with other colours, and it is not a free value. Tradition confines colours to its own parochial meanings and draws the strictest of boundary-lines about them. Even in the freer ceremonial of fashion, colours generally derive their significance from outside themselves: they are simply metaphors for fixed cultural meanings. At the most impoverished level, the symbolism of colours gets lost in mere psychological resonance: red is passionate and

aggressive, blue a sign of calm, yellow optimistic, and so on; and by this point the language of colours is little different from the languages of flowers, dreams or the signs of the Zodiac.

The traditional treatment of colour negates colour as such, rejects it as a complete value. Indeed, the bourgeois interior reduces it for the most part to discreet 'tints' and 'shades'. Grey, mauve, garnet, beige – all the shades assigned to velours, woollens and satins, to the profusion of fabrics, curtains, carpets and hangings, as also to heavier materials and 'period' forms, imply a moral refusal of both colour and space. But especially of colour, which is deemed too spectacular, and a threat to inwardness. The world of colours is opposed to the world of values, and the 'chic' invariably implies the elimination of appearances in favour of being:[2] black, white, grey – whatever registers zero on the colour scale – is correspondingly paradigmatic of dignity, repression, and moral standing.

'Natural' Colour

Colours would not celebrate their release from this anathema until very late. It would be generations before cars and typewriters came in anything but black, and even longer before refrigerators and washbasins broke with their universal whiteness. It was painting that liberated colour, but it still took a very long time for the effects to register in everyday life. The advent of bright red armchairs, sky-blue settees, black tables, multicoloured kitchens, living-rooms in two or three different tones, contrasting inside walls, blue or pink façades (not to mention mauve and black underwear) suggests a liberation stemming from the overthrow of a global order. This liberation, moreover, was contemporary with that of the functional object (with the introduction of synthetic materials, which were polymorphous, and of non-traditional objects, which were polyfunctional). The transition, however, did not go smoothly. Colour that loudly announced itself as such soon began to be perceived as over-aggressive, and before long it was excluded from model forms, whether in clothing or in furnishing, in favour of a somewhat relieved return to discreet tones. There is a kind of obscenity of colour which modernity, after exalting it briefly as it did the explosion of form, seems to end up apprehending in much the same way as it apprehends pure functionality: labour should not be discernible anywhere – neither should instinct be allowed to show its face. The dropping of sharp contrasts and the return to 'natural' colours as opposed to the violence of 'affected' colours reflects this compromise solution at the level of model objects. At the level of serially produced objects, by contrast, bright colour is always apprehended as a sign of emancipation – in fact it often compensates for the absence of more fundamental qualities (particularly a lack of space). The discrimination here is obvious: associated with primary values, with functional objects and synthetic materials, bright, 'vulgar' colours always tend to predominate in the serial interior. They thus partake of the same anonymity as the functional object: having once represented something approaching a liberation, both have now become signs that are merely traps, raising the banner of freedom but delivering none to direct experience.

Furthermore – and this is their paradox – such straightforward and 'natural' colours turn out to be neither. They turn out to be nothing but an impossible echo of the state of nature, which explains why they are so aggressive, why they are so naïve – and why they so very quickly take refuge in an order which, for all that it is no longer the old moral order with its complete rejection of colour, is nevertheless a puritanical order of compromise with nature. This is the order, or reign, of *pastels*. Clothing, cars, showers, household appliances, plastic surfaces – nowhere here, it seems, is the 'honest' colour that painting once liberated as a living force now to be found. Instead we encounter only the pastels, which aspire to be living colours but are in fact merely *signs* for them, complete with a dash of moralism.

All the same, even though these two compromises, the flight into black and white and the flight into pastels, ultimately voice the same disavowal of pure colour as the direct expression of instinctual life, they do not do so in accordance with the same system. The first is systematized by reference to an unequivocally moral and anti-natural black/white paradigm, whereas the pastel solution answers to a system with a larger register founded *not on opposition to nature but on naturalness*. Nor do the two systems have the same function. Black (or grey) retains the meaning of distinction, of culture, as opposed to the whole range of vulgar colours.[3] As for white, it remains largely pre-eminent in the 'organic' realm: bathrooms, kitchens, sheets, linen – anything that is bound up with the body and its immediate extensions has for generations been the domain of white, a surgical, virginal colour which distances the body from the dangers of intimacy and tends to neutralize the drives. It is also in this unavoidable area of hygiene and down-to-earth tasks that the use of synthetic materials, such as light metals, formica, nylon, plastiflex, aluminium, and so forth, has experienced its most rapid growth and achieved a dominant position. Of course the lightness and practical utility of these materials have much to do with their success, but the very convenience they offer does not merely lighten the burden of work, it also helps to drain value from this whole basic area. The fluid, simplified lines of our refrigerators or similar machines, with their plastic or artificial lightweight material, operate likewise as a kind of 'whiteness' – as a non-stressed indicator of the presence of these objects that bespeaks the radical omission from our consciousness of the responsibilities they imply, and of bodily functions in general, which are never innocent. Little by little colour is making inroads here, too, but resistance to this development is very deeply felt. In any case, even if kitchens are blue or yellow, even if bathrooms are pink (or even black – a 'snobbish' black as a reaction to the former 'moral' white), we may still justifiably ask to what nature such colours allude. For even if they do not turn pastel, they do connote a kind of nature, one that has its own history: the 'nature' of leisure time and holidays.

It is not 'real' nature which suddenly transfigures the atmosphere of daily life, but holidays – that simulacrum of nature, the reverse side of everyday routine, thriving not on nature but on the Idea of Nature. It is holidays that serve as a model here, holidays whose colours devolve into the primary everyday realm. And it was indeed in the fake natural environment of holidays, with its caravan, tents and camping gear, experienced as a model and as a zone of freedom, that the tendency towards bright colours, to plasticity, to the ephemeral practicality of labour-saving gadgets, and so on, first came to the fore. We began by transplanting our little house into Nature, only to end up bringing the values of leisure and the idea of Nature back home with us. There has been a sort of flight of objects into the sphere of leisure: freedom and the absence of responsibilities are thus inscribed both in colours and in the transitory and insignificant character of materials and forms.

'Functional' Colour

Thus, after a few brief episodes of violent liberation (notably in the world of art, with, in the end, but mild impact upon everyday life – except, of course, for the spheres of advertising and commerce, where colour's power to corrupt enjoys full rein), colour was immediately taken back in hand by a system in *which nature no longer plays any part except as naturalness* – as a mere connotation of nature behind whose screen instinctual values continue to be subtly disavowed. Nevertheless, the very abstractness of these now 'free' colours means that they are at last able to play an active role. It is towards this third stage that colour is at present orientating itself so far as model objects are concerned: a stage characterized by colour as an atmospheric value. Certainly an 'atmospheric' interplay of this kind is already pre-figured in the colours associated with leisure, but these colours still refer too clearly to a system directly experienced, namely holidays and the primary level of everyday life; consequently they are subject to external constraints. In the fully fledged system of atmosphere, by contrast, colours obey no principle but that of their own interaction; no longer constrained in any way, whether by ethical considerations or by nature, they answer to one imperative only – the gauging of atmosphere.

Indeed, in a sense we are no longer dealing with colours *per se* but with more abstract values. The combination, matching and contrast of tones are the real issues when it comes to the relationship between colour and atmosphere. Blue can go with green – all colours are capable of combination – but only certain blues with certain greens; furthermore, it is not so much a question of blue and green as one of *hot and cold*. At the same time, colour is no longer a way of emphasizing each object by setting it off from the décor; colours are now contrasting ranges of shades, their value has less and less to do with their sensory qualities, they are often dissociated from their form, and it is their tonal differences

that give a room its 'rhythm'. Just as modular furniture loses its specific functions so much that at the logical extreme its value resides solely in the positioning of each movable element, so likewise colours lose their unique value, and become relative to each other and to the whole. This is what is meant by describing them as 'functional'.

Consider the following descriptions from a practical guide to interior decoration:

> The framework of the seats has been painted in the same shade as the walls, while the shade chosen for the upholstery echoes that of the hangings. There is harmony between the cold tones, off-white and blue, but certain touches supply the necessary warm response: the gold frame of the Louis XVI mirror, the light-coloured wood of the table, the parquet floor, and the bright red of the carpets. Red here constitutes a sort of upward movement – the red of the carpet, the red of the seats, the red of the cushions – to which is opposed a downward movement in the blues of hangings, settees and chairs.[4]
> A plain matte white background interrupted by great blue surfaces (on the ceiling). White and blue are repeated in the arrangement of the décor: a white marble table, a screen partition. . . . A warm touch is supplied by the bright red doors of a low storage unit. In fact we find ourselves in a space handled entirely in plain colours, devoid of any nuances of tone or of any softness (all the softness having taken refuge in the picture on the left), albeit balanced by large areas of white.[5]

Here is another example: 'The little indoor tropical garden is not just protected but also lent rhythm by a slab of black enamelled glass.' (Notice that black and white in these descriptions retain nothing of their traditional value; they have escaped from the white-black polarity and taken on a *tactical* value within the extended range of all colours.) When one considers the advice to 'choose a particular colour because your wall is large or small, because it contains such and such a number of doors, because your furniture is antique or modern, or designed in a European or an exotic tradition, or for some other precise reason',[6] it becomes clear that the third stage we have been discussing is indeed characterized by an objectivity of colour; strictly speaking, colour is now one more or less complex factor among others – just one element of a solution. Once again, this is what makes colour 'functional' – that is to say, reduced to an abstract conceptual instrument of calculation.

Hot and Cold

So far as colours are concerned, 'atmosphere' depends upon a calculated balance between hot and cold tones. This is a fundamental distinction which – along with a few others (components/seats,[7] design/atmosphere) – helps to endow the discursive system of furnishing with a high degree of coherence, and thus makes it into a determining category of the overall system of objects. (We shall see that this coherence is perhaps merely that of a manifest discourse beneath which a latent discourse is continually deploying its contradictions.) To get back to the warmth of warm tones: this is clearly not a warmth grounded in confidence, intimacy or affection, nor an organic warmth emanating from colours or substances. Warmth of that kind once had its own density and required no opposing cold tones to define it negatively. Nowadays, on the other hand, both warm and cold tones are required to interact, in each ensemble, with structure and form. When we read that 'The warmth of its materials lends intimacy to this well-designed bureau', or when we are told of 'doors of matte piled Brazilian rosewood traversed by chrome-plated handles [and] chairs covered in a buff leatherette that blends them perfectly into this austere and warm ensemble', we find that warmth is always contrasted with rigour, organization, structure, or something of the sort, and that every 'value' is defined by this contrast between two poles. 'Functional' warmth is thus a warmth that no longer issues forth from a warm substance, nor from a harmonious juxtaposition of particular objects, but instead arises from the systematic oscillation or abstract synchrony of a perpetual 'warm-and-cold' which in reality continually defers any real 'warm' feeling. This is a purely *signified* warmth – hence one which, by definition, is never realized: a warmth characterized, precisely, by the absence of any source.

Atmospheric Values: Materials

Natural Wood/Cultural Wood

The same sort of analysis applies to materials – to wood, for example, so sought after today for nostalgic reasons. Wood draws its substance from the earth, it lives and breathes and 'labours'. It has its latent warmth; it does not merely reflect, like glass, but burns from within. Time is embedded in its very fibres, which makes it the perfect container, because every content is something we want to rescue from time. Wood has its own odour, it ages, it even has parasites, and so on. In short, it is a material that has *being*. Think of the notion of 'solid oak' – a living idea for each of us, evoking as it does the succession of generations, massive furniture and ancestral family homes. The question we must ask, however, is whether this 'warmth' of wood (or likewise the 'warmth' of freestone, natural leather, unbleached linen, beaten copper, or any of the elements of the material and maternal dream that now feeds a high-priced nostalgia) still has any meaning.

By now functional substitutes for virtually all organic and natural materials have been found in the shape of plastic and polymorphous substances: wool, cotton, silk and linen are thus all susceptible of replacement by nylon and its countless variants, while wood, stone and metal are giving way to concrete and polystyrene.[8] There can be no question of rejecting this tendency and simply dreaming of the ideal warm and human substance of the objects of former times. The distinction between natural and synthetic substances, just like that between traditional colours and bright colours, is strictly a value judgement. Objectively, substances are simply what they are: there is no such thing as a true or a false, a natural or an artificial substance. How could concrete be somehow less 'authentic' than stone? We apprehend *old* synthetic materials such as paper as altogether natural – indeed, glass is one of the richest substances we can conceive of. In the end, the inherited nobility of a given material can exist only for a cultural ideology analogous to that of the aristocratic myth itself in the social world – and even that cultural prejudice is vulnerable to the passage of time.

The point is to understand, apart from the vast horizons opened up on the practical level by these new substances, just how they have changed the 'meaning' of the materials we use.

Just as the shift to shades (warm, cold or intermediate) means that colours are stripped of their moral and symbolic status in favour of an abstract quality which makes their systematization and interplay possible, so likewise the manufacture of synthetics means that materials lose their symbolic naturalness and become polymorphous, so achieving a higher degree of abstractness which makes possible a universal play of associations among materials, and hence too a transcendence of the formal antithesis between natural and artificial materials. There is thus no longer any difference 'in nature' between a Thermoglass partition and a wooden one, between rough concrete and leather: whether they embody 'warm' or 'cold' values, they all now have exactly the same status as component materials. These materials, though disparate in themselves, are nevertheless homogeneous as cultural signs, and thus susceptible of organization into a coherent system. Their abstractness makes it possible to combine them at will.[9]

The Logic of Atmosphere

This 'discourse of atmosphere' concerning colours, substance, volume, space, and so on mobilizes all these elements simultaneously in a great systematic reorganization: it is because furniture now comprises movable elements in a decentralized space, and because it has a correspondingly lighter structure based on assembly and veneers, that there is a case for more 'abstract' woods – teak, mahogany, rosewood or certain Scandinavian woods.[10] And it so happens that the colours of these woods are not traditional either, but lighter or darker variations, often varnished, lacquered, or left deliberately unfinished; the main point, though, is that the colour in question, like the wood itself, is always *abstract* – an object of mental manipulation along with everything else. The entire modern environment is thus transposed onto the level of a sign system, namely ATMOSPHERE, which is no longer produced by the way any particular element is handled, nor by the beauty or ugliness of that element. That used to be true for the inconsistent and subjective system of tastes and colours, of *de gustibus non est disputandum*, but under the present system the success of the whole occurs in the context of the constraints of abstraction and association.

Whether or not you care for teak, for example, you are obliged to acknowledge that its use is consistent with the organization of component elements, that its shade is consistent with a plane surface, hence also with a particular 'rhythm' of space, etc., etc. – and that this is indeed the law of the system. There is nothing at all – not antiques, not rustic furniture in solid wood, not even precious or craft objects – that cannot be incorporated into the interactions of the system, thus attesting to the boundless possibilities of such abstract integration. The current proliferation of such objects does not constitute a contradiction in the system:[11] they enter the system precisely as the most 'modern' materials and colours, and as atmospheric elements. Only a traditional and fundamentally

naïve view would find inconsistency in the encounter, on a teak-veneered chest, of a futuristic cube in raw metal and the rotten wood of a sixteenth-century carving. The point is, though, that *the consistency here is not the natural consistency of a unified taste but the consistency of a cultural system of signs*. Not even a 'Provençal' room, not even an authentic Louis XVI drawing-room, can attest to anything beyond a vain nostalgic desire to escape from the modern cultural system: both are just as far removed from the 'style' they ape as any formica-topped table or any black-metal and leatherette tubular chair. An exposed ceiling beam is every bit as abstract as a chrome-plated tube or an Emauglas partition. What nostalgia paints as an authentic whole object is still nothing but a combining variant, as is indeed signalled by the language used in speaking of provincial or period 'ensembles'. The word 'ensemble', closely related to 'atmosphere', serves to reintroduce any conceivable element, whatever subjective associations it may carry, into the logic of the system. That this system is affected by ideological connotations and latent motives is indisputable, and we shall return to this question later. But it is incontestable, too, that its logic, which is that of a combination of signs, is irreversible and limitless. No object can escape this logic, just as no product can escape the formal logic of the commodity.

A Model Material: Glass

One material sums up the idea of atmosphere and may be thought of as embodying a universal function in the modern environment. That material is glass. Advertising calls it 'the material of the future' – a future which, as we all know, will itself be 'transparent'. Glass is thus both the material used and the ideal to be achieved, both end and means. So much for metaphysics. Psychologically speaking, glass in its practical, as in its imaginary uses has many merits. It is the ideal modern recipient: it does not 'pick up the taste', it does not change over time as a function of its content, as do wood and metal, nor does it shroud that content in mystery. Glass eliminates all confusion in short order, and does not conduct heat. Fundamentally it is less a recipient than an isolator – the miracle of a rigid fluid – a content that is also a container, and hence the basis of a transparency between the two: a kind of transcendence which, as we have seen, is the first priority in the creation of atmosphere. Moreover, glass implies a symbolism of access to a secondary state of consciousness, and at the same time it is ranked symbolically at zero level on the scale of materials. Its symbolism is one of solidification – hence of abstractness. This abstractness opens the door to the abstractness of the inner world: the crystal of madness; to the abstractness of the future: the clairvoyant's crystal ball; and to the abstractness of nature: the other worlds to which the eye gains entry via microscope or telescope. And certainly, with its indestructibility, immunity to decay, colourlessness, odourlessness, and so on, glass exists at a sort of zero level of matter: glass is to matter as a vacuum is to air. We have already noted the operation of the values of play and calculation, combined with abstraction, apropos of the system of atmosphere. Above all, though, glass is the most effective conceivable material expression of the fundamental ambiguity of 'atmosphere': the fact that it is at once proximity and distance, intimacy and the refusal of intimacy, communication and non-communication. Whether as packaging, window or partition, glass is the basis of a transparency without transition: we see, but cannot touch. The message is universal and abstract. A shop window is at once magical and frustrating – the strategy of advertising in epitome. The transparency of jars containing food products implies a formal satisfaction, a kind of visual collusion, yet basically the relationship is one of exclusion. Glass works exactly like atmosphere in that it allows nothing but the *sign* of its content to emerge, in that it interposes itself in its transparency, just as the system of atmosphere does in its abstract consistency, between the materiality of things and the materiality of needs. Not to mention glass's cardinal virtue, which is of a moral order: its purity, reliability and objectivity, along with all those connotations of hygiene and prophylaxis which make it truly the material of the future – a future, after all, that is to be one of disavowal of the body, and of the primary and organic functions, in the name of a radiant and functional objectivity (of which hygiene is the moral version for the body).

> Live in a garden in close intimacy with nature – experience the charm of every season totally, without giving up the comforts of a modern living space. This is the new heaven on earth, the grace bestowed by houses with picture windows.
>   Glass tile or block set in concrete makes it possible to construct translucent walls, partitions, arches and ceilings that are as strong as if they were built of stone. Such 'transpartitions' allow the passage of light, which is thus able freely to permeate the whole house. But, since the glass used is not see-through, the privacy of each room is preserved.

Clearly the age-old symbolism of the 'house of glass' is still with us, even though in the modern version it has lost much of its sublime aspect. *The distinction accorded transcendence has given way to that accorded atmosphere* (just as in the case of mirrors). Glass facilitates faster communication between inside and outside, yet at the same time it sets up an invisible but material caesura which prevents such communication from becoming a real opening onto the world. Indeed, the modern 'house of glass' does not open onto the outside at all; instead it is the outside world, nature, landscape, that penetrates, thanks to glass and its abstractness, into the intimate or private realm inside, and there 'plays freely' as a component of atmosphere. The whole world thus becomes integrated as spectacle into the domestic universe.[12]

The Man of Relationship and Atmosphere

From the foregoing account of colours and materials we may already draw a number of conclusions. The systematic alternation between hot and cold is fundamentally a defining trait of the concept of 'atmosphere' itself, for *atmosphere is always both warmth and distance*.

The 'atmospheric' interior is designed to permit the same alternation between warmth and non-warmth, between intimacy and distance, to operate not only between the objects that comprise it but also between the human beings who live in it. Friend or relative, family or customer – *some* relationship is always required, but it is supposed to remain mobile and 'functional'; in other words, the aim is that relating should be possible at every instant, but its subjective aspects should no longer be problematic, and the various relationships should therefore be freely interchangeable. Such is the nature of functional relationships, from which desire is (in theory) absent, having been neutralized for the sake of atmosphere.[13] This, however, is where ambiguity begins.[14]

Seats

This ambiguity is attested to by the objects that best express the relationship of atmosphere: *seats*, which we see continually alternating in the system of modern furnishing with modular *components*. These antithetical kinds of objects concretize the opposition between the concepts of interior design and atmosphere (although they do not constitute the sole underpinnings of that opposition).

The minimal function of the countless seats that fill the furnishing and home-decorating magazines is unquestionably to permit people to sit down: to sit down to rest, or sit down at a table to eat. But chairs no longer gravitate towards a table; these days seats take on their own meaning, while tables – typically low coffee tables – are subordinate to them. This meaning, moreover, refers not to the posture of the body but to the position of interlocutors relative to each other. The general arrangement of the seating and slight changes in people's positions in the course of an evening may be said, for example, to constitute a discourse in themselves. Modern seating – pouf or settee, wall-sofa or easy chair – invariably lays the stress on sociability and conversation, promoting a sort of all-purpose position, appropriate to the modern social human being, which de-emphasizes everything in the sitting posture that suggests confrontation. No more beds for lying in, no more chairs for sitting at[15] – instead, 'functional' seats which treat all positions, and hence all human relationships, as a free synthesis. All moral overtones are gone: one no longer sits opposite anyone. It is impossible to become angry in such seats, or to argue, or to seek to persuade. They dictate a relaxed social interaction which makes no demands, which is open-ended but above all open to play. From their depths one is no longer obliged to meet another person's gaze or to look directly at them: these seats are so designed that one's eyes are entitled simply to look people over in a general way, for their positioning and depth combine to keep everyone's eye level 'naturally' at half the usual altitude – at an ill-defined elevation which is also that of the flow of words. Seats of this kind may well respond to a basic current concern, namely the wish never to be alone – but never to be face to face with another person either. The body is invited to relax, but it is above all the gaze, with all its perils, that must be put out to grass. Even as modern society frees us in large measure from the promiscuity of primary functions, it exacerbates the promiscuity of secondary ones, especially that of the gaze and its tragic dimension. Accordingly, just as primary demands are veiled, so likewise every effort is made to relieve social intercourse of all its rough edges, contradictoriness and, ultimately, obscenity – what is obscene here being the direct play of aggression and desire in the gaze.

The binary opposition between 'components' and 'seats' thus amounts to a complete system: modular components are the vehicle of modern man's organizing discourse, while from the depths of his chairs he proffers a discourse of relationship.[16]

So 'man the interior designer' is always coupled with the 'man of relationship and atmosphere', and the two together give us 'functional man'.

Cultural Connotation and Censorship

For seats, then, but also for all other objects, cultural connotation is now as essential a requirement as calculation. In earlier times furniture stated its function. The fundamental nurturing function of the house found unequivocal expression in tables and sideboards that were heavy, round-bellied – overloaded with connotations of motherhood. Furniture whose function was taboo was flatly withdrawn from view, as in the case of a bed concealed in an alcove. As for the bed in the middle of the room, it was even more eloquent in its embodiment of bourgeois marriage (and not, of course, of sexuality). Today the bed is no more – in its place we have only couches, divans, settees and banquettes. Some 'beds' now disappear into the wall, bowing not to moral stricture but to abstract logic.[17] Tables are low, no longer centrally placed, weightless. The whole kitchen has lost its culinary function and is now a functional laboratory. This is progress, moreover, because the traditional environment, for all its directness, was an environment of moral obsession that bespoke the material difficulty of living. We do have more freedom in the modern interior, but this freedom is accompanied by a subtler formalism and a new moralism: everything here indicates the obligatory shift from eating, sleeping and procreating to smoking, drinking, entertaining, discussing, looking and reading. Visceral functions have given way to functions determined by culture. The sideboard used to hold linen, crockery or food; the functional elements of today house books, knick-knacks, a cocktail bar, or nothing at all. The term 'refined' – which, like 'functional', is a catchword of manipulated interior decoration – sums up this cultural constraint perfectly. Rooms have traded in the symbols of family for signs of social relationship. Once a solemn backdrop for affection, they are now an equally ritualistic décor of reception. A close reading of modern house-furnishings reveals that they converse among themselves with an ease in every way comparable to that of the dinner guests, that they mingle and drift apart with the very same freedom, and that they convey the same message: namely, that it is quite possible to live without working.

Of course, culture has always played the ideological role of pacifier, sublimating tensions associated with functional imperatives and answering the need for being to take on recognizable form beyond the material reality and conflicts of the world. Such a form – which attests, despite everything, to the existence of a purpose, and ensures the direct memory of a fundamental security – is no doubt even more urgently needed in a technological civilization. It is just that, like the reality it simultaneously reflects and disavows, this form is now being systematized. Systematic technicity calls forth systematic cultural connotation. And *this systematic cultural connotation at the level of objects is what I am calling* atmosphere.

NOTES

1 To the extent that arrangement involves dealing with space, it too may be considered a component of atmosphere.
2 'Loud' colours are meant to strike the eye. If you wear a red suit, you are more than naked – you become a pure object with no inward reality. The fact that women's tailored suits tend to be in bright colours is a reflection of the social status of women as objects.
3 Already, however, there are quite a few cars that are simply no longer available in black; apart from mourning or other ceremonial uses, black has almost completely disappeared from American life (except where it is brought back as a combining element).
4 Betty Pepys, *Le guide pratique de la décoration*, p. 163.
5 Ibid, p. 179.
6 Ibid., p. 191.
7 Jean Baudrillard, *The System of Objects*, pp. 44 ff.
8 This development at least partially realizes the substantialist myth which, beginning in the sixteenth century, informed the stucco and the worldly demiurgy of the baroque style: the notion that the whole world could be cast from a single ready-made material. This substantialist myth is one aspect of the functionalist myth that I discuss elsewhere, and the equivalent on the material plane of automatism on the functional one. The idea is that a 'machine of machines' would replace all human gestures and institute a synthetic universe. It should be borne in mind, however, that the 'substantialist' dream is the most primitive and repressive aspect of the myth as a whole, for it continues to enshrine a premechanist alchemy of transubstantiation.
9 And this is the difference, for instance, between the 'solid oak' of old and the present-day use of teak. Teak is not fundamentally distinct from oak in respect of origin, exoticism or cost; it is its use in the creation of atmosphere which means that it is no longer a primary natural material, dense and warm, but, rather, *a mere cultural sign of such warmth*, and by virtue of that fact reinstated *qua* sign, like so many other 'noble' materials, in the system of the modern interior: no longer wood-as-material but wood-as-component. And now, instead of the quality of presence, it has atmospheric value.
10 Certainly these woods are technically better suited than oak to the needs of veneering and assembling. It must also be said that exoticism plays the same role here as the idea of holidays does in the use of bright colours: it evokes the myth of an escape via 'naturalness'. The essential point, however, is that for all these reasons these woods are 'secondary' woods, embodying a cultural abstraction that enables them to partake of the logic of the system.
11 It does indicate a *shortcoming* of the system – but a successfully integrated one.
12 The ambiguity of glass becomes especially clear when we shift our focus from living-spaces to consumption and packaging – areas where its use is ever on the increase. Here too glass has all the desirable qualities: it protects the product against deterioration, letting nothing in but the appraising glance. 'To contain the product properly and let it be seen': a perfect definition of the goal of packaging. Mouldable to any form, glass offers unlimited options from the aesthetic point of view. We may confidently expect that before long it will be used to 'present' fruit and vegetables, ensuring that they remain as fresh as the morning dew. Very likely it will soon be enclosing even ordinary steaks with its transparent sheath. Invisible yet ubiquitous, it will constitute the ideal analogue of a more beautiful and limpidly clear life. Further, whatever purpose it may serve, glass can never become true refuse because it is without odour. It is a 'noble' material. All the same, the consumer is invited to throw it out after using it: 'No deposit – no return'. Glass thus cloaks the purchase in its 'indestructible' prestige – yet must be destroyed immediately. Is there a contradiction here? Not really, because glass is still playing its part as a component of atmosphere, but in this case 'atmosphere' has attained its full economic

meaning, that of *packaging*. Glass sells things, it is functional in that sense, but it must also be consumed itself and, indeed, consumed at an accelerated rate. The psychological function of glass (its transparency and purity) is thus totally recuperated and submerged by its economic function. The sublime ends up as a motivation to buy.

13 Even sexuality itself in its modern conception is subsumed by the functional relationship. As distinct from sensuality, which is warm and instinctual, sexuality is at once hot and cold – by virtue of this it ceases to be a passion and becomes nothing but an atmospheric value.

14 In the system of objects, as in all directly experienced systems, the major structural antitheses are always in effect more complicated than they seem, for what appears as a structural antithesis from the standpoint of the system may well be simply a consistent rationalization of an underlying conflict.

15 Except for chairs at the dining-table – which are upright and have peasant-like overtones. But this evidences a reflex cultural process.

16 Or perhaps, after all, simply a *passive* discourse – for we should not forget that advertising is far less inclined to enjoin the active arrangement of furniture than to stress the passive joys of relaxation. On this point the notion of atmosphere is similarly ambiguous, for it has both active and passive implications. 'Functional man' is exhausted from the start. And the millions of leather and Dunlopillo armchairs, each deeper than the last, whose modern virtues of atmosphere and repose fill the pages of the glossy magazines, amount to a sort of massive invitation from our future civilization to resolve all our tensions and bask in a placid seventh-day euphoria. The whole ideology of that civilization – still far distant, yet imminent in model objects – is to be found in these images of an idyllic, neo-pastoral modernity in which the inhabitant communes with his atmosphere from the mellow depths of his chair. Having solved the problems of his emotions, his functions and his contradictions, so that all that is left are relationships, a system of relationships whose structure he rediscovers in a system of objects; having infused the space around him with life and 'created' a multiplicity of ways to integrate his modules into the room as a whole (much as he himself is integrated into the social whole); having thus put together a world absolved of drives and primary functions but overloaded with social connotations of calculation and prestige – having done all this, and tired out by his efforts, the modern home-dweller is ready to cosset his ennui by plunging into an easy chair whose form is a perfect match for the form of his body.

17 An exception here is an object reintroduced with a new connotation that occludes its earlier obscenity, a case in point being the old free-standing eighteenth-century Spanish bed.

7
History, Craft, Invention

George Ranalli

Source: *Carlo Scarpa Architect: Intervening with History.* The Monacelli Press, 1999, pp. 39–43

In the work of Carlo Scarpa
'Beauty'
The first sense
Art
The first word
Then wonder
Then the inner realization of 'Form'
The sense of the wholeness of inseparable elements.
Design consults nature
To give presence to the elements.
A work of art makes manifest the wholeness of 'Form'
The symphony of the selected shapes of the elements.
In the elements
The joint inspires ornament, its celebration.
The detail is the Adoration of Nature.[1]

Louis I. Kahn

By the late 1950s, two architects – Louis I. Kahn in the United States and Carlo Scarpa in Italy – had begun to distance themselves decisively from the functionalist aesthetic and machine technology of the modern movement. They commenced what was essentially an alternative discourse – establishing a dialogue with the history of architecture, entering a new realm of thinking about interventions into the historic fabric, and returning to the idea of craft, construction method, and on-site invention as the ultimate creative acts in architecture. Both Kahn and Scarpa were grounded in the modernist aesthetic, and this return to the origins of building was shared in spirit with Ludwig Mies van der Rohe, the reigning master builder of the mid-twentieth century. But they gradually developed a different sensibility, in which chance, mythology, and the irrational were permitted to have a role. They argued for the persistent force of ancient forms and structures and of the classic fundamentals of design – as Scarpa listed them, "the wall, the joint, the window, stair, and door." At the same time, they countered the prevailing emphasis on transparency and ephemerality with a new emphasis on materiality. In proposing an alternative to the post-war doctrine of light construction and mass-production techniques and in rejecting the prevailing assumption of architectural transience – short life-cycles for new buildings – they initiated, in tandem with Frank Lloyd Wright, one of the most radical shifts in architectural thought since the origins of the modern movement.

It is clear that Kahn and Scarpa recognized a kinship of purpose. Each wrote in admiration of the other, and the two sustained an ongoing dialogue. But their approaches were markedly different. Where Kahn tried to rethink the question of permanence through inventing new monumental forms, Scarpa chose to weave new work into its historical setting. Unlike Kahn's rigorously geometrical organization of form, Scarpa's projects seem casually organized and based on an experiential method. Spatial cohesion results from a procession of discrete ideas held together by an uncanny ability to judge the essence of each part and orchestrate its relation to a whole. This approach evolved from Scarpa's long association with traditional artisanship and depended on his readiness to push the boundaries of the maker's craft. To achieve his effects he delved into extreme methods of construction, often demanding radical adaptations of established craft techniques. In effect, Scarpa reinvented traditional technology by returning to a dialogue with craftsmen, who worked with him in close and constant communication on every project. The idea of an architecture that was rooted in artisanal traditions, involved in transforming those traditions into a contemporary language, stood in opposition to other modernist work being produced at the time, centered around a belief in mass-production methods appropriated from industrial-design practice. In opposition to the quest for lightness and the recognition of ephemerality that marked the orthodoxies of post-war modernism, Scarpa proposed textured, solid, often opaque and sculptural structures that would take their place in the continually changing fabric of the city. At the same time, his meticulous creation of a dialogue between an architectural intervention and its setting opened up a new sense of the relationship between old and new. Together, this recombination of history, craft, and invention, applied to the conditions of the latter half of the twentieth century, marks Scarpa's major contribution to the discipline of architecture.

In all of this work, the relationship between artisanry and drawing, design, and construction is indivisible. Scarpa's formative works were glass objects produced for the Venini firm in Murano. These designs show an experimental approach that still respected the conventions established by the glassmakers. Communicating with the artisans was essential, as it informed Scarpa of the limitations of methods and materials. The intricate balance between drawing upon craft traditions and the necessity to explore new territory in design would later become Scarpa's architectural working method.

Scarpa looked to several architects whose built works exemplified a close involvement with both artisans and construction techniques. The most important of these was Frank Lloyd Wright. Wright's Southern California concrete-block buildings of the early 1920s – the Millard, Storer, Freeman, and Ennis houses, in which Wright began to explore the complete integration of decoration and form – were seminal works for Scarpa. Cast concrete, which Wright had used in the Unity Temple, re-emerged in these California projects as a precast material. Scarpa must also have looked closely at Wright's A.D. German warehouse in Wisconsin, of 1915, whose frieze shows a use of concrete casting startlingly similar to that found in the Brion family tomb. These themes in Wright's work were observed and studied by Scarpa, who developed them from the 1950s onward to culminate in a remarkable transformation away from the original source. Scarpa was able to develop a working method with artisans that tempered the reference to Wright and made it more directly applicable to his own intentions. Unlike Wright, who moves on from arts and crafts research to embrace the machine and to explore mass production, Scarpa remains in the manual craft tradition and works with the same artisans all his life. As a result, each work represented new research into the joining of materials in an astonishing set of "interdisciplinary" relationships that revealed new ways of making architecture.

This is borne out in interviews with artisans, many of whom had an intense working relationship with Scarpa that spanned more than twenty-five years. Each spoke of long conversations with the architect even before projects began, dialogues that often focused on a material to be used or a problem Scarpa had anticipated. Scarpa worked consistently with three Venetian firms: Zanon for iron and other metal work, Anfodillo for woodwork, and De Luigi for plasterwork. These craftsmen contributed to Scarpa's projects in ways that move them into the role of collaborators rather than simply fabricators of architectural detail. Scarpa turned to them as experts in the realm of what was possible, as sources of knowledge used to attain specific ends.

At the Museo di Castelvecchio, for example, on many of the iron and metal brackets a small circle appears at the point where the metal changes shape or direction. In discussions with Zanon about how the steel was to be cut, Scarpa realized that when the saw ran into the metal there would be no place to stop and achieve a clean cut; drilling a hole first would give the saw blade a stopping point, permitting a neat crosscut from two directions. This analysis of the artisan's working method provided a basis from which to create form.

Throughout his research, Scarpa's drawings were a vivid representation of his ability to visualize form and material. His own words are clear: "I want to see things, I don't trust anything else, I want to see and that's why I draw. I can see an image only if I draw it."[2] His craftsmen remember that he would design six or seven solutions on paper very quickly, then put them away "to season" while he explored others, gradually developing a pile of alternative drawings until the final choice began to appear "as a necessity." These drawings are also a by-product of Scarpa's own love of craft. Full of information, they are at the same time deliberately exquisite.

One of the most interesting aspects of Scarpa's drawings is his preference for working in orthographic projection. The integration of plan, section, and elevation in this tripartite system coded all objects and buildings so that they could be measured immediately and transformed into material reality. The didactic precision of the engineering drawing was combined with shading, shadow, and the human figure (providing scale) in order to produce a drawing of extraordinary legibility without sacrificing overt sensuality and atmosphere. The use of orthographic projection was essential to Scarpa's architecture, in which every surface was worked out with details and joinery that wrapped from walls to floor to ceiling, allowing each design iteration to be followed through all necessary planes.

Often these drawings were the very documents used for construction, as they also contained dimensions and notes to the artisans. The scale of the drawing was frequently pushed toward full size, enhancing Scarpa's ability to delve more fully into material, joinery, and surface treatment. His drawing exemplifies the idea of representation as inquiry. In the drawing for the canopy of the water pavilion at the Brion tomb, for example, Scarpa designed the wood cover, cor-ten steel supports, and concrete footings with intricate detail and a heightened sense of construction and craft. The pattern of fasteners in the wood was studied along with the complex joinery of the split cor-ten steel legs.

The struggle for clarity of thought through drawing was explored with great rigor, yet with a desire to make the drawing a pure expression of thought and feeling; pattern, texture, weight, and color were represented in real terms but also with their metaphysical and lyrical characteristics. Scarpa thus allowed the drawing to become the external manifestation of his internal process – rich, varied, sometimes moving between several ideas, but at all times precise. In each drawing the didactic information is overtaken by the poetry and emotional quality of the sketch. This mix of illustrative and expressive information was achieved not only by the addition of color, but with the incorporation of figures and vegetation and by a looseness of technique not usually seen in mechanical drawings. The margins around the orthographic drawing are sometimes filled with sketches and studies visualizing the perspectival aspects of a particular area or detail. In the plan drawings of the Brion tomb, for example, the buildings and elements are organized on the site with surrounding sketches that illustrate the forms in their three-dimensional reality. In some cases drawings were so thoroughly worked over that white paint was needed to obscure their earlier states. These densely drawn sheets are constructions in themselves. They resemble shop drawings made for construction purposes, and at the same time are detailed maps of a mental process and objects of great force and sensibility.

The artisans responded to the logic and lucidity of the drawings, replicating Scarpa's effort in their own work in a true collaboration of passion, talent, and conviction. Scarpa, a craftsman of the highest order, saw himself as one of the artisans. For this reason his work could develop and evolve through a primary dialogue between like-minded creators, clearly and loudly reasserting that the medium of architecture involves design and building as a single, indivisible act.

NOTES

1 Cited in *Carlo Scarpa*. Vicenza: Academia Olympica, 1974.
2 Sergio Los, *Carlo Scarpa: Architect, Poet*. Venice: Edizione Clova 1967.

8
The Exercise of Detailing

Vittorio Gregotti

Source: *Casabella*, no. 492, June 1983, p.11

Detailing is, surely, one of the more revealing components of changing architectural language. We have often stated our opinion on how this language has, in recent years, lost its capacity to signify structural changes in the architectural field. Its manifest redundance and its obsession with the new and the different, has nullified any meaningful differences. Nevertheless, things that get made are given a form, which automatically has a capacity to communicate through language.

For this reason it is important to examine its constitution which, to take August Perret's famous saying "Il n'y a pas de détail dans la construction," detail is certainly not just a matter of detail. Obviously detailing does not necessarily depend on an overall guiding concept; even if it has inherent relations with such a concept, it is not simply a declination of general decisions; but gives them form, rendering them recognizable and articulated in their various parts.

In the Fifties and Sixties the detail had some great and very diverse protagonists in Italy such as Franco Albini, Carlo Scarpa, and Mario Ridolfi, in which the analysis and displays of material, provided by the laws of construction and formation of the architectural object, constituted its principal support. One can easily see how the eloquent detail of that period has been followed by one of reduced expressive content, one could say the return of the architectural detail to guiding concept.

It was not a case of its elimination but a different approach to the hierarchy of the detail to the whole, which was occasionally a great deal more sophisticated and complex. The connection between the floors, the relation of the materials and the differences in the use, both practical and symbolic, thus became more explicit and for the first time expressive. This has taken on a double meaning. On the one hand, a negation of the value of construction as a subject of importance regarding architectural expression, resulting in a gradual increase in the abstraction of detailing, and the progressive lack of interest in the handling of materials according to a model of modernity, going back to the architecture of the end of the nineteenth century and that of the Enlightenment. On the other hand, there has been discussion, not so much of the detail's possible eloquence as its different expressive value and technical composition, in relation to a crisis of architectural language as an objectual language, towards the revaluation of the notion of relation and modification, of physical and historical place and context of specificity and difference. In both cases the resulting eloquent aphasia, though with very different meanings, has been hastily taken over by a reawakening of interest in decoration, or the ornate (according to [Ernesto N.] Rogers's distinction between these two terms) in the peculiar acceptance of stylistic quotation, often as a breaking of the constitutional methodological rules of contemporary architecture.

There have been hurried reconciliations with tradition and history, false cures derived from communication processes, searching for a consent at the lowest level of mass culture, as well as, and worse for architecture, the loss of practice, tradition, and knowledge. There was the illusion that quotation is a sufficient substitute for the detail as a system of articulation in architectural language, and that an overall "grand conception" can dominate and automatically permeate every aspect of the project and its realization, but the very abstention of the detail, thus polemically underlining the lack of influence of building techniques as an expressive component. Often the outcome of this idea in built terms is an unpleasant sense of an enlarged model, a lack of articulation of the parts at different scales: walls that seem to be made of cut-out cardboard, unfinished windows and openings; in sum, a general relaxing of tension from the drawing to the building. It is false to think that culture of industry or building (by now distant cultures from design) could solve the problem of detailing; this might be convenient or economic to the architect, but lead to unprecedented downfall of architecture. There is no wonder that in classical architecture, on the contrary, the "general, the proportioned, and the measured project" (i.e. the outline sketch project, the project to scale and the model, according to [Antonio Averlino] Filarete) were coupled with very few indications of detail: both construction detail and decorative detail were expressions of a cultural heritage common to design and building in a unity of intent unknown today.

With regard to this point, we know that the dissociation between decoration and detail was practiced for many centuries, sometimes with great success. This was in the past the acting out of a continuing dialogue about classical rules on "ornament in architecture," whose object lay in their comprehension and re-articulation. But according to theories held by someone, the notion of ornament was, for example with [Leon Battista] Alberti, much closer in meaning to expressive form than that of the ornate, and the memory of the original links between ornament and construction was always there to testify to the integrity of architecture. Even the marvellous medieval use of classical fragments, as exemplary architectural details, was the testimony of the perfection of that integrity. Both technology and culture of design (in the production sense from industry's point of view) have "improperly" flooded the architectural field. This is due to the weakness of our discipline and its inability to reintegrate the sum of those techniques, which certainly form an indestructible base of today's building process, and therefore of the exercise in detailing, to architectural horizons.

9
Spolia
Inappropriate Appropriations

Graeme Brooker and Sally Stone

Source: *Interior Tools Interior Tactics: Debates in Interior Theory and Practice*. Libri Publishing, 2011, pp. 223–233

Abstract

Spolia, an archaic term rarely used outside of the study of Roman and medieval antiquities, describes the practice of recycling existing architectural elements by incorporating them into new buildings.

The word itself is derived from the Latin *spoils*, a phrase used to describe the act of taking trophies, usually armour and weaponry, from the enemy after a battle. The spoils of war would be either worn as trophies or used to decorate the victors' houses and temples. In architecture and design spolia traditionally refers particularly to the reuse of the elements of the classical column: the shaft, base, capital and entablature. Spolia is a tactic that relies on contingency, availability and ease of supply. It relies on the materials that are to hand and the ease of their reuse and it is a tactic that relies on a collage-like approach to reconfiguring buildings.

The use of spolia is a device that can be seen in the practice of many contemporary designers and architects. The appropriation of elements from different sources, and the reuse of details or fragments from other contexts, can be seen in the work of Ben Kelly, LOT/EK, and many other designers. This paper will explore the work of those and others.

Spolia accepts traditions, patterns and language. It suggests the application of a meaningful approach to design that reads and then revises existing meaning in a place. In this paper we will suggest that spolia is a device that has been long neglected, and we shall examine various techniques of using it as a viable tactic for building reuse and the creation of interior space.

An early scene within the film *Indiana Jones and the Last Crusade*, finds Indy on a quest to discover the whereabouts of his kidnapped father. He visits the place where he was last seen, an academic library in Venice. It is a quiet point within the film, intended to both progress the narrative of the story and fill the lull between the episodes of action. It is a period of the film which contains conjecture, speculation and mistaken assumptions, and as always within Indiana Jones films, it plays upon the ambiguity between illusion and reality.

The sequence of scenes contains a collection of appropriated images, statements and facts. Indy arrives by boat into a clichéd vision of Venice, the surprisingly female Dr Schneider is the image of Veronica Lake; she says that he "has his father's eyes" and he claims to have "his mother ears". The flower that Indy swipes from a canal-side stall is a gardenia and is a direct reference to *Summertime*, another much earlier film set in Venice and the library is a reused church. But it is the interior of this building that encapsulates this attitude of appropriation; Dr Schneider when showing Indy and his companion Marcus Brody around describes how ". . . these columns were brought as spoils of war, after the sacking of Byzantium after the Crusades".

These "spoils of war" give the scene an authenticity; they appear to be old, relevant to the study of antiquities and are described as Byzantine, and yet they are the only things in this series of incongruous episodes and elements that are openly admitted as out of place.

The very act of appropriating images, elements and facts, and then reusing them with little regard for authenticity or continuity is symptomatic of today's information age. Everything is valid, everything is available and everything can be reused.

The Indiana Jones films are typical of this contemporary "both/and" approach; all styles, traditions and cultures are valid. These "spoils of war" or "spolia" could be described as the epitome of the post-modern culture that we inhabit.

Spolia, an archaic term rarely used outside of the study of Roman and Medieval antiquities, describes the recycling of existing architectural elements by incorporating them into new buildings. *Spolia* is derived from the Latin word *spoils,* a phrase used to describe the act of taking trophies, usually armour and weaponry, from the enemy after a battle. The *spolia opima,* the weaponry and parts of ships stripped from the enemy, would be either worn as trophies or used to decorate the victors' houses and temples after battle.

Spolia, and its study, is a little known discipline or practice, and one that is largely confined to the fields of archaeology and antiquity. It is usually only referred to by archaeologists when analysing historic monuments, such as the temples, churches and fortifications. Within architecture, spolia particularly refers to the reuse of the elements of the classical colonnade: the shaft, base, capital and entablature. Roman builders often built a colonnade in fragments, a practice that not only facilitated construction but one that also valued contingency and the potential for reuse (Kinney, 2001, pp. 138–150). Roman and Greek architecture is characterised by the use of spolia. Evidence of spolia can also be found in other periods of history such as the Byzantine or Moorish eras.

However, spolia can be seen as a thoroughly contemporary tactic. It is an integral element of the process of creating interior design, and is a method that is used by many contemporary interior architects and designers. The appropriation of elements from different sources, the reuse of details or fragments from other contexts, sampling, specifying, and the selection of key elements to be incorporated into a new design, is one of the fundamental skills in the armoury of an interior designer. The act of creating interior compositions composed of a selection of elements is an elemental skill. The use of spolia is a method of design that has been neglected and we shall examine various techniques of using it as a tactic for building reuse and the creation of interior space.

Spolia is a tactic that relies on contingency, availability and ease of supply. It relies on the materials that are to hand and the ease of their reuse, and therefore it is a tactic that uses a collage-like approach to reconfiguring buildings. The use of spolia accepts traditions, patterns and a particular spatial design language, which suggests the application of a meaningful approach to design that reads and then revises existing meaning in a place.

The many methods and variations of the use of spolia can be distributed into three different categories. These are deliberately vague and, of course, not exhaustive, they are: Ready-mades, Persistent or Residual Meaning, Continuity and Permanence.

READY-MADES

> The ready-mades are anonymous objects which the gratuitous gesture of the artist, by the simple act of choosing them, converts into "works of art". At the same time this gesture dissolves the notion of work.
>
> (Paz, 1987, p. 84)

Both the designer and the artist will utilise "Found Objects" when creating works of art or interior space. This connection is central to close relationship between interior design and other creative practices, such as painting, sculpture and installation art. The "Ready-made" is an approach to the creative act of making which allows the artist and designer to recreate, reinterpret and reproduce any existing elements to make something new. In his book *Postproduction* Nicholas Bourriaud suggests that this method of creating, taken from the film and TV production terminology, and based on the set of processes applied to recorded material such as montage, voice-over and subtitles after production is completed, is the dominant method of artistic production since the 1990s. He argues:

> These artists who insert their own work into that of others contribute to the eradication of the traditional distinction between production and consumption, creation and copy, ready-made and original work. The material they manipulate is no longer primary.
>
> (Bourriaud, 2002, p. 17)

Of course, the use of the "Ready-made" as Art was first argued by Marcel Duchamp. He instigated the use of the ready-made, creating artworks from appropriated mundane utilitarian objects such as a bottle rack and a urinal; this deliberately provoked the art world by removing the human hand from the creative or production process. Duchamp coined this method as "Retinal" art as opposed to "crafted" or hand-made, a process that allowed him to elevate mundane or everyday objects by lifting them:

. . . Out of the earth and place them onto the planet of aesthetics.

(Paz, 1987, p. 19)

The use of spolia within interior design is a ready-made approach to the reuse of existing buildings and is a tactic that is based on the creation of appropriating and using what is already to hand. Contemporary interior design is characterised by this approach. When using an off-the-peg approach to designing interiors Ben Kelly uses "Ready-mades" such as traffic bollards, factory-standard plastic screens, telegraph poles, industrial glazed bricks and hazard signs appropriated from motorway hard shoulders. Kelly uses "Ready-mades" in order to create distinct interior space, examples of which include the Hacienda nightclub, Dry Bar, and the Science Museum Basement Galleries. The use of contemporary spolia creates a distinct collage-like identity for a space. It also poses difficult questions about the selection of objects and taste and value:

> The ready made doesn't postulate a new set of values: it is a spanner in the works of what we call "valuable". It is an active criticism.
>
> (Paz, 1987, p. 84)

The reuse of a found object can greatly enhance the atmosphere and quality of a space. It can add a sense of nostalgia and remembrance to what would otherwise be a fairly anodyne place or add to an eclectic collection of elements and spaces. The found object may be totally suitable for the interior, but from a different era or culture, it would then become subtly prominent, but it could also be totally alien to the space, it then becomes a dramatic statement or critique of the space.

The ready-made is a process of spolia that can take place at a variety of scales. Bunny Lane House by the architect and self-titled "American Anarchist" Adam Kalkin is exactly that. Designed in 2001 the existing house on the rural site was a traditional New Jersey two-storey clapperboard house with shingle cladding. Rather than demolish this undistinguished building, Kalkin completely enclosed it within a corrugated steel shed, a massive structure of the type usually found on an industrial estate. Kalkin viewed the house as a found object, a historical fragment that was left entirely intact within the portal frame of the shed.

The building has now become a strange collection of different types of enclosure; interior spaces within other interior spaces. This ambiguity has produced a new building that is familiar while being equally surreal. What was once the front garden is now the living room and the front porch is the dining room. Walls and roofs that previously battled with the elements have, in a single stroke, now been relieved of that. The scale and brutality of the shed contrasts strongly with the traditional quality of the original house, and also with that of the furniture, which is carefully positioned within the expanse of the ground floor. The shed was positioned to accommodate the house at the northern end and, at the other, a tall very modern three-storey frame structure was inserted, which contains offices and bedrooms. This leaves the "courtyard" of a lounge in between the two internal structures. Huge sliding glazed doors allow natural light into this central space and reinforce the connection with the scale of the shed and the surrounding landscape. An extraordinary approach to a found object that revives and enlarges a conventional structure in a most dramatic manner.

> We come from a culture of sampling. I'm just out there in the world picking out things and reusing things—sampling—from my experience and from what other people have already invested a lot of time and energy in. I think there's a tremendous amount of richness out there.
>
> (Kalkin, 2002)

Ready-mades can be used as spolia purely because they happen to conform to exact sizes or measurements that ensure that they are fit for use. LOT/EK use found objects such as shipping containers to create new elements within or around existing buildings. The Bohen Foundation in New York is a gallery that is inhabited by three moveable shipping crates that become an office, a meeting room and a bookshop; they are flexible and can be moved to create more gallery space (Fig. 9.1). In other projects the designers have used tankers from petroleum lorries to make bedrooms, and stainless steel kitchen sinks to create partitions in a New York publishing house. The off-the-peg process of creating spaces and elements by utilising existing objects is very much a process of the assimilation of the designers' context. Contingency and the elements to hand are important for the designers:

> I get inspiration from the view of the West Side highway from the studio windows, the machines for moving meat, the water tanks on the roof,

Figure 9.1 The Bohen Foundation, New York, LOT/EK 2002. Ready-made objects can be removed from their original location and reused in a fresh and dramatic manner. [Credit: ©Graeme Brooker]

the fire escapes and air conditioners that seem to grow out of the sides of buildings.
(Toller, 2002, p. 141)

Ready-mades suggest a *fit for usefulness* approach or a potential for adaptation to new uses. This type of spolia may manifest itself in reuse of a variety of different found objects and elements. The idea of contingency or potential for reuse is important; the reading and then subsequent manipulation of a ready-made can then create distinct identities for the building or interior.

PERSISTENT MEANING

Spolia could be used as a method for creating form by appropriating objects where meaning is lost, is inadvertently forgotten or has become obscured over time. This approach often provokes reflections, whether intentional or inadvertent, on the new use or meaning of the appropriated fragment.

The church of Santa Catalina in Valencia is one of the city's oldest churches. The church was built over a mosque in the 13th Century and then remodelled in the 18th Century in a Baroque style. In the west wall of the church, facing Placa De Santa Catalina, are three pointed windows that were closed during the 18th Century remodelling. Two of the windows were sealed with stone and rendered

whilst the middle window has been filled in with the rubble of the Baroque era renovation. The spolia that is used consists of fragments such as plinths, the head from a statue, the shaft of a column and an eroded entablature. The fragments were deemed as superfluous and therefore they were appropriated into the window to become *in-fill*.

On the small Venetian island of Torcello is the Santa Maria Assunta Cathedral. Rebuilt in the 9th Century, it was abandoned in the 13th Century as the growth of Venice, the silting up of its canals and the onset of malaria decimated its population. The cathedral pulpit is fabricated from spolia. Its steps are made from a series of reliefs that have been sawn and cut to provide an edge and balustrade to the stair. The carvings are datable to the 11th and the 12th Centuries and subsequent research uncovered the fact that they were dedicated to Kairos, in antiquity the symbol of time as an opportunity. The reinstatement of these fragments was not an entirely arbitrary gesture and Patricia Fortini Brown suggests:

The restitution of the fragments to a certain degree of wholeness within the larger program calls attention to another occurring, and consummately Venetian, concern: to create a density of time within their major monuments through the employment of rediscovered relics.
(Fortini Brown, 1996, p. 9)

Both the *in-fill* in Valencia and the steps of the Torcello pulpit have been formulated using a series of leftover fragments (Fig. 9.2). Both sets of remains are valued but for different reasons. In Valencia the fragments are used as *in-fill*; they are no longer of any use, their meaning is lost and they fix a space that needed covering. In Torcello the carvings were also brutally treated. They were cut to fit the steps and then edged with a reclaimed frieze detail, yet they were retained for their residual meaning; their connection to time. In both examples spolia is used as a meaningful link to the past but both are treated quite differently.

The historical understanding of using spolia is also found in contemporary interior design. One of the fundamental principles of interior design is that the discipline is concerned with the understanding and the subsequent reuse of existing spaces. Objects and spaces are "valued" for their previous meaning and retained or reused in a space. This principle lends an air of the fetishisation of existing space, as Fred Scott suggests in *On Altering Architecture*:

> The atmosphere of all preserved buildings is unavoidably instilled with the qualities of fetish. The idea of alteration is to offer an alternative to preservation or demolition, a more general strategy to keep buildings beyond their time.
>
> (Scott, 2008, p. 113)

In 1990 the American designer Ben Nicholson made Appliance House: an installation created to reflect the modern home. The house was conceived and designed with the use of collage; the working drawings for the construction of the house are made using appropriated images from a Sears Catalogue. Spolia is used in order not only to generate the appearance of the house but also to suggest an exaggerated distortion of a normal house. As Nicholson suggests:

> By assembling frail and barely recognisable traits of urban existence into firm gestures, the Appliance House is formed into a Sub-Urban Home.
>
> (Nicholson, 1990, p. 42)

Nicholson conceived the most important room of the house as the "Kleptoman Cell" (the trophy room). He invented a mythical inhabitant, the Kleptoman, who would decorate this room with his trophies. The room was designed to be an armature that would contract and swell with the contents of the booty which the Kleptoman had collected from his travels. His spolia would become the interior content, decoration and eventually the structure of the room as the frame of the space accepted the contents and displayed them as *in-fill*. In the centre of the room was the Telemon cupboard; a device that allowed forty of the Kleptoman's favoured spoils to be displayed. The cupboard acts as a barometer for the space, monitoring the collection and displaying his finds, selecting the most meaningful objects that have an "afterlife" of memories, meanings, associations and connections.

The use of spolia can create a particular aesthetic in a space. In a nondescript 1970s school building in Omaha, Nebraska, Randy Brown has installed an autonomous object that has a number of different uses: an office for three designers and a home for his wife and himself. Brown and his wife lived in the building when it was being built and the hands-on approach to project management led to a particular off-the-peg D.I.Y. aesthetic. The elegant timber and steel element is assembled using off-the-peg sections of material from the local hardware store. Its off-the-peg aesthetic lends itself to a temporary piece of furniture, a detail that helped Brown to persuade the local council that it was furniture rather than new-build and hence ease its transition through planning.

The formal or surface properties of the existing building in this case are basic and the anonymity of the school merely provides the container for the new interior. Rather than disguising these attributes the studio and residence accepts these qualities and therefore places importance on them as a design feature. Brown retained the existing wall surfaces. In fact the bland qualities of the host has informed the off-the-peg solution to its reuse. Whilst assembling the interior Brown would work with plans but then while the structure was being built he would move the elements around until they achieved a satisfactory relationship within the space.

Interiors built using elements and objects with an off-the-peg aesthetic are spaces that are designed as an independent element, using the envelope and its qualities as a container that contrasts or juxtaposes with the new space. Persistent meaning is evident in pervasive elements that are often designed as enigmatic one-offs or sequential elements that enclose new functions yet do not make contact with the walls of the existing space. Their character is to appear at odds with the host and heighten the contrast between them.

Figure 9.2 Pulpit of the Santa Maria Assunta Cathedral, Torcello. The steps are constructed from ornate elements that have been salvaged from other buildings and cut to size. [Credit: ©Graeme Brooker]

CONTINUITY AND PERMANENCE

Artists today program more forms than they compose them; rather than transfigure a raw element (blank canvas, clay etc.), they remix available forms and make use of data. In a universe of products for sale, preexisting forms, signals already emitted, buildings already constructed, paths marked out by their predecessors, artists no longer consider the artistic field ... a museum containing works that must be cited or surpassed as the Modernist ideology of originality would have it, but so many storehouses filled with tools that should be used, stockpiles of data to manipulate and present.

(Bourriaud, 2002, p. 17)

The third category of spolia is the enhancement of the narrative of the host building by the appropriation of fragments or objects of distinct meaning. These fragments might have important associations with the past, links to other ideologies or traditions, or distinct meaning or value. Continuity in the making of buildings advocates the reading of a place in order to understand meaning and then act appropriately. This implies an acceptance of patterns, traditions, forms and the language of a site, yet it does not necessarily advocate a straightforward copy of those conditions. Making buildings with spolia allowed Roman architects to express their strengths through their connections with the past. As Kinney states:

Making had not yet been problematized as creativity, and the crafting of a new object from traditional – perused – elements could give satisfaction. Building with spolia was just the instantiation of tradition, and the knowledge that the language of architecture had already been spoken and could only be repeated, never invented, was contentedly embraced, to the extent that repetition was enacted as verbatim quotation. Spolia are not symptoms of influence, but symbols of the acceptance of the authority of the Latin/Roman past.

(Kinney, 2001, pp. 138–150)

In *Postproduction* Bourriaud states that the current artistic practice of making connections to historicist forms and inhabiting past styles is a process of making sense of the vast flows of information in our daily lives. Whereas the Roman builder was happy with carrying on with traditional forms, today the artist and designer are willing to adapt and remix the existing in order to shape it to fit their lives:

All of these artistic practices . . . have in common the recourse to already produced forms. They testify to a willingness to inscribe the work of art within a new network of signs and significations, instead of considering it an autonomous form. It is no longer a matter of starting with a blank slate . . . but finding a means of insertion into the innumerable flows of production.

(Bourriaud, 2002, p. 17)

When designing the University Library in Ljubljana in 1936, Jose Plecnik's interest in Roman antiquity and Semper's theory of cladding led him to produce a solution that incorporated spolia from the site. The library façade is studded with remnants of the old Palais Auersperg and the medieval city walls that once occupied the site (Fig. 9.3). Granite, marble, Podec stone and spolia were combined with brick and concrete blocks to complete the façades. Plecnik wanted to ensure that the profile of the building retained its associations not only to its immediate history but also to its allusions to connections with Italy and Rome. He placed Etruscan concrete vessels above the side entrances in order to suggest an association between Slovenian culture and its Mediterranean roots.

The recycling of the existing building and elements can involve the reuse of unusual spaces, sometimes with extremely odd results. Interiors are usually created to service a specific function and the design of the space will reflect the particular activities happening within it. Sometimes the functional requirements are so specific, that is difficult to convert without completely losing the essence and honesty of the interior. However, the designer can choose to retain the character and indeed the obvious function of a space and use it as the starting point for the redesign. One of the most outrageous examples of the new and old fitting together very well, but each still retaining a distinct and individual identity, is Klein Dytham's project for an advertising agency situated within an operational bowling alley.

In the dense, ever changing metropolis of Tokyo, KDa were engaged to design the new HQ for global recently merged advertising company TWBA/Hakuhodo; this included finding space for the 300 strong workforce. The site was in an eight-storey amusement complex and the company had to share their venture with a reception for the gaudy gaming halls and endure a still working bowling alley situated around them. The designers adapted the single span, 30-lane bowling hall into a studio

Figure 9.3 University Library, Ljubljana, Josip Plecnik,1936. The façade of the building is studded with blocks from the Palais Auersperg, the building that once occupied the site. [Credit: ©Graeme Brooker]

for the company. They worked within the existing grain of the building using the extended, timber lanes of the alley for the distribution of work and meeting spaces. Each lane provided a long narrow length of space for work activities and the space between the lanes, previously used for returning the bowling balls, became circulation. A folded office room was positioned in each lane to provide an element of private meeting space for each team.

In both of these projects spolia is used to further connections and links with either the past or already established meanings. In all of the projects spolia is used as a method of constructing buildings in a way that makes associations with existing meanings. The use of spolia accepts traditions, patterns and the language of either a site or an existing object. It suggests the application of a meaningful approach to design that reads and then revises existing meaning in a place; the appropriate use of appropriation as a strategy for reuse.

CONCLUSION

The use of spolia as a tactic for interiors is another element in the attempt to reclaim the theory of interiors. Interior architecture and design has often been regarded as a superficial practice that lacks any particular histories, design theories or principles. Interior architecture, interior design and building reuse are very closely linked subjects, all of them deal in varying degrees with the transformation of a given space, whether that is the crumbling ruins of an ancient building or the drawn parameters of a building proposal. This alteration or conversion is a complex process of understanding the qualities of the given space whilst simultaneously combining these factors with the functional requirements of new users.

This distinctive attribute creates a unique set of issues, theories and processes that are different to many other disciplines. Spolia is just one of the tactics.

The use of spolia is an enduring strategy and one that can underpin the creation of interior space, especially within the practice of remodelling existing buildings. Spolia is an overlooked and meaningful tactic for reuse, and is a method of designing that is particular and unique to the creation of interior space. Interiors is a subject that encompasses the analysis and understanding of existing buildings, the nature and qualities of an interior space, and an intimate examination of the characteristics of the decoration. The creation of new interior environments from fragments, existing objects, new materials as well as found elements, is as much a thoroughly postmodern, contemporary process of design.

REFERENCES

Bourriaud, N. *Postproduction: Culture as Screenplay: How Art Reprograms the World* (Lukas and Sternberg 2002).

Fortini Brown, P. *Venice and Antiquity* (Yale University Press, New Haven 1996).

Kalkin, A. *Architecture and Hygiene* (Batsford Publishers 2002).

Kinney, D. Roman Architectural Spolia. *Proceedings of the American Philosophical Society*, 145(2): 138–150 (2001).

Nicholson, B. *Appliance House* (MIT Press 1990).

Paz, O. *Marcel Duchamp: Appearance Stripped Bare* (Seaver Books 1987).

Scott, F. *On Altering Architecture* (Routledge 2008).

Tolla, A. *LOT/EK* (Blueprint May 2002).

SECTION 1.3
HISTORY AND PHILOSOPHY

Introduction

The history of interior decoration is a difficult subject to study for the reason that very few interiors survive the test of time. This is because they are easily altered; whether this is with fashion, with a change of occupants or a shift in the manner in which people occupy space. The sometimes overzealous or vigorous practice of conservation means that it is often impossible to actually identify the original elements of the interior and distinguish the chronology of the changes. So information about the nature and character of these historic interiors has to be gleaned from more than just the original source. The most obvious starting point is paintings, but writings can also provide clues to the nature of the interior. The artist, for whatever reason, will create a painting to communicate a message, so when using these as the basis for a theoretical study, the historian must always be aware that there must be an element of mistrust in the piece. But since these are the best evidence available they just have to be read in a circumspect manner. The paintings depict the kind of space our ancestors surrounded themselves with, the artefacts and furniture that they used and the manner in which they occupied the interior.

The history of interior decoration could also be described as social commentary upon the manner in which people lived. Historically homes were constructed to fit the people who occupied them and the design and the decoration of the interior was dependent upon the needs and customs of the occupants. Peter Thornton in his *Authentic Decor: the Domestic Interior 1620–1920* describes a wish for topographers to have spared a few pages from their higher pretentions to tell us what the parlours and bedchambers of our ancestors looked like. It is, of course, almost impossible for someone from the twenty-first century to understand what it was like to occupy these spaces, we can of course theorise, but to actually think and feel as a member of an earlier time is out of the question. We have a different attitude to comfort, to occupation, to social hierarchy, we can but attempt to empathise with those occupants of a different era, based upon our readings of these paintings and other types of description.

It was Mario Praz in *An Illustrated History of Interior Decoration: from Pompeii to Art Nouveau*, who first drew widespread attention to the question of the history of the interior, although strangely, it is purported that he did not regard his book as an authoritative work about history, more a discursive conversation upon the subject. This may be because he was completely reliant upon the secondary information of contemporary paintings, or it may have been his loquacious style of writing.

The concept of interior decoration as a creative entity within the visual arts is essentially a product of the twentieth century. Up until this point, it was the architect working with the upholsterer who were responsible for the interior decoration. It was expected that they could create sumptuous works of art, whether inside or out. The divorce between architecture and decoration occurred with mass-production and the lack of contact with the individual craftsmen. However, the rise of decorative finishes both within and outside the building in the twenty-first century has seen a rise in the status of the interior decorator; it will be interesting to see whether the link between architecture and decoration becomes smaller, or will protective practices mean that the chasm will become greater?

There are three essays in this section; each deals in a slightly different manner with the historic interior. Mario Praz, in his usual florid style, describes the history and nature of the intense interiors of the Soane Museum. It would have been possible to select almost any building study from his highly influential book; this one seemed the most appropriate to this publication. Edith Wharton and Ogden Codman discuss the influence that the historic European interior has had upon American designers and Witold Rybczynski traces the origins of the concept of comfort.

An Illustrated History of Interior Decoration: from Pompeii to Art Nouveau by **Mario Praz** is an extremely comprehensive survey of the western domestic interior. The author exclusively uses paintings and drawings that were created contemporaneously with the interiors to illustrate his discussion. Praz reputedly took 19 years to write the excellent, if a little gossipy, introduction to what is a rivetingly good examination of the subject.

The essay selected from this thorough account is the description of the home of the neo-classical architect Sir John Soane. The building, which was actually the conversion of two town houses, is now a museum dedicated to the work and the collection of this renowned architect, and is well worth a visit.

Praz begins his study of the house by tracing Soane's affinity with the bold French eighteenth century architects, Ledoux and Boullée, before quoting John Summerson's glowing description of an architect at the forefront of the classical movement. Praz then describes how Soane's collection of objects, paintings and books had been an obvious influence upon his own style of architecture. The house itself is the documentation of taste and also failure. The all-encompassing style of the author allows him to dwell upon the disappointment that Soane felt when he realised that none of his sons were to follow him into the architectural profession, an act that eventually led him to leave this home to the nation rather than to his family, as well as a detailed description of the lineage of the objects and a discussion of the architectural itself. The essay is a florid portrayal of a flamboyant building constructed by a complex architect.

Edith Wharton and **Ogden Codman, Jr.** open their book *The Decoration of Houses* by stating that "Rooms may be decorated in two ways: by a superficial application of ornament totally independent of structure, or by means of those architectural features which are part of the organism of every house, inside as well as out." They then proceed to explain why the second method is preferable, while also bemoaning the belittled position of the home-decorator. (How little has changed since the end of the nineteenth century!)

This essay, "The Historical Tradition", which is actually the first chapter of the book, is a quick survey of European domestic decoration from a North American perspective. The authors discuss the American idea of using totally unsuitable precedents that were chiefly to be found among the buildings erected in Italy after the beginning of the sixteenth century. These were inappropriate, they argue, because the manner in which people lived had so radically changed. Much of European architecture and interiors were initially based upon the need to protect the occupants from invasion and feudal conflict. As a gradual peace spread through Europe, then a more Roman civic way of life was re-introduced, but still Wharton and Codman contend, these houses could hardly, in the modern sense, be called convenient. The same argument applied to furniture, it needed to be portable, or at least be able to be carried from place to place as the landowner travelled from one estate to another. Thus strength was more greatly regarded than comfort and, prior to the seventeenth century, even the most affluent people had to content themselves with hard straight-backed seats.

Wharton and Codman argue that the modern house ought to be constructed in strict accordance with its purpose, and then the decoration will harmonise with the architecture. The plan for the room should be based upon rhythm and logic, rather than the prevailing style of the day. The authors conclude that proportion, common sense and reasonable conformity will produce a great variety of decoration without losing sight of purpose. If novelist Edith Wharton and architect Ogden Codman, Jr. had written this book today rather than over a hundred years ago (published in 1898), no doubt it would be a sumptuous volume filled with glossy coloured photos because they offer timeless advice on so many important matters of interior decoration.

Witold Rybczynski's *A Short History of Home* traces the manner in which social and cultural changes have influenced the decoration of the domestic interior, and the chapter "Comfort and Well-Being", clearly sets out the distinction between comfort, culture and decoration.

Rybczynski claims that decoration is primarily a product of fashion, something ephemeral that can be measured in decades or even less, while comfort and cultural ideas have "a life measured in centuries". Social behaviour, which is built upon habits and customs, is more long-lived; he cites the acceptability or not of special places to smoke as an example. He argues that a simple copying of the style of decoration cannot recapture the past. The style of the room was designed around a particular type of behaviour, which in turn was conditioned by the way that people thought about comfort. Technology has brought massive changes to our ideas of how space should be occupied. Hot water and electricity introduced in the late nineteenth century meant a massive shift in the manner in which domestic spaces were used, but interestingly, as the text was published in 1986, Rybczynski doesn't touch upon the implications of the computer. The author discusses also the role of the woman within the home and argues that domesticity was a feminine concept and that the modernist idea of the home as machine for living in was one that was built to fit the female form.

Rybczynski ponders upon the definition of comfort. It is well recognised that it wasn't really until the eighteenth century that the concept of comfort became widely recognised, but "What," he asks, "is comfort?" Rybczynski surveys the history of the idea, before concluding that the definition of comfort is as ephemeral as fashion itself.

Sally Stone

Edith Wharton (1862–1937)

Edith Wharton was a novelist, garden designer and interior decorator. She made her name with the book *The House of Mirth* in 1905 and won the Pulitzer Prize for Literature in 1921 for her novel *The Age of Innocence*. She wrote widely on many subjects, including *The Decoration of Houses* (with Ogden Codman), which is a sort of interior design manual. Here they denounced Victorian interior design with its bric-a-brac and cluttered opulent furniture, and advocated clean interiors that were inspired by simple classicalism, accentuated by carefully selected furniture. They were probably the first to use the term 'Interior Architect' in this book, and it helped to characterise the work of interior decorators as a separate professional entity from upholsterers.

Building Study: Teatro Olimpico

Vicenza, Italy
Andrea Palladio
1580

The Teatro Olimpico in Vicenza is one of the oldest surviving Renaissance theatres in the world. It is based on the ancient Roman principle of a fixed and elaborate architectural backdrop with a stage in front of it. The stage contains a permanently fixed street set. It is of a classical urban scene, complete with arches, columns and windows. Seven streets appear to recede with exaggerated perspective from behind the proscenium and away from the viewer. The narrowing of the space between the walls and the gradual raising of the floor creates this illusion. This scenery is constructed from wood and plaster, but as with all Roman theatres, has the appearance of permanent stone; in this case it matches exactly the white marble that is used elsewhere in the city. The scene continues behind the audience, so that they are completely enclosed by it. The trompe l'oeil clouds painted onto the flat ceiling contribute to this sense of enclosure. The spectators are very much part of the performance; they are enveloped by the air of theatricality, which helps to reinforce the sense of suspended belief, so important for all dramatic performances. Palladio has created a vision of classical theatre within the tight confines of a city context.

Palladio studied the classical texts and also the remains of Roman theatres in Italy, Istria and Provence. It was one of the last projects that he designed; indeed, he died before it was completed. However, his knowledge of classical antiquity was such that it is often considered as his masterpiece.

10
Sir John Soane

Mario Praz

Source: *An Illustrated History of Interior Decoration: From Pompeii to Art Nouveau.*
Thames and Hudson, 2008, pp. 246–249

Almost as startling as the Brighton Pavilion is an English building decorated in the period of George IV: the house and museum of the Neoclassical architect Sir John Soane (1753–1837). An architect who belonged to the innovating, revolutionary current of Neoclassicism rather than to the academic school, Sir John had some affinities with the bold French architects of the 18th century, Ledoux and Boullée. "In 1792," writes John Summerson, "when the style arrived suddenly, at maturity, there was not, anywhere in Europe, an architecture as unconstrained by classical loyalties, as free in the handling of proportion and as adventurous in structure and lighting as that which Soane introduced at the Bank of England in that year."[1] Between the end of the 18th and the beginning of the 19th centuries Soane began to collect the objects of art which he was later to arrange in his museum, and at the same time (probably under the influence of the theories of Payne Knight and Uvedale Price concerning the picturesque) he introduced picturesque effects in greater quantity into his buildings. Illumination from above was one of the most important of these effects. The arrangement of Soane's House and Museum, a work of his last years, expresses a certain ideal of archeological abundance, an ideal already exemplified by Piranesi in his *Different Ways of Decorating Fireplaces,* 1769 *(Diverse maniere d'adornare i camini)* and by John Zoffany in pictures like *Charles Townley and His Friends in His Library* (1790) where the classical sculptures scattered in various parts of the house were assembled in the same room for the painting. Though Soane was rather unfortunate in his attempts at Gothic architecture, he greatly admired Gothic effects and tried to introduce some into his house. Speaking for example of the Breakfast Room, Soane says: "The views from this room into the Monument Court [a little court in the center of which Soane had erected an "Architectural Pasticcio," as he called it, formed of classical, Gothic, and even Indian fragments] and into the

Museum, the mirrors in the ceiling, and the looking-glasses, combined with the variety of outline and general arrangement in the design and decoration of this limited space, present a succession of those fanciful effects which constitute the poetry of Architecture."[2] His virtuosity in uniting varied motifs can be seen in the combination of two semicircles and an arch-segment which divides the Dining Room from the Library. This tripartite arch recalls a section of the ceiling of Edward VII's chapel in Westminster Abbey.

The Sir John Soane Museum is the documentation of a taste and also of a failure. Soane had collected works of art to furnish his house, Pitzhanger Manor, which he had imagined as the ideal setting for the education of young architects, particularly of his sons, whom he meant to train for that career. But his sons were a disappointment to him, and in 1833 Soane, by a special act of Parliament, left his house and its contents to the nation, to become a public institution after his death. Since he had been unable to found a dynasty of architects, at least the Museum would enshrine his memory for posterity. The minute, loving description of his house and its treasures contains, in a sense, his spiritual testament and the expression of his pleasure in handsome furnishings, which he at times naïvely displayed, as in this passage on the *Dining Room and Library:* "The general effect of those rooms is admirable; they combine the characteristics of wealth and elegance, taste and comfort, with those especial riches which belong expressly to literature and art,—to the progressive proofs of human intellect and industry, given, from age to age, in those works which most decisively evince utility and power." Among the works in the Library was the Shakespeare that had once belonged to Garrick. In this room, as in the others of the house, there is no spot where the eye can light without finding a mass of things: books, statues, pictures, or objects, whose presence is multiplied by the round mirrors set here and there throughout the house. The eye cannot find repose from the windows, either, for the window of the Dining Room gives on the Monument Court, occupied by the "Architectural Pasticcio." The problem which Soane had to solve in making a Museum out of his house in Lincoln's Inn Fields was rather like the problem which faced Pietro da Cortona with the Piazza della Pace in Rome: to create space where there wasn't any. For this reason, in *The Painting Room,* Sir John arranged the paintings on movable panels which could be opened out like doors. "By this arrangement, the small space of thirteen feet eight inches in length, twelve feet four inches in breadth, and nineteen feet six inches in height, which are the actual dimensions of this room, is rendered capable of containing as many pictures as a gallery of the same height, twenty feet broad and forty-five feet long. Another advantage of this arrangement is, that the pictures may be seen under different angles of vision." The four ivory chairs had belonged to Tippoo Sahib, the Sultan of Mysore, whose territory fell under English domination in 1779. In this room there is Hogarth's *The Rake's Progress* series and the Nymph who can be seen in front of the window is a statue by R. Westmacott. *The Monk's Cell,* or *parlour* of Father Giovanni, whose statue stands on a chest of drawers in a niche opposite the fireplace, was decorated with fragments of architecture and religious sculpture meant to "impress the spectator with reverence for the Monk," while the Scriptural subjects on glass were "suited to the destination of the place, and increase its sombre character."

In the sepulchral chamber, the *Belzoni Room,* we see the sarcophagus that Giovanni Belzoni, an adventurer much talked about in England at the beginning of the century, had brought from Egypt and exhibited in the Egyptian Hall in Piccadilly.[3] Sir John Soane bought it for two thousand pounds. Like the *Monk's Cell,* this room, too, is so crammed with sculptures, vases, and fragments that its teeming appearance is extraordinarily Piranesian. In accordance with the principle of having a room's decoration follow its character, this room contains a death-mask of Parker the mutineer and a life-mask of Mrs. Siddons, one corner of her mouth a little distorted by the unpleasant sensation caused by the plaster's pressure. From the gallery under the cupola of the museum one can look down to see the sarcophagus. From this vantage point various other rooms can be seen as well. The play of arches, recesses, and depths among walls covered with a veritable eruption of carved stones follows the same principle which made Soane place mirrors here and there to multiply the views. Perhaps a psychoanalyst, more than a student of esthetics, could explain this obsession. In any case, these bizarre English constructions, the Brighton Pavilion and the Soane House-Museum, the first with its proliferation of serpents and dragons, the second with its profusion of carved stones scattered as in a cemetery, tend surely to make a sinister impression on the spirit of the visitor.[4]

NOTES

1 John Summerson, *Sir John Soane*, London (1952).
2 *Description of the House and Museum ... Residence of Sir John Soane*, London (1835) p. 54.
3 Cf. M. Willson Disher, *Pharoah's Fool, The Story of Giovanni Belzoni*, London (1957) and also Stanley Mayer, *The Great Belzoni*, New York (1959).
4 On the Soane Museum see also the richly illustrated article by Philippe Julian, "L'extraordinaire amoncellement du Soane Museum à Londres," *Connaissance des Arts* (Oct. 1962) p. 65.

11
The Historical Tradition

Edith Wharton and Ogden Codman

Source: *The Decoration of Houses*. B.T. Batsford, 1898, pp. 1–16

The last ten years have been marked by a notable development in architecture and decoration, and while France will long retain her present superiority in these arts, our own advance is perhaps more significant than that of any other country. When we measure the work recently done in the United States by the accepted architectural standards of ten years ago, the change is certainly striking, especially in view of the fact that our local architects and decorators are without the countless advantages in the way of schools, museums and libraries which are at the command of their European colleagues. In Paris, for instance, it is impossible to take even a short walk without finding inspiration in those admirable buildings, public and private, religious and secular, that bear the stamp of the most refined taste the world has known since the decline of the arts in Italy; and probably all American architects will acknowledge that no amount of travel abroad and study at home can compensate for the lack of daily familiarity with such monuments.

It is therefore all the more encouraging to note the steady advance in taste and knowledge to which the most recent architecture in America bears witness. This advance is chiefly due to the fact that American architects are beginning to perceive two things that their French colleagues, among all the modern vagaries of taste, have never quite lost sight of: first that architecture and decoration, having wandered since 1800 in a labyrinth of dubious eclecticism, can be set right only by a close study of the best models; and secondly that, given the requirements of modern life, these models are chiefly to be found in buildings erected in Italy after the beginning of the sixteenth century, and in other European countries after the full assimilation of the Italian influence.

As the latter of these propositions may perhaps be questioned by those who, in admiring the earlier styles, sometimes lose sight of their relative unfitness for modern use, it must be understood at the outset that it implies no disregard for the inherent beauties of these styles. It would be difficult, assuredly, to find buildings better suited to their original purpose than some of the great feudal castles, such as Warwick in England, or Langeais in France; and as much might be said of the grim machicolated palaces of republican Florence or Siena; but our whole mode of life has so entirely changed since the days in which these buildings were erected that they no longer answer to our needs. It is only necessary to picture the lives led in those days to see how far removed from them our present social conditions are. Inside and outside the house, all told of the unsettled condition of country or town, the danger of armed attack, the clumsy means of defence, the insecurity of property, the few opportunities of social intercourse as we understand it. A man's house was in very truth his castle in the middle ages, and in France and England especially it remained so until the end of the sixteenth century.

Thus it was that many needs arose: the tall keep of masonry where the inmates, pent up against attack, awaited the signal of the watchman who, from his platform or *échauguette*, gave warning of assault; the ponderous doors, oak-ribbed and metal-studded, with doorways often narrowed to prevent entrance of two abreast, and so low that the incomer had to bend his head; the windows that were mere openings or slits, narrow and high, far out of the assailants' reach, and piercing the walls without regard to symmetry—not, as Ruskin would have us believe, because irregularity was thought artistic, but because the mediæval architect, trained to the uses of necessity, knew that he must design openings that should afford no passage to the besiegers' arrows, no clue to what was going on inside the keep. But to the reader familiar with Viollet-le-Duc, or with any of the many excellent works on English domestic architecture, further details will seem superfluous. It is necessary, however, to point out that long after the conditions of life in Europe had changed, houses retained many features of the feudal period. The survival of obsolete customs which makes the study of sociology so interesting, has its parallel in the history of architecture. In the feudal countries especially, where the conflict between the great nobles and the king was of such long duration that civilization spread very slowly, architecture was proportionately slow to give up many of its feudal characteristics. In Italy, on the contrary, where one city after another succumbed to some accomplished condottiere who between his campaigns read Virgil and collected antique marbles, the rugged little republics were soon converted into brilliant courts where, life being relatively secure, social intercourse rapidly developed. This change of conditions brought with it the paved street and square, the large-windowed palaces with their great court-yards and stately open staircases, and the market-place with its loggia adorned with statues and marble seats.

Italy, in short, returned instinctively to the Roman ideal of civic life: the life of the street, the forum and the baths. These very conditions, though approaching so much nearer than feudalism to our modern civilization, in some respects make the Italian architecture of the Renaissance less serviceable as a model than the French and English styles later developed from it. The very dangers and barbarities of feudalism had fostered and preserved the idea of home as of something private, shut off from intrusion; and while the Roman ideal flowered in the great palace with its galleries, loggias and saloons, itself a kind of roofed-in forum, the French or English feudal keep became, by the same process of growth, the modern private house. The domestic architecture of the Renaissance in Italy offers but two distinctively characteristic styles of building: the palace and the villa or hunting-lodge.[1] There is nothing corresponding in interior arrangements with the French or English town house, or the *memoir* where the provincial nobles lived all the year round. The villa was a mere perch used for a few weeks of gaiety in spring or autumn; it was never a home as the French or English country-house was. There were, of course, private houses in Renaissance Italy, but these were occupied rather by shopkeepers, craftsmen, and the *bourgeoisie* than by the class which in France and England lived in country houses or small private hotels. The elevations of these small Italian houses are often admirable examples of domestic architecture, but their planning is rudimentary, and it may be said that the characteristic tendencies of modern house-planning were developed rather in the mezzanin or low-studded intermediate story of

the Italian Renaissance palace than in the small house of the same period.

It is a fact recognized by political economists that changes in manners and customs, no matter under what form of government, usually originate with the wealthy or aristocratic minority, and are thence transmitted to the other classes. Thus the *bourgeois* of one generation lives more like the aristocrat of a previous generation than like his own predecessors. This rule naturally holds good of house-planning, and it is for this reason that the origin of modern house-planning should be sought rather in the prince's mezzanin than in the small middle-class dwelling. The Italian mezzanin probably originated in the habit of building certain very high-studded saloons and of lowering the ceiling of the adjoining rooms. This created an intermediate story, or rather scattered intermediate rooms, which Bramante was among the first to use in the planning of his palaces; but Bramante did not reveal the existence of the mezzanin in his façades, and it was not until the time of Peruzzi and his contemporaries that it became, both in plan and elevation, an accepted part of the Italian palace. It is for this reason that the year 1500 is a convenient point from which to date the beginning of modern house-planning; but it must be borne in mind that this date is purely arbitrary, and represents merely an imaginary line drawn between mediæval and modern ways of living and house-planning, as exemplified respectively, for instance, in the ducal palace of Urbino, built by Luciano da Laurano about 1468, and the palace of the Massimi alle Colonne in Rome, built by Baldassare Peruzzi during the first half of the sixteenth century.

The lives of the great Italian nobles were essentially open-air lives: all was organized with a view to public pageants, ceremonies and entertainments. Domestic life was subordinated to this spectacular existence, and instead of building private houses in our sense, they built palaces, of which they set aside a portion for the use of the family. Every Italian palace has its mezzanin or private apartment; but this part of the building is now seldom seen by travellers in Italy. Not only is it usually inhabited by the owners of the palace but, its decorations being simpler than those of the *piano nobile*, or principal story, it is not thought worthy of inspection. As a matter of fact, the treatment of the mezzanin was generally most beautiful, because most suitable; and while the Italian Renaissance palace can seldom serve as a model for a modern private house, the decoration of the mezzanin rooms is full of appropriate suggestion.

In France and England, on the other hand, private life was gradually, though slowly, developing along the lines it still follows in the present day. It is necessary to bear in mind that what we call modern civilization was a later growth in these two countries than in Italy. If this fact is insisted upon, it is only because it explains the relative unsuitability of French Renaissance or Tudor and Elizabethan architecture to modern life. In France, for instance, it was not until the Fronde was subdued and Louis XIV firmly established on the throne, that the elements which compose what we call modern life really began to combine. In fact, it might be said that the feudalism of which the Fronde was the lingering expression had its counterpart in the architecture of the period. While long familiarity with Italy was beginning to tell upon the practical side of house-planning, many obsolete details were still preserved. Even the most enthusiastic admirer of the French Renaissance would hardly maintain that the houses of that period are what we should call in the modern sense "convenient." It would be impossible for a modern family to occupy with any degree of comfort the Hôtel Voguë at Dijon, one of the best examples (as originally planned) of sixteenth-century domestic architecture in France.[2] The same objection applies to the furniture of the period. This arose from the fact that, owing to the unsettled state of the country, the landed proprietor always carried his furniture with him when he travelled from one estate to another. Furniture, in the vocabulary of the middle ages, meant something which may be transported: "Meubles sont apelez qu'on peut transporter";—hence the lack of variety in furniture before the seventeenth century, and also its unsuitableness to modern life. Chairs and cabinets that had to be carried about on mule-back were necessarily somewhat stiff and angular in design. It is perhaps not too much to say that a comfortable chair, in our self-indulgent modern sense, did not exist before the Louis XIV armchair; and the cushioned bergère, the ancestor of our upholstered easy-chair, cannot be traced back further than the Regency. Prior to the time of Louis XIV, the most luxurious people had to content themselves with hard straight-backed seats. The necessities of transportation permitted little variety of design, and every piece of furniture was constructed with the double purpose of being easily carried about and of being used as a trunk. As Havard says, "Tout meuble se traduisait par un coffre." The unvarying design of the cabinets is explained by the fact that they were made to form two trunks,[3] and even the chairs and settles had hollow seats which could be packed with the owners' wardrobe. The king himself, when he went from one château to another, carried all his furniture with him, and it is thus not surprising that lesser people contented themselves with a few substantial chairs and cabinets, and enough arras or cloth of Douai to cover the draughty walls of their country-houses. One of Madame de Sévigné's letters gives an amusing instance of the scarceness of furniture even in the time of Louis XIV. In describing a fire in a house near her own hôtel in Paris, she says that one or two of the persons from the burning house were brought to her for shelter, because it was known in the neighborhood (at that time a rich and fashionable one) that she had an extra bed in the house!

It was not until the social influences of the reign of Louis XIV were fully established that modern domestic life really began. Tradition ascribes to Madame de Rambouillet a leading share in the advance in practical house-planning; but probably what she did is merely typical of the modifications which the new social conditions were everywhere producing. It is certain that at this time houses and rooms first began to be comfortable. The immense cavernous fireplaces originally meant for the roasting of beeves and the warming of a flock of frozen retainers,—"les grandes antiquailles de cheminées," as Madame de Sévigné called them,—were replaced by the compact chimney-piece of modern times. Cushioned bergères took the place of the throne-like seats of Louis XIII, screens kept off unwelcome draughts, Savonnerie or moquette carpets covered the stone or marble floors, and grandeur gave way to luxury.[4]

English architecture having followed a line of development so similar that it need not here be traced, it remains only to examine in detail the opening proposition, namely, that modern architecture and decoration, having in many ways deviated from the paths which the experience of the past had marked out for them, can be reclaimed only by a study of the best models.

It might of course be said that to attain this end originality is more necessary than imitativeness. To this it may be replied that no lost art can be re-acquired without at least for a time going back to the methods and manner of those who formerly practised it; or the objection may be met by the question, What is originality in art? Perhaps it is easier to define what it is not; and this may be done by saying that it is never a wilful rejection of what have been accepted as the necessary laws of the various forms of art. Thus, in reasoning, originality lies not in discarding the necessary laws of thought, but in using them to express new intellectual conceptions; in poetry, originality consists not in discarding the necessary laws of rhythm, but in finding new rhythms within the limits of those laws. Most of the features of architecture that have persisted through various fluctuations of taste owe their preservation to the fact that they have been proved by experience to be necessary; and it will be found that none of them precludes the exercise of individual taste, any more than the acceptance of the syllogism or of the laws of rhythm prevents new thinkers and new poets from saying what has never been said before. Once this is clearly understood, it will be seen that the supposed conflict between originality and tradition is no conflict at all.[5]

In citing logic and poetry, those arts have been purposely chosen of which the laws will perhaps best help to explain and illustrate the character of architectural limitations. A building, for whatever purpose erected, must be built in strict accordance with the requirements of that purpose; in other words, it must have a reason for being as it is and must be as it is for that reason. Its decoration must harmonize with the structural limitations (which is by no means the same thing as saying that all decoration must be structural), and from this harmony of the general scheme of decoration with the building, and of the details of the decoration with each other, springs the rhythm that distinguishes architecture from mere construction. Thus all good architecture and good decoration (which, it must never be forgotten, *is only interior architecture*) must be based on rhythm and logic. A house, or room, must be planned as it is because it could not, in reason, be otherwise; must be decorated as it is because no other decoration would harmonize as well with the plan.

Many of the most popular features in modern house-planning and decoration will not be found to stand this double test. Often (as will be shown further on) they are merely survivals of earlier social conditions, and have been preserved in obedience to that instinct that makes people cling to so many customs the meaning of which is lost. In other cases they have been revived by the archæologizing spirit which is so characteristic of the present time, and which so often leads its possessors to think that a thing must be beautiful because it is old and appropriate because it is beautiful.

But since the beauty of all such features depends on their appropriateness, they may in every case be replaced by a more suitable form of treatment without loss to the general effect of house or room. It is this which makes it important that each room

(or, better still, all the rooms) in a house should receive the same style of decoration. To some people this may seem as meaningless a piece of archaism as the habit of using obsolete fragments of planning or decoration; but such is not the case. It must not be forgotten, in discussing the question of reproducing certain styles, that the essence of a style lies not in its use of ornament, but in its handling of proportion. Structure conditions ornament, not ornament structure. That is, a room with unsuitably proportioned openings, wall-spaces and cornice might receive a surface application of Louis XV or Louis XVI ornament and not represent either of those styles of decoration; whereas a room constructed according to the laws of proportion accepted in one or the other of those periods, in spite of a surface application of decorative detail widely different in character,—say Romanesque or Gothic,—would yet maintain its distinctive style, because the detail, in conforming with the laws of proportion governing the structure of the room, must necessarily conform with its style. In other words, decoration is always subservient to proportion; and a room, whatever its decoration may be, must represent the style to which its proportions belong. The less cannot include the greater. Unfortunately it is usually by ornamental details, rather than by proportion, that people distinguish one style from another. To many, persons, garlands, bow-knots, quivers, and a great deal of gilding represent the Louis XVI style; if they object to these, they condemn the style. To an architect familiar with the subject the same style means something absolutely different. He knows that a Louis XVI room may exist without any of these or similar characteristics; and he often deprecates their use as representing the cheaper and more trivial effects of the period, and those that have most helped to vulgarize it. In fact, in nine cases out of ten his use of them is a concession to the client who, having asked for a Louis XVI room, would not know he had got it were these details left out.[6]

Another thing which has perhaps contributed to make people distrustful of "styles" is the garbled form in which they are presented by some architects. After a period of eclecticism that has lasted long enough to make architects and decorators lose their traditional habits of design, there has arisen a sudden demand for "style." It necessarily follows that only the most competent are ready to respond to this unexpected summons. Much has to be relearned, still more to be unlearned. The essence of the great styles lay in proportion and the science of proportion is not to be acquired in a day. In fact, in such matters the cultivated layman, whether or not he has any special familiarity with the different schools of architecture, is often a better judge than the half-educated architect. It is no wonder that people of taste are disconcerted by the so-called "colonial" houses where stair-rails are used as roof-balustrades and mantel-friezes as exterior entablatures, or by Louis XV rooms where the wavy movement which, in the best rococo, was always an ornamental incident and never broke up the main lines of the design, is suffered to run riot through the whole treatment of the walls, so that the bewildered eye seeks in vain for a straight line amid the whirl of incoherent curves.

To conform to a style, then, is to accept those rules of proportion which the artistic experience of centuries has established as the best, while within those limits allowing free scope to the individual requirements which must inevitably modify every house or room adapted to the use and convenience of its occupants.

There is one thing more to be said in defence of conformity to style; and that is, the difficulty of getting rid of style. Strive as we may for originality, we are hampered at every turn by an artistic tradition of over two thousand years. Does any but the most inexperienced architect really think that he can ever rid himself of such an inheritance? He may mutilate or misapply the component parts of his design, but he cannot originate a whole new architectural alphabet. The chances are that he will not find it easy to invent one wholly new moulding.

The styles especially suited to modern life have already been roughly indicated as those prevailing in Italy since 1500, in France from the time of Louis XIV, and in England since the introduction of the Italian manner by Inigo Jones; and as the French and English styles are perhaps more familiar to the general reader, the examples given will usually be drawn from these. Supposing the argument in favor of these styles to have been accepted, at least as a working hypothesis, it must be explained why, in each room, the decoration and furniture should harmonize. Most people will admit the necessity of harmonizing the colors in a room, because a feeling for color is more general than a feeling for form; but in reality the latter is the more important in decoration, and it is the feeling for form, and not any archæological affectation, which makes the best decorators insist upon the necessity of keeping to the same style of furniture and decoration. Thus the massive dimensions and heavy panelling of a seventeenth-century room would dwarf a set of eighteenth-century furniture; and the wavy, capricious movement of Louis XV

decoration would make the austere yet delicate lines of Adam furniture look stiff and mean.

Many persons object not only to any attempt at uniformity of style, but to the use of any recognized style in the decoration of a room. They characterize it, according to their individual views, as "servile," "formal," or "pretentious."

It has already been suggested that to conform within rational limits to a given style is no more servile than to pay one's taxes or to write according to the rules of grammar. As to the accusations of formality and pretentiousness (which are more often made in America than elsewhere), they may probably be explained by the fact that most Americans necessarily form their idea of the great European styles from public buildings and palaces. Certainly, if an architect were to propose to his client to decorate a room in a moderate-sized house in the Louis XIV style, and if the client had formed his idea of that style from the state apartments in the palace at Versailles, he would be justified in rejecting the proposed treatment as absolutely unsuitable to modern private life; whereas the architect who had gone somewhat more deeply into the subject might have singled out the style as eminently suitable, having in mind one of the simple panelled rooms, with tall windows, a dignified fireplace, large tables and comfortable arm-chairs, which were to be found in the private houses of the same period. It is the old story of the two knights fighting about the color of the shield. Both architect and client would be right, but they would be looking at the different sides of the question. As a matter of fact, the bed-rooms, sitting-rooms, libraries and other private apartments in the smaller dwelling-houses built in Europe between 1650 and 1800 were far simpler, less pretentious and more practical in treatment than those in the average modern house.

It is therefore hoped that the antagonists of "style," when they are shown that to follow a certain style is not to sacrifice either convenience or imagination, but to give more latitude to both, will withdraw an opposition which seems to be based on a misapprehension of facts.

Hitherto architecture and decoration have been spoken of as one, as in any well-designed house they ought to be. Indeed, it is one of the numerous disadvantages of the present use of styles, that unless the architect who has built the house also decorates it, the most hopeless discord is apt to result. This was otherwise before our present desire for variety had thrown architects, decorators, and workmen out of the regular routine of their business. Before 1800 the decorator called upon to treat the interior of a house invariably found a suitable background prepared for his work, while much in the way of detail was intrusted to the workmen, who were trained in certain traditions instead of being called upon to carry out in each new house the vagaries of a different designer.

But it is with the decorator's work alone that these pages are concerned, and the above digression is intended to explain why his task is now so difficult, and why his results are so often unsatisfactory to himself as well as to his clients. The decorator of the present day may be compared to a person who is called upon to write a letter in the English language, but is ordered, in so doing, to conform to the Chinese or Egyptian rules of grammar, or possibly to both together.

By the use of a little common sense and a reasonable conformity to those traditions of design which have been tested by generations of architects, it is possible to produce great variety in the decoration of rooms without losing sight of the purpose for which they are intended. Indeed, the more closely this purpose is kept in view, and the more clearly it is expressed in all the details of each room, the more pleasing that room will be, so that it is easy to make a room with tinted walls, deal furniture and dimity curtains more beautiful, because more logical and more harmonious, than a ball-room lined with gold and marbles, in which the laws of rhythm and logic have been ignored.

NOTES

1 Charming as the Italian villa is, it can hardly be used in our Northern States without certain modifications, unless it is merely occupied for a few weeks in mid-summer; whereas the average French or English country house built after 1600 is perfectly suited to our climate and habits. The chief features of the Italian villa are the open central *cortile* and the large saloon two stories high. An adaptation of these better suited to a cold climate is to be found in the English country houses built in the Palladian manner after its introduction by Inigo Jones. See Campbell's *Vitruvius Britannicus* for numerous examples.

2 The plan of the Hôtel Voguë has been greatly modified.

3 Cabinets retained this shape after the transporting of furniture had ceased to be a necessity.

4 It must be remembered that in describing the decoration of any given period, we refer to the private houses, not the royal palaces, of that period. Versailles was more splendid than any previous palace; but private houses at that date were less splendid, though far more luxurious, than during the Renaissance.

5 "Si l'on dispose un édifice d'une manière convenable à l'usage auquel on le destine, ne différera-t-il pas sensiblement d'un autre édifice destiné à un autre usage? N'aura-t-il pas naturellement un caractère, et, qui plus est, son caractère propre?" J. L. N. Durand. *Précis des Leçons d'Architecture données à l'École Royale Polytechnique*. Paris, 1823.

6 It must not be forgotten that the so-called "styles" of Louis XIV, Louis XV and Louis XVI were, in fact, only the gradual development of one organic style, and hence differed only in the superficial use of ornament.

12
Comfort and Well-Being

Witold Rybczynski

Source: *Home: A Short History of an Idea.* Penguin, 1987, pp. 217–232

> . . . lately I have been thinking how comfort is perhaps the ultimate luxury.
>
> (Billy Baldwin
> as quoted in the *New York Times*)

Domestic well-being is a fundamental human need that is deeply rooted in us, and that must be satisfied. If this need is not met in the present, it is not unnatural to look for comfort in tradition. In doing so, however, we should not confuse the idea of comfort with decor—the external appearance of rooms—nor with behaviour—how these rooms were used. Decor is primarily a product of fashion, and its longevity is measured in decades or less. A decorating style like Queen Anne lasted at the most thirty years; Art Nouveau barely more than a decade; Art Deco even less than that. Social behavior, which is a function of habits and customs, is more durable. The male practice of withdrawing to a special room to smoke, for example, began in the mid-nineteenth century and continued well into the twentieth. As late as 1935, the steamship *Normandie* was provided with a smoking room, although by then women were beginning to smoke in public. Public smoking has lasted about forty years, but it is likely that before long it will cease altogether, and we will return to the time when it was considered impolite to smoke in the company of others. Cultural ideas like comfort, on the other hand, have a life that is measured in centuries. Domesticity, for example, has existed for more than three hundred years. During that time the "density" of interior decoration has varied, rooms have changed in size and function and have been more or less crowded with furniture, but the domestic interior has always demonstrated a feeling of intimacy and hominess.

Changes in fashion occur more frequently than changes in behavior; cultural ideas, because they last so long, are more resistant to change, and consequently tend to constrain both behavior and decor. Although new fashions are often called revolutionary, they are rarely that, for they can only alter social customs slightly, and traditional culture not at all. Long hair, that symbol of 1960s rebellion, was heralded as a major cultural shift; it turned out to be what we should have known it was all the time—a short-lived fashion. When fashion does attempt to change social behavior, it does so at its peril. Paper clothing, for example, another fad of the 1960s, could not satisfy people's traditional use of dress as status symbol, and did not last long. The power of culture to constrain behavior is evident when foreign customs are borrowed from abroad. The Japanese hot tub, for example, is currently an American fashion—it may eventually become a custom—but the traditions of bathing in Japan and America are tremendously different. The hot tub has consequently been turned from an oriental semireligious, contemplative ritual to a western social recreation. This adaptation occurs in both directions, and just as the hot tub has been westernized, the Japanese have altered our domestic customs to suit their own habits and culture.[*]

Borrowing from the past must similarly accommodate itself to contemporary customs. That is why period revivals, even when they were not outright inventions, were never intended to be authentic recreations of the past; they were always, in the strict sense of the word, "superficial." When the Gothic style returned to favor in the eighteenth century it affected room decoration, but it was not meant to revive the "big house," or the medieval lack of privacy—the basic arrangement of the Victorian house remained intact. When Renaissance interiors became fashionable in America in the 1880s, there was no attempt to turn back the clock; the style was always used selectively, and only in specific rooms. There were no Renaissance kitchens, for example—the idea of convenient and efficiently planned work areas was by then too strong a part of domestic culture.

One cannot recapture the comfort of the past by copying its decor. The way that rooms looked made sense because they were a setting for a particular type of behavior, which in turn was conditioned by the way that people thought about comfort. Reproducing the former without the latter would be like putting on a play and only building the stage set, but forgetting the actors and script. It would be a hollow and unsatisfying experience. We can appreciate the interiors of the past, but if we try to copy them we will find that too much has changed. What has changed the most is the reality of physical comfort—the standard of living—largely as the result of advances in technology. Technological changes have affected the evolution of comfort throughout history, of course, but ours is a special position. The evolution of domestic technology that has been traced in the preceding chapters demonstrates that the history of physical amenities can be divided into two major phases: all the years leading up to 1890, and the three following decades. If this sounds outlandish, it is worth reminding ourselves that all the "modern" devices that contribute to our domestic comfort—central heating, indoor plumbing, running hot and cold water, electric light and power and elevators—were unavailable before 1890, and were well known by 1920. We live, like it or not, on the far side of a great technological divide. As John Lukacs reminds us, although the home of 1930 would be familiar to us, it would have been unrecognizable to the citizen of 1885.[2] Until then, recreating the past was plausible—even if it was rare—after 1920 it became an eccentricity.

Comfort has changed not only qualitatively, but also quantitatively—it has become a mass commodity. After 1920, especially in America (somewhat later in Europe), physical comfort in the home was no longer the privilege of a part of society, it was accessible to all. This democratization of comfort has been due to mass production and industrialization. But industrialization has had other effects—it has made hand-work a luxury (in that regard Le Corbusier's analysis was correct). This, too, separates us from the past. As the Art Deco designers discovered, a reliance on craftsmanship was expensive and meant an extremely limited clientele. We can admire Mrs. Lauder's Louis XV office, but how many could afford even good reproductions, let alone authentic antiques? If we insist on Rococo we must be content with ersatz— a poor imitation that is neither commodious nor delightful. Only the wealthy or the very poor can live in the past; only the former do so by choice. If one has enough money—and enough servants—a Georgian country home is just the ticket. But the reality of small, servantless households makes it

impossible for most people to undertake such wholesale restorations: who will dust all those pretty moldings, who will shake the carpets and polish the brass?

The current fashion for decorating interiors with bits and pieces of traditional-looking ornament, without adhering to any particular historical style, seems, at least on the surface—and it is mostly surface—to be an acceptable alternative. It is an inexpensive if halfhearted compromise—neither out-right revivalism nor unadulterated modernism. But so-called postmodernism has missed the point; putting in a stylized strip of molding or a symbolic classical column is not really the issue. It is not watered-down historical references that are missing from people's homes. What is needed is a sense of domesticity, not more dadoes; a feeling of privacy, not neo-Palladian windows; an atmosphere of coziness, not plaster capitals. Postmodernism is more interested in (mostly obscure) architectural history than in the evolution of the cultural ideas that history represents. Moreover, it is reluctant to question any of the basic principles of modernism—it is aptly named, for it is almost never antimodern. Despite its visual wit and fashionable insouciance, it fails to address the basic problem.

What is needed is a reexamination not of bourgeois styles, but of bourgeois traditions. We should look at the past not from a stylistic point of view, but regarding the idea itself of comfort. The seventeenth-century Dutch bourgeois interior, for example, has much to teach us about living in small spaces. It suggests how simple materials, appropriately sized and placed windows, and built-in furniture can create an atmosphere of cozy domesticity. The way that Dutch homes opened up onto the street, the careful variety of types of windows, the planned gradient of increasingly private rooms, and the sequence of small sitting places are architectural devices that are applicable still.[3] The Queen Anne house offers similar lessons in informal planning. The Victorians were faced with technical devices more innovative than our own, and the ease with which they incorporated new technology into their homes without sacrificing traditional comforts is instructive. The American home of 1900 to 1920 shows that convenience and efficiency can be dealt with effectively without in any way creating a cold or machinelike atmosphere.

Reexamining bourgeois traditions means returning to house layouts that offer more privacy and intimacy than the so-called open plan, in which space is allowed to "flow" from one room to another. This produces interiors of great visual interest, but there is a price to be paid for this excitement. The space flows, but so also does sight and sound—not since the Middle Ages have homes offered as little personal privacy to their inhabitants. It is difficult for even small families to live in such open interiors, especially if they are using the large variety of home entertainment devices that have become popular—televisions, video recorders, audio equipment, electronic games, and so on. What is needed are many more small rooms—some need not be larger than alcoves—to conform to the range and variety of leisure activities in the modern home.

It also means a return to furniture that is accommodating and comfortable; not chairs that make an artistic statement, but chairs that are a pleasure to sit in. This will involve going both forward and backward—backward, to recover the eighteenth century's knowledge of ergonomics, and forward to devise furniture which can be adjusted and modified to suit different individuals. It means returning to the idea of furniture as practical rather than aesthetic object, and as something enduring rather than a passing novelty.

Another tradition that should be reexamined is that of convenience. In many parts of the house, the pragmatism of the early domestic engineers has been lost in the emphasis on visual appearance. Aesthetics, not practicality, predominate. The modern kitchen, in which everything is hidden in artfully designed cabinets, looks well organized, like a bank office. But a kitchen does not function like an office; if anything, it is more like a workshop. Tools should be out in the open where they are accessible, near those places where the work is done, not secreted below counters or in deep, difficult-to-reach cupboards. The need for different work-surface heights was identified a long time ago, but kitchens continue to have uniform counters, of standardized height and width, finished in the same material. This neatness and uniformity follow the modern dictum requiring lack of clutter and visual simplicity, but they do little to improve working comfort.

The small standardized bathroom (whose layout is unchanged since the 1850s) looks efficient, but it is ill suited to the modern home. The combination of tub and shower is awkward, the fixtures are neither particularly comfortable nor safe nor even easy to clean. For functional and hygienic reasons the water closet would be better separated, as it is in Europe. When houses contained many more rooms, bathrooms could be small. Today, the bathroom must accommodate activities which previously took place in dressing rooms, nurseries, and boudoirs (even washing machines are now located in bathrooms). In small houses, the bathroom may be the only totally private room, and although bathing may not be a ritual in America as it is in Japan, it is certainly a form of relaxation, and yet this activity takes place in a room that is devoid of both charm and commodity. The modern kitchen is also too small. Early studies of kitchen efficiency focused on reducing the amount of walking done during food preparation. This has produced the tiny, so-called efficient kitchen—often without windows—in which there is little countertop area, but where one can work almost without moving. If such an arrangement was ever convenient, which is arguable, it has outlived its usefulness. There is not enough space for the large number of appliances—mixers, blenders, pasta makers, and coffee grinders—required by the time-conscious housekeeper.

Ever since the seventeenth century, when privacy was introduced into the home, the role of women in defining comfort has been paramount. The Dutch interior, the Rococo salon, the servantless household—all were the result of women's invention. One could argue, with only slight exaggeration, that the idea of domesticity was principally a feminine idea. So was the idea of efficiency. When Lillian Gilbreth and Christine Frederick introduced management and efficiency to the home, they took it for granted that this work would be done by a woman whose main occupation would be taking care of the family. Domestic management may have been more efficient, but housework was still a full-time job—the woman's place was in the home. The desire of women for careers—and not just for economic reasons—has changed all that. This does not mean that domesticity will disappear, although it may mean that the home will cease to be "the woman's place." The scarcity of servants in the early 1900s prompted an interest in machines that would help the homemaker and reduce the tedium of housework; the reduced presence of women in the home requires machines that can do chores on their own. Most recently developed home appliances, such as automatic clothes washers, ice-cube makers, self-cleaning ovens, and frost-free refrigerators, are intended to replace manual operations with self-regulating mechanical ones—they are all partially automated. This development—from tools to machines to automatons—is a characteristic of all technologies, in the home no less than in the workplace.[4] The drying rack leads to the manual- and then the machine-driven wringer, which is replaced by the automatic dryer. The availability of inexpensive microchips is hastening the day when full-scale automation will enter the home in the form of domestic robots—mechanical servants.

A reexamination of the bourgeois tradition of comfort is an implicit criticism of modernity, but it is not a rejection of change. Indeed, the evolution of comfort will continue. For the moment, this evolution is dominated by technology, though to a lesser degree than in the past. This need not dehumanize the home, any more than effective fireplaces or electricity did in the past. Can we really have coziness and robots? That will depend on how successful we are in turning away from modernism's shallow enthusiasms, and developing a deeper and more genuine understanding of domestic comfort.

What is comfort? Perhaps the question should have been asked earlier, but without a review of the long evolution of this complex and profound subject the answer would almost certainly have been wrong, or at least incomplete. The simplest response would be that comfort concerns only human physiology—feeling good. Nothing mysterious about that. But this would not explain why, although the human body has not changed, our idea of what is comfortable differs from that of a hundred years ago. Nor is the answer that comfort is a subjective experience of satisfaction. If comfort were subjective, one would expect a greater variety of attitudes toward it; instead, at any particular historical period there has always been a demonstrable consensus about what is comfortable and what is not. Although comfort is experienced personally, the individual judges comfort according to broader norms, indicating that comfort may be an objective experience.

If comfort is objective, it should be possible to measure it. This is more difficult than it sounds. It is easier to know when we are comfortable than why, or to what degree. It would be possible to identify comfort by recording the personal reactions of large numbers of people, but this would be more like a marketing or opinion survey than a scientific study; a scientist prefers to study things one at a time, and especially to measure them. It turns out that in practice it is much easier to measure discomfort than comfort. To establish a thermal "comfort zone," for example, one ascertains at which temperatures most people are either too cold or too hot, and whatever is in between automatically becomes "comfortable." Or if one is trying to identify the appropriate angle for the back of a chair, one can subject people to angles that are too steep and too flat, and between the

points where they express discomfort lies the "correct" angle. Similar experiments have been carried out concerning the intensity of lighting and noise, the size of room dimensions, the hardness and softness of sitting and lying furniture, and so on. In all these cases, the range of comfort is discovered by measuring the limits at which people begin to experience discomfort. When the interior of the Space Shuttle was being designed, a cardboard mock-up of the cabin was built. The astronauts were required to move around in this full-size model, miming their daily activities, and every time they knocked against a corner or a projection, a technician would cut away the offending piece. At the end of the process, when there were no more obstructions left, the cabin was judged to be "comfortable." The scientific definition of comfort would be something like "Comfort is that condition in which discomfort has been avoided."

Most of the scientific research that has been carried out on terrestrial comfort has concerned the workplace, since it has been found that comfortable surroundings will affect the morale, and hence the productivity, of workers. Just how much comfort can affect economic performance is indicated by a recent estimate that backaches—the result of poor working posture—account for over ninety-three million lost workdays, a loss of nine billion dollars to the American economy.[5] The modern office interior reflects the scientific definition of comfort. Lighting levels have been carefully controlled to fall within an acceptable level for optimal reading convenience. The finishes of walls and floors are restful; there are no garish or gaudy colors. Desks and chairs are planned to avoid fatigue.

But how comfortable do the people feel who work in such surroundings? As part of an effort to improve its facilities, one large pharmaceutical corporation, Merck & Company, surveyed two thousand of its office staff regarding their attitudes to their place of work—an attractive modern commercial interior.[6] The survey team prepared a questionnaire that listed various aspects of the workplace. These included factors affecting appearance, safety, work efficiency, convenience, comfort, and so on. Employees were asked to express their satisfaction, or dissatisfaction, with different aspects, and also to indicate those aspects that they personally considered to be the most important. The majority distinguished between the visual qualities of their surroundings—decoration, color scheme, carpeting, wall covering, desk appearance—and the physical aspects—lighting, ventilation, privacy, and chair comfort. The latter group were all included in a list of the ten most important factors, together with size of work area, safety, and personal storage space. Interestingly, none of the purely visual factors was felt to be of major importance, indicating just how mistaken is the notion that comfort is solely a function of appearance or style.

What is most revealing is that the Merck employees expressed some degree of dissatisfaction with *two-thirds* of the almost thirty different aspects of the workplace. Among those about which there was the strongest negative feelings were the lack of conversational privacy, the air quality, the lack of visual privacy, and the level of lighting. When they were asked what aspects of the office interior they would like to have individual control over, most people identified room temperature, degree of privacy, choice of chair and desk, and lighting intensity. Control over decor was accorded the lowest priority. This would seem to indicate that although there is wide agreement about the importance of lighting or temperature, there is a good deal of difference of opinion about exactly how much light or heat feels comfortable to different individuals; comfort is obviously both objective and subjective.

The Merck offices had been designed to eliminate discomfort, yet the survey showed that many of the employees did not experience well-being in their workplace—an inability to concentrate was the common complaint. Despite the restful colors and the attractive furnishings (which everyone appreciated), something was missing. The scientific approach assumes that if background noises are muffled and direct view controlled, the office worker will feel comfortable. But working comfort depends on many more factors than these. There must also be a sense of intimacy and privacy, which is produced by a balance between isolation and publicness; too much of one or the other will produce discomfort. A group of architects in California recently identified as many as nine different aspects of workplace enclosure that must be met in order to create this feeling.[7] These included the presence of walls behind and beside the worker, the amount of open space in front of the desk, the area of the workspace, the amount of enclosure, a view to the outside, the distance to the nearest person, the number of people in the immediate vicinity, and the level and type of noise. Since most office layouts do not address these concerns directly, it is not surprising that people have difficulty concentrating on their work.

The fallacy of the scientific definition of comfort is that it considers only those aspects of comfort that are measurable, and with not untypical arrogance denies the existence of the rest—many behavioral scientists have concluded that because people experience only discomfort, comfort as a physical phenomenon does not really exist at all.[8] It is hardly surprising that genuine intimacy, which is impossible to measure, is absent in most planned office environments. Intimacy in the office, or in the home, is not unusual in this respect; there are many complicated experiences that resist measurement. It is impossible, for example, to describe scientifically what distinguishes a great wine from a mediocre one, although a group of wine experts would have no difficulty establishing which was which. The wine industry, like manufacturers of tea and coffee, continues to rely on nontechnical testing— the "nose" of an experienced taster—rather than on objective standards alone. It might be possible to measure a threshold below which wine would taste "bad"—acidity, alcohol content, sweetness, and so on—but no one would suggest that simply avoiding these deficiencies would result in a good wine. A room may feel uncomfortable—it may be too bright for intimate conversation, or too dark for reading—but avoiding such irritations will not automatically produce a feeling of well-being. Dullness is not annoying enough to be disturbing, but it is not stimulating either. On the other hand, when we open a door and think, "What a comfortable room," we are reacting positively to something special, or rather to a series of special things.

Here are two descriptions of comfort. The first is by a well-known interior decorator, Billy Baldwin: "Comfort to me is a room that works for you and your guests. It's deep upholstered furniture. It's having a table handy to put down a drink or a book. It's also knowing that if someone pulls up a chair for a talk, the whole room doesn't fall apart. I'm tired of contrived decorating."[9] The second is by an architect, Christopher Alexander: "Imagine yourself on a winter afternoon with a pot of tea, a book, a reading light, and two or three huge pillows to lean back against, Now make yourself comfortable. Not in some way which you can show to other people, and say how much you like it. I mean so that you *really* like it, for *yourself*. You put the tea where you can reach it: but in a place where you can't possibly knock it over. You pull the light down, to shine on the book, but not too brightly, and so that you can't see the naked bulb. You put the cushions behind you, and place them, carefully, one by one, just where you want them, to support your back, your neck, your arm: so that you are supported just comfortably, just as you want to sip your tea, and read, and dream."[10]

Baldwin's description was the result of sixty years of decorating fashionable homes; Alexander's was based on the observation of ordinary people and ordinary places.[†] Yet they both seem to have converged in the depiction of a domestic atmosphere that is instantly recognizable for its ordinary, human qualities.

These qualities are something that science has failed to come to grips with, although to the layman a picture, or a written description, is evidence enough. "Comfort is simply a verbal invention," writes one engineer despairingly.[11] Of course, that is precisely what comfort is. It is an invention—a cultural artifice. Like all cultural ideas—childhood, family, gender—it has a past, and it cannot be understood without reference to its specific history. One-dimensional, technical definitions of comfort, which ignore history, are bound to be unsatisfactory. How rich, by comparison, are Baldwin's and Alexander's descriptions of comfort. They include convenience (a handy table), efficiency (a modulated light source), domesticity (a cup of tea), physical ease (deep chairs and cushions), and privacy (reading a book, having a talk). Intimacy is also present in these descriptions. All these characteristics together contribute to the atmosphere of interior calm that is a part of comfort.

This is the problem with understanding comfort and with finding a simple definition. It is like trying to describe an onion. It appears simple on the outside, just a spheroidal shape. But this is deceptive, for an onion also has many layers. If we cut it apart, we are left with a pile of onion skins, but the original form has disappeared; if we describe each layer separately, we lose sight of the whole. To complicate matters further, the layers are transparent, so that when we look at the whole onion we see not just the surface but also something of the interior. Similarly, comfort is both something simple and complicated. It incorporates many transparent layers of meaning—privacy, ease, convenience— some of which are buried deeper than others.

The onion simile suggests not only that comfort has several layers of meaning, but also that the idea of comfort has developed historically. It is an idea that has meant different things at different times. In the seventeenth century, comfort meant privacy, which lead to intimacy and, in turn, to domesticity. The eighteenth century shifted the emphasis to leisure and ease, the nineteenth to mechanically aided comforts—light, heat, and ventilation. The twentieth-century domestic engineers stressed efficiency and convenience. At various times, and in response to various outside forces—social, economic, and technological—the idea of comfort has changed, sometimes drastically. There was nothing foreordained or inevitable about the changes. If seventeenth-century Holland had been less egalitarian and its women less independent, domesticity would have arrived later than it did. If eighteenth-century England had been aristocratic rather than bourgeois, comfort would have taken a different turn. If servants had not been scarce in our century, it is unlikely that anyone would have listened to Beecher and Frederick. But what is striking is that the idea of comfort, even as it has changed, has preserved most of its earlier meanings. The evolution of comfort should not be confused with the evolution of technology. New technical devices usually—not always—rendered older ones obsolete. The electric lamp replaced the gasolier, which replaced the oil lamp, which replaced candles, and so on. But new ideas about how to achieve comfort did not displace fundamental notions of domestic well-being. Each new meaning added a layer to the previous meanings, which were preserved beneath. At any particular time, comfort consists of *all* the layers, not only the most recent.

So there it is, the Onion Theory of Comfort— hardly a definition at all, but a more precise explanation may be unnecessary. It may be enough to realize that domestic comfort involves a range of attributes—convenience, efficiency, leisure, ease, pleasure, domesticity, intimacy, and privacy—all of which contribute to the experience; common sense will do the rest. Most people—"I may not know why I like it, but I know what I like"—recognize comfort when they experience it. This recognition involves a combination of sensations—many of them subconscious—and not only physical, but also emotional as well as intellectual, which makes comfort difficult to explain and impossible to measure. But it does not make it any less real. We should resist the inadequate definitions that engineers and architects have offered us. Domestic well-being is too important to be left to experts; it is, as it has always been, the business of the family and the individual. We must rediscover for ourselves the mystery of comfort, for without it, our dwellings will indeed be machines instead of homes.

NOTES

*   According to George Fields, an Australian marketing consultant, appliances such as washing machines and refrigerators have a higher "psychological positioning" for the Japanese, who attach the same importance to these utilitarian devices as Americans do to furniture; in

a Japanese home, the refrigerator is just as likely to be placed in the living room as in the kitchen.[1]

† Baldwin, until his death in 1983, was generally considered to be the foremost high-society decorator; his clients included Cole Porter and Jacqueline Kennedy. Alexander is the author of the iconoclastic *A Pattern Language*, a critique of modern architecture.

1 George Fields, *From Bonsai to Levi's: When West Meets East, an Insider's Surprising Account of How the Japanese Live* (New York: Macmillan, 1983), pp. 25–26.

2 John Lukacs, *Outgrowing Democracy: A History of the United States in the Twentieth Century* (Garden City, NY: Doubleday, 1984), p. 170.

3 Many of the patterns described in Christopher Alexander et al., *A Pattern Language: Towns, Buildings, Construction* (New York: Oxford University Press, 1977), are derived from seventeenth-century interiors.

4 See the author's *Taming the Tiger: The Struggle to Control Technology* (New York: Viking, 1983), p. 25.

5 J. Douglas Phillips, "Establishing and Managing Advance Office Technology: A Holistic Approach Focusing on People," paper presented to the annual meeting of the Society of Manufacturing Engineers, Montreal, September 16–19, 1984, p. 3.

6 S. George Walters, "Merck and Co., Inc. Office Design Study, Final Plans Board," unpublished report (Newark, NJ: Rutgers Graduate School of Management, August 24, 1982).

7 Alexander, *Pattern Language*, pp. 847–52.

8 Henry McIlvaine Parsons, "Comfort and Convenience: How Much?" paper presented to the annual meeting of the American Association for the Advancement of Science, New York, January 30, 1975, p. 1.

9 Quoted in George O'Brien, "An American Decorator Emeritus," *New York Times Magazine: Home Design*, April 17, 1983, p. 33.

10 Christopher Alexander, *The Timeless Way of Building* (New York: Oxford University Press, 1979), pp. 32–33.

11 Parsons, "Comfort and Convenience," p. 1.

PART 2
INTERIOR DESIGN

Introduction

> The modern interior can be linked to architecture . . . to the idea of theatre, as, that is, a "stage set" for its occupants which invokes discussions about interiority; as an extension of the body, linked to the world of fashion: and as a represented, mediated ideal connoting a modern lifestyle.[1]

It is widely acknowledged that the design of the interior is a multidisciplinary and diverse practice. It is a field of study that is primarily engaged with the creation of a range of environments that articulate a multiplicity of spatial functions and identities. As Sparke suggests in *Designing the Modern Interior* (quoted above), the understanding of inside space can involve a broad and expansive inquiry: it is one that touches upon a wide range of spatial subjects, including buildings, stage sets and issues concerning the body in space. Whatever form or function an interior adopts, it might involve pragmatic issues, such as fabrication, or it might concern more esoteric circumstances, such as the psychological or atmospheric conditions of inside space. Whichever form or function the interior is manifest as, whatever character it adopts, in this chapter it is our suggestion that the interior is the location of a variety of diverse, assorted, spatial processes. It is a subject that delineates a multidisciplinary and varied approach to the fabrication and occupation of inside space.

In this book we use the term *interior* in relation to: architecture, design, and decoration. The difference between these areas ranges from legal and structural responsibilities to associations of taste and consumption. In short, in this chapter, we suggest that *Interior Design* bridges architecture and decoration. It is an interdisciplinary practice that is formed with the primary concern of the functional reorganization of a space, in order to house new use. Its underlying concerns are pragmatic, with function and professionalism forming two of its essential or core issues. In this chapter, in order to reflect this, we have collated a series of essays that are organised into three sections: **Histories and Identity**, **Organisation**, and **Function**. All three sections contain essays that explore the diversity and multiplicity of the discipline, but which have an emphasis on the more pragmatic issues involved in the designing of interior space. In *Interior Design: A Critical Introduction*, Clive Edwards recognises these views. He states:

> Interior design is a professionally conducted, practice-based process of the planning and realization of interior spaces and all the elements within. Interior design is concerned with the function and operation of the space, its safety and efficiency, its aesthetics and its sustainability.[2]

Whilst interior design shares similar processes and practices with both interior architecture and decoration, it is our suggestion that it embodies a closer connection to the more pragmatic and functional elements involved in the designing of interior space. In other words, in this chapter, we have collated a series of essays that view interior design as a practice that is fundamentally concerned with the pragmatic and more realistic affairs of the design of inside space. The term *design* is ascribed importance in the context of this chapter because it has a particular bearing on the meaning of *process* in the creation of an interior. Design is a term that is used to describe the construction of an object or environment that has been *crafted* to achieve a desired act or effect. It is normal to understand the *designed* object, or space, as an item that is a considered and calculated entity. The interior designer, as opposed to the interior architect or decorator, is an agent who *in abundance* practises and masters these processes. They are primarily tasked with the functional adaptation of a site with which to house a new programme. To *design* an interior is to *craft* a very particular environment and one that must achieve its aims often in relation to a brief: the creation of a space that reflects the requirements and desires of the client through functional and material form. Whilst the interior architect and decorator will also be tasked with the same aims we would suggest that the pragmatic and functional dimensions of the creation of interior space are most closely allied to the role of the *designer*.

Because of its close connection to function, programming, organisation and the crafting of particular environments that communicate particular meanings, such as a retail space, or a place of work, interior design is often defined by *materiality*. The selection of elements, materials, objects and furnishings, with which to communicate particular meaning and narratives, is a very important part of the process of design. The material concerns of interior design are space, planning, furnishing, light, colour and detail. As Alfoldy and Holland suggest in *Craft, Space* and *Interior Design*:

> Constructed space is defined by its shape, by the materials with which it is enclosed and by the objects that are placed within or decorate its exterior or interior. Like architecture, craft and interior design emphasise the absolute importance of materiality. All three work together to develop perceptions of space.[3]

The deployment of materials and the organisation of the interior are both fundamental skills and very important techniques in the proficiency of the interior designer. Without either it is not possible to design interior space.

Whilst the material elements of the interior are furnishings, light and details, the immaterial rudiments of the interior are its histories and theories. Because of its wide-ranging and diverse qualities, the interior is often understood as an instrument or measure of cultural, economic, political and technological change. Not only can the interior be read as a construct of the organisation of space, along with the deployment of an atmosphere through material selection, but it can also be read as a crafted environment for social interaction. This will include the manipulation of spatial volume, the placement of specific elements such as furniture and the treatment of either applied or existing surfaces. Therefore central concerns in interior design incorporate the desire for a better understanding of human interaction in space, via the critical examination of its histories of use, manifestations of societal spatial organisation and cultural and economic representation through material and technological choices. In other words the interior has always formed the backdrop for narratives of lifestyle, consumption and capital. The emphasis on the human aspect of the interior is all-important as it is clear that the interior is a backdrop for all types of human engagement. As Salcedo suggests:

> There is no way of isolating living experience from spatial experience.[4]

As in interior architecture and decoration, an understanding of the existing space is an important part of the process of creating an interior. But instead of an emphasis on structural reconfiguration, or just surface modification, interior design will often involve the nominal adaptation of a host building, in order to adapt it to accept a new inserted interior. A typical interior design would encompass such projects as retail, exhibition and domestic interiors, spaces that are designed to be a sign of current forms of occupation, reflect cultures and reflect ideas as complex as social habits and behaviours. Therefore rapid and substantial change is often a distinguishing feature of the identity of the discipline. Interior design is realised through the processes of creating spaces for working, health/wellbeing, leisure, retail, exhibition, performance and living. Because of this interior design has an ephemeral quality, a temporal dimension that is reflected in the transient and often fashion-led emphasis of the spaces that it creates. The essays in this chapter have been chosen to reflect these concerns.

Histories and identity

. . . The interior emerged in addition to constructional, ornamental and surface definitions of inside space that were architectural. The interior was articulated through decoration, the literal covering of the inside of an architectural "shell" with the soft "stuff" of furnishing.[5]

The first section in this chapter is entitled "Histories and Identity". It consists of a series of essays on interior design that explore the complex history and distinctiveness of the discipline. The history and the identity of interior design has always been an elusive and diverse tale. In the past it has been approached in a number of different ways: as a history of forms and styles, often in relation to architectural history; as social, cultural and political history; as a gender-specific narrative, closely related to domesticity; and as a history of the profession. As Charles Rice suggested in *The Emergence of the Interior* (quoted above), the interior has often been constructed as a result of the architectural envelope in which it is contained. But at the same time it is quite disconnected from this envelope and has often been constructed at quite a different chronological timescale to the shell in which it is placed. The history of the interior is a subject that can be construed as developed in contrast to as opposed to in conjunction with the history of the architectural shell.

The many strands of the history of interior design form a rich and multi-dimensional character that is in stark contrast to the notion of a sharply defined *canon* of exemplary works or ideas. It is in this spirit that we have chosen a wide-range of essays, drawn from books and magazines, which we feel symbolise the diverse range of ideas on this subject. The five essays that have been chosen to illustrate this section touch on many of these themes and will give a broad overview of issues and moments in the history of the subject. We have not chosen essays that merely illustrate a time-line of chronological development but on the contrary have tried to illustrate the diversity of the many voices that characterise the history and identity of the discipline. The history of the subject is contentious and is formed from a variety of sources and whilst one view of history may inform the subject this may exclude other voices or narratives. Therefore each essay has been chosen because it unpacks different issues in the subject utilising different voices or perspectives.

Organisation

Aside from the proverbial "four walls" that demarcate the space, determine the proportions and thus set the basic tenor of the effect, interiors are rendered experiential through the layout of the floor plan and the path through the building.[6]

The second part of this chapter explores ideas and strategies in relation to the organisation of interior space. The planning of rooms, the deployment of furniture, the application of materials and the management of both natural and artificial light, manifest the organisation and planning of an interior space. It is the organisation of these components in a congruent manner that constitutes the construction of interior space.

Whilst the design of interior space is often closely connected to the reuse of existing buildings, a significant amount of its practical work takes place in the design of yet-to-be built projects. In existing buildings organisation might already be determined by the layout and structure of the extant space. In a new build project the interior might be able to be more freely determined. Whatever the case the functional organisation of the inside space, in such a way to ensure its efficient use by its occupants, is of paramount importance. In this section of the chapter we examine the complex ideas involved in organising interior space. As well as this, this chapter examines issues such as the threshold between inside and out, the symbolic dimension of the aesthetics of an interior and the choice of objects with which to furnish and produce interior atmosphere through light and materiality.

Function

Broadly speaking, for the interior designer, there will be two approaches: the first is the integrated, where the interior is indivisible from the structure and where pattern, form, texture and lighting are part of the architecture, and qualities of permanence and monumentality are sought. The second, which may be termed the 'Superimposed', is where the interior is required to be more flexible and easily modified or even transformed without mutilating the architecture in which it is temporarily contained.[7]

The third and final part of this chapter examines function: the variety of uses with which an interior is constructed to accommodate. The particular requirements of the interior that is to be designed will vary with each functional need that is to be contained. In this final section of the chapter we have assembled five essays on the various functions of the interior. The first essay looks at the design of the workplace. The evolution of workspaces can be viewed in parallel to stylistic, programmatic, material and environmental changes that evolve from one decade to another. Most notably, the modernist era ushered in new forms of workspaces as seen in open floor plans, the emergence of office-based furniture and lighting solutions. The chosen essay explores the development of patterns of occupation in office environments, and it suggests new ways of understanding the development of ever-increasing sophisticated interior designs for working environments.

Exhibition design, the creation of environments that narrate a theme through the display of a series of objects or settings, is a fundamental practice in the design of interior space. The requirement for visitors to be enthralled and dazzled, in an age of increasingly spectacular and accessible forms of media, emphasises the need for the exhibition designer to devise increasingly sophisticated narrative environments. The essay in this chapter explores the communication of knowledge through different methods of display, and the various typologies of exhibition design. Issues in the relationship between private and public space are personified in the design of interiors that contain both types of places. Hotel designs are a mixture of both private and public rooms, often contained within one building. The essay "The Hotel Lobby" explores the most public space, the lobby. The function that interior design is often associated with is the domestic realm. The use and function of domestic rooms has remained consistent over time, yet the integration of new technologies, housing types and product design have altered the traditional domestic realm into one that allows for new media, materials and voyeuristic activities to span private and public realms. The evolution of the domestic realm has seen the thick protective wall give way to thin glass resulting in increased visibility into private spaces. The final essay in this section examines the work of one of the most celebrated designers of houses in the twentieth century: Adolf Loos. The complexities of the interiors of the Muller and Moller houses are examined and explained in detail.

The emergence of interior design as a discipline results in foundational issues that give this subject a distinct identity. Inherent to this identity is the intimate nature of interiors as seen through the close proximity of people, objects, and spatial elements. All of the essays chosen in this chapter focus on core topics and include historical, organisational, identity and functional issues. This collection of essays seeks to ground core issues pertinent to the interior design discipline and it aims to connect and overlap with the contexts that are established in the other chapters of this book.

Graeme Brooker

REFERENCES

1 Sparke, Penny. *Designing the Modern Interior: From the Victorians to Today.* Cited in Sparke, P., Massey, A., Keeble, T. and Martin, B. (Eds), *Designing the Modern Interior: From the Victorians to Today.* Berg 2009, p. 3.
2 Edwards, Clive. *Interior Design: A Critical introduction.* Berg 2011, p. 1.
3 Alfoldy, Sandra and Helland, Janice. *Craft, Space and Interior Design, 1855–2005.* Ashgate Publishers 2008, p. 1.
4 Doris Salcedo quoted in an interview with Carlos Basualdo in *Doris Salcedo*, Phaidon Press, London 2000, p. 17.
5 Rice, Charles. *The Emergence of the Interior.* Routledge 2007, p. 3.
6 Holz, Christoph. *The Architect as Designer of Space: Classic Modernism. Interior Spaces.* Birkhauser. Edition detail 2002, p. 17.
7 Casson, Hugh. *Inscape.* Architectural Press 1968, p. 17.

Andrée Putman (1925–)

The interiors of the French designer Andrée Putman encapsulated the urbane and debonair character of the 1980s. Her designs epitomised the age of New Wave, they were uncompromisingly bold, but also cool, controlled and most of all, elegant. She designed the playgrounds for the young and the affluent including the Morgans Hotel and the Palladium Night-club, both in New York, shops for Yves St Laurent and Karl Largerfield, and, of course, she redesigned the interior of Concorde. Putman's designs were not based upon whimsy, she was knowledgeable about preservation and had already undertaken a number of important conservation projects including the restoration Villa Turque which was originally designed by le Corbusier. But Putman is best known for the cool black and white hotel interiors that set the standard for interior design in the late twentieth century.

SECTION 2.1
HISTORIES AND IDENTITY

Introduction

The interior and its design is a subject that encompasses a vast and diverse range of spatial histories, theories and practices. It is a discipline that spans ideas as complex and diverse as psychology, cultural geography and technology. Its history and subsequently quite often its identity are often contested. On the one hand, interiors is a multi-disciplinary practice that overlaps with architecture, furniture, exhibition design, graphics and installation art. On the other it is a vehicle to study patterns of consumption, notions of gender, spatial and human identity and politics. Multiplicity is at the core of interior design's history and ultimately this is what nourishes its identity. In this chapter five essays have been selected that will convey the unusual and often convoluted qualities of the various narratives of interior histories and identities.

Interior Design of the Twentieth Century was one of the earliest books to clarify the complex social, political and economic histories of the history of interior design. In the chapter entitled "The Emergence of Interior Decoration as a Profession", the author **Anne Massey** describes the beginnings of the roots of the profession at the turn of the twentieth century in relation to the guilds and trades of upholsters and cabinet-makers. She then charts the role of the emergence of the decorator and the advent of the profession in relation to the emancipation of women, particularly in relation to their role in the house in the early part of the twentieth century.

In "Rethinking Histories of the Interior", first published in the *Journal of Architecture* in 2004, the author **Charles Rice** examines the domestic interior's relationship to media, or its image, to its setting, by using the example of the nineteenth century bourgeois house. Rice recognises Walter Benjamin and Charles Baudelaire's writings on the doubled or the de-realised state of the domestic setting in their work, employing these ideas to provide an alternative critique on the histories of interior design.

"Inscape", edited by **Hugh Casson**, was published as a special issue of the Architectural Review in 1968. Casson was the architect of the Festival of Britain in London in 1951 and was a Professor of Interior Design at the Royal College of Art. This publication was a product of that highly respected course. Inscape is very much of its time and is included in this chapter as it offers the opportunity for a timely reflection on the status of the discipline over forty years after the article was first written. Its clear and concise language offers an insight into the beginnings of discourse in the subject and its search for independence.

In the early 1990s a series of articles featured in a set of talks called "The Inside Edge", published in *The Designers Journal*. The four articles were each titled "Towards a New . . ." and featured educators and designers of the day opening up the debate regarding the discipline. In "Towards a New Agenda", **Fred Scott** identifies the subtle shifts in territories that distinguish the discipline of interiors from other spatial disciplines such as architecture. He suggests that the distinction of working with existing buildings ensures that the successful practice of interiors requires different skills and sensibilities, ideas regarding services, construction and history.

Finally, in "Towards a New Equilibrium", **Patrick Hannay** and **Oliver Lewis** argue that it is foolish to define an identity of interiors in relation to what architecture is not. Instead they suggest that an identity should be formed through celebrating its close connections to its clients, its sustainable credentials, its embracing of temporality, its collaborative nature, its un-protectionist agenda and its inclusive approach to patrons and inhabitants.

Graeme Brooker

Philippe Starck (1949–)

Born in 1949 in Paris, France, Starck is the apotheosis of the designer as a celebrity icon. He is a prolific designer, responsible for a wide and diverse range of buildings, interiors, furniture and objects such as motorbikes, watches and toothbrushes. Starck started his first company at the age of twenty and was initially responsible for designing inflatables. Starck is probably best known for his most popular and mass produced objects, such as the tripod orange juice squeezer, designed for Alessi, often derided as impossible to use due to its proclivity to fall over during squeezing.

His most famous interiors are the theatrical and extravagant hotels in New York, LA and London designed for the Ian Schrager chain of hotels.

Building Study: St Martin's Lane Hotel

London, UK
1999
Philippe Starck

A seven storey 1960s concrete frame tower block, just north of Trafalgar Square, was originally the head-quarters of an advertising agency. The concrete slab frame and post building offered the designers a relatively blank slate with which to work. Non-structural internal partitions could be swept away and the building could be adapted in order to house 204 rooms and 18,000 square metres of hotel. The grid of the structural frame presented a framework of opportunities for the designer Philippe Starck. The lobby on the ground floor is conceived as a "stage set". Upon entrance, the visitor becomes an actor as they enter the hotel. The ground floor of the hotel flows from the lobby and is conceived as a series of over-lapping fluid spaces that are counterpointed by the angular grid of the building's columns. Six exagger-ated columns in the entrance have been beefed up to become almost two metres in diameter. These punctuate the entrance lobby. To the side of these columns is a long thin glass and sandstone desk. Amongst the columns is an assortment of novelty furniture. Stools are shaped like molar teeth; gnomes on toadstools and huge vases of plants lend a theatrical atmosphere to the interior. The lobby drifts into the main restaurant. As you walk through the ground floor, the "hypostyle" of columns sequence the space, choreographing the different environments within the lobby. This is a condition that the designers exaggerate by utilising different furniture and lighting in each space. The main restaurant, "Asia De Cuba", is full of typically idiosyncratic furniture and is prefaced by a series of tall thin tables in the Rum bar at the front of the restaurant. The main dining area is populated with Scandinavian plywood chairs and tables, illuminated by naked light bulbs artfully hung by their flex from the ceiling. In this space shelves bursting with books, radios and pictures wrap the overstated columns. This over-emphasises their cumbersome and ungainly qualities. The light bar sits centrally in the lobby space. In contrast to the restaurant it is designed to appear as if it is an atmospheric "cellar bar". A series of voids puncturing the ceiling at regular intervals alleviates the overbearing enclosed atmosphere of the bar. These allow natural light to spill into the space from the second floor of the building.

At night the façade of the hotel springs to life. As the guests adjust the interior lighting of their room, the exterior is also changed. The mood and ambience of the rooms and the requirements of the guests of the hotel transform the visual drama of the exterior of the hotel.

13
The Emergence of Interior Decoration as a Profession

Anne Massey

Source: *Interior Design of the 20th Century*. Thames and Hudson, 1990

Before the twentieth century the profession of 'interior decoration' simply did not exist. Traditionally it was the upholsterer, cabinetmaker or retailer who advised on the arrangement of interiors. In London, the firm of Lenygon and Morant, founded in 1915, was typical. Francis Lenygon was primarily a furniture dealer, supplying chiefly Americans through the art dealer Joseph Duveen. His decorating work was a marginal part of the business which he shared with Morant, the traditional upholsterer. Their London showroom was situated in a Palladian house, and was used to display English antique furniture from the sixteenth to mid-eighteenth centuries, when, it was generally considered, the production of 'good' furniture came to an end. Twentieth-century interior decorators consistently worked within the styles of the past, and until the First World War decorating was almost synonymous with the antique trade.

The rise of the interior decorator during the twentieth century was the result of changed social and economic circumstances. The employment of an interior decorator was, and remains, an expensive luxury, available only to the upper echelons of society. There is a certain status attached to using a professional to advise on the appearance of your home or workplace. During the early years of the century American millionaires sought to express power and prestige by using professional decorators to recreate Renaissance palaces or French châteaux. In the 1920s and 1930s, the heyday of the decorator, there was a greater emphasis than ever before on entertaining, and decorators were employed to create suitable backdrops for the lavish cocktail parties then fashionable. Their services remained in demand during the Depression because it was cheaper to redecorate an existing house than build a new one.

The rôle of interior decorator has always been one of adviser and even confidante. Because of the consultative nature of the work it has been one of the few professions in which women have led and excelled. In the years preceding the First World War interior decoration emerged as an acceptable new profession for women. Inspired by the suffragette movement in America, women strove to establish economic independence from husbands or fathers, and one of the means open to them was the orchestration of the overall appearance of pre-existing rooms. This rôle has changed little since the 1900s. Decorators are chiefly responsible for selecting suitable textiles, floor- and wall-coverings, furniture, lighting and an overall colour-scheme for rooms which may already contain some of these elements. The interior decorator is rarely responsible for structural alterations which are the preserve of the architect.

Interior decoration never enjoyed the status of architecture or even interior design, being regarded as a branch of fashion. This could be explained by its ephemeral nature, for few schemes remain intact for any length of time. The lack of seriousness associated with interior decoration could also be explained by the dominance of women in the profession's early days. The Victorian middle-class woman was expected to stay at home and manage the household and servants. The decoration of the domestic interior was a respectable pastime which allowed women some control over their environment. Periodicals such as *Home Chat* (1895–1968) as well as various home manuals advised on the selection of furniture and furnishings and the application of decorating techniques such as stencilling. As Jacob von Falke, vice-director of the Austrian Museum of Art and Industry, described the position in the popular American edition of *Art in the House* (1879): 'taste in woman may be said to be natural to her sex. She is the mistress of the house in which she orders like a queen.'

Interior decoration gained status with the publication in 1897 of *The Decoration of Houses* by the future novelist Edith Wharton and architect Ogden Codman. The book set a precedent for all subsequent decorating activity by equating 'natural good taste' with English, Italian and French models from the Renaissance onwards. There was particular emphasis in the book on French eighteenth-century interiors which was to inspire a lasting admiration among decorators and their clients for the 'Old French look'. The comparative simplicity of Louis XV, Louis XVI and Directoire furniture was preferred to the overblown revivalism of the later nineteenth century. Wharton and Codman identified the principles of proportion and harmony as the most significant for the planning of interior schemes. Taken from classical architecture, such laws have had an enduring appeal for the decorator. During the late nineteenth century classicism had been identified as the most appropriate style to symbolize the American Republic. It evoked qualities of solidity, endurance and universal harmony.

The craft of the interior decorator became associated with the elegant, if not entirely accurate, recreation of antique interiors. Such historicism was inextricably bound up with the notion of 'good taste', which the decorator possessed by virtue of studying the decorative styles of the past and being a member of the same social circles as his or her patrons. The criterion of 'good taste' was to dominate the profession throughout the twentieth century, with decorators rarely designing wholly modern interiors. *The House Beautiful* magazine included a long-running series entitled 'The House in Good Taste', and numerous books appeared on the subject, including *Furnishing the Home in Good Taste* (1912) by Lucy Abbot Throop, *Good Taste in Home Decoration* (1954) by Donald D. MacMillen, and in 1968 a contribution by Britain's leading decorator, David Hicks: *On Living – With Taste*.

Elsie de Wolfe (1865–1950), a pioneer of the profession of interior decoration in America, contributed to the trend in 1913 with her book *The House in Good Taste*, which included the advice that 'It is the personality of the mistress that the home expresses. Men are forever guests in our homes, no matter how much happiness they may find there.' De Wolfe began her professional life as an actress, attracting attention less by her performances than by her dress-sense, bringing the latest Parisian creations of Paquin and the House of Worth to New York. By her own efforts she gained an entrée to New York high society, at that time dominated by the Vanderbilts.

The leading New York Beaux-Arts architect, Stanford White, admired De Wolfe's achievements, and in 1905 secured for her the contract for the interior decoration of his building for New York City's Colony Club, a new club open only to women-members. This was the first public interior to be designed by a professional interior decorator, rather than by an architect or antique dealer. De Wolfe was inspired by the elegant rooms she had seen in English country houses in the 1880s. She visited both England and France to acquire suitable antique furniture and samples of the chintzes which were to become her trade mark. The bedrooms, private dining room and library all had the same refined look. The walls were painted in pale tones, the furniture was mainly slender and light, and the large prints of the chintzes added an English country atmosphere. In the tea room the green-painted trellis work, tiled floor and wicker furniture evoked a conservatory rather than a city-centre club.

De Wolfe's scheme was a success and guaranteed her further commissions.

Elsie de Wolfe established the working pattern for subsequent interior decorators. Her trips to Europe to gather antique furniture and fabrics, the extensive social contacts with potential clients, her adherence to the Wharton and Codman approach and taste for the 'Old French', set a standard. A group of professional decorators emerged during the 1920s and 1930s in America and England, eager to emulate her success. Nancy McClelland (1876–1959) established the decorating section for Wanamakers department store, New York, in 1913, the first of its type in America, and in 1922 went on to establish a decorating firm which specialized in the accurate recreation of period interiors for the domestic market and museums. Eleanor McMillen (b.1890, Brown from 1935) worked within the same classical idiom, and founded McMillen Inc. in 1924 as 'the first professional full-service interior decorating firm in America'. She had taken courses in art history and business practice, and was determined not to be identified with the rather amateurish approach of her contemporaries. The firm survives into the 1990s.

Women also played an important rôle in founding the profession of interior decoration in Britain. Betty Joel (1896–1985) established her own furniture-making and interior decoration business after the First World War, eventually opening a showroom in Knightsbridge with twelve room-settings. She was inspired by Art Deco to create bold designs such as ziggurat-shaped bookcases and curved sofas. Her interiors reflected the geometrical inspiration of Art Deco mingled with the smoothness and glamour of the Moderne, as in the all-silver bedroom at Elveden Hall, Suffolk. The firm undertook a wide variety of commercial decorating work for shops, hotels and board-rooms. In contrast, the two women who contrib-uted most towards the establishment of interior decoration in Britain, Syrie Maugham (1879–1955) and Lady Sybil Colefax (1875–1950), worked largely on private commissions.

Syrie Maugham was the wife first of Henry Wellcome, the founder of the pharmaceutical firm, and then of the novelist Somerset Maugham. After the end of her second marriage she learned the basics of the trade by working under Ernest Thornton Smith, head of Fortnum and Mason's antique department, and went on to become the most fashionable interior decorator in London.

Like Elsie de Wolfe, with whom she had visited India, Maugham created elegant interiors using eighteenth-century French furniture with elements of the Moderne and light colours. She created the fashion for 'pickling' furniture – that is, stripping antique chairs and tables of their original dark polish and finishing them with light paint or wax.

Her rival Lady Sybil Colefax created very English interiors, inspired by the chintz and solid furniture of the English country house. She had turned from life as London hostess to become a professional decorator in 1933, after losing money in the Wall Street Crash. In 1938 she took on a partner, John Fowler (1906–1977), an expert on eighteenth-century decoration and one of the most influential figures for the period decoration of houses.

While some British decorators were excelling in recreating the past, others in Britain, France and America were finding novel sources of inspiration, such as Surrealism, for the creation of witty rooms. The Surrealist movement began in 1924 with the publication of the Manifesto du Surréalisme in Paris. Surrealist painters including René Magritte and Salvador Dali attempted to illustrate the threatening world of the subconscious in their paintings, most often by juxtaposing incongruous elements within the picture-frame to startle the viewer and undermine everyday expectations. The Surrealist influence first came to the fore in Paris, where Surrealism had been conceived. The Mexican millionaire collector Charles de Beistigui had commissioned an apartment from Le Corbusier in 1931 and by the time it was completed, and de Beistigui came to decorate the interior, he had developed an interest in the style. In collaboration with architect-decorator Emilio Terry he created a Surreal interior with out-of-scale furniture.

Ornate Second Empire gold-and-white chairs in the Cinema Room overpower the simple lines of Le Corbusier's spiral staircase, and on the roof-terrace, artificial grass formed the carpet for baroque garden furniture. The walls were painted blue, and a mirror set above the fireplace reflected views of the Champs Elysées.

In the 1930s the influence of Surrealism also affected France's leading interior decorator, Jean-Michel Frank (1895–1941), renowned for his supremely simple but expensively elegant inte-riors. He had influenced and supplied leading American decorators, including Elsie de Wolfe, Syrie Maugham, Frances Elkins and Eleanor Brown, with Art Deco emphasis on the quality and rarity of the materials used. The Cinema Ballroom he designed for Baron Roland de l'Espée (1936) was a major departure. The colour scheme was startling: there was a bright red carpet and one pink, one pale blue, one sea-green and one yellow wall. The theatre-boxes hung with purple velvet flanked the ultimate in Surrealist seating, the 'Mae West Lips' sofa (c.1936) designed by Dali and based on his painting, *Mae West* (1934, Art Institute of Chicago), which had depicted the film star's lips as a sofa, her nose as a fireplace and her eyes as framed oil-paintings. The British versions were commissioned in deep and pale-pink felt by the great collector of Surrealist art, Edward James, for Monkton House near Chichester, the country home he furnished and decorated as a monument to Surrealism. A series of strange room-settings used quilting on the walls, and a stair carpet was specially woven to reproduce James's dog's paw-prints.

Edward James also commissioned the painter Paul Nash to design a bathroom for his wife, the Viennese dancer Tilly Losch, at his London house. Like many artists during the Depression, Nash was forced to take on design-work in order to make a living. He wrote passionately on the subject of design in his *Room and Book* (1932), decrying the British taste for historical revivals: 'It is time we woke up and took an interest in our times. Just as the modern Italian has revolted against the idea that his country is nothing but a museum, so we should be ashamed to be regarded by the Americans as a charming old-world village.'

By the 1930s the whole profession had become more formalized. The American Institute of Interior Decorators (now the American Society of Interior Designers) was established in 1931, and trade magazines were founded in America including *Home Furnishing* from 1929 and *The Decorators' Digest* in 1932 (renamed *Interior Design* in the

1950s). A new generation entered the profession in the 1930s with more formal training in design and a more business-like approach. Terence Harold Robsjohn-Gibbings (1909–73) for instance had an architectural training. He was brought to America by Charles Duveen, the antique-dealer and brother of art-dealer Joseph Duveen, and set up his own practice on Madison Avenue, New York City, in 1936. His designs were inspired by Ancient Greece and Moderne.

The rise in status of the interior decorator was halted for a time after the Second World War by shortages, and then aided by the emergence of the new profession of 'interior designer'. Entrants to the profession would now usually be trained, relying less on 'natural good taste' and more on graduate education. Such designers increasingly worked on non-domestic commissions, as the commercial sector realized the value of good interior design.

In the grand milieu, John Fowler was succeeded as principal adviser to the National Trust in Britain in 1969 by David Mlinaric, who did not aim for the faded elegance of Fowler, but re-created period interiors with new textiles and gilding. Mlinaric's private commissions reveal an eclectic use of antiques from different centuries. Another new figure on the post-war decorating scene, Michael Inchbald (b. 1920), showed the same disregard for historical accuracy, and incorporated a varied mixture of past styles in his interiors. He designed the luxury interior of the QE2, and his own London home provides a slightly quirky setting for an important collection of antique furniture and *objets d'art*. Perhaps the best known of all British *115–16* interior decorators and designers, David Hicks (1929–98), was an admirer of Inchbald's work, and he shows the same skill in combining antiques with modern design.

Hicks's career was launched in 1954 when the decoration of the interior of his mother's house in London was published in *House and Garden*. The combination of strong colours such as scarlet, black and cerulean blue in the library, the emphasis on crisp outline, and the careful table-top arrangements or 'tablescapes', all characterize Hicks's work. After a four-year partnership with Tom Parr, who went on to run Colefax & Fowler, he established his own business, David Hicks Ltd, in 1959. During the 1960s he contributed to the renaissance in British culture at a time when British pop groups, fashion designers, photographers and models dominated the international scene. His photograph appeared in *David Bailey's Box of Pin-Ups* in 1965 as one of the young fashion-leaders working in London.

Post-war interior decorators have found lasting inspiration in the working practices of the women who founded the profession.

14
Rethinking Histories of the Interior

Charles Rice

Source: *Journal of Architecture*, 9:3, Autumn 2004

INTRODUCTION

Our contemporary image-saturated culture revolves around the domestic interior. Sitting comfortably at home, we are constantly offered images of how we should live our domestic lives, or of how others live theirs. As a society, we seem at once threatened by, but also totally at ease with, this close fit between mechanisms of publicity and the private sphere. The correlation between images of the domestic and the domestic setting of their consumption is at the core of our contemporary fascination with lifestyle, a fascination we might often disavow in the search for a supposedly more authentic mode of living.

Yet this correlation between the domestic and the media is not purely the result of the current prominence of, say, Martha Stewart or *Big Brother*. Several authors have sought to understand what underpins this correlation. For Paul Virilio, the bourgeois home 'is an intersection, a nodal point, a fixed pole on which inertia begins to renew the ancient sedentary ways of townspeople, legal citizens for whom the liberty to come and go is suddenly replaced by the liberation of home reception.'[1] In Margaret Morse's work, revolutions in technology, cyberspace and cyber culture come to figure immersive environments in terms of the house-machine as itself an interactive subject, a mixture of virtual and material space.[2] Terence Riley's 1999 Museum of Modern Art exhibition and catalogue figures this mediatised condition within the notion of the un-private house.[3] And in looking at historical antecedents for this condition, Beatriz Colomina has argued that modern architecture, especially in relation to its domestic innovations, emerged in the early twentieth century as a mass medium.[4]

Yet I want to make a different claim about domesticity's relation to media. It is not through the technological colonisation of an existing private space that domesticity enters into its relationship with the media, nor through an avant-gardism that opened up an introverted domestic realm to spatial and image-based possibilities beyond its strict boundaries. Rather, the realisation of a domesticity wherein images interact with a spatial context came about through the historical emergence of the bourgeois domestic interior at the beginning of the nineteenth century. The very context for a bourgeois sense of domesticity emerges as a doubled interior, an interior that is consciously understood as both an image and a spatial condition.

In this paper, I shall look specifically at the historical emergence of this doubled interior: how it developed both as the spatial context for the rise of bourgeois domesticity, and as an image that was able to circulate within this context. In the same way that it challenges current diagnoses of domesticity's relation to the culture of the image, the interior's double sense poses questions for how histories of privacy, domesticity and the interior have traditionally been written. While on the one hand contemporary characterisations of domesticity are inclined to present media infiltration as a novelty, on the other hand, histories of domesticity are inclined to emphasise those aspects of domesticity that are considered timeless. In focusing on the problems inherent in the latter, we may come to appreciate domesticity within a frame of reference that neither essentialises nor trivialises the idea that the domestic interior has a history.

THE HISTORICAL EMERGENCE OF THE BOURGEOIS INTERIOR

The word 'interior' has undergone several shifts in meaning. It had come into use in English from the late fifteenth century to mean basic divisions between inside and outside, and to describe the spiritual and inner nature of the soul. From the early eighteenth century, interiority was used to designate inner character and a sense of individual subjectivity, and from the middle of the eighteenth century the interior came to designate the domestic affairs of a state, as well as the interior sense of territory that belongs to a country or region. It was only from the beginning of the nineteenth century, however, that the interior came to designate what the *Oxford English Dictionary* (*OED*) records as: 'The inside of a building or room, esp. in reference to the artistic effect; also, a picture or representation of the inside of a building or room. Also, in a theatre, a "set" consisting of the inside of a building or room'.

The first use of the word in this domestic sense is dated 1829 from a publication entitled *Companion To Theatres*: 'A few interiors, two or three streets, and about the same number of country views; would last as stock scenery for several seasons'. An entry from George Eliot's diary of 1858 has a use in the sense of a genre of representation: 'The two interiors of Westminster Abbey by Ainmueller admirable'. The *OED* entry for interior decoration suggests a usage for interior which is more specifically domestic: 'The planned co-ordination for artistic effect of colours and furniture, etc., in a room or building'.[5] The first use given is *Household Furniture and Interior Decoration*, the title of Thomas Hope's 1807 publication, which, along with Charles Percier and Pierre Fontaine's *Receuil de décorations intérieurs* of 1801, marked the newly emergent interior as a site of professional struggle between architects and upholsterers. Through the nineteenth century, interior decoration began to articulate itself separately from architecture.[6]

In this way, the interior emerges with conceptual specificity in the context of bourgeois domesticity. It is not simply architectural, but it borrows on the enclosure provided by architecture to be articulated through decoration, the literal covering of the inside of an architectural 'shell'. In this sense the interior is also not simply spatial, but is equally an image-based phenomenon.

There are further doubled conditions of the interior that consolidate the significance of its historical emergence. A sense of doubled experience, the way in which an inhabitation of the interior is caught between material and immaterial registers, is captured in 'The Twofold Room', a prose poem of 1862 by Charles Baudelaire. It begins with a description of 'A room just like a daydream, a truly spiritual room, in which the air is tinged with rosiness and blue'.

The furniture takes on elongated shapes, prostate and languorous. Each piece seems to be dreaming, as if living in a state of trance, like vegetable and mineral things. The draperies speak an unvoiced language, like flowers and skies and setting suns.[7]

In a similar vein to this poetic evocation, Walter Benjamin's 1939 exposé of the bourgeois domestic interior describes it as a material space which produces de-realised experiences.[8] For the bourgeoisie, the interior emerges as a space separated from sites of work and productive labour, and becomes a place of refuge from the city and its new, alienating forms of experience. In the interior, subjects confront themselves in psychologically charged ways through the medium of objects and furnishings. Benjamin writes of the private individual inhabiting the interior by 'taking possession' of things in divesting them of their character as commodities: 'The collector proves to be the true resident of the interior'. By bestowing a 'connoisseur's value', rather than a 'use value' on objects, the collector 'delights in evoking a world that is not just distant and long gone but also better – a world in which, to be sure, human beings are no better provided with what they need than in the real world, but in which things are freed from the drudgery of being useful'.[9] These things become what Benjamin calls the traces of inhabitation.

Yet Baudelaire's interior is sealed off from the everyday world only in reverie. The internal coherence of his animate, nature-like room changes with the intrusion of reality into the room and its interiorised world. This intrusion comes with 'a terrible, heavy thump' on the door, at which point he remembers:

Yes, this hovel, this home of everlasting boredom, is indeed my own. Look, there are the fatuous bits of junk, my dusty and chipped furniture; the fireless hearth with not even a glowing ember in the grate all fouled with spit; the dingy windows down which the rain has scrawled runnels in the grime; the manuscripts riddled with cross-outs or left half done; the calendar on which the evil days of reckoning are underlined in pencil.[10]

A space of immaterial, de-realised experience, Baudelaire's interior is also the space of his work, and of his relation to the productive cycle. His plight figures the way in which the increased awareness of the bourgeois interior as a space removed from the everyday world also produced a measure for assessing the living conditions of the working classes, those for whom the domestic and the productive spheres were not necessarily separated.[11] More broadly, this relation between reverie and the reality of the onward march of time gives a context for understanding the bourgeoisie's relation to the world of objects as commodities, to the industrialising city, and to their social and political identity through the nineteenth century.

Baudelaire and Benjamin's immaterial experience occurs in relation to a space for and of the psyche, a space that borrows on the material attributes of the everyday domestic interior – its furnishings – and imbues them with a transformed, psychological significance.

The bourgeois domestic interior emerges historically in the nineteenth century through an accumulation of traces, and in relation to occluded meanings. At one level, we can understand these aspects of its historical emergence as intrinsic to the bourgeoisie's experience of domesticity in the nineteenth century. But what does the doubleness of the interior, and the idea that the interior is historically emergent in this way, mean for how we might write a history of this domestic experience? In other words, how can we gain access to and evaluate an historical experience which is complicated by a condition of doubleness?

The primary complicating factor is the idea that the interior's spatial and imagistic senses do not map directly onto each other. As we learn from Baudelaire, the imagistic sense of the interior is not simply transparent to its spatial sense. This presents problems for conventional ways in which the evidence of the interior is gathered to reconstruct and interpret historical conditions of domesticity. In what follows, I shall look at the two main ways in which evidence is dealt with to construct histories of privacy, domesticity and the interior. The first has to do with understanding the interior as the site for articulating the nineteenth-century's domesticity through an historical recording of the evidence of everyday life. The second has to do with the interior itself being seen to have a history that can be constructed through the collection of visual representations of the interior.

PRIVACY AND THE EVIDENCE OF EVERYDAY LIFE

Domestic privacy has become an important topic of historical research largely through the seminal multi-volume study *A History of Private Life*.

Volume IV constitutes the major work on the rise of privacy and domesticity through the nineteenth century.[12] Evidence of everyday life is drawn together into a broad and inclusive picture of the terrain of privacy and domesticity in the nineteenth century. Particular parts of the text reveal this method, but also its shortcomings in terms of how we might appreciate the bourgeois domestic interior as a particular historical emergence.

Michelle Perrot and Roger-Henri Guerrand broaden the formation of the domestic interior beyond specifically bourgeois practices of decoration. They describe the first impulses towards decoration by the French working class of the nineteenth century, arguing that 'Moving meant changing wallpaper', the low price of wallpaper in that context having a significant impact.[13] They suggest that it was the choosing and arranging of objects more than the physical nature of space that marked off a private, individualised interior. Perrot and Guerrand note with respect to elderly people who were confined to hospice care in the nineteenth century, and who hoarded old household objects and utensils, that 'The only value these things have for them is that they are not part of the house-issued clothing and furnishings. These things belong to them, and taken together they symbolise a kind of home'.[14]

In turning their focus specifically to bourgeois practices, Perrot and Guerrand go on to suggest that the significance for the Parisian bourgeoisie of decoration as 'trimming' or covering lay in its symbolic protection from the violence and danger of the streets of Paris, and as a way of banishing the look of poverty:

> People became obsessed with the desire that no wall or floor be left bare; bare floors became a mark of poverty. The leading bourgeois magazine, *L'Illustration*, described the new conception of space in its February 15, 1851 issue: 'We gathered in a small saloon, which was tightly sealed by door curtains, silk pads, and double drapes. . . . A good carpet lies underfoot . . . a profusion of fabrics graces the windows, covers the mantle piece and hides the woodwork. Dry wood and cold marble are concealed beneath velvet and plush'.[15]

Yet even as these motivations to decorate stem from a desire to establish the interior as a stable, personalised space, further on in volume IV of *A History of Private Life*, Alain Corbin identifies the development of certain neuroses within this interior condition. He likens the 'bourgeoisie's obsession with drapery, slipcovers, casings and upholstery' with the 'perverse effects of modesty' seen in the increasing sumptuousness and complexity of fastenings in lingerie, and the subsequent negotiations and rituals of dressing and undressing. Corbin suggests: 'The desire to preserve, the concern to leave a trace of one's existence, the fear of castration, and the omnipresent reminder of the menace of desire joined in a neurotic encounter'.[16] This account of the claiming of a space through the leaving of traces sets up a charged and ambivalent relation between an inhabitant's objects, and the inhabitant's subjectivity. A mark of this ambivalence is that the other side of the menace of private space – or perhaps the menace of private space is the other side of this dominant tendency – is the desire for a private space in which to define and cultivate one's individuality. Volume IV of *A History of Private Life* does much to emphasise the interior as a setting for crucial aspects of private life in the nineteenth century, with activities such as: the keeping of a diary, reading, whether in private or as a family (partaking of both secular and religious texts), the cultivation of gendered domestic duties, and the habits of grooming.[17]

Even from these brief expositions, we can see how arguments about domestic privacy are drawn from the minutiae of daily life.

VISUAL REPRESENTATION AND THE HISTORY OF THE INTERIOR

It was from the beginning of the nineteenth century that interior views were painted and drawn as ends in themselves, as a specific genre. Charlotte Gere has argued that practices of interior decoration were directly linked to the emergence of this genre: 'That this interest in interior decoration [prompted by the publications from Percier and Fontaine, and Hope] had a direct bearing on the taste for interior views is evidenced by the fact that so many of them show rooms that must just have been decorated and newly arranged'.[18] Gere's album of interior water colours provides a history of the decoration of the nineteenth-century interior evidenced through its representation, but this project hides an essentialist view of the interior which betrays the historical specificity of the bourgeois interior doubled between representational and spatial practices. In the following passage, Gere shifts from describing the historical conditions for the emergence of the genre of the interior view, to describing how these representations

become evidence for a much broader conception of the history of the interior:

> The depiction of rooms for their own sake, rather than as a background to a narrative, anecdotal or portrait painting, germinated, reached its fullest flowering and died within the space of one century. It was not unusual for such interiors to form a group, representing different aspects of several rooms. They were intended to be placed in albums rather than to be framed and hung, and remained an almost secret possession. . . . When the interior view went out of fashion in the second half of the nineteenth century, their very existence seems to have been forgotten. They were rendered obsolete by the development of a photographic camera capable of focusing on a great depth of field and thus able to do the job of the interior view-painter much more quickly and no less efficiently. Some of these [photographic] albums survive, giving an invaluable picture of decorating taste in the period 1880–1910, before they too were forgotten, like the albums of paintings they had superseded. Mario Praz's rediscovery of this minor but fascinating art barely thirty years ago (his pioneering *Illustrated History of Interior Decoration* was published in 1964) was a revelation, and the historic no less than aesthetic importance of the subject is now recognised by a group of informed collectors.[19]

While Perrot realised the ultimately private nature of the evidence of privacy, Gere is signalling the shift of visual representations of the interior from being familial possessions to becoming historical, and therefore public, documents. The implications of this shift can be seen most clearly in relation to Mario Praz's seminal work. His *Illustrated History of Interior Decoration* provides a selection of visual representations of domesticity from ancient Greece through to Art Nouveau, and a commentary upon them.[20] The introduction to Praz's book muses on the literary and representational evocation of furniture, the home and the interior. Praz sees the house and its interior as a continuum, which is always in need of furnishing. In witnessing the destruction of houses after the second world war, their interiors laid open with 'some still furnished corner, dangling above the rubble, surrounded by ruin',[21] Praz sees that:

> The houses will rise again, and men will furnish houses as long as there is breath in them. Just as our primitive ancestor built a shapeless chair

with hastily-chopped branches, so the last man will save from the rubble a stool or a tree stump on which to rest from his labours; and if his spirit is freed a while from his woes, he will linger another moment and decorate his room.[22]

Such an observation of the timeless qualities of 'human nature' is the platform upon which Praz launches his history of the interior. He writes quite directly of the interior and its furnishing as reflecting the 'character' or 'personality' of the occupant, working from a basic division of human nature between those who 'care about their house, and those who care not at all about it'.[23] Based on his reading of decorative tendencies from visual representations, Praz sees that:

perhaps even more than painting or sculpture, perhaps even more than architecture itself, furniture reveals the spirit of the age. And there is nothing like a retrospective exhibition of furnished rooms in a chronological sequence to declare to us, at first glance, the varying personalities of the rooms' occupants.[24]

Praz's book aims to provide the published equivalent of this 'retrospective exhibition', taking the idea of the inhabiting subject, and the interior and its decoration, as pre-given concepts for the construction of this history, not ones that have emerged out of particular historical conditions. Referring to Benjamin, whose exposé on the interior he cites at length,[25] Praz collects traces of the inhabitant through their visibility in the interior. Yet he generalises this bourgeois condition as one obtaining across all history. He ignores the historical specificity of the genre of the interior view, and how it might relate to specific spatial practices of inhabitation, by rendering the idea of visual representation across many genres transparent to spatial conditions of domesticity. What has been tacitly recognised as a particular historical emergence has been used to authorise a transhistorical and essentialised view of the domestic interior.

We must ask: what is the impetus behind this sort of essentialised historiography? An answer may be found in another history of the interior, Peter Thornton's *Authentic Décor: The Domestic Interior 1620–1920*. Thornton takes the cue for his investigation from this quotation from Macaulay's 1848 *History of England*:

Readers who take an interest in the progress of civilisation and of the useful arts will be grateful

to the humble topographer who has recorded these facts [about the meanness of the lodgings of those taking the waters at Bath, early in the eighteenth century], and will perhaps wish that historians of far higher pretensions had sometimes spared a few pages from military evolutions and political intrigues, for the purpose of letting us know how the parlours and bedchambers of our ancestors looked.[26]

In these terms, a history of the interior supplements traditional grand historical narratives, whereby one's supposed innate appreciation of domesticity would colour the background of past events. What is common in all of these histories of privacy, domesticity and the interior is that they attest to a post-nineteenth-century way of seeing. This way of seeing authorises a general historical retrospection which is itself not appreciated within an historical context. This situation approaches what Michel Foucault terms traditional history:

We believe in the dull constancy of instinctual life and imagine that it continues to exert its force indiscriminately in the present as it did in the past. But a knowledge of history easily disintegrates this unity, depicts its wavering course, locates its moments of strength and weakness, and defines its oscillating reign.[27]

A 'knowledge of history' relates to what Foucault terms effective history. It is a history of discontinuity, for the sake of breaking tendencies for recognition and 'rediscovery of ourselves'[28] in acts of constructing narrative-driven traditional histories. In Foucault's terms, the emergence of the interior, in its doubleness, can be cast as an event in the schema of effective history, an event that, when perceived as such, enables a 'reversal of a relationship of forces'.[29] By returning to Benjamin's exposé of the bourgeois domestic interior, we shall see the importance of understanding the historical emergence of the interior within this schema of effective history. And far from providing an increased consciousness of everyday domesticity within the continuum of history, we shall see that essentialised histories of the interior, privacy and domesticity have produced a sleep of historical consciousness.

TRACING THE INTERIOR

The larger historical project to which Benjamin's exposé belongs seeks to preserve the fragmentary and occluded nature of the historical evidence of the everyday as a radical critique of narratives of historical progress. Embedded within Benjamin's fragmentary history of the nineteenth century, the interior takes on the role of estranging us from, rather than connecting us to, bourgeois domesticity. In showing this, Benjamin is able to provide an account of the historical emergence of the bourgeois interior that seeks to understand precisely its historical emergence. The trace is a key concept of this historiography:

> Ever since the time of Louis Philippe, the bourgeois has shown a tendency to compensate for the absence of any trace of private life in the big city. He tries to do this within the four walls of his apartment. It is as if he made it a point of honour not to allow the traces of his everyday objects and accessories to get lost. Indefatigably, he takes the impression of a host of objects; for his slippers and his watches, his blankets and his umbrellas, he devises coverlets and cases. He has a marked preference for velour and plush, which preserve the imprint of all contact. In the style characteristic of the second empire, the apartment becomes a sort of cockpit. The traces of its inhabitant are moulded into the interior. Here is the origin of the detective story, which inquires into these traces and follows these tracks.[30]

At one level, this description does not differ greatly from those that contribute to the histories of privacy, domesticity and the interior discussed above. Yet the above passage is a summary or exposé of a much larger collection of notes and documents that form one section of his voluminous historical study of the nineteenth century, the *Arcades Project*. This collection, or convolute, is entitled 'The Interior, the Trace',[31] and contains fragmentary accounts of the culture and materiality of the bourgeois interior. As we see from the above passage, the concept of the trace is central in Benjamin's articulation of how the interior is both formed by its inhabitant, as well as forming an impression of the inhabitant. Prior to the *Arcades Project*, Benjamin had developed the idea of the trace of the inhabitant in his quasi-autobiographical work *One Way Street*. In this account, the trace is related to the kind of evidence that begins the detective story:[32]

> The bourgeois interior of the 1860s to the 1890s, with its gigantic chests distended with carvings, the sunless corners where palms

stand, the balcony embattled behind its balustrade, and the long corridors with their singing gas flames, fittingly houses only the corpse. 'On this sofa the aunt cannot but be murdered'. The soulless luxuriance of the furnishings becomes true comfort only in the presence of a dead body.[33]

For Benjamin, the act of reading a trace in terms of the evidence it provides mortifies the object positioned by those traces, as with the corpse. The interior is the space of this kind of mortification. Via a double action, this fragmentary comment on the interior becomes mortified in Benjamin's own text. The *Arcades Project* itself acts like an interior for the collected fossil-like fragments of the nineteenth century – traces of things long dead, rather than living things which could provide a point of continuity for the culture of interwar Europe. Thus Benjamin's history of the nineteenth century is like an ancient, natural history, rather than a history of forward progress which might explain 'where we are today'.

For Benjamin, as for Foucault, the danger of a progressivist history is that we are lulled into a dream of progress. Benjamin's idea of history is to wake us up to the present, to shock us out of the complacency of such a dream of progress. Thus his history is not a synthesis of documents from which a smooth narrative of 'living history' is produced. It is, rather, a fragmentary collection, a literal mass of archaic matter barely sorted into basic divisions, or convolutes. These can be sifted in order to understand the radical separations between a present moment and the nineteenth century as the ancient past. Such an historiography allows us to understand that very few things of value can be carried forward out of such a wreckage of history.[34] In the words of Michael Jennings: 'Only this sort of ongoing purgative labour which "mortifies" the past can reveal those few images that might have a positive effect in the present'.[35]

Yet the context of the present is always shifting; we are no longer living in Benjamin's present. I began this paper by highlighting the mediatisation of the interior as a dominant characterisation of contemporary domesticity. In Benjamin's terms, what we need to awaken to in this contemporary context is the precise relationship between the domestic and the media. On one level, the media are seen as a threat to the interior's private world. They open the interior up to an array of forces and influences beyond its supposedly strict boundaries. On another level, the adoption of domestic content into the media (say, once again, Martha Stewart and

Big Brother) is a means to domesticate the media, to soften their presence within the domestic by interiorising the media loop. Yet I have argued that the bourgeois interior emerges historically at the beginning of the nineteenth century to underpin this mediatisation of the interior: the interior is unthinkable outside of a relation between images and space. The supposed novelty of the current mediatisation of the domestic, or the architectural avant-gardism which aligned modern architecture with the mass media, are situations that are only conceptualisable within this bourgeois interior condition.

In Benjamin's terms, understanding this condition is akin to awakening from a kind of bourgeois 'dream' of domesticity. We might begin to estrange ourselves from, and therefore critically engage this condition if we understand bourgeois domesticity as a particular historical formation. This would enable the contours of current domesticity to be 'traced' most clearly, opening the domestic to a mode of inquiry whereby relationships between images and spaces are seen precisely as constructors of the interior, rather than either natural or novel aspects of domesticity. The aim in this mode of inquiry is not to recognise ourselves, but to reveal such a traditional historiographical ideal as itself a construction, and to reverse the relationship of forces that blind us to the precisely constructed condition of the interior, and of our historical relationship to it.

NOTES AND REFERENCES

1 Paul Virilio, *The Lost Dimension* (New York, Semio-text(e), 1991), pp. 72–73.
2 Margaret Morse, *Virtualities: Television, Media Art and Cyberculture* (Bloomington and Indianapolis, Indiana University Press, 1998), p. 8. These themes have a connection to the larger issue of the supposed dematerialisation of architecture itself.
3 Terence Riley, *The Un-Private House* (New York, Museum of Modern Art, 1999).
4 Beatriz Colomina, *Privacy and Publicity: Modern Architecture as Mass Media* (Cambridge, MA and London, MIT Press, 1994).
5 *Oxford English Dictionary*, 2nd ed. (Oxford, Clarendon Press, 1989).
6 Peter Thornton, *Authentic Décor: The Domestic Interior, 1620–1920* (New York, Viking, 1984), pp. 10–12.
7 Charles Baudelaire, 'The Twofold Room', in Francis Scarfe (ed. and trans.), *The Poems in Prose, with La Fanfarlo* (London, Anvil Press, 1989), p. 37.
8 Walter Benjamin, 'Paris: Capital of the Nineteenth Century (exposé of 1939)', in Rolf Tiedemann (ed.), *The Arcades Project*, trans. Howard Eiland and Kevin McLaughlin (Cambridge, MA and London, The Belknap Press of Harvard University Press, 1999), pp. 19–20.
9 *Ibid.*, p. 19.
10 Baudelaire, 'The Twofold Room', *op. cit.*, p. 39.
11 Important here is the sociological research conducted by Henry Mayhew into slums in London in the middle of the nineteenth century. Against a bourgeois consciousness of domestic comfort, Mayhew's research points to where basic standards of comfort in dwellings are not achieved amongst the working classes. See Henry Mayhew, 'Home is home, be it never so homely', in Viscount Ingestre (ed.), *Meliora, or Better Times to Come* (London, 1851), pp. 258–280. See also Martin Hewitt, 'District Visiting and the Constitution of Domestic Space in the Mid-Nineteenth Century', in Inga Bryden and Janet Floyd (eds), *Domestic Space: Reading the Nineteenth-Century Interior* (Manchester and New York, Manchester University Press, 1999), pp. 121–141, for an account of the surveillance of the working class by the middle classes in Britain.
12 Michelle Perrot, (ed.), *A History of Private Life. Volume IV: From the Fires of Revolution to the Great War*, trans. Arthur Goldhammer (Cambridge, MA and London, The Belknap Press of Harvard University Press, 1990). See also Norbert Elias, *The Civilizing Process: The History of Manners*, trans. Edmund Jephcott (Oxford, Basil Blackweli, 1978), for a seminal account of the history of domesticity, privacy and manners in Western civilisation.
13 Michelle Perrot and Roger-Henri Guerrand, 'Scenes and Places', in *A History of Private Life. Volume IV, op. cit.*, p. 354.
14 *Ibid.*, p. 356.
15 *Ibid.*, p. 369.
16 Corbin 'Backstage', *A History of Private Life, op. cit.*, p. 487.
17 See especially *ibid.*, pp. 479–502, 519–547.
18 Charlotte Gere, *Nineteenth Century Interiors: An Album of Watercolours* (London, Thames and Hudson, 1992), p. 13.
19 *Ibid.*, p. 14. Peter Thornton puts this argument thus: 'It was fashionable, from about 1815 to about 1840, to draw and paint views of interiors. Grand people instructed a draughtsman to make pictures of their favourite rooms; the

less grand did it themselves'. (Thornton, *Authentic Décor, op. cit.*, p. 217.) Gere recognises that there are precedents for interior view-painting in examples from the eighteenth century. She suggests that these earlier examples were either isolated representations that were informational sources in relation to the rooms they depicted (rather than having 'artistic' merit, which would define a genre in Gere's terms), were representations of well-known houses in periodicals and other publications, or were representations produced to accompany visits to well-known buildings. Thornton argues that the practice of allowing visits to well-known houses, and the attendant publications, ceased around 1840, when the interior shifted from being a space for the display of taste and wealth, to being the space of familial privacy and the cultivation of domestic virtues. See Thornton, *Authentic Décor, op. cit.*, p. 210, For an in-depth discussion of one particular eighteenth century drawing type, see Robin Evans, 'The Developed Surface', in *Translations from Drawing to Building and Other Essays* (London, Architectural Association, 1997), pp. 55–91.

20 Mario Praz, *An Illustrated History of Interior Decoration from Pompeii to Art Nouveau*, trans. William Weaver (London, Thames and Hudson, 1964). Alternative edition: *An Illustrated History of Interior Furnishing from the Renaissance to the 20th Century*, trans. William Weaver (New York, George Braziller, 1964). The two editions are identical, and despite the supposed 'Renaissance' beginning of the American edition, it still includes the plates 'from Pompeii'.

21 *Ibid.*, p. 17.

22 *Ibid.*, p. 18.

23 *Ibid.*, p. 19.

24 *Ibid.*, p. 25.

25 *Ibid.*, pp. 25–29.

26 T. B. Macaulay, *History of England from the Accession of James II* (London, 1848), vol. 1, ch. 111. Quoted in Thornton, *Authentic Décor, op. cit.*, p. 8.

27 Michel Foucault, 'Nietzsche, Genealogy, History', in Paul Rabinow (ed. and trans.), *The Foucault Reader* (London, Penguin, 1984), p. 87.

28 *Ibid.*, p. 88.

29 *Ibid.*, p. 88.

30 Benjamin, 'Paris: Capital of the Nineteenth Century', *op. cit.*, p. 20.

31 Benjamin, *The Arcades Project, op. cit.*, pp. 212–227.

32 For a thorough consideration of the detective novel as a literary genre, see Ernst Bloch, 'A Philosophical View of the Detective Novel', in *The Utopian Function of Art and Literature: Selected Essays*, trans. Jack Zipes and Frank Mecklenburg (Cambridge, MA and London, MIT Press, 1988), pp. 245–264. Within the narrative logic of the detective novel, Bloch describes the obligatory murder as *'the un-narrated factor'*, which occurs prior to the beginning of the novel, and which is then reconstructed within it: 'The story arrives on the scene with the corpse'. This aspect is, for Bloch, the *'most decisive* criterion' of the detective novel as a genre (p. 255, emphasis in original).

33 Walter Benjamin, *One Way Street and Other Writings*, trans. Edmond Jephcott and Kingsley Shorter (London, Verso, 1992), p. 49.

34 See especially Walter Benjamin, 'Poverty and Experience', in M. Jennings, H. Eiland and G. Smith (eds), *Selected Writings Volume 2, 1927–1934*, trans. R. Livingstone (Cambridge, MA and London, The Belknap Press of Harvard University Press, 1999), pp. 731–736.

35 Michael W. Jennings, *Dialectical Images: Walter Benjamin's Theory of Literary Criticism* (Ithaca and London, Cornell University Press, 1987), p. 38. In relating the trace to Benjamin's rendering of the complexity of time, Pierre Missac suggests: '[Benjamin] distinguished between two kinds of time: the time of a pre- or proto-history, marked by an indisputably positive evolution; and the time of human history, which we have to shape – and which we can spoil – by taking our fate into our own hands. The first leaves its traces in the second – especially, in fact, in the most "human" or advanced areas, such as that of literary or artistic creation, where the unsupervisable process of maturation plays an essential role'. (Pierre Missac, *Walter Benjamin's Passages*, trans. Shierry Weber Nicholson (Cambridge, MA and London, MIT Press, 1995), p. 107.)

15
Inscape

Hugh Casson

Source: *Inscape: the Design of Interiors*. Architectural Press: London, 1968

WHY 'INSCAPE'? . . .

Lack of confidence perhaps in the subject? Certainly not. It is surely by now generally accepted that the design of interiors is a, serious and justifiably expert, field, with its own history and traditions and with a future of expanding possibilities. Cowardice, then, in the face of orthodox nomenclature? A faint shiftiness here perhaps. Authors always feel uneasy in the presence of words, which have a tendency, under pressure of fatigue or fashion or rethinking, to run downhill and to finish—as Rose Macaulay put it—in a 'pejorative puddle'. Nowhere is this process more swift than in the world of art and architecture. Brutalism has already clumped over the horizon in pursuit of the New Empiricism. Image, Node, Plug-in and Environment are doomed to tumble inevitably behind Ornament, Neighbourhood Unit and Sketch Design into a discredited exile to await perhaps future rebirth. 'Interior Design', afforded a legitimate reprieve by changing its name from 'Interior Decoration' (and all those disagreeable associations with amateurism and lampshades), need not yet be discarded, though its position is precarious and its future threatened.

Again one asks then: why 'Inscape'? The answer is a simple one—because it indicates something more than a timely reassessment of a recognized creative activity. It represents an attitude of mind. Put briefly, it reasserts the Ruskinian formula that the first duty of the artist is 'to see and to feel', and that of the three attacking points in the designer's armoury of weapons—Professor Guyatt's 'Head, Heart and Hand'—the second is, on this particular battlefield, the sharpest and the most powerful. The architect need not be alarmed by this, for it is not the first time it's happened. Many historians and critics have observed that new conceptions and new forms in architecture spring quite as often, if not more often, from the experiments of poets and painters as from new materials, new techniques or new problems to be solved. These last may suggest new solutions or even create new limitations which themselves become exciting, but fundamentally in architecture, as in any other art, there is no substitute for insight and inspiration, and it is in these two irreplaceable qualities that the architect, possibly because he is trained to distrust them, is often so woefully weak. It is perhaps this weakness, in part, that whips up his antagonism and helps to explain why many architects refuse to believe that such a thing as interior design exists at all. Some place it on a par with the art of the milliner, or pastrycook; others seem to regard its claims for separate consideration as a personal affront. It is true that the forms and materials with which the interior designer deals are often, but by no means always, less permanent than those handled by the architect and become thus morally suspect and contemptible to the orthodox. Every architect has a perfect right to contract out of such responsibilities as the design of furniture, textiles and fittings and their assembly into coherent interiors, if he feels they are beyond his powers or outside his interests. He has no right, however, to claim that such matters are so trivial as to be unworthy of his attention. Few architects, of course, will argue upon such weak grounds as this. Much more defensible, and indeed at times impregnable, is the attitude of the architect who says quite simply that architecture, interpreted as the imaginative handling of space, *is* interior design. Here the shrug of indifference is replaced by the bland blue-eyed stare of the confident artist who will claim, quite rightly, that a building should grow first from an understanding of its use, through an expression of its use in the shape of a plan into its final three-dimensional form—a process which at all stages and in every detail should be in the unassisted hands of the architect. With only a momentary twitch of an eyebrow over the word 'unassisted', this view is ideally surely the right one. It clearly depends for its success upon the architect being of the highest calibre and of great versatility. Historically, too, there are many precedents for this 'soap-bubble' conception: some Gothic cathedrals—but not the façade of Lincoln—and the work, say, of Palladio or Perret, or Mies van der Rohe. But the fact that nobody would dispute this approach to interior design does not mean that it is necessarily the only approach. Just as from time to time (some would say more often than not) buildings are needed which must be flexible in use or impermanent in form, so too, and perhaps even more often, interiors are needed which can be unrelated, superimposed and entirely independent of their structural enclosure. The architect may dislike this, or regard it as morally indefensible, but he cannot call upon either History or Function to support him. Historically, there are many splendidly successful examples, from the Pyramids and the blind houses of Pompeii to Frank Lloyd Wright's glass showroom in San Francisco, or the lecture hall of the Royal College of Physicians, in London, where the exterior appearance of the building bears no relation whatever to what lies inside, and there are many buildings, hotels, department stores, and particularly ships, whose function demands that the structure is divorced from, or at any rate more permanent than, the interiors which must change as often as public demand may require.

Obviously there are many estimable and inspiring examples to be found in both camps. Let us then have no more talk of morality and admit that no justificatory gymnastics are needed to prove that the interior designer is as necessary—and must therefore be as well-trained, imaginative and skilful—as his colleagues, the town-planner, the sociologist, the services consultant and the landscape-architect. If this should, however reluctantly, be agreed, how does the interior designer, once given his brief, go about his task, and what are the tools, elements, ploys and resources at his command?

First he must start with that architectural anathema, a preconception—not one of actual form, arrangement or technique, for these will be drastically affected by his limitations of the problem, many of them not yet apparent—but a preconception of the 'character' or 'mood' of the project. This preconception, or, as the OED puts it, this 'anticipation in thought' (not, please note, anticipation *of* thought), is the reverse of the normal architectural process. Although it is born of intuition or, if you prefer to term it, instant rationalization, it is not a mystic personal revelation, but the disciplined and imaginative application of *Insight*,

which is the ability to penetrate with understanding into the character and circumstances of a problem. This 'mood assessment' is in itself a product of two elements—the mood inherent in the problem, and the mood that the designer intends to impart to it in order to emphasize or play down what is already there. Together these combine into the mood that the final job presents to all the senses when completed.

Broadly speaking, for the interior designer, there will be two approaches: the first is the 'Integrated', where the interior is indivisible from the structure and where pattern, form, texture and lighting are part of the architecture, and qualities of permanence and monumentality are sought. The second, which may be termed the 'Superimposed', is where the interior is required to be more flexible, and easily modified or even transformed without mutilating the architecture in which it is temporarily contained. Within these two groups the variations are limitless, but in each one atmosphere is all. 'An apartment,' wrote Robert de Montesquiou, 'is a mood.' A series of apartments may be a series of moods or variations upon one theme, but once determined—usually as part of the brief—it must be consistently pursued with every weapon that lies to hand—colour, texture, scale, heat, light sound, movement, even perhaps smell. This can never be merely a visual matter, for a mood thus captured and expressed in space is totally experienced and must, therefore, be totally conceived.

This moment of insight is for the interior designer perhaps almost the most important one in the whole design process. To succeed he must be something of an impresario, a mixture of architect and illusionist, scholar and artist, medicine man and psychologist, acutely sensitive to gradations of character, to atmosphere and to the *genius loci et temporis*. This does not mean that he is blown helplessly about by the whims of fashion, but it does mean that he must keep his mind sensitively and constantly attuned to the values and attitudes of the times in which he lives. All art, as Arthur Koestler has pointed out, is appreciated through twin lenses, one of which is personal and biologically-based aesthetic judgement; the other, the result of the pressures and atmosphere and creative influences of contemporary society. It may be disturbing to reflect that one's sense of beauty, far from being absolute, is continually being diverted or, as it may seem, warped, by a social process. The only real danger in this lies when unequal weight is given to what is perceived by one of the two lenses, and quality is measured as it were by the wrong instrument. This danger is one particularly to be guarded against in interior design with its implication of impermanence and its vulnerability to charges of modishness. Architects seem to accept without a qualm their role as shapers of our human environment, but, as many critics repeatedly tell us, there is nothing in their training or personal experience that would seem particularly to fit them for this self-appointed task. Too often, as aestheticians, they are preoccupied with arbitrary and self-created criteria or, as technicians they pursue the illusion that there must be a technical solution to every question. Too seldom do they remember—as the sociologist, theologian and politician always must—that human creativeness is not confined to experts, and that the creation of an interior, like the building of a city, is a process, not an act, in which the user's contribution must be recognized and anticipated. People are complicated and infinitely adaptable, and architects will therefore pursue in vain the chimera of 'the optimum environment'. Even if such a thing were obtainable other than within the broadest limits, it would fail to satisfy each man's natural wish to have some personal say in the appearance and climate of his own surroundings.

Success or failure does not lie alone with the designer. Space creates its own emotions. It can mean different things to different people at different ages or in different circumstances—and these, as every artist knows, can be physically, if vicariously, sensed as he draws them on paper; but the client—whether banker, restaurateur, shoe-salesman or personnel-officer—must be encouraged to add his own important contribution. The designer cannot by himself create success. He can only create conditions in which, if he and his client have guessed correctly, success can be achieved. This is vital. Most designers, because they are trained to believe this, tend to underestimate or ignore the essentially powerful influence of human creativeness. Human society is founded on the belief that so far as is organizationally possible everybody must be allowed to have his say in the important things of life—education, religion, politics, social behaviour. Why, asks N. J. Habraken, is environment so often, and so conveniently for architects and designers, considered the private province of the specialist? An interior (or a building or a city) that carries too heavily and for ever the

professional signature of its designer, and permits no contribution from its users, may be a fine monument, but it is nevertheless a tomb. Insight, then, born of knowledge and understanding, sets the mood. Once the mood is established, strategy follows. The principles are familiar enough—Design Consistency in every form, material and detail, and Economy in its true sense—the achievement of the maximum of aims (simple or elaborate) by the minimum of means. The formula has a medical directness—Diagnosis, Prescription and Treatment. Get this first one right, and then, with that insight-based decision correct and out of the way, it is possible afterwards to experiment. Get the diagnosis wrong, and only luck or the impervious indifference of the patient will save the day.

Inevitably, since we are dealing with an evasive subject, rules are impossible to prescribe. Even commonsense rules, if not questioned or occasionally broken, can be at times misleading or constricting. For instance, if required, could not drama be enhanced—by equating brilliant lighting with dead (and therefore menacing) silence, rather than by opposing the more orthodox solutions of noise and light with quiet and twilight? Is not a successful restaurant sometimes made even more successful by the deliberate playing-up of noise and overcrowding than by the conventional remedies designed to cure these faults? Is the quantity of daylight provided so significant so long as, by the light of a window, an illusion of daylight is created? Could not more be done by surprise or by support in playing with what psychologists call 'the mental set', that interplay between expectation and observation upon which—as Gombrich has observed—all culture, communication and thus the experience of art depend?

This partnership between designer and user is a subtle never-ending game. Sometimes the user must be coaxed and taken by the hand—sometimes he can be left safely to take a hint. The designer is in charge and must choose his weapons.

The interior can be 'a mirror of the soul', or, more imaginatively, a reinforcement of the soul—opening new possibilities into new and unexpected worlds. It can be spontaneous or contrived, magical or formal, mysterious intricate, impersonal or dotty.

16
Towards a New Agenda

Fred Scott

Source: The Inside Edge, *The Designers Journal*, September 1991

Certain vested interests would wish the idea of interior design to be fragmented, considered for instance as an aspect of retailing or as an instrument of the client's fantasies, so as to contain it within an assumption that it is faster and shallower than proper architecture. The pressures supporting this containment may come from both designers and architects. Without wishing to defuse the tension between the two, I would like to identify a few basic characteristics that differentiate interior design from architecture and in so doing put them on a more equal footing.

Architecture is an undertaking, like furniture design, which strives to be archetypical; other practices which deal with the built environment, such as interior design and urban design, essentially begin with an apprehension of the world as it exists. This is not to say that one is more open to compromise or the other more prone to blind assertiveness, but rather to suggest that there are two separate territories, containing different issues, attitudes and approaches and sharing a long common border and a common culture.

Interior design is generally concerned with changing existing buildings because they have become in some way obsolete. Obsolescence in buildings is a complex idea made up of social, technological and contextual aspects; that is to say, related to change and temporality. In this condition, buildings face three possible fates: for a few, transcendence into museum pieces, conserved and unchanging, and for the rest demolition or change to make them once more contemporary, usually by adaptation to a new use. An example of the latter would be Michelangelo's conversion of the Diocletian baths into the church of Santa Maria degli Angeli in Rome. The alteration process has been given several names, among them, rehabilitation, remodelling, adaptive re-use, interior design and so on. Probably the difficult problem of nomenclature can be best resolved by employing the old analogy between architecture and music. Just as music is the inclusive and generic term for a variety of separate forms of expression, so equally architecture can flourish by means of different specialisms.

Not everyone will be happy with a designation which confers extra status but arguments for a more restricted and trivial role for interior design cannot be sustained without recourse to a sort of class prejudice, the suggestion that the interior designer is congenially or inherently incapable of superior work. This would also miss the point. Just as great works of architecture can be achieved by sculptors, and great furniture designed by architects, interior design is not necessarily exclusively the realm of interior designers. One can perhaps discern a difference between work done by art school trained designers and those from an architectural background – Ben Kelly Design compared with Stanton Williams for instance. But these are niceties within a common undertaking, adding to its richness, complexity and strength. Art students are more knowing about art, as are secondary-mod girls about relationships, and architects are more literate, like grammar school boys.

The differentiation between designing new buildings and working with existing buildings is important and opportune for the issues raised are to some degree different. One might add that at the moment the issues to be addressed within interior design are clearer than those confronting architecture. Probably the subject consists of a set of natural antagonisms which have to be confronted and dealt with in the work. The primary questions are these: What are the conditions that govern and what are the processes of determining how much a building can be changed? How is the designer on the one hand to clarify the nature of the host building and on the other to work cogently within it and make the outcome coherent? Against this complex background it is clear that the practice of interior design requires an equal and in some aspects different knowledge of services, construction and history.

Interior design is as difficult and as slow as architecture and as equally fraught with dangers in uncertain hands. For these reasons more post-graduate courses should be established, despite the present misconceived attempts to contract design and architectural education.

As for definitions, while I hope I have been able to show that it is possible to discriminate between the distinct disciplines of architecture and interior design it is much more difficult to say where interior design ends and urban design begins.

17
Towards a New Equilibrium

Patrick Hannay and Oliver Lewis

Source: The Inside Edge, *The Designers Journal*, September 1991

Interior design does not exist. It has yet to be defined. To do so may risk ossifying what is on the edge of being a radical activity; but not to do so will leave it wallowing in its own doubts and confusions or prey to media pundits, already keen to forecast its demise.

> *Our own epoch is determining, day by day, its own style. Our eyes, unhappily, are unable yet to discern it.*
>
> Le Corbusier

Interior design will not be running away ashamed of interior decoration, nor running titleless into the arms of architecture. It will intelligently address and confront both, and more. Its identity will be a positive rebuttal and critique of a particular set of dominant architectural values. For it is no good arguing as some do that it is a fool's task to define interior design in terms of what architecture is not. Such a task on the contrary is very necessary. These dominant values need confronting for the health of environmental design in general.

Look at the photos and drawings in architectural magazines and you see what is highly valued – the middle distance, the building in relation to the horizon. The scale is 1:100 and above. Micro scale elements internally are rarely made visible and are thus implicitly not treasured or valued.

The focus of the architectural mind is to 60 years and beyond, and in that period 'time' is suspended. Day to day habitation is thus trivialised, low valued. It is the big costly fixed elements which might leak that get the attention. They require expert knowledge. It is assumed that the transient small elements and the not so transient medium sized elements close to the inhabitants' touch, do not. We are all supposedly expert at choosing sofas and rugs; low value again.

There is a prevailing tendency to put high value on universal systems. If you can reduce the door schedule to two types this is valued. Everything else becomes a 'special,' expensive to account for on the office time sheet. What is highly valued is what can be influenced by the senior partners' felt pen. The annotated conceptual sketch is treasured. The legal liability for the high value big elements is increasingly pushed out on to the subcontractor. In-house detailing becomes low value, risky, it's a self-fulfilling prophecy. The results of all this are visible everywhere. A poverty of imagination is evident beyond the first big moves. No wonder it is open house, as agencies from other fields, management consultancy, corporate identity, graphics, and furniture design colonise the vital and neglected middle and small scale aspects of buildings.

All this stacks up to form a formidable prevailing ideology. Architects continue to tolerate a shallow sort of interior design as an additional service. This is hardly surprising. Interior designers haven't done themselves any favours. You have to search long and hard for a serious historical or theoretical treatise about the design of interiors published in a periodical by a practitioner. Where do you find a respectable debate about the subject's boundaries? There isn't a professional association; the title interior designer is not legally protected, not that it necessarily needs to be but others with such titles are bound to devalue those who don't have them. Their 'conditions of engagement' are written in the same spirit as the architects' rather than starting afresh. There is little sense of a community; too much of their education is organised by architects, and they have allowed themselves to become too much associated with capitalist excesses. No wonder no one takes them seriously.

Of course elements of tomorrow's interior design exist today. Its practitioners are largely unknown. They will remain so. 'Late Show' TV producers' attempts to market the faces should be resisted. At stake is a more important goal.

When credit is due it should be offered in the context of the expressed vision of the commissioning client. The work will be particular because it identifies with the particular client's culture, and not because it offers another recognisable variation on a single 'named' designer's hidden agenda, spotted only by the cognoscenti. Interim-designers aim to be selected because clients trust their interpretations and flexibility, not because 'I want one of those.'

Interior design will continue to use existing architectural skills ecologically. It will operate in a semi-private world behind the public facades, addressing itself to particular inhabitants and to places rather than to 'the masters,' the media and the void beyond.

Most important of all it will continue to be transient or temporal, permanent or secure to the particular degree required by the circumstances. This also tends to reduce the possibility of prominence for its practitioners and confounds simplistic categorisation.

The work will revel in the passage of time; it will consciously and explicitly participate in the 'now' and the 'tomorrow'. It will enjoy the unpredictability of habitation. It will know when to embrace fashion and when to anticipate it. It will accept the concept of design redundancy on its own terms, not on the terms of those who deliberately do it to increase consumption. It will service those with excess capital and those who have had their interior design service downmarketed to be just 'rehab' or 'refurbishment,' the term architects have assigned to council tenants. It will seek out and rid our nation of a mean and patronising welfare aesthetic.

It will be wryly amused at the ridiculous notion, so often expressed, that the 'spirit of the age' and 'timelessness' are somehow compatible. It will be wary of art galleries as timeless shops or shops as timeless art galleries. Irony in such places will be explicit and provocative and the particular 'time' of the 'timelessness' made evident.

It will look outwards to all of society's signals as clues and inspiration, not inwards to an increasingly monastic language obscured by the conversation of the 'initiated'. It will embrace and respond to change not with universal systems and neutered, neutral backdrop-to-life frameworks, but by understanding and expressing unresolved conflicts, relationships and frictions. It will not be burdened by a guilt-ridden search for a utopia and universal happiness fuelled by an overweening belief in design as saviour of the world. It knows that people with a progressive vision have to carry their arguments to the populace and convince them first. Design will merely confirm that degree of agreed agenda instead of forcing it on an unwilling and unconvinced constituency. It will design 'angst' with élan in recognition of the discipline's artistic origins. It will be honest about what it cannot deliver. It will be joyously collaborative; unfussed about protectionist boundaries and legal titles; it will be inclusive of craft, design and art, exhibition and theatre, workshop and studio, corporate identity and furniture design. The practice of interior design will not be driven by the desire to carve out another specialism in the already over-specialised construction jungle. Practice will be inclusive of patrons and inhabitants.

It will revel in the micro-environment, the bits that matter close to people. It will reinstate the importance of destination and the room to rebalance design energy away from the domination of large scale circulation and spatial diagrams. Focus at 1:1 and 1:100 will be equalised.

It will be energised by a multitude of decisions made with a colossal, and changing palette of materials, artefacts and atmospheres, tuned to the appropriate culture. Each moment, element and place will be special. The architecturally favoured term 'a special' will be redundant.

Could it be that a major shift is taking place? Might the recent focus on urban design soon be balanced by a drive for that which can be used and touched? Book on shelf as well as library in city; flower, chair, desk, wall, lighting and radiator as well as landmark. A certain well known polemicist summarised – presented here with a slight shift of emphasis – what might come to pass:

There exists a mass of work conceived in the new spirit; it is to be met with particularly in individual production. [The author actually wrote 'industrial production'] . . . *Style is a unity of principle animating all work of an epoch, the result of a state of mind which has its own special character.*
Le Corbusier, *'Towards a new architecture'*

SECTION 2.2
ORGANISATION

Introduction

The organisation of an interior is a process that relies upon a number of considerations. Firstly, whether an existing building or an outline of a project yet to be built, a thorough analysis of the potential of that space is required. This involves an evaluation of the scale, composition and features of the space that are to be adapted. Secondly, the organisation of a new interior requires a complete understanding of the details of the new function. The designer needs to be fully aware of the requirements of the new occupants in order to organise the interior in a suitable manner. Finally, a coherent material strategy, with which to form a particular and appropriate spatial language, is vital. Meaningful occupation relies on a tacit understanding of the requirements of the new function, a process that informs the careful and considered arrangement of spaces that will adequately fulfil the duties of the brief. A thorough analysis of a brief, space and materials are required in order to create a suitably appropriate well-organised interior space.

This chapter explores ideas and strategies regarding the organisation of interiors. The opening essay is one of three articles featured in a set of talks called 'The Inside Edge', published in *The Designers Journal* in 1991. In 'Towards a New Aesthetic', **Drew Plunkett** outlines a desire for a socially responsive and better organised interior profession, one that acknowledges its social responsibilities. In **Robert Venturi**'s seminal book *Complexity and Contradiction in Architecture*, first published in 1966, the chapter entitled 'Inside/Outside' analysed the modern movement's orthodox position when proposing continuity between the interior and exterior of a building. Venturi suggested that the contradiction between the essential purpose of an interior, one that was to direct space, and the building's exterior, an essential purpose that is to enclose space, was the moment of tension between the two states. The threshold between interior and exterior is where, as Venturi suggests, the architectural event occurs.

First published in 1968 in the book *The System of Objects*, the French theorist **Jean Baudrillard** examined the organisation of consumer appetites in relation to the consumption of everyday household goods. The organisation of the interior through elements such as furniture, and the attainment of other household objects through advertising, allowed Baudrillard to study the organisation of notional structures of class and taste. 'Structures of Interior Design' examines the psychological imperatives of consumption in an advanced capitalistic economy. Baudrillard argues that meaning, not use, is primarily transferred through consumer objects and that the individual in effect buys a group identity and a metaphysical order with each over-determined purchase. In the seminal book, *From Translations from Drawing to Building and Other Essays* published in 1978, the essay 'Figures, Doors, Passages' by **Robin Evans** examines the organisation and development of the room and its occupation. Primarily tasked with examining interior space through figures in painting, the author explores the development of movement through interior space by examining the plans of a number of seventeenth and eighteenth century houses.

The final essay in this chapter is from **Jun'ichirō Tanizaki**'s *In Praise of Shadows*, originally published in 1933. The book offers a subtle and rewarding reflection on the importance of light and darkness in the organisation of rooms and objects in Japanese interior space. In this excerpt Tanizaki considers darkness and shadow as primary elements in the formation and organisation of interior space.

Graeme Brooker

George Ranalli (1946–)

George Ranalli opened his office in New York City in 1977. In over thirty years of existence the practice has developed a reputation for carefully crafted, elegantly realised design work, both at the scale of furniture and interiors and at a larger scale of buildings and urbanism. Both Frank Lloyd Wright and Carlo Scarpa, exemplars of highly crafted space and sophisticated detailing, inform Ranalli's work. Ranalli's most recent project is the Saratoga Avenue Community Centre in Brooklyn, NYC. The project involved the reworking of an existing community facility to provide a new, strong, durable public building, one that the community could take pride in and in turn also be proud of.

Building Study: Apartment

New York
1975
George Ranalli

The manner in which people inhabit domestic space is continually evolving. The family home has become the test-bed for innovatory interiors that accommodate new patterns of living. In small domestic spaces, the type often found in large cities where large expanses of domestic space can be out of reach financially for most of the inhabitants, a careful and considered organisation of space is required to satisfy the occupiers' requirements and expectations of their home. In a small space it can be a useful strategy to design a freestanding object that can be organised to accommodate a number of different functions. Separate activities can be collected together to form a tight single element. In a small domestic space, it can be economical to combine the seating, storage, eating, and sleeping activities together, to create one piece of furniture that can contain all of these needs.

In a tiny apartment in a warehouse in New York, George Ranalli created such a piece of furniture. He was commissioned to design a small apartment in a tiny space in a converted furniture warehouse. A new element is inserted into the apartment. It consists of a dining space below a raised sleeping platform, which is accessed by a stair that contains bookshelves, with steps that are wide and deep enough to relax upon. This concentrated element contained all the basic functions of the living space. The sleeping, dining and working areas were combined into the piece of furniture; this maximised the amount of free space, both horizontally and vertically, within the tiny flat for relaxing. Bookcases were accommodated into a set of steps that led up to the elevated bed level that in turn sheltered a small dining table and seating. The elegant autonomous object was positioned off centre, so that the kitchen could occupy the smaller space next to the door, while the larger, naturally lit area was used for lounging in. Home condensed into a petite element in a tiny space with no wastage. The scale of the host, a neutral, white walled space, informs the Ranalli element. The new element also adopts this neutral tone and is white; the space is animated by the timber stairs and the upholstered seating and of course the occupants.

The distinct object combines many of the functions necessary to create a suitable space for living.

18
Towards a New Aesthetic

Drew Plunkett

Source: The Inside Edge, *The Designers Journal*, September 1991

First an attempt at definition: community projects are perhaps those where the commissioning client's primary impulse is not to make a profit. A designer may or may not be interested in making money, although it is gratifying when virtue is seen to be rewarded.

Correspondents to this magazine suggest that interior designers can only cosmeticise honest squalor and are waiting impatiently for a return to big budget commercialism. These may be no more than expressions of resentment by those whose bandwagon is becoming crowded but they do suggest that the concept of the idealistic interior designer is not unthinkable. However idealism alone does not make good designers. The best always ignore profit margins when they sniff the possibility of a creative opportunity.

Ten years ago interior design became exciting. We set about inventing and learning a richer visual language and, because the eighties were what they were, used it to make commercial projects. Now we are bored by shops with pretensions to be galleries and no great ingenuity is required to churn out another one. A fresh excitement will be found in examining new building types and because of the economic and attitudinal changes that have come with the nineties these are less likely to be purely commercial. Public services look set to respond to residual market psychology and the concept of second class accommodation for those reclassified as 'customers' will be eroded. We now have to think about a new language, or perhaps just a dialect, something inoffensive to people who are a bit hard up, a low budget aesthetic that deals with cheaper materials and simpler means of production.

A demonstrable, almost urgent, demand already exists for community interior design. In the last year, students at Glasgow School of Art have been asked to make proposals for a community café, a job training centre, an old people's home, a prison. The requests come from publicly-funded and voluntary organisations. Students are asked because the school is seen to be approachable, very affordable and part of the community, though it should be said that any serious client might be better advised to invest modestly in a good experienced designer.

Unfortunately for many clients the process of engaging a designer remains mysterious, even when made very simple. For example, one interior designer working in London, bored with retail, approached local authorities with an offer to consider design for community spaces. Replies were all negative. Local authorities are locked into a routine of commissioning architects. Interior designers have yet to establish themselves as capable of making a distinctive, essential contribution. Designers determined to contribute may need to be devious and may even have to do some work for nothing.

At the risk of interior design defining itself again in terms of architecture, there is something encouraging to be learnt from the community architecture movement. It began at the greenest of grass roots and everyone was a volunteer. Given that few people can afford, or are inclined, to be indefinitely idealistic it is worth remembering that several architectural practices have grown from idealistic beginnings (CRHP in London, Assist in Glasgow) and that such practices have learnt to generate projects and to find finance to pay fees and build buildings.

Some manifestations of community architecture also offer a warning, about pandering to clients. Designers are not required to outrage perfectly normal people but they are obliged to offer them more than their first expectations. People do seem more relaxed about innovation in interiors than in exteriors (Prince Charles is not on record) and designers have the great advantage of being interested in revitalising well-regarded buildings. The successful rehabilitation of a decent building can generate peripheral improvement (and more work). Covent Garden is the obvious example but most cities now boast a particularly vibrant area, usually associated with shopping, centred around a building of historical significance. This is the contribution interior design can make to urban design. It can even save communities.

Over the last ten years, almost the life span of the profession in its present incarnation, there has been a pervading sense of astonishment and delight that it was all so easy, so lucrative. The regurgitation of formulaic responses to repetitive briefs encourages scepticism about interior design's capacity for a social role. But it can be done – if we take our responsibilities seriously.

19
Inside/Outside

Robert Venturi

Source: *Complexity and Contradiction in Architecture*. New York: Museum of Modern Art, 1988

The external configuration is usually rather simple, but there is packed into the interior of an organism an amazing complexity of structures which have long been the delight of anatomists.

The specific form of a plant or animal is determined not only by the genes in the organism and the cytoplasmic activities that these direct but by the interaction between genetic constitution and environment. A given gene does not control a specific trait, but a specific reaction to a specific environment.*

Contrast between the inside and the outside can be a major manifestation of contradiction in architecture. However, one of the powerful twentieth century orthodoxies has been the necessity for continuity between them: the inside should be expressed on the outside. But this is not really new—only our means have been new. The Renaissance church interior, for instance, has a continuity with its exterior; the interior vocabulary of pilasters, cornices, and drip mouldings is almost identical in scale and sometimes in material with its exterior vocabulary. The result is subtle modification but little contrast and no surprise.

Perhaps the boldest contribution of orthodox Modern architecture was its so-called flowing space, which was used to achieve the continuity of inside and outside. The idea has been emphasized by historians ranging from Vincent Scully's discovery of its early evolution in Shingle Style interiors to its flowering in the Prairie House and its culmination in De Stijl and the Barcelona Pavilion. Flowing space produced an architecture of related horizontal and vertical planes. The visual independence of these uninterrupted planes was scored by connecting areas of plate glass: windows as holes in the wall disappeared and became, instead, interruptions of wall to be discounted by the eye as a positive element of the building. Such cornerless architecture implied an ultimate continuity of space. Its emphasis on the oneness of interior and exterior space was permitted by new mechanical equipment which for the first time, made the inside thermally independent of the outside.

But the old tradition of enclosed and contrasted inside space, which I want to analyze here, has been recognized by some Modern masters, even if it has not been much emphasized by the historians. Although Wright did in fact "destroy the box" in the Prairie House, the rounded corners and solid walls of the Johnson Wax Administration Building are analogous to the diagonal and rounded corners of Borromini's interiors and those of his eighteenth century followers—and for the same purpose: to exaggerate a sense of horizontal enclosure and to promote the separateness and unity of the interior space by the continuity of the four walls. But Wright, unlike Borromini, did not puncture his continuous walls with windows. That would have weakened the bold contrast of horizontal enclosure and vertical openness. And it also would have been too traditional and structurally ambiguous for him.

The essential purpose of the interiors of buildings is to enclose rather than direct space, and to separate the inside from the outside. Kahn has said: "A building is a harboring thing." The function of the house to protect and provide privacy, psychological as well as physical, is an ancient one. The Johnson Wax Building fosters a further tradition: the expressive differentiation of the inside and outside spaces. Besides enclosing the inside with walls, Wright differentiated the interior light, an idea with a rich evolution from Byzantine, Gothic, and Baroque architecture to that of Le Corbusier and Kahn today. The inside *is* different from the outside.

But there are other valid means of differentiating and relating inside and outside space which are foreign to our recent architecture. Eliel Saarinen said that just as a building is the "organization of space in space. So is the community. So is the city."[1] I think this series could start with the idea of a room as a space in space. And I should like to apply Saarinen's definition of relationships not only to the spatial relationships of building and site, but to those of interior spaces within interior spaces. What I am talking about is the baldacchino above the altar and within the sanctuary. Another classic building of Modern architecture, again admittedly not typical, illustrates my point. The Villa Savoye with its wall openings which are, significantly, holes rather than interruptions, restricts any flowing space rigidly to the vertical direction. But there is a spatial implication beyond that of enclosure which contrasts it with the Johnson Wax Building. Its severe, almost square exterior surrounds an intricate interior configuration glimpsed through openings and from protrusions above. In this context the tense image of the Villa Savoye from within and without displays a contrapuntal resolution of severe envelope partly broken and intricate interior partly revealed. Its inside order accommodates the multiple functions of a house, domestic scale, and partial mystery inherent in a sense of privacy. Its outside order expresses the unity of the idea of house at an easy scale appropriate to the green field it dominated and possibly to the city it will one day be part of.

A building can include things within things as well as spaces within spaces. And its interior configurations can contrast with its container in other ways besides those of the Villa Savoye's.

Contradiction between the inside and the outside may manifest itself in an unattached lining which produces an additional space between the lining and the exterior wall. Plan diagrams illustrate that such layers between the inside space and the outside space can be more or less contrasting in shape, position, pattern, and size. A different material inside, wainscoting in this case, provides the contrast. The Byzantine mosaics inside the chapel of Galla Placidia represent a lining attached but contrasting in richness of texture, pattern, and color with the drab brickwork of the exterior. The pilasters, architraves, and arches of Renaissance walls, such as Bramante's façade in the Belvedere Court in the Vatican, can imply layers while the colonnade of the loggia of the south façade of the Louvre makes spatial layers. The colonnettes in the interior of the cathedral at Rouen or the disengaged pilasters in the anteroom of Syon House represent more detached kinds of layers also, but their subtle contrast to the outside depends more on scale than on form and texture. The lining becomes semidetached in Percier and Fontaine's curtained bedroom at Malmaison, which is derived from a Roman military tent. The graduated series of symbolic doors at Karnak are multiple linings in

relief similar in two dimensions to the generic idea of nests of toy eggs or wooden dolls. These doors within doors, like the multi-framed doors in Gothic porches, differ from multi-pedimented Baroque openings, which juxtapose triangular and segmental shapes.

Residual space that is open might be called "open poché." Kahn's "servant space," which sometimes harbors mechanical equipment, and the poché in the walls of Roman and Baroque architecture are alternative means of accommodating an inside different from the outside. Aldo van Eyck has said: "Architecture should be conceived of as a configuration of intermediary places clearly defined. This does not imply continual transition or endless postponement with respect to place and occasion. On the contrary, it implies a break away from the contemporary concept (call it sickness) of spatial continuity and the tendency to erase every articulation between spaces, i.e., between outside and inside, between one space and another (between one reality and another). Instead the transition must be articulated by means of defined in-between places which induce simultaneous awareness of what is significant on either side. An in-between space in this sense provides the common ground where conflicting polarities can again become twin phenomena."[2]

Residual space is sometimes awkward. Like structural poché it is seldom economic. It is always leftover, inflected toward something more important beyond itself. The qualifications, contrasts, and tensions inherent in these spaces are perhaps cogent to Kahn's statement that "a building should have bad spaces as well as good spaces."

Redundant enclosure, like crowded intricacies, is rare in our architecture. With some significant exceptions in the work of Le Corbusier and Kahn, Modern architecture has tended to ignore such complex spatial ideas. The "utility core" of Mies or early Johnson is not relevant because it becomes a passive accent in a dominant open space, rather than an active parallel to another perimeter. Contradictory interior space does not admit Modern architecture's requirement of a unity and continuity of all spaces. Nor do layers in depth, especially with contrapuntal juxtapositions, satisfy its requirements of economic and unequivocal relationships of forms and materials. And crowded intricacy within a rigid boundary (which is not a transparent framework) contradicts the modern tenet which says that a building grows from the inside out.

What are the justifications for multiple enclosure and for the inside's being different from the outside? When Wright expressed his dictum: "an organic form grows its structure out of conditions as a plant grows out of the soil, both unfold similarly from within,"[3] he had a long precedent behind him. Other Americans had advocated what was at the moment a healthy thing—a needed battle cry:

Greenough: Instead of forcing the functions of every sort of building into one general form, adopting an outward shape for the sake of the eyes or association, without references to the inner distribution, let us begin from the heart as a nucleus and work outward.[4]

Thoreau: What of architectural beauty I now see, I know has grown gradually from within outward, out of the necessities and character of the indweller.[5]

Sullivan: [The architect] must cause a building to grow naturally, logically, and poetically out of its condition.[6] . . . Outward appearances resemble inner purposes.[7]

Even Le Corbusier has written: "The plan proceeds from within to without; the exterior is the result of an interior."[8]

Designing from the outside in, as well as the inside out, creates necessary tensions, which help make architecture. Since the inside is different from the outside, the wall—the point of change—becomes an architectural event. Architecture occurs at the meeting of interior and exterior forces of use and space. These interior and environmental forces are both general and particular, generic and circumstantial. Architecture as the wall between the inside and the outside becomes the spatial record of this resolution and its drama. And by recognizing the difference between the inside and the outside, architecture opens the door once again to an urbanistic point of view.

NOTES

* Edmund W. Sinnott, *The Problem of Organic Form.* Yale University Press, New Haven, 1963.
1 Eliel Saarinen. *Search for Form.* Reinhold Publishing Corp, New York, 1948, p. 254.
2 Aldo Van Eyck. *Architectural Design 12.* Vol xxxii, December 1962, p. 602.
3 Frank Lloyd Wright. *Modern Architecture.* Princeton University Press, 1931 (front piece).
4 Horatio Greenough. *Roots of Contemporary American Architecture.* Lewis Mumford (ed). Grove Press Inc, New York, 1959, p. 37.
5 Henry David Thoreau. *Walden and other Writings.* The Modern Library. Random House, New York, 1940, p. 42.
6 Louis H. Sullivan. *Kindergarten Chats.* Wittenborn Schultz Inc, New York, 1947, p. 140.
7 Ibid, p. 43.
8 Le Corbusier. *Towards a New Architecture.* The Architectural Press, London, 1927, p. 31.

20
Structures of Interior Design

Jean Baudrillard

Source: *The System of Objects*. Translated by James Benedict. Verso: London, 1996

THE TRADITIONAL ENVIRONMENT

The arrangement of furniture offers a faithful image of the familial and social structures of a period. The typical bourgeois interior is patriarchal; its foundation is the dining-room/bedroom combination. Although it is diversified with respect to function, the furniture is highly integrated, centring around the sideboard or the bed in the middle of the room. There is a tendency to accumulate, to fill and close off the space. The emphasis is on unifunctionality, immovability, imposing presence and hierarchical labelling. Each room has a strictly defined role corresponding to one or another of the various functions of the family unit, and each ultimately refers to a view which conceives of the individual as a balanced assemblage of distinct faculties. The pieces of furniture confront one another, jostle one another, and implicate one another in a unity that is not so much spatial as moral in character. They are ranged about an axis which ensures a regular chronology of actions; thanks to this permanent symbolization, the family is always present to itself. Within this private space each piece of furniture in turn, and each room internalizes its own particular function and takes on the symbolic dignity pertaining to it – then the whole house puts the finishing touch to this integration of interpersonal relationships within the semi-hermetic family group.

All this constitutes an organism whose structure is the patriarchal relationship founded on tradition and authority, and whose heart is the complex affective relationship that binds all the family members together. Such a family home is a specific space which takes little account of any objective decorative requirements, because the primary function of furniture and objects here is to personify human relationships, to fill the space that they share between them, and to be inhabited by a soul.[1] The real dimension they occupy is captive to the moral dimension which it is their job to signify. They have as little autonomy in this space as the various family members enjoy in society. Human beings and objects are indeed bound together in a collusion in which the objects take on a certain density, an emotional value – what might be called a 'presence'. What gives the houses of our childhood such depth and resonance in memory is clearly this complex structure of interiority, and the objects within it serve for us as boundary markers of the symbolic configuration known as home. The caesura between inside and outside, and their formal opposition, which falls under the social sign of property and the psychological sign of the immanence of the family, make this traditional space into a closed transcendence. In their anthropomorphism the objects that furnish it become household gods, spatial incarnations of the emotional bonds and the permanence of the family group. These gods enjoyed a gentle immortality until the advent of a modern generation which has cast them aside, dispersed them – even, on occasion, reinstated them in an up-to-date nostalgia for whatever is old. As often with gods, furniture too thus gets a second chance to exist, and passes from a naïve utility into a cultural baroque.

THE MODERN OBJECT LIBERATED IN ITS FUNCTION

The style of furniture changes as the individual's relationships to family and society change. Corner divans and beds, coffee tables, shelving – a plethora of new elements are now supplanting the traditional range of furniture. The organization of space changes, too, as beds become day-beds and sideboards and wardrobes give way to built-in storage. Things fold and unfold, are concealed, appear only when needed. Naturally such innovations are not due to free experiment: for the most part the greater mobility, flexibility and convenience they afford are the result of an involuntary adaptation to a shortage of space – a case of necessity being the mother of invention. Whereas the old-fashioned dining-room was heavily freighted with moral convention, 'modern' interiors, in their ingeniousness, often give the impression of being mere functional expedients. Their 'absence of style' is in the first place an absence of room, and maximum functionality is a solution of last resort whose outcome is that the dwelling-place, though remaining closed to the outside, loses its internal organization. Such a restructuring of space and the objects in it, unaccompanied by any reconversion, must in the first instance be considered an impoverishment.

The modern set of furniture, serially produced, is thus apparently destructured yet not restructured, nothing having replaced the expressive power of the old symbolic order. There is progress, nevertheless: between the individual and these objects, which are now more supple in their uses and have ceased to exercise or symbolize moral constraint, there is a much more liberal relationship, and in particular the individual is no longer strictly defined through them relative to his family.[2] Their mobility and multifunctionality allow him to organize them more freely, and this reflects a greater openness in his social relationships. This, however, is only a partial liberation. So far as the serial object is concerned, in the absence of any restructuring of space, this 'functional' development is merely an emancipation, not (to go back to the old Marxian distinction) a liberation proper, for it implies *liberation from the function of the object only, not from the object itself.* Consider a nondescript, light, foldable table or a bed without legs, frame or canopy – an absolute cipher of a bed, one might say: all such objects, with their 'pure' outlines, no longer resemble even what they are; they have been stripped down to their most primitive essence as mere apparatus and, as it were, definitively secularized. What has been liberated in them – and what, in being liberated, has liberated something in man (or rather, perhaps, what man, in liberating himself, has liberated in them) – is their function. The function is no longer obscured by the moral theatricality of the old furniture; it is emancipated now from ritual, from ceremonial, from the entire ideology which used to make our surroundings into an opaque mirror of a reified human structure. Today, at last, these objects emerge absolutely clear about the purposes they serve. They are thus indeed free as *functional objects* – that is, they have the freedom to function, and (certainly so far as serial objects are concerned) that is practically the *only* freedom they have.[3]

Now, *just so long as the object is liberated only in its function, man equally is liberated only as user of that object.* This too is progress, though not a decisive turning-point. A bed is a bed, a chair is a chair, and there is no relationship between them so long as each serves only the function it is supposed to serve. And without such a relationship there can be no space, for space exists only when it is opened up, animated, invested with rhythm and expanded by a correlation between objects and a transcendence of their functions in this new structure. In a way space is the object's true freedom, whereas its function is merely its formal freedom. The bourgeois dining-room was structured, but its structure was closed. The functional environment is more open, freer, but it is destructured, fragmented into its various functions. Somewhere between the two, in the gap between integrated psychological space and fragmented functional space, serial objects have their being, witnesses to both the one and the other – sometimes within a single interior.

THE MODEL INTERIOR

Modular Components

This elusive space, which is no longer either a confined externality nor an interior refuge, this freedom, this 'style' which is indecipherable in the serial object because it is subordinated to that object's function, may nevertheless be encountered in *model interiors*, which embody a new emerging structure and a significant evolution.[4]

Leafing through such glossy magazines as *Maison Française* or *Mobilier et Décoration* [Furniture and Decoration],[5] one cannot fail to notice two alternating themes. The first reaches for the sublime, presenting houses beyond compare: old eighteenth-century mansions, miraculously well-equipped villas, Italian gardens heated by infra-red rays and populated by Etruscan statuettes – in short, the world of the unique, leaving the reader no alternative (so far as sociological generalization is concerned, at any rate) but contemplation without hope. Aristocratic models such as these, by virtue of their absolute value, are what underpin the second theme, that of modern interior decoration and furnishing. The objects and furniture proposed here, though they are high in 'status' value, do impinge on sociological reality: they are not dream creations without commercial significance but, rather, *models* in the proper sense of the word. We are no longer in a world of pure art, but in a world which (potentially, at least) is of interest to the whole of society.

These models of the home-furnishing avant-garde are organized around the basic distinction between components and seating; the practical imperative they obey is that of interior design, or syntagmatic calculation, to which may be contrasted, as seats are to components, the general concept of atmosphere.

Walls and Daylight

The rooms and the house themselves now transcend the traditional dividing-line of the wall, which formerly made them into spaces of refuge. Rooms open into one another, everything communicates, and space is broken up into angles, diffuse areas and mobile sectors. Rooms, in short, have been liberalized. Windows are no longer imposed upon the free influx of air and light – a light which used to come *from outside* and settle upon objects, illuminating them *as though from within*. Now there are quite simply no windows, and a freely intervening light has become a universal function of the existence of things. In the same way objects have lost the substantiality which was their basis, the form which enclosed them whereby man made them part of his self-image: it is now space which plays freely between them; and becomes the universal function of their relationships and their 'values'.

Mirrors and Portraits

Another symptomatic change is the disappearance of looking-glasses and mirrors. A psycho-sociology of the mirror is overdue, especially in the wake of so much metaphysics. The traditional peasant milieu had no mirrors, perhaps even feared them as somewhat eerie. The bourgeois interior, by contrast, and what remains of that interior in present-day serially produced furniture, has mirrors in profusion, hung on the walls and incorporated into wardrobes, sideboards, cabinets or panelling. As a source of light, the mirror enjoys a special place in the room. This is the basis of the ideological role it has played, everywhere in the domestic world of the well-to-do, as redundancy, superfluity, reflection: the mirror is an opulent object which affords the self-indulgent bourgeois individual the opportunity to exercise his privilege – to reproduce his own image and revel in his possessions. In a more general sense we may say that the mirror is a symbolic object which not only reflects the characteristics of the individual but also echoes in its expansion the historical expansion of individual consciousness. It thus carries the stamp of approval of an entire social order: it is no coincidence that the century of Louis XIV is epitomized by the Hall of Mirrors at Versailles, nor that, in more recent times, the spread of mirrors in apartments coincided with the spread of the triumphal Pharisaism of bourgeois consciousness, from Napoleon III to Art Nouveau. But things have changed. There is no place in the functional ensemble for reflection for its own sake. The mirror still exists, but its most appropriate place is in the bathroom, unframed. There, dedicated to the fastidious care of the appearance that social intercourse demands, it is liberated from the graces and glories of domestic subjectivity. By the same token other objects are in turn liberated from mirrors; hence, they are no longer tempted to exist in a closed circuit with their own images. For mirrors close off space, presuppose a wall, refer back to the centre of the room. The more mirrors there are, the more glorious is the intimacy of the room, albeit more turned in upon itself. The current proliferation of openings and transparent partitions clearly represents a diametrically opposed approach. (Furthermore, all the tricks that mirrors make possible run counter to the current demand for a frank use of materials.) A chain has definitely been broken, and there is a real logic to the modern approach when it eliminates not only central or over-visible light sources but also the mirrors that used to reflect them; by thus eschewing any focus on or return to a central point, it frees space of the converging squint which gave bourgeois décor – much like bourgeois consciousness in general – such a crosseyed view of itself.[6]

TOWARDS A SOCIOLOGY OF INTERIOR DESIGN?

It is the whole world of *Stimmung* that has disappeared, the world of 'natural' harmony between movements of the emotions and the presence of things: an internalized atmosphere as opposed to the externalized atmosphere of modern 'interiors'. Today, value resides neither in appropriation nor in intimacy but in information, in inventiveness, in control, in a continual openness to objective messages – in short, in the syntagmatic calculation which is, strictly speaking, the foundation of the discourse of the modern home-dweller.

The entire conception of decoration has changed too. Traditional good taste, which decided what was beautiful on the basis of secret affinities, no longer has any part here. That taste constituted a poetic discourse, an evocation of self-contained objects that responded to one another; today objects do not respond to one another, they communicate – they have no individual presence but merely, at best, an overall coherence attained by virtue of their simplification as components of a code and the way their relationships are calculated. An unrestricted combinatorial system enables man to use them as the elements of his structural discourse.

In the case of serial objects, the possibilities of this functional discourse are reduced. Objects and furniture of this kind are dispersed elements whose syntactic links are not evident; to the degree that they are arranged in a calculated way, the organizing principle is penury, and the objects appear impoverished in their abstraction. This is a necessary abstraction, however, for it provides the basis, at the level of the model, for the homogeneity of the elements in functional interaction. First of all man must stop mixing himself up with things and investing them with his own image; he will then be able, beyond the utility they have for him, to project onto them his game plan, his calculations, his discourse, and invest these manoeuvres themselves with the sense of a message to others, and a message to oneself. By the time this point is reached the mode of existence of 'ambient' objects will have changed completely, and *a sociology of furnishing will perforce have given way to a sociology of interior design.*[7]

MAN THE INTERIOR DESIGNER

We are beginning to see what the new model of the home-dweller looks like: 'man the interior designer' is neither an owner nor a mere user – rather, he is an active engineer of atmosphere. Space is at his disposal like a kind of distributed system, and by controlling this space he holds sway over all possible reciprocal relations between the objects therein, and hence over all the roles they are capable of assuming. (It follows that he must also be 'functional' himself: he and the space in question must be homogeneous if his messages of design are to leave him and return to him successfully.) What matters to him is neither possession nor enjoyment but responsibility, in the strict sense which implies that it is at all times possible for him to determine 'responses'. His praxis is exclusively external. This modern home-dweller does not 'consume' his objects. (Here again, 'taste' no

longer has the slightest part to play, for in both its meanings it refers us back to self-contained objects whose form contains an 'edible' substance, so to speak, which makes them susceptible of internalization.) Instead of consuming objects, he dominates, controls and orders them. He discovers himself in the manipulation and tactical equilibration of a system.

What we glimpse today in modern interiors is the coming end of this order of Nature; what is appearing on the horizon, beyond the break-up of form, beyond the dissolution of the formal boundary between inside and outside and of the whole dialectic of being and appearance relating to that boundary, is a qualitatively new kind of relationship, a new kind of objective responsibility. As directly experienced, the project of a technological society implies putting the very idea of genesis into question and omitting all the origins, received meanings and 'essences' of which our old pieces of furniture remained concrete symbols; it implies practical computation and conceptualization on the basis of a total abstraction, the notion of a world no longer given but instead produced – mastered, manipulated, inventoried, controlled: a world, in short, that has to be *constructed.*[8]

NOTES

1 They may also have taste and style – or not, as the case may be.
2 We cannot help but wonder, however, whether he is not henceforward strictly defined through them relative to society at large. On this point, see 'Models and Series' below.
3 Similarly, the bourgeois and industrial revolution gradually freed the individual from his involvement with religion, morality and family. He thus acceded to a freedom in law as an individual, but also to an actual freedom as labour-power – that is, the freedom to sell himself as labour-power. This parallel has nothing coincidental about it, for there is a profound correlation here: both the serially produced 'functional' object and the social individual are liberated in their 'functional' objectification, not in their singularity or in their totality as object or person.
4 In other words, these things happen at a privileged level. And there is a sociological and a social problem with the fact that a restricted group should have the concrete freedom to present itself, through its objects and furniture,

as a model in the eyes of an entire society. This problem will be addressed later, however – see 'Models and Series' below.

5 A glossy magazine devoted to mass-produced products is unthinkable, the only appropriate form here being a catalogue.

6 The mirror occasionally makes a comeback, but it does so in a baroque cultural mode, as a secondary object – a romantic looking-glass, say, or an antique or bull's-eye mirror. The function is no longer the same (and will be addressed below apropos of antiques in general).

7 Roland Barthes describes this new stage as it affects cars:

> . . . the uniformity of models seems to belie the very idea of technical performance, so 'normal' driving becomes the only possible field in which phantasies of power and invention can be invested. The car thus transfers its phantasied power to a specific set of practices. Since we can no longer tinker with the object itself, we are reduced to tinkering with the way it is driven . . . it is no longer the car's forms and functions that call forth human dreams but, rather, its handling, and before long, perhaps, we shall be writing not a mythology of the automobile but a mythology of driving. ('La voiture, projection de l'ego', *Réalités,* no. 213, October 1963)

8 As a matter of fact this model of praxis emerges clearly only when a high technical level has been attained, or in the context of very advanced everyday objects, such as tape recorders, cars or household appliances, whose dials, dashboards or control panels bespeak the degree of mastery and coordination required to operate them. It should be noted that everyday life is still very largely governed by the traditional forms of praxis.

21
Figures, Doors, Passages

Robin Evans

Source: *Translations from Drawing to Building and Other Essays*. AA Documents, 1997

Ordinary things contain the deepest mysteries. At first it is difficult to see in the conventional layout of a contemporary house anything but the crystallization of cold reason, necessity and the obvious, and because of this we are easily led into thinking that a commodity so transparently unexceptional must have been wrought directly from the stuff of basic human needs. Indeed, practically all housing studies, whatever their scope, are founded on this assumption. 'The struggle to find a home', declares a prominent expert, 'and the desire for the shelter, privacy, comfort and independence that a house can provide, are familiar the world over.'[1] From such a vantage-point the characteristics of modern housing appear to transcend our own culture, being lifted to the status of universal and timeless requisites for decent living. This is easily enough explained, since everything ordinary seems at once neutral and indispensable, but it is a delusion, and a delusion with consequences too, as it hides the power that the customary arrangement of domestic space exerts over our lives, and at the same time conceals the fact that this organization has an origin and a purpose. The search for privacy, comfort and independence through the agency of architecture is quite recent, and even when these words first came into play and were used in relation to household affairs, their meanings were quite different from those we now understand. So the following article is a rather crude and schematic attempt to uncover just one of the secrets of what is now so ordinary.

THE PLAN AND ITS OCCUPANTS

If anything is described by an architectural plan, it is the nature of human relationships, since the elements whose trace it records – walls, doors, windows and stairs – are employed first to divide and then selectively to re-unite inhabited space. But what is generally absent in even the most elaborately illustrated building is the way human figures will occupy it. This may be for good reasons, but when figures do appear in architectural drawings, they tend not to be substantial creatures but emblems, mere signs of life, as, for example, the amoebic outlines that turn up in 'Parker-Morris' layouts.

Surely, though, if the circle were widened to take in material beyond architectural drawings, one might expect there to be some tally between the commonplaces of house-planning and the ordinary ways in which people dispose themselves in relation to each other. This might seem an odd connection to make at first, but however different they are – however realistic and particular the descriptions, pictures or photographs of men, women, children and other domestic animals doing what they do, however abstract and diagrammatic the plans – both relate back to the same fundamental issue of human relationships.

Take the portrayal of human figures and take house plans from a given time and place: look at them together as evidence of a way of life, and the coupling between everyday conduct and architectural organization may become more lucid. That is the simple method adopted in what follows, and that is the hope contained in it.

THE MADONNA IN A ROOM

The work of Raphael as painter and architect offers a convenient opening into the subject, if only because it gives a clear indication that the ideal of secluded domesticity is rather more local than we are inclined to think. Of course this is not an attempt to review Raphael's entire work; the intention is simply to extract from his art and architecture the evidence of a particular *temperament towards others* which is implicit in it and indicative of the time, not just in art but in daily transactions.

During the Italian High Renaissance the interplay of figures in space began to dominate painting.

Previous to this, the fascination with the human body had centred on physiological detail: the articulation of limbs, the modelling of sinew, flesh and muscle, and the rendering of individual comeliness. It was only in the sixteenth century that bodies were attenuated into the graceful or magnified into the sublime, then brought together in peculiarly intense, carnal, even lascivious poses by Leonardo, Michelangelo, Raphael and their followers. Subject-matter, too, was often modified in favour of this new conception. The treatment of the Virgin and Child illustrates this well.

So if the tally between figures and plans is to be sought anywhere, it might as well be sought here, in a painting where personal relationships were translated into a compositional principle transcending subject-matter, and where solicitations between saints and mortals alike seem so exaggerated to us – or rather they would do so if we were to think of them as plausible illustrations of conduct.

In 1518 or 1519 Cardinal Giuliano de' Medici commissioned an ambitious project for a villa sited on the slopes of Monte Mario in Rome. Only part of this vast scheme, later to be called the Villa Madama, was completed. The supervision of the work was carried out by Antonio da Sangallo, but the conception was unquestionably Raphael's. Here, then, was a sumptuous setting for daily life produced by an artist who had helped to desecrate the Virgin in his paintings. A laboured reconstruction of the villa published by Percier and Fontaine in 1809 emphasized axial symmetries, making the whole complex into one unified pile of building stuck into the hillside, adjusting the layout of rooms to fit what was, at that time, the established idea of strict classical conformity. How could Raphael have designed it any other way?[2] Yet the portion that was actually built, and the earliest surviving plan,[3] show something quite different.

Overall symmetry would have created repetitions, with each room and each situation having its mirrored counterpart on the other side of the building, but in the early plan this never occurs. Although most spaces within the villa were symmetrically composed, there were no duplications; every room was different. Uniformity was restricted to the parts where it could be immediately apprehended; the building as a whole was diverse. Yet, despite this striving to create singularity of place, it is very difficult to tell from the plan which parts are enclosed, and which are open, as the relationship between all the spaces is much the same throughout. The chambers, loggias, courts

and gardens all register as walled shapes – like large rooms – which add up to fill the site. The building seems to have been conceived as an accumulation of these enclosures, with the component spaces being more regular than the overall pattern. This could not have come from the ultimately classical Raphael dreamed up by eighteenth-century academicians and preyed upon by nineteenth-century romantics.

DOORS

Looking at the Villa Madama plan as a picture of social relationships, two organizational characteristics become apparent. Though numbered amongst the things we would nowadays never do, these are crucially important evidence of the social milieu the villa was meant to sustain.

First, the rooms have more than one door – some have two doors, many have three, others four – a feature which, since the early years of the nineteenth century, has been regarded as a fault in domestic buildings of whatever kind or size. Why? The answer was given at great length by Robert Kerr. In a characteristic warning he reminded readers of The Gentleman's House (1864) of the wretched inconvenience of 'thoroughfare rooms', which made domesticity and retirement unobtainable. The favoured alternative was the terminal room, with only one strategically placed door into the rest of the house.[4]

Yet exactly the opposite advice had been furnished by the Italian theorists who, following ancient precedent, thought that more doors in a room were preferable to fewer. Alberti, for instance, after drawing attention to the great variety and number of doors in Roman buildings, said, 'It is also convenient to place the doors in such a Manner that they may lead to as many Parts of the edifice as possible.'[5] This was specifically recommended for public buildings, but applied also to domestic arrangements. It generally meant that there was a door wherever there was an adjoining room, making the house a matrix of discrete but thoroughly interconnected chambers. Raphael's plan exemplifies this, though it was in fact no more than ordinary practice at the time.

So, between the Italians and Kerr, there had been a complete inversion of a simple notion about convenience. In sixteenth-century Italy a convenient room had many doors; in nineteenth-century England a convenient room had but one. The change was important not only because it necessitated a rearrangement of the entire house, but also because it radically recast the pattern of domestic life.

Along with the limiting of doors came another technique aimed at minimizing the necessary intercourse between the various members of a household: the systematic application of independent access. In the Villa Madama, as in virtually all domestic architecture prior to 1650, there is no qualitative distinction between the way through the house and the inhabited spaces within it. The main entrance is at the southern extremity of the villa. A semicircular flight of steps leads through a turreted wall into a forecourt, up another flight of steps into a columned hill, through a vaulted passage into the central circular court; thus far a prescribed sequence through five spaces preliminary to the more specific and intimate areas of the household. From the circular court, however, there are ten different routes into the villa apartments, none with any particular predominance. Five lead directly off the court or its annexes, three go via the magnificent loggia with the walled garden beyond, and two via the belvedere. Once inside it is necessary to pass from one room to the next, then to the next, to traverse the building. Where passages and staircases are used, as inevitably they are, they nearly always connect just one space to another and never serve as general distributors of movement. Thus, despite the precise architectural containment offered by the addition of room upon room, the villa was, in terms of occupation, an open plan relatively permeable to the numerous members of the household,[6] all of whom – men, women, children, servants and visitors – were obliged to pass through a matrix of connecting rooms where the day-to-day business of life was carried on. It was inevitable that paths would intersect during the course of a day, and that every activity was liable to intercession unless very definite measures were taken to avoid it. As with the multiplying of doors, there was nothing unusual about this; it was the rule in Italian palaces, villas and farms – a customary way of joining rooms that hardly affected the style of architecture (which could equally well be gothic or vernacular), but most certainly affected the style of life.

From the Italian writers who described contemporary events, nothing is more evident than the large numbers of people who congregated to pass the time, watch, discuss, work or eat, and the relative frequency of recountable incident amongst them. At one end of the spectrum of manners, Castiglione, a close friend of Raphael, recorded in *The Courtier* four consecutive evening conversations supposed to have taken place during March 1507 at the Ducal Palace of Urbino (itself an example of the matrix planning described above). Nineteen men and four women participated and apparently there were similar gatherings every day after supper.[7] No doubt *The Courtier* was a purified, elaborated and sentimentalized account of actual events, but the portrayal of the group as a natural recourse for passing the time is in perfect accord with other sources. It is known that the majority of characters were palace guests at the time.

The nether end of the spectrum was described by Cellini (1500–71) in his autobiography. The passionate, violent and intemperate creatures in this work hardly resemble the refined, witty conversationalists in the other: so vivid is the contrast, they could easily be mistaken for separate species. Yet Cellini, like Castiglione, required an active flow of characters on whom to impress his own illimitable ego. In both, company was the ordinary condition and solitude the exceptional state.

There is another telling similarity which at first seems to contradict the gist of this article; neither writer ever described a place. In *The Courtier* a few hyperbolic sentences suffice to eulogize the Urbino Palace, one of the great works of Italian Renaissance architecture, and not one word is said from beginning to end, either directly or indirectly, about the appearance, contents, form or arrangements of the apartments which serve as the setting. This is all the more strange because Castiglione likened himself to a painter of a scene in his preamble. Cellini's autobiography, too, is so packed with relationships of enmity, love, ambition and exploitation that they entirely fill the space of his book. He locates events by saying where they occurred, but these indications are like references to a mental map. No landscape or cityscape is mentioned in even the most cursory terms. Topography, architecture and furnishings are likewise absent, not even raised as backdrops to the intrigues, cabals, triumphs and catastrophes that he recites. Here are the most explicit references to architecture outside of his solitary confinement in the Castello S. Angelo. The first is an account of the circumstances surrounding a robbery:

> . . . as was only fitting at the age of twenty-nine, I had taken a charming and very beautiful young girl as my maidservant . . . Because of this, I had my room at quite a distance from where the workmen slept, and also some way from the shop. I kept the young girl in a tiny ramshackle bedroom adjoining mine. I used to sleep very heavily and deeply . . . So it happened when one night a thief broke into the shop.

The second is an attempt to engineer a reconciliation with a patron while bedridden:

> I had myself carried to the Medici Palace, up to where the little terrace is: they left me resting there, waiting for the Duke to come past. A good few friends of mine from the court came up and chatted with me.

The third describes a confrontation with a potential assassin:

> I left home in a hurry, though as usual I was well armed, and I strode along Strada Giulia not expecting to meet anyone at this time of day. I had reached the end of the street, and was turning towards the Farnese Palace – giving the corner a wide berth as usual – when I saw the Corsican stand up and walk into the middle of the road.[8]

Rarely did architecture penetrate into the narrative and then only as an integral feature of some misadventure or encounter. The Cellini autobiography and *The Courtier* share a total absorption with the dynamics of human intercourse to the exclusion of all else, and that is why their physical setting is so hard to discern.

The same predominance of figure over ground, the same over-whelming of objects by animation, can be observed in painting.

All of this raises an unexpected difficulty: it is not easy to explain how, when the Italians were so wrapped up in human affairs, they developed a refined, elaborate architecture which they hardly had time to notice and which seemed to lie outside the orbit of social life. Perhaps that is an exaggeration, but the paradox remains. The marvellous modelling and exquisite decoration of the Villa Madama loggia based on Nero's Golden House and the combined work of Raphael, Giulio Romano and Giovanni da Udine, cannot be explained by the urge to impress or in terms of iconography alone. These must have played their part, but such sensibility to form does not issue from status or symbolism like water from a tap. However, it could be that the incidental and accessory nature of architecture was precisely what led it to become so visually rich. Of all the senses, sight is the most appropriate for things at the boundary of experience, and that is exactly what a room, particularly a large room, provides; an edge to perception. In the immediate precincts of the body, the other senses prevail.

The examples given above, though hardly furnishing a proof, serve to indicate that the fondness for company, proximity and incident in sixteenth-century Italy corresponded nicely enough with the format of architectural plans. It is perhaps too easy for historians of domestic architecture to look back and see in the matrix of connected rooms a primitive stage of planning that begged for evolution into something more differentiated, since little attempt was made to arrange the parts of the building into independently functioning sets or to distinguish between 'serving' and 'served'. But this was not the absence of principle: for all the different sizes, shapes and circumstances of the rooms in the Villa Madama, the connectivity was the same throughout. This did not happen by accident. It, too, was a principle. And maybe the reason why it was not thrown into high relief by theorists was simply that it was never put in question.[9]

PASSAGES

The history of the corridor as a device for removing traffic from rooms has yet to be written. From the little evidence I have so far managed to glean, it makes its first recorded appearance in England at Beaufort House, Chelsea, designed around 1597 by John Thorpe.[10] While evidently still something of a curiosity, its power was beginning to be recognized, for on the plan was written 'A longe Entry through all'. And as Italianate architecture became established in England so, ironically enough, did the central corridor, while at the same time staircases began to be attached to the corridors and no longer terminated in rooms.

After 1630 these changes of internal arrangement became very evident in houses built for the rich. Entrance hall, grand open stair, passages and back stairs coalesced to form a penetrating network of circulation space which touched every major room in the household. The most thoroughgoing application of this novel arrangement was at Coleshill, Berkshire (c. 1650–67) built by Sir Roger Pratt for his cousin. Here passages tunnelled through the entire length of the building on every floor. At the ends were back stairs; in the centre, a grand staircase in a double-storey entrance hall which, despite its portentous treatment, was really no more than a vestibule, since the inhabitants lived their lives on the other side of its walls.

Every room had a door into the passage or into the hall. In his book of architecture Pratt maintained that the 'common way in the middle through the whole length of the house' was to prevent 'the offices [i.e. utility rooms] from one molesting the other by continual passing through them' and, in the rest of the house, to ensure that 'ordinary servants may never publicly appear in passing to and fro for their occasions there'.[11]

According to him, the passage was for servants: to keep them out of each other's way and, more important still, to keep them out of the way of gentlemen and ladies. There was nothing new in this fastidiousness, the novelty was in the conscious employment of architecture to dispel it – a measure in part of the antagonism between rich and poor in turbulent times, but also an augury of what was to render household life placid in years to come.

As to the main apartments, they were to be enfiladed into as long a vista of doors as could be obtained. The corridor was not, therefore, an exclusive means of access at this time, but was installed parallel to interconnecting rooms. Even so, at Coleshill the corridor predominated to the extent of becoming a necessary route through a large part of the house. A more elegant plan, balancing the two types of circulation, was John Webb's Amesbury House, Wiltshire, where the central passage served the whole house, while all the rooms, on the principal floor at least, were also interconnected. From these plans it can be seen how the introduction of the through-passage into a domestic architecture first inscribed a deeper division between the upper and lower ranks of society by maintaining direct sequential access for the privileged family circle while consigning servants to a limited territory always adjacent to, but never within the house proper; where they were always on hand, but never present unless required.

Its effects were even more pervasive than this would suggest. The architectural solution to the servant problem (the problem of their presence being part of their service, that is) had wider ramifications. With Pratt a similar caution can be detected in all matters relating to 'interference', as if from the architect's point of view all the occupants of a house, whatever their social standing, had become nothing but a potential source of irritation to each other. It is true that he made the magnanimous gesture of putting doors between some of the rooms at Coleshill, as noted above, but then he did so explicitly to obtain the visual effect of a receding perspective through the whole house:

> As to the smaller doors within, let them all lie in a direct line one against another out of one room into another so that they being all open you may see from one end of the house to the other; answerable to which if the windows be placed at each end, the vista of the whole will be so much the more pleasant.[12]

Accordingly, the integration of household space was now for the sake of beauty, its separation was for convenience – an opposition which has since become deeply engraved into theory, creating two distinct standards of judgement for two quite separate realities: on the one hand, an extended concatenation of spaces to flatter the eye (the most easily deceived of the senses, according to contemporary writers); on the other, a careful containment and individual compartments in which to preserve the self from others.

This split between an architecture to look through and an architecture to hide in cut an unbridgeable gap dividing commodity from delight, utility from beauty, and function from form. Of course in Raphael's work the distinction between those aspects of architecture affecting daily intercourse and those concerned solely with visual form can just as easily be made. What is so different is that in his work they were in general accord with one another, whereas at Coleshill they began to pull in quite contrary directions.

Why the innovation of independent access should have come about at all is not yet clear. Certainly it indicated a change of mood concerning the desirability of exposure to company; whether exposure to all in the house, or to just some, was at this point a matter of emphasis. Its sudden and purposeful application to domestic planning shows that it did not turn up at the end of a long, predictable evolutionary development of vernacular forms, as is often alleged, nor did it have anything to do with the importation of the Italian style or Palladianism, though these were its vehicles. It came apparently out of the blue.

These were the years when the puritans talked of 'armouring' the self against a naughty world. They of course meant spiritual armour, but here was another sort, outside of body and soul: the room made into a closet. The story of Cotton Mather, a New England puritan, gives some idea of how hard it is to distinguish morality from sensibility in this voluntary sequestration. He was said to have made it a rule 'never to enter any company . . . without endeavouring to be useful in it', dropping, as opportunities arose, instructive hints, cautions or reproofs. He was later portrayed as a domestic paragon, 'doing all the good in his power to his brothers, sisters and servants'. But in order to do so much good he found it best to avoid the paying or receiving of any unnecessary or 'impertinent' visits. To prevent useless intrusions, he inscribed in large letters above the door of his room these admonitory words: 'BE SHORT'.[13]

Dividing the house into two domains – an inner sanctuary of inhabited, sometimes disconnected rooms, and an unoccupied circulation space – worked in the same way as Mather's sign, making it difficult to justify entering any room where you had no specific business. With this came a recognizably modern definition of privacy, not as the answer to a perennial problem of 'convenience', but quite possibly as a way of fostering a nascent psychology in which the self was, for the first time, felt to be not just at risk in the presence of others, but actually disfigured by them.

There was a commonplace analogy in seventeenth-century literature that compared a man's soul to a privy chamber,[14] but it is hard to tell now which became more private first, the room or the soul. Certainly, their histories are entwined.

All the same, the logic of containment was not pursued with any rigour during the eighteenth century. Large households tended to follow the pattern of Amesbury, attempting to reconcile independent access and interconnection by providing both, though rarely in as methodical a way. Only at the approach of the nineteenth century was there a move back toward greater systematization of access, observable for example in the plans of Soane and Nash. In this respect Soane's work, perhaps more than that of any other architect, lies on the edge of modernity.

Soane, like Pratt, contrived vistas from his interiors, only he was not content with the aligning of doors. He also layered space upon space, so that the eye was no longer constrained into a telescopic recession of portals and could wander wide, up, across and through from one place to another. Or to be more exact, this was the architectural effect he was able to achieve in his own house at Lincoln's Inn Fields: in other people's houses, the yearning for extension was often held in check by an equal persuasion that all rooms should be sufficiently enclosed to be independent of one another for the purposes of daily use. As the room closed in, so the aesthetic of space unfolded, as if the extensive liberty of the eye were a consolation for the closer confinement of body and soul; a form of compensation which was to become more familiar and more pronounced in twentieth-century architecture. Thus, when characteristically Soanian vistas occurred, they did so most often in circulation space or out of windows, not in occupied space. As at Coleshill, the most studied and impressive parts were generally stairs, landings, halls and vestibules – spaces which housed nothing but the way from one place to another, together with ensigns of occupation in the form of statuary or paintings.

Half a century later, when Robert Kerr was informing his readership of the perils attending thoroughfare rooms, the issue had been resolved once and for all: the corridor and the universal requirement of privacy were firmly established and principles of planning could be advanced with more or less equal application to all dwellings in all circumstances: large houses, small houses, servant quarters, family apartments, rooms for business, for leisure – these discriminations were subsidiary to the key distinction between route and destination that would henceforth pervade domestic planning. Kerr made diagrams that reduced house plans to these two categories of trajectory and position, proposing that their proper arrangement was the substratum upon which both architecture and domesticity were to be raised.

On the face of it, there would seem to be little difference between the complaints made by Alberti, who valued privacy far more than did the sixteenth-century theorists, and those in Kerr's book about the irritations of daily life. Both deplore the mixing of servants and family, the racket of children, and the prattle of women.

The real difference was the way architecture was used to overcome these annoyances. For Alberti, it was a matter of arranging proximity within the matrix of rooms. The expedients of installing a heavy door with a lock, or of locating the household's most tiresome members and most offensive activities at the greatest distance served his purpose, and these were conceived of as secondary adjustments to bring harmony to the cacophony of home life rather than silence it. Kerr, for his part, mobilized architecture in its entirety against the possibility of commotion and distraction, bringing to bear a range of tactics involving the meticulous planning and furnishing of each part of the building under a general strategy of compartmentalization on the one hand, coupled with universal accessibility on the other.

Oddly enough, universal accessibility was as necessary an adjunct to privacy as was the one-door room. A compartmentalized building had to be organized by the movement through it, because movement was the one remaining thing that could give it any coherence. If it were not for the paths making the hyphen between departure and arrival, things would have fallen apart in complete irrelation. With connected rooms, the situation had been quite different. There, movement through architectural space was by filtration rather than canalization, which meant that although great store might be set on sequential passage from one place to the next, movement was not necessarily a generator of form. Considering the difference in terms of composition, one might say that, with the matrix of connected rooms, spaces would tend to be defined and subsequently joined like the pieces of a quilt, whilst with the compartmentalized plans the connections would be laid down as a basic structure to which spaces could then be attached like apples to a tree.[15]

Hence, in the nineteenth century, 'thoroughfares' could be regarded as the backbone of a plan not only because corridors looked like spines, but because they differentiated functions by joining them via a separate distributor, in much the same way as the vertebral column structures the body: 'The relation of rooms to each other being the relationship of their doors, the sole purpose of the thoroughfares is to bring these doors into a proper system of communication.'[16]

This advanced anatomy made it possible to overcome the restrictions of adjacency and localization. No longer was it necessary to pass serially through the intractable occupied territory of rooms, with all the diversion, incidents and accidents that they might harbour. Instead, the door of any room would deliver you into a network of routes from which the room next door and the furthest extremity of the house were almost equally accessible. In other words these thoroughfares were able to draw distant rooms closer, but only by disengaging those near at hand. And in this there is another glaring paradox: in facilitating communication, the corridor reduced contact. What this meant was that purposeful or necessary communication was facilitated while incidental communication was reduced, and contact, according to the lights of reason and the dictates of morality, was at best incidental and distracting, at worst corrupting and malignant.

BODIES IN SPACE

Since the middle of the nineteenth century there have been no great changes in domestic planning – only accentuations, modifications and restatements, at least until very recently. Neither the radical Victorian medievalists nor the modernists made any noticeable attempt to go back or forward from the accepted conventions of the nineteenth century, despite reams of bombast from each quarter on the great improvements in daily life that would ensue either from the complete rejection of industrial production or from its wholesale affirmation; it did not matter much which, because medievalists and modernists shared a conviction that deliverance lay

in the way the house was built. Thus the social aspect of architecture, which surfaced for the first time as an integral feature of theory and criticism, was more concerned with the fabrication of buildings than with their occupation.

And so with the house considered first and foremost as an item of production, the stage was set for the arrival of 'housing' in the current sense of the term (housing, as has recently been pointed out, is an activity, not a place).[17] Emphasis shifted from the nature of the place to the procedures of its assembly. Nevertheless, beneath this or that revolutionary, workmanlike programme of reconstruction, the house itself remained unaltered in all its essentials. Because of the undeniable dynamism of the modern movement and the crusading utopianism of the arts and crafts movement, this has tended to be overlooked.

The Red House at Bexley Heath by William Morris and Philip Webb is the set-piece of craft revivalism. It was begun in 1859, not long after Morris had completed his only easel painting, *La Belle Iseut*. The real subject of both these works was Morris's new wife, Jane. Isolde was her portrait and the Red House was to be her setting, an altogether romantic project in which Morris sought a medieval authenticity to replace the stylistic shams of contemporary gothic and Elizabethan. Yet his commitment to past practice only went so far. The morality of craft and beauty might transform the procedures of building and the appearance of the finished work, but medievalism did not percolate into the plan, which was categorically Victorian and utterly unlike anything built in the fourteenth or fifteenth centuries. Indeed the Red House illustrates the principles laid down by the bourgeois Robert Kerr better than Kerr's own plans: rooms never interconnect, never have more than one door, and circulation space is unified and distinct.

So even though Morris was regarded as a bohemian, a radical leading an unorthodox life, flaunting bourgeois standards, the planning of the Red House was perfectly contemporary and conventional: its eccentricities lay elsewhere.

Not that Morris refused to pursue medievalism to the point where it would change men's lives. Even at this early date the idea was at the core of his work. What he envisaged, however, was not so much a change as a transfiguration; a fulfilment of medieval literary idealizations rather than a recreation of medieval conditions of life. These were idealizations of extreme spirituality, so it is not altogether surprising that the more carnal aspects of medievalism, such as interconnecting rooms, had been subtracted from his architecture. When he later moved to a genuine medieval house at Kelmscott he accepted such things with a show of bravado:

> The first floor . . . has the peculiarity of being without passages, so that you have to go from one room into another to the confusion of some of our casual visitors, to whom a bed in the close neighbourhood of a sitting room is a dire impropriety. Braving this terror we must pass through . . .[18]

But though it may have been a good test of squeamishness, he found nothing else to commend it.

Similar expurgations were made in his poetry and painting. In *La Belle Iseut*, as in a great deal of Victorian art, the body was treated as a sign of its invisible occupant. Jane, in the guise of the legendary heroine, was turned into a languid effigy of an overwrought spirit, radiating that peculiar Pre-Raphaelite loveliness through her listless, distracted expression and lethargic posture. The soul might overflow with febrile energy but the body had been abandoned to lassitude. Everything in the painting is emblematic, more like a still-life than an illustration of an event. As in Raphael's *Madonna*, the room is barely decipherable, but now for quite different reasons. The space has not been eclipsed by a tangle of figures. In Morris's picture, furniture, fittings, drapes, ornaments and other objects, not figures, stand in the way. They, too, are there as emanations of an exquisite psyche, symbolizing a life but not engaging with it in any way. In the heroine's absence this display of lovingly embellished articles would represent her well enough. Her physical isolation from others was in any case complete, and these items served as her proxy.

No wonder that the apostles of modernity, who also expressed an unfathomable distaste for the stultifying oppressiveness of nineteenth-century family life, were left with only two possibilities. The first was to dissipate the clammy heat of intimate relationships by collectivizing them; the second, more applicable to the house, as it turned out, was to atomize and individualize and separate each person yet further. Here were two solutions, the one ultimately politic, the other ultimately private. From a certain angle they appear remarkably alike, so it was quite logical for Le Corbusier, Hilberseimer and the constructivists to use the individual private cell as the basic building block for entire new cities in which all other facilities would be collectivized.[19]

After the brave rhetoric and utopian visions, more pedestrian investigations with less exalted aims would continue, in the name of modernity, the effort undertaken a century earlier – only now even the Victorians were taken to task for their salacious domestic arrangements. 'The Functional House for Frictionless Living' was designed from researches carried out for a German housing agency in 1928 by Alexander Klein, who compared his proposal with an odious, if typical, nineteenth-century layout.[20] Flow-line diagrams revealed the superiority of Klein's improved plans. In the nineteenth-century example, the 'necessary movements' of persons from room to room cross and intersect like rails in a shunting yard, but in the House for Frictionless Living they remain entirely distinct and do not touch at all; paths literally never cross. The journey between bed and bath – where trod the naked to enact the rawest acts of the body – was treated with particular caution and isolated from all other routes. The justification for Klein's plan was the metaphor hidden in its title, which implied that all accidental encounters caused friction and therefore, threatened the smooth running of the domestic machine: a delicately balanced and sensitive device it was too, always on the edge of malfunction. But however attenuated this logic appears to be, it is nevertheless the logic now buried in the regulations, codes, design methods and rules-of-thumb which account for the day-to-day production of contemporary housing.

There is not much difference between Klein's terror of bodies in collision and Samuel Butler's description of the nausea of touch, except that Butler records experience while Klein defines it. Nor is there much distance between Butler's sour point of view and the condemning of all intimacy as a form of violence, all relationships as forms of bondage – and it is really in this direction that we have advanced from the nineteenth century, finding liberty always in the escape from the tyranny of 'society'. It is exactly the word 'bondage' that Dr R. D. Laing now uses to describe, in terms of radical psychiatry, the knots and binds that tie us to other people.[21] What better than to untie them? And it is the above passage from *The Way of All Flesh* that Edward Hall now uses to examine, from the standpoint of proxemics,[22] the psychological response to intrusions into personal space, a territorial envelope in which we are said to shroud our bodies against the assaults of intimacy.[23] What better than to design things so that no such violations would ever occur? In these and in many other behavioural and psychological studies, attempts are being made to categorize only recently conceived and nurtured sensibilities as if they were immutable laws of an incontrovertible reality. But perhaps before they are definitively classified by the 'Linnaeus of human bondage',[24] those same sensibilities will have sunk once more into oblivion, taking with them their counterparts in architecture.

As yet, however, no way of altering the modern arrangement of domestic space has been found; true, there are some very interesting recent projects which flaunt the principles, rules and methods that combine to fix the normal dwelling; true, there are many more which extrapolate the same principles, rules and methods, either for the sake of irony and parody or in the vain hope of discovering their ultimate value, but they tend to be offered as commentaries on reality, as alternatives to convention, as eccentric investigations or as momentary escapes from the necessary banality of ordinariness. We still do not have the courage to confront the ordinary as such. Yet for all that, the increasing number of attempts to circumvent it signify that we may well be approaching the outer edge, not just of the modern movement in architecture (for of that there can hardly be much doubt), but of a historical modernity which extends back to the Reformation. It was with a decisive shift of *sensibility* that we entered that phase of civilization, and it will be with an equally decisive shift that we shall leave it.

CONCLUSION

The matrix of connected rooms is appropriate to a type of society which feeds on carnality, which recognizes the body as the person, and in which gregariousness is habitual. The features of this kind of life can be discerned in Raphael's architecture and painting. Such was the typical arrangement of household space in Europe until it was challenged in the seventeenth century and finally displaced in the nineteenth by the corridor plan, which is appropriate to a society that finds carnality distasteful, which sees the body as a vessel of mind and spirit, and in which privacy is habitual. This mode of life was so pervasive in the nineteenth century that it coloured the work even of those who recoiled from it, as did William Morris. In this respect modernity itself was an amplification of nineteenth-century sensibilities.

In reaching these conclusions architectural plans have been compared with paintings and various sorts of literature. There is a lot to be said for making architecture once more into art; rescuing it from the semiology and methodology under which it has largely disappeared. But too often this restitution has been attempted by taking it out from under one stone and putting it back under another. This is sometimes done in a rather guileless way, by equating architecture with literature or painting so that it becomes an echo of words and shapes; sometimes in a more sophisticated way, by adopting the vocabulary and procedures of the literary critic or art historian and applying them to architecture. The result is the same: like novels, like portraiture, architecture is made into a vehicle for observation and reflection. Overloaded with meaning and symbolism, its direct intervention in human affairs is spuriously reduced to a question of practicality.

Yet architecture is quite distinct from painting and writing, not simply because it requires the addition of some extra ingredient such as utility or function, but because it encompasses everyday reality, and in so doing inevitably provides a format for social life. In the foregoing I have tried to avoid treating buildings as if they were paintings or writings. A different kind of link has been sought: plans have been scrutinized for characteristics that could provide the preconditions for the way people occupy space, on the assumption that buildings accommodate what pictures illustrate and what words describe in the field of human relationships. This, I know, is a broad assumption, but it is the article of faith around which all these words have been wrapped.

This may not be the only way of reading plans but, even so, such an approach may offer something more than commentary and symbolism by clarifying architecture's instrumental role in the formation of everyday events. It hardly needs to be said that giving architecture this kind of consequentiality would not entail the reinstatement of functionalism or behavioural determinism. Certainly it would be foolish to suggest that there is anything in a plan which could compel people to behave in a specific way towards one another, enforcing a day-to-day regime of gregarious sensuality. It would be still more foolish, however, to suggest that a plan could not prevent people from behaving in a particular way, or at least hinder them from doing so.

The cumulative effect of architecture during the last two centuries has been like that of a general lobotomy performed on society at large, obliterating vast areas of social experience. It is employed more and more as a preventive measure; an agency for peace, security and segregation which, by its very nature, limits the horizon of experience – reducing noise-transmission, differentiating movement patterns, suppressing smells, stemming vandalism, cutting down the accumulation of dirt, impeding the spread of disease, veiling embarrassment, closeting indecency and abolishing the unnecessary; incidentally reducing daily life to a private shadow-play. But on the other side of this definition, there is surely another kind of architecture that would seek to give full play to the things that have been so carefully masked by its anti-type; an architecture arising out of the deep fascination that draws people towards others; an architecture that recognizes passion, carnality and sociality. The matrix of connected rooms might well be an integral feature of such buildings.

NOTES

1 D.Y. Donnison, *The Government of Housing* (Harmondsworth, 1967), p. 17.

2 This is especially true of Bafile's reconstruction, but it applies also to that of Percier and Fontaine.

3 Ground plan drawn by Antonio da Sangallo.

4 Christian Norberg-Schulz, *Meaning in Western Architecture* (London, 1975).

5 L.B. Alberti, *The Ten Books of Architecture*, translated by Leoni, edited by Rykwert (London, 1955), Book i, Chapter xii.

6 An interesting study of a cardinal's household has been made by D.S. Chambers. See *Journal of the Warburg & Courtauld Institute*, vol. 39, 1976, pp. 27–58, 'The Housing Problems of Cardinal Francesco Gonzaga'.

7 Baldessare Castiglione, *The Courtier* (Harmondsworth, 1967), p. 44.

8 *The Life of Benvenuto Cellini, written by himself* (London, 1956), pp. 110, 161, 138.

9 W.E. Greenwood, *Villa Madama* (London, 1928).

10 *The Book of Architecture of John Thorpe*, edited by J. Summerson (Glasgow, 1966).

11 *Sir Roger Pratt on Architecture,* edited by R.T. Gunther (Oxford, 1928), pp. 62, 64.

12 Ibid. p. 19.

13 William Davis, *Hints to Philanthropists* (Bath, 1821), p. 157.

14 A collection of these can be found in the OED under 'Privy'.

15 Only after writing this did it occur to me how similar the matrix of connected rooms is to the multiple connectivity proposed for the city by Chris Alexander in 'The City is not a Tree', *Architectural Forum*, vol. 122, April 1965, pp. 58–62, and May 1965, pp. 52–61.

16 Robert Kerr, *The Gentleman's House* (London, 1864), concluding paragraph.

17 John Turner, *Architects' Journal*, 3 September 1975, p. 458.

18 Morris, *Gossip About an Old House on the Upper Thames* (Birmingham, 1895), p. 11.

19 Collectivization, far from being the opposite of privatization, is just another way of obtaining the same psychic homogeneity. Peter Serenyi ('Le Corbusier, Fourier and the Monastery of Ema', *Art-Bulletin*, vol. 49, no. 4, pp. 227–86) has drawn attention to the similarities between Le Corbusier's early proposals for housing and the monastic organization of daily life, where solitary and collective both represent renunciation of worldliness.

20 Catherine Baur, *Modern Housing* (New York, 1935), p. 203.

21 R.D. Laing, *Knots* (London, 1970).

22 Proxemics is the study of the spatial organization of behaviour.

23 Edward T. Hall, *The Hidden Dimension* (London, 1969), pp. 89–90.

24 As predicted by Laing in the introduction to *Knots*, op. cit.

22
In Praise of Shadows

Jun'ichirō Tanizaki

Source: *In Praise of Shadows*. New Haven: Leetes Island Books, 1977

I possess no specialized knowledge of architecture, but I understand that in the Gothic cathedral of the West, the roof is thrust up and up so as to place its pinnacle as high in the heavens as possible—and that herein is thought to lie its special beauty. In the temples of Japan, on the other hand, a roof of heavy tiles is first laid out, and in the deep, spacious shadows created by the eaves the rest of the structure is built. Nor is this true only of temples; in the palaces of the nobility and the houses of the common people, what first strikes the eye is the massive roof of tile or thatch and the heavy darkness that hangs beneath the eaves. Even at midday cavernous darkness spreads over all beneath the roof's edge, making entryway, doors, walls, and pillars all but invisible. The grand temples of Kyoto—Chion'in, Honganji—and the farmhouses of the remote countryside are alike in this respect: like most buildings of the past their roofs give the impression of possessing far greater weight, height, and surface than all that stands beneath the eaves.

In making for ourselves a place to live, we first spread a parasol to throw a shadow on the earth, and in the pale light of the shadow we put together a house. There are of course roofs on Western houses too, but they are less to keep off the sun than to keep off the wind and the dew; even from without it is apparent that they are built to create as few shadows as possible and to expose the interior to as much light as possible. If the roof of a Japanese house is a parasol, the roof of a Western house is no more than a cap, with as small a visor as possible so as to allow the sunlight to penetrate directly beneath the eaves. There are no doubt all sorts of reasons—climate, building materials—for the deep Japanese eaves. The fact that we did not use glass, concrete, and bricks, for instance, made a low roof necessary to keep off the driving wind and rain. A light room would no doubt have been more convenient for us, too, than a dark room. The quality that we call beauty, however, must always grow from the realities of life, and our ancestors, forced to live in dark rooms, presently came to discover beauty in shadows, ultimately to guide shadows towards beauty's ends.

And so it has come to be that the beauty of a Japanese room depends on a variation of shadows, heavy shadows against light shadows—it has nothing else. Westerners are amazed at the simplicity of Japanese rooms, perceiving in them no more than ashen walls bereft of ornament. Their reaction is understandable, but it betrays a failure to comprehend the mystery of shadows. Out beyond the sitting room, which the rays of the sun can at best but barely reach, we extend the eaves or build on a veranda, putting the sunlight at still greater a remove. The light from the garden steals in but dimly through paper-paneled doors, and it is precisely this indirect light that makes for us the charm of a room. We do our walls in neutral colors so that the sad, fragile, dying rays can sink into absolute repose. The storehouse, kitchen, hallways, and such may have a glossy finish, but the walls of the sitting room will almost always be of clay textured with fine sand. A luster here would destroy the soft fragile beauty of the feeble light. We delight in the mere sight of the delicate glow of fading rays clinging to the surface of a dusky wall, there to live out what little life remains to them. We never tire of the sight, for to us this pale glow and these dim shadows far surpass any ornament. And so, as we must if we are not to disturb the glow, we finish the walls with sand in a single neutral color. The hue may differ from room to room, but the degree of difference will be ever so slight; not so much a difference in color as in shade, a difference that will seem to exist only in the mood of the viewer. And from these delicate differences in the hue of the walls, the shadows in each room take on a tinge peculiarly their own.

Of course the Japanese room does have its picture alcove, and in it a hanging scroll and a flower arrangement. But the scroll and the flowers serve not as ornament but rather to give depth to the shadows. We value a scroll above all for the way it blends with the walls of the alcove, and thus we consider the mounting quite as important as the calligraphy or painting. Even the greatest masterpiece will lose its worth as a scroll if it fails to blend with the alcove, while a work of no particular distinction may blend beautifully with the room and set off to unexpected advantage both itself and its surroundings. Wherein lies the power of an otherwise ordinary work to produce such an effect? Most often the paper, the ink, the fabric of the mounting will possess a certain look of antiquity, and this look of antiquity will strike just the right balance with the darkness of the alcove and room.

A Japanese room might be likened to an inkwash painting, the paper-paneled shoji being the expanse where the ink is thinnest, and the alcove where it is darkest. Whenever I see the alcove of a tastefully built Japanese room, I marvel at our comprehension of the secrets of shadows, our sensitive use of shadow and light. For the beauty of the alcove is not the work of some clever device. An empty space is marked off with plain wood and plain walls, so that the light drawn into it forms dim shadows within emptiness. There is nothing more. And yet, when we gaze into the darkness that gathers behind the crossbeam, around the flower vase, beneath the shelves, though we know perfectly well it is mere shadow, we are overcome with the feeling that in this small corner of the atmosphere there reigns complete and utter silence; that here in the darkness immutable tranquility holds sway. The "mysterious Orient" of which Westerners speak probably refers to the uncanny silence of these dark places. And even we as children would feel an inexpressible chill as we peered into the depths of an alcove to which the sunlight had never penetrated. Where lies the key to this mystery? Ultimately it is the magic of shadows. Were the shadows to be banished from its corners, the alcove would in that instant revert to mere void.

This was the genius of our ancestors, that by cutting off the light from this empty space they imparted to the world of shadows that formed there a quality of mystery and depth superior to that of any wall painting or ornament. The technique seems simple, but was by no means so simply achieved. We can imagine with little difficulty what extraordinary pains were taken with each invisible detail—the placement of the window in the shelving recess, the depth of the crossbeam, the height of the threshold. But for me the most

exquisite touch is the pale white glow of the shoji in the study bay; I need only pause before it and I forget the passage of time.

The study bay, as the name suggests, was originally a projecting window built to provide a place for reading. Over the years it came to be regarded as no more than a source of light for the alcove; but most often it serves not so much to illuminate the alcove as to soften the sidelong rays from without, to filter them through paper panels. There is a cold and desolate tinge to the light by the time it reaches these panels. The little sunlight from the garden that manages to make its way beneath the eaves and through the corridors has by then lost its power to illuminate, seems drained of the complexion of life. It can do no more than accentuate the whiteness of the paper. I sometimes linger before these panels and study the surface of the paper, bright, but giving no impression of brilliance.

In temple architecture the main room stands at a considerable distance from the garden; so dilute is the light there that no matter what the season, on fair days or cloudy, morning, midday, or evening, the pale, white glow scarcely varies. And the shadows at the interstices of the ribs seem strangely immobile, as if dust collected in the corners had become a part of the paper itself. I blink in uncertainty at this dreamlike luminescence, feeling as though some misty film were blunting my vision. The light from the pale white paper, powerless to dispel the heavy darkness of the alcove, is instead repelled by the darkness, creating a world of confusion where dark and light are indistinguishable. Have not you yourselves sensed a difference in the light that suffuses such a room, a rare tranquility not found in ordinary light? Have you never felt a sort of fear in the face of the ageless, a fear that in that room you might lose all consciousness of the passage of time, that untold years might pass and upon emerging you should find you had grown old and gray?

Why should this propensity to seek beauty in darkness be so strong only in Orientals? The West too has known a time when there was no electricity, gas, or petroleum, and yet so far as I know the West has never been disposed to delight in shadows. Japanese ghosts have traditionally had no feet; Western ghosts have feet, but are transparent. As even this trifle suggests, pitch darkness has always occupied our fantasies, while in the West even ghosts are as clear as glass. This is true too of our household implements: we prefer colors compounded of darkness, they prefer the colors of sunlight. And of silver and copperware: we love them for the burnish and patina, which they consider unclean, unsanitary, and polish to a glittering brilliance. They paint their ceilings and walls in pale colors to drive out as many of the shadows as they can. We fill our gardens with dense plantings, they spread out a flat expanse of grass.

But what produces such differences in taste? In my opinion it is this: we Orientals tend to seek our satisfactions in whatever surroundings we happen to find ourselves, to content ourselves with things as they are; and so darkness causes us no discontent, we resign ourselves to it as inevitable. If light is scarce then light is scarce; we will immerse ourselves in the darkness and there discover its own particular beauty. But the progressive Westerner is determined always to better his lot. From candle to oil lamp, oil lamp to gaslight, gaslight to electric light—his quest for a brighter light never ceases, he spares no pains to eradicate even the minutest shadow.

SECTION 2.3
FUNCTION

Introduction

The creation of an environment in which meaningful occupation can be accommodated is one of a number of primary concerns for an interior designer. Whether an office, exhibition, hotel or home, the requirements of the inhabitant, as well as the facilitating of different functions, are of the utmost importance in the formulation of a new interior space. Therefore, a careful and rigorous scrutiny of the requirements of the functional aspects of a new design is an essential component within the design process.

The five essays that have been selected to form this section all explore functionalism in various ways. This section starts with an essay written by the authors **Graeme Brooker** and **Sally Stone**, who interview the prominent British interior designer Ben Kelly. In this essay they discuss how the previous function of a building is as important as the proposed use of the project that he is working on. The designer outlines the importance of the properties of the existing space, within which the new interior is to be accommodated, and how any interesting qualities can become influential components in the design process. He describes how elements that are found in the existing buildings can ultimately inform the function and the identity of the new interior.

"The New Office" was an important essay written in 1997 by the prominent workspace theoretician **Frank Duffy**. The essay suggested a new way of understanding the design logic and organisational culture of a workspace. Duffy suggests that a new model by which the work environment can be understood involves the analysis of a variety of work environment cultures. This analysis is then translated into a series of typologies that can be used to form the basis of the design of a new office. These patterns of occupation, referred to as "Hives, Cells, Dens and Clubs" are designed to reflect the variety of both inhabitants and companies' cultures.

In the essay "Exhibition Design as Metaphor of a New Modernity", written in 2002 and first published in *Lotus* magazine, its author **Andrea Branzi** explores interior urbanism, the temporal transformation of interior parts of the city through adaptation. Branzi suggests that the descriptions such as interior design are limited and do not adequately portray the fluidity of the postindustrial city. Instead Branzi suggests that understanding "display", and the design of "ambient technologies" might offer a more coherent solution to the issues of the interior and the city.

The functional requirements of an interior will vary, and will depend on the form and identity of the inhabitant's requirements. Initially published in *Das Ornament der Masse*, in 1963, the essay 'The Hotel Lobby' by **Siegfried Kracauer** examines the effects that the entrance and reception area of a hotel has on its inhabitants. He compares the space of the church with the foyer of a hotel and examines the rituals and aesthetics of both sets of occupants. In the fourth essay in this chapter Kracauer describes the hotel lobby as a transient place, a buffer zone where the exterior environment is jettisoned and the occupants of the lobby can adopt relaxation and indifference. This is in stark comparison to the occupants of a church, where a single unifying theme is all prevailing.

In the final essay of this chapter, **Johan Van De Beek** analyses the spatial strategies utilised by Adolf Loos in the design of a series of exemplary domestic interiors. The author describes the various strategies by which Loos could form the complex patterns of interior occupation of the houses he designed for his clients. The author, using a series of simple line drawings, demonstrates the complexities of the combinations of rooms, circulation between these rooms, and the view into the interior spaces in the houses he created.

Graeme Brooker

Ben Kelly (1949–)

Principal Ben Kelly founded BKD in the mid-1970s. The practice was founded to initially work within the fields of retail and leisure. BKD built their reputation producing high-profile and innovative spaces, including flagship fashion stores, museum and exhibition design and most recently a chain of fitness clubs. The practice rose to prominence in the 1980s and 1990s with the design of three legendary interiors in Manchester: The Haçienda, Dry Bar and the Factory Records HQ. All three projects were based upon the innovative adaptation of existing buildings and the creation of a distinct spatial and material language.

   What all these projects have in common is a design approach derived from the conviction that all built spaces have the potential to be improved and if needed rehabilitated for new uses. With that in mind BKD strive to retain the best features of any given site, while employing a comprehensive palette of materials, textures, finishes and colours.

Building Study: Haçienda Nightclub

Manchester, UK
1982
Ben Kelly Design (BKD)

In the early 1980s Factory Records, a company run by the partners Anthony Wilson, Alan Erasmus, Peter Saville and Rob Gretton, decided to consolidate their increasing importance within the music industry in the north west of England by creating a club: a new venue for music, drinking, eating, dancing. With a brief that the club was to be like no other club in Manchester, Peter Saville enlisted Ben Kelly to devise the interior and to translate the label's innovative visual identity into a three-dimensional spatial entity. The club was to be contained in an enormous old yachting showroom on Whitworth Street, central Manchester, a site that was found by accident and which was available on a cheap rent. Working on a perfunctory brief of a "big bar, small bar, food, stage, dance-floor, balcony and a cocktail bar in the basement", Kelly was required to create a functional space that also exemplified the company's ethos and visual identity.

The Haçienda, like many of Kelly's projects, was rigorously organised around the designer's response to the unique features of the existing building. The original warehouse building was arranged into two main spaces, a cavernous top-lit hall originally used to display boats, which was entered from Whitworth Street via a curved red brick four-storey office building. This simple organisation of building elements subsequently informed the organisation and consequent sequencing of the journey from outside the club into the interior. This is a journey that is carefully planned and rigorously executed. From the discreet plaque on the outside wall announcing the club, the visitor passes underneath the retracted galvanised steel roller shutter and is into the small lobby. Once a ticket was bought they enter through the black Fac51 doors and into the antechamber of the main hall. The next part of the journey is framed by the joke "monolithic arch" requiring you to pass through a plastic curtain, found in most warehouses, to be confronted by the tall double bay top-lit warehouse space full of people, light and noise. The dynamic of the space was articulated by a powerful design language that mixed the language of the everyday such as traffic bollards and motorway catseyes, with gaudy colours and robust materials such as yellow and black chevrons, steel tread plate, and the now infamous Pigeon Blue BS409.

A rigorous and expansive analysis of the functional requirements of the project, and a detailed analysis of the building to be adapted, ensured that Kelly created a seminal design that years later, and subsequently demolished, is still regarded as a classic.

Ben Kelly Design, The Haçienda, Manchester, 1982
Once inside, the clubber emerged from the dark constrained entrance into the massive warehouse-type space. It was only at this point that the noise, sweat and frenetic energy became apparent. © Ben Kelly Design.

23
Off-The-Peg: The Bespoke Interiors of Ben Kelly

Graeme Brooker and Sally Stone

Source: Interior Atmospheres, *Architectural Design*, May/June 2008

A series of discussions between some of the founding instigators of the famous Manchester record label Factory were recently posted on YouTube. The conversations were recorded to celebrate 25 years since the opening of the label's infamous nightclub, the Haçienda, and the commemorative launch of a pair of trainers. Not training shoes, not footwear for organised sport or activity, but a bright and glaring pair of striped casual dance shoes, as worn by those who were/are part of the post-punk rave culture.

The industrial language of the Haçienda represented a massive shift in the sensibilities of a generation of club-goers. Before the 1980s, nightclubs did not exist; instead there were discos, which were glamorous, pretentious places with severe door policies that restricted entry to anybody not wearing the right clothes or footwear. The Haçienda, which was once described as the world's best nightclub, predicted the need for the postindustrial society to populate the warehouse-type spaces that they were on the cusp of losing.

Although the films were recorded at the studio of Ben Kelly, who designed the commemorative trainers, he is an almost silent character within the performance. While the rest of the group lean forwards, eager to share their anecdotes or insights into that strange and wonderful time, Kelly leans affably back from the table. Indeed, until video four of the set of nine, his contribution seems to be limited to ensuring that everyone has enough tea to drink and knows the whereabouts of the sugar. Only when the discussion is specifically about design does he really contribute. His direct prose is a welcome relief from the more florid and gossipy detailed explanations of his fellow conspirators. His description of the shoe is telling. He does not discuss the ironic or historical qualities of the design or the appropriateness of it as a symbol of our postindustrial society. Nor does he mention that when the Haçienda opened it was probably the only club that would let anyone in who was wearing trainers. Instead he manages to sum up the whole design aesthetic as he carefully explains the choice of colours and the minutiae of the design, at one point actually bringing out one of the trainers that he had made earlier. He says: 'The main body of the trainer is the same colour as the club – pigeon blue . . . the black and yellow stripes are synonymous with the club . . . inevitably some orange . . . different coloured eyelets and the laces could be striped.' And then, with affection for a small detail of a design that was constructed 25 years ago: 'I really wanted the graphic from the entrance to the club; a granite plaque with silver leaf, red enamel and the cedilla on the C.'[1]

Kelly does not engage in elaborate explanations of theories and ideas; he just has a clear and direct explanation of what was designed. Not since the late great James Stirling has a designer used so few words to convey so much. He is a designer who has a need to control every detail, almost obsessively. He is renowned for his response to the given and the exposure of the existing while inserting a totally new and appropriate layer of radical design. He is known for his passion for materials and for the manipulation of light.

The Ben Kelly Design (BKD) timeline of major projects is well documented. Projects from the early Howie store on the King's Road in London to the Manchester triumvirate of the Haçienda (1982), Dry 201 (1989) and Factory Headquarters (1990) established him at the forefront of contemporary design. The list continues: Bar Ten in Glasgow

Ben Kelly Design, The Haçienda, Manchester, 1982
The small and discreet plaque that signals the entrance. From the outside the club was hardly noticeable; little more than a factory-produced roller-shutter door. © Ben Kelly Design.

Ben Kelly Design, The Haçienda Trainers, June 2007
The trainers, designed to commemorate the 25th anniversary of the founding of the Haçienda in Manchester, are detailed to reflect the industrial quality of the legendary nightclub. The pigeon blue with hazard-warning details is reminiscent of the finishes in the club. © Ben Kelly Design.

(1991), the Basement Children's Gallery at the Science Museum (1995), followed by the Design Council Offices (1997), an apartment for Peter Saville (1996), Halfords Depots (1999), the Discovery Gallery in Walsall (2000), Borough Hotel, Edinburgh (2001) and the latter-day Gymbox projects (2003–06). BKD has worked through the usual spectrum of interior design project types: exhibition, offices, leisure, residential and retail. Throughout each project there are common themes including interesting relationships with clients, a thorough understanding of the nuances of the existing building, fastidious organisation with a real understanding of how people use spaces and, of course, materials. It is the assemblage of these appropriate, well-thought-out finishes that generates a unique design language – off-the-peg to create bespoke identities.

The BKD office is situated next to Borough Market, which is underneath the main viaduct leading out of London Bridge Station. The studio is on the first floor of an adjacent market building and, as befits the most taciturn man in design, the office is accessed from a side street, through a discreet door and up a dark staircase. However, once inside, just like Kelly's brain the studio is overflowing with drawings, materials, ideas and light. Initially the office appears chaotic – a wall of full-height windows dominates the room while the vast piles of stacked samples, rolled plans, books and catalogues all jostle with little mementoes of travels. The lampshades really are plastic buckets. A French hazard-sign warning of imminent electrocution is propped next to an orange shovel, leaning against a folded-up ping-pong table. But there is an underlying order to the chaos – this office is built to be worked in. Things are close to hand. The chance arrangement of samples, products and objects provokes ideas. The underlying atmosphere of the space is work-manlike and unpretentious. It is obvious that Kelly is a man who needs to touch, to feel, to see, to sense the materials, finishes and products that he specifies.

In response to our opening discussion about the general perception of interiors practice and education, Kelly introduces himself as 'an old-fashioned interior designer'.[2] He describes the subject as something that has integrity far beyond just surface consideration and he regards it as something that is 'very close to architecture, but it's not architecture', that actually has little to do with surface treatment, but has its basis in the manipulation and control of space. He explains that the starting point for any project is in the analysis and understanding of the unique qualities of the existing space, and suggests that there is a resonating element that springs from the original building that is crucial for the development of the project. This interpretive attitude can be traced back to the work of the well-known Italian interior architect Carlo Scarpa, although of course with vastly different visual results.

'When I get the plan then this is when the project begins. We sit around the table and discuss what it's telling us, what's possible, what can we keep and what has to go,' says Kelly. The site-specific qualities of the existing building that can be teased out and repossessed in the transformation of a space are one of the major sources of atmosphere in his work. It is from these readings that the process of organisation and assembly can begin. Kelly could be accused of not really doing very much; the basic spaces are relatively unaltered, many of the finishes are pre-existing and the new bits are very much the same as the old. He makes it look too easy. But that is exactly the point – he liberates the existing, not just in the way the space is exposed and manipulated, but also, and most importantly, the manner in which the new elements, insertions and materials echo the existing qualities.

The Basement Children's Gallery at the Science Museum in London exhibits these bare and uncovered characteristics. BKD robustly stripped away much of the accumulated junk to reveal the bones of the space, the natural light and the structural finishes. The raw space was then quite simply organised with a new long, raked terrace floor that runs the length of the room, and animated by the deliberate and conscious application of materials. Brightly coloured surfaces are applied to embellish interesting features, which complement the exposed elements. The new elements emphasise the rawness; they use the same basic and crude language and yet are incredibly well-thought-out and designed. The language is of a warehouse or factory for kids; it is totally suitable for children without being childish. The workings and mechanics of the place are (necessarily) revealed and relished; the electrical cables become decorative, the air-conditioning units are prominently displayed and even the lift panels are transparent. It is robust, truthful, unrefined and happy.

The work of the practice is often typecast as beginning and ending with a bold, varied and graphic palette of materials. But this underplays a crucial element of the work and Kelly should

Ben Kelly Design, The Haçienda, Manchester, 1982
Traffic bollards signal the edge of the dance floor. These were 'found objects',
appropriated from the streets of Manchester, promoting a connection between the post-
punk, postindustrial generation and the warehouse-type space. © Ben Kelly Design.

Ben Kelly Design studio, London, 2007
Kelly values the relative privacy of working at the large meeting table beneath the bucket lampshades.
© Graeme Brooker.

Stacked piles of materials and samples litter the floor of the BKD studio. © Ben Kelly Design.

be given much greater credit for the careful and masterful planning of the spaces. Bar Ten in Glasgow has a European character. A large window on to the street makes it suitable for visiting during the day and at night, but once inside the space is very internally focused. A very crucial metre of transitional space at the entrance allows the visitor to mentally adjust to a new atmosphere.

This focus on the movement of the entrance space also exists at Dry 201. Once again the big shop-window frames the activity within, thus creating a strong relationship with the street. But the visitor is once more moved into the darkness of the shadows at the side of the space to become accustomed to the enclosure and inward concentration of the room. As Kelly explains: 'I think it needed to be as public as it could be to the street, so people would be drawn into it, and also that kind of Continental bar, very open to the street. We wanted people to see in for sure.' This notion was reinforced and the memory of the previous furniture showroom was solidified through the reuse of an enormous plaster curtain. The

detritus from an earlier existence was painted red and blatantly displayed in the shop window of the bar.

Within the Haçienda, now demolished, existed the most theatrical architectural promenade. The presence of the club on the street was almost nonexistent. The clubber would pass through a small dark door into a tight lobby, from there into a slightly larger area and 'then into a massive cathedral-like space which heightened and magnified the experience, you became over-whelmed once you were in there, it took you over'. This is typical of BKD's work, where the movement is linear and spaces are designed in series, as a progression of scenes for the user to inhabit, each connected to the last through the themed use of materials, textures and colours, but each with a distinct and identifiable atmos-phere.

In all of Ben Kelly's work, the atmospheric condition of each project is born out of a mixture of the pragmatic use of the qualities of the existing space, the planning and organisation of the new function, and the fabrication of an identity through the creative use of specific materials. He enjoys the

Ben Kelly Design, Bar 10, Glasgow, 1991
The interior was designed as a culmination of a journey that progresses from the busy shopping area,
through a narrow alley and, finally, into the bar. Material selection and placement within the bar reinforce
this narrative as they repeat and mimic materials found along the journey's path. © Ben Kelly Design.

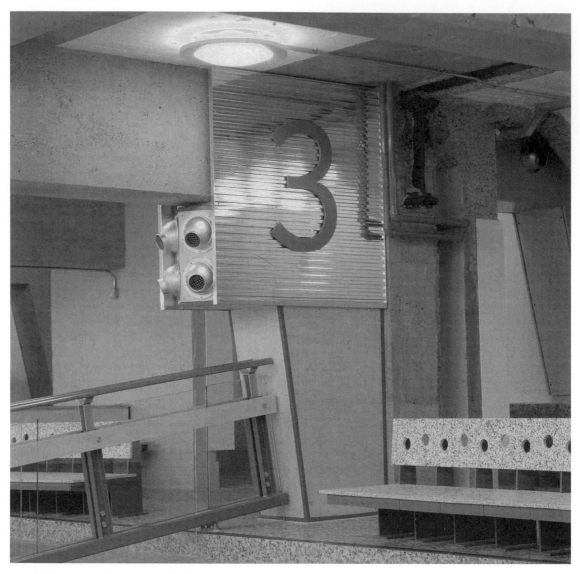

Ben Kelly Design. Basement Childrens Gallery, Science Museum
The designers have transformed the space into a stimulating place for children to investigate. The new and the existing materials are raw and robust, and the applied finishes are as tough as the stripped-down space. © Ben Kelly Design

conversation between new and old, the act of bringing life to the redundant, the process of remembering, of revealing and of constructing a new contemporary layer of meaning and animation.

NOTES

1   www.youtube.com/watch?v=evaCQLEuZQs& mode=related&search=
2   In conversation with the authors.

24
Old and New Office Cultures

Frank Duffy

Source: *The New Office*. Conran Octopus, 1997

The physical differences between the old work culture and the new are striking. The physical features of the former tell us very clearly how work was assumed to be done, the level of technology, who was important and who was not, and, most importantly, the cultural values in the management of human resources that determined what was appropriate to make the work force, despite the low level of expectations, carry out such routine and often mindless tasks.

Conventional offices:

- assume that clerical tasks are the staple of office work;
- offer limited settings because the work is homogenous and undifferentiated;
- accommodate one person per workstation, and then only from nine to five;
- are excellent at expressing boundaries through physical barriers designed to keep functions and people apart;
- are even better at reinforcing hierarchy through an apparatus of physical signs that indicate precisely how important – or unimportant – everyone is;
- suit big groups – departments, businesses – rather than small;
- say nothing about teamwork because little individual, let alone collective, initiative is necessary and very few resources are shared;
- are unconvinced by the logic or potential of advanced forms of information technology.

The physical features and appearance of the new office will depend upon, and be stimulated by, powerful, integrated, interconnected, and ubiquitous information technology. The new office will express:

- much greater attention to the economic importance of better use of time, taking advantage, for example, of office work as a parallel and serial, rather than a linear, process, leading to moves towards intensifying the use of space;
- impatience with boundaries, because advanced organizations want more communication between departments and between specialisms in order to solve more complex problems more quickly;
- little love of hierarchies, and even less of status, because, more often than not, what you can do is more important than who you are;
- a tendency towards smaller, more rapidly changing organizational units, the result of stripping organizations back to the core by 'out-sourcing' whatever activities are non-central and ruthlessly weeding out anything that is redundant;
- the importance of group activity, reflected in the provision of work settings that are the focus for, and encourage, interactive, complex, open-ended teamwork – these are expected to be mostly open-plan and only partially cellular but with much more specialized support, often in the form of several different kinds of meeting and project areas;
- the obsolescence of clerks and clerical ways because routine clerical tasks have been automated or exported off-site, away from the creative teams and decision-makers;
- total confidence in the creative use of information technology;
- a new flexibility, with an ever-wider range of work settings in response to choices in the timing of work and in the ways in which it is carried out.

Many office organizations are already working in unconventional and very different ways. Some, just by doing what seems to them in their new circumstances to be sensible, are already far ahead of many designers in their thinking about what the new kind of office should be like. They are developing different and higher expectations involving employees' control of time and place, and the quality of their working environments and life-styles.

The chart below summarizes the ways in which such organizations are changing how and where they work, how they use information technology, how they are using space over time in new ways, and what the implications are for the design of office layouts.

A variety of office layouts – as well as ways of owning or sharing space – is implied by these fundamental shifts in the shape and patterns of work. It would be a grave mistake to assume that the conventional office, which fails not least because it is attempting to solve all organizational problems with a single solution, should be replaced by a similarly singular stereotype. To anyone who recognizes the size and complexity of the emerging world of work it is clear that not all organizations are likely to use space in the same way. The reverse is more likely to be true. Nor is the rate of

take-up of new forms of space-use likely to be modelled on the past. Some companies, or parts of companies, will rush to innovate; others will have legitimate reasons to move more slowly towards adopting new ways of working and new ways of accommodating themselves. Timing, as in all aspects of management, is everything.

THE DESIGN LOGIC OF THE NEW OFFICE

The new kinds of offices are likely to be perceived by management to be closely related to increasing the potential for organizational survival. The diagram displayed on page 158 explains why. It demonstrates the direct and dynamic relationship between client priorities and broad types of office layout. It explains why contemporary managerial thinking should be leading not only to richer and more diverse office layouts, but also to a particular

	Conventional office assumptions	New ways of working
Patterns of work	Routine processes Individual tasks Isolated work	Creative knowledge work Groups, teams, projects Interactive work
Patterns of occupancy of space over time	Central office locations in which staff are assumed to occupy individually 'owned' workstations on a full-time basis, typically over the course of the 9–5 day. The office assumes one desk per person; provides a hierarchy (planned or enclosed); and is occupied typically at levels at least 30% below full capacity.	Distributed set of work locations (which may be nomadic, mobile, in the office or at home) linked by networks of communication in which autonomous individuals work in project teams. Daily timetable is extended and irregular. Multifunctional work settings are occupied on an as-needed basis. Daily occupancy of space near to capacity.
Type of space layout, furniture systems, and use of space and buildings	Hierarchy of space and furniture related to status. Individual allocation of space predominates over interactive meeting spaces.	Multiple shared group work and individual task-based settings. Setting, layout and furniture of the office geared to work process and its tasks.
Use of information technology	Technology used for routine data-processing, terminals in fixed positions served by mainframes.	Focus on mobility of IT equipment used in a wide variety of settings. Technology used to support creative knowledge work, both individual and group. File servers serve a variety of IT tools, including PCs and laptops and shared specialized equipment.

The contrast between the assumptions that underpinned the conventional office and the expectations that are creating new office environments is very marked.

sequence in which new kinds of layout are likely to be adopted.

Interaction and autonomy

The diagram overleaf is based upon two organizational variables: interaction and autonomy. Taken together, these throw light on the ways in which office layouts are likely to differ and to change, and also explain the dynamics of change in office design. Since most companies differ within themselves the diagram can also be used as a means of measuring the state of all the parts of any complex organization at any given moment – and also of predicting how the proportions of different kinds of office-use are likely to change over time.

Interaction is the personal, face-to-face contact that is necessary to carry out office tasks. As the amount of interaction increases, there is more pressure to accommodate and support such encounters. Even more pressure is exerted as the quality – the intellectual content and the significance – of interaction increases. Forms of interaction vary as the complexity, urgency, and importance of the tasks being carried out increase, so settings for interaction can range from the most informal to the most formal meetings and from the most casual to the most structured encounters. Interactions that are not face-to-face, i.e. are via the computer, telephone, or other virtual media, are not directly significant, although they are likely to supplement, or become a substitute for, face-to-face interaction both now and in the future.

Interaction outside the organization is also relevant because it has a direct impact on occupancy: heavy interaction with clients and colleagues outside the office is often connected with intermittent space occupancy.

Autonomy is the degree of control, responsibility, and discretion each office worker has over the content, method, location, and tools of the work process. The more autonomy office workers enjoy, the more they are likely to want to control their own working environments, singly and collectively, and the more discretion they are likely to want to exercise over the kind and quality of their surroundings in their places of work.

Interaction and autonomy are strongly correlated with many aspects of office design because they affect workers' expectations about the layout, the work settings – the heights of the space-dividing elements, for example – and their control over environmental services and lighting.

Four types of office work

The dominant organizational mode of the conventional office was 'the office as factory' – a place where individuals processed work, under supervision, at their own workstations. Such work is low in interaction – apart from social chatter – as well as low in the autonomy given to individual office workers. In the USA and the UK a great deal of basic clerical work has either been automated out of existence or been exported to economies where it can be carried out more cheaply. Hence the arrow pointing downwards to indicate that such work is already sifting like sand out of the box. Higher-level office activities of this type are being transmuted – re-engineered – into more intellectually demanding activity where working together and teamwork are all important. In such 'group process' work, interaction increases while individual autonomy remains relatively low. Another persistent, and respectable, form of office work – found, for example, in the legal profession and in research institutes – uses the office as a place primarily for 'concentrated study'. In such offices autonomy is high and interaction low. It is expected, as information technology changes work, that many examples of the offices now identified as being for 'group processes' and 'concentrated study' will tend to converge into what has been called the 'transactional' office where, through deft management of time and space, both interaction and autonomy will be maximized. Out of the top right-hand corner of the diagram is escaping, like steam, the growing amount of office work that is becoming virtual, more or less independent of space and even time.

Hives, cells, dens, and clubs

The diagram identifies four major organizational types and, as a shorthand way of capturing the distinct work patterns and distinctive design features of each, has characterized them as hive, cell, den, and club. 'Hive' because such offices can be compared to beehives occupied by busy worker bees; 'cell' because these recall the monks' cloister or the venerable, highly cellular, offices of the Inns of Court in London; 'den' because these are busy and interactive places where it is easy to work informally in teams; 'club' because one of the nearest models to the new transactional office, despite its unfortunate and outmoded élitist overtones, is the old-fashioned gentlemen's club. This categorization is, of course, only a convenient simplification. In the real world any organization of any

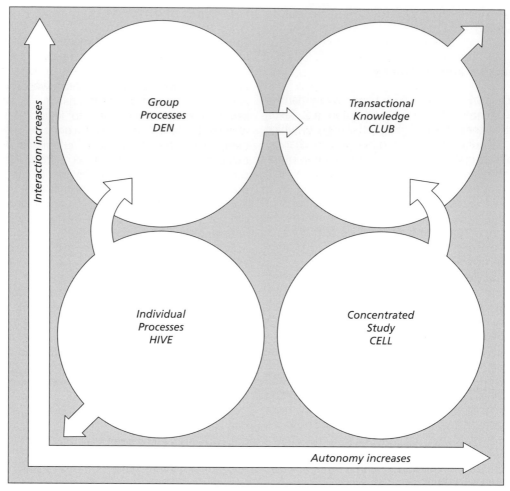

The workplace forum: the ever-increasing power of technology will eventually lead to the elimination of Individual Processes – unless they are transformed into Group Processes. As Information Technology enhances group competence, so Group Processes will tend towards Transactional Knowledge. Concentrated Study also tends towards Transactional Knowledge, or even home working, while Transactional Knowledge places emphasis on better relations with clients and making full use of all available facilities. The diagram identifies four major organizational types: HIVES, CELLS, DENS, and CLUBS. They are a shorthand way of describing affinities between work patterns, the use of space, and the demands likely to be made by these groups on environmental services.

size or complexity is likely to be characterized by a shifting mixture of all four. The terms hive, cell, den, and club can refer either to a whole organization occupying a whole building or to part of an organization occupying a floor or even part of a floor. In most companies there will be found combinations of these work patterns. For example, many have 'back office' staff engaged in data-entry or routine administrative functions – typically accommodated in hives, or in cheaper office accommodation out of town – while other groups within the same organi-zation are dens or clubs and are more likely to be located in a headquarters office near the city centre. Also, while there are clearly many affinities between certain sectors of work and the types of office – between advertising and dens, for example – the limits of the typology must be recognized since, even within the same professions, there may be sufficient differences in workstyle to preclude straightforward associations between particular sectors and the individual types defined here.

THE HIVE

Hives are characterized by individual, routine-process work with low levels of interaction and low autonomy. Hive office workers sit continuously at simple workstations for long periods of time on a regular nine-to-five schedule. Variants of hive offices include 24-hour shift working. Workplace settings are typically uniform, open-plan, screened, and impersonal. Typical organizations or work groups include telesales, data-entry or processing, routine banking, financial and administrative operations, and basic information services.

THE CELL

Cell offices accommodate individual, concentrated work with little interaction. Highly autonomous people occupy them in an intermittent, irregular pattern with extended working days – and often work elsewhere some of the time (possibly at home, at a client's office, or on the road). Each person typically occupies either an enclosed cell or a highly screened workstation in a more open-plan office. Each individual work place must be designed to provide for a complex variety of tasks. The autonomous pattern of work, implying sporadic and irregular occupancy, means that the potential exists for such work settings to be shared. Typical occupiers of cellular offices include accountants, lawyers, management and employment consultants, and computer scientists.

THE DEN

Den offices are associated with group work, typically highly interactive but not necessarily highly autonomous. Den spaces are designed for group working and often provide a range of several simple settings, usually arranged in an open-plan office or in group rooms. While the settings are normally designed on the assumption that individual office workers occupy their 'own' desks, such groups also like to have access to local ancillary space for meetings and project work, and for shared equipment such as printers and copiers and other special technical facilities. Tasks are often short-term and intense. Sometimes they are more long-term; and they always involve much team effort. Typical work requiring dens includes design, insurance processing, some media work, particularly radio and television, and advertising.

THE CLUB

Club organizations are for knowledge work, i.e. far office work that transcends data-handling because it can only be done through exercising considerable judgment and intelligence. Typically, work in such organizations is both highly autonomous and highly interactive. The pattern of occupancy tends to be intermittent over an extended working day. A wide variety of time-shared task-based settings serve both concentrated individual and group interactive work. Individuals and teams occupy space on an 'as-needed' basis, moving around it to take advantage of a wide range of facilities. The ratio of sharing depends on the precise content of the work activity and the mix of in-house versus out-of-office working, possibly combining tele-working, home-working, and working at client and other locations. Typical organizations include creative firms such as advertising and media companies, information technology companies, and many management consultancies. What such organizations have in common are highly intellectual staff, open-ended problem-solving, and, above all, constant access to a vast array of shared knowledge.

PATTERNS OF WORK AND OFFICE SPACE

Each of the work patterns characteristic of the four different types of organization implies its own and particular way of using space and furniture. To get the most out of any organization, different kinds of office layouts must be designed to support these patterns. The chart below is intended as a key to the design decisions that follow from this logic. Thus, while hives need relatively simple workstations, cells need richer individual work settings; dens require several relatively simple settings and clubs need many rich and complex ones. Layouts that best support the different patterns of work are also likely to be used in characteristically different ways over time: more interactive and more highly autonomous work patterns are more likely to lead to time-sharing space – what is often called 'space use intensification' – because occupancy is intermittent or irregular.

Patterns of work, space occupancy, office layout and use of information technology for each of the four organizational types may be summarized as shown in the chart.

An inevitable direction of development?

The design of the material office and the direction of organizational change are intimately bound together, and must be closely correlated to achieve business success – not to mention business survival.

The first steps in thinking about how this can be done are obvious. Think about organizational structure, work processes, and physical consequences in an integrated, systematic way. The diagrams on the right show two stages in the process of change, from the present-day situation in which most offices are predominantly hives towards a new distribution of office space in which there will be a far higher proportion of cells, dens and clubs. This process involves shifts in the total office population, from lower to higher levels of

	Hive	Cell	Den	Club
Pattern of work	Work broken down into smallest components and carried out by staff who are given precise instructions and little discretion.	High-level work carried out by talented independent individuals (isolated knowledge work).	Project or other group work of a straightforward kind needing a changing balance of different, independent skills.	High-level work carried out by talented independent individuals who need to work both collaboratively and individually: work process constantly being redesigned.
Occupancy of space over time, capacity for sharing space over time	Conventional 9–5, but tending towards shift work. Routine timetable, low interaction, and full-time occupancy of space offer little scope for shared space use except for 24-hour shift work.	Increasingly ragged and variable, more extended working days, depending on individual arrangements. If occupancy of space is low, opportunities exist for shared individual settings (enclosed or open).	Conventional 9–5, but becoming more varied by subgroup activities. Opportunity for sharing space over time increases since interactive staff more likely to be away from desks or out of building.	Complex and dependent on what needs to be done and on individual arrangements, but expect high-occupancy pattern of use over extended periods of time. Highly intermittent pattern of occupancy supports shared use of task settings.
Type of space layout	Open, ganged (4 or 6 pack), minimal partitions, maximal filing, imposed simple space standards.	Cellular enclosed offices or individually used open workstations with high screening or partitions.	Group space or group rooms, medium filing. Complex and continuous spaces incorporating meeting spaces and work spaces.	Diverse, complex and manipulate range of settings based on wide variety of tasks.
Use of IT	Simple dumb terminals or networked PCs.	Variety of individual PCs on networks and widespread use of laptops.	PCs and some shared specialized group equipment.	Variety of individual PCs on networks and widespread use of laptops.

No one organization can be categorized as being completely a Hive, Cell, Den or Club. Most are combinations. Similarly the sum of all offices at any one time must consist of a proportion of all four types. As time goes on this proportion is likely to change. For example, if the vast majority of offices today are Hives, with some Cells and Dens but few Clubs, it is expected that, over the coming years, the proportion of Hives will have significantly diminished in favour of a higher proportion of Cells, even more Dens and a huge increase in Clubs.

interaction and from lower to higher levels of autonomy for workers. As this happens, the relationship between the workstyles will change, from the old clerical pattern (hive) in the bottom left-hand quadrant of the top diagram, to more group work (den) or more concentrated individual work (cell). Ultimately, as the diagrams show both of these more complex forms of workstyles are likely to combine in the most communicative and collaborative work processes and environments (club).

A more practical way of using this form of analysis for a particular project is to identify the relative proportions of organizational types found within one company or location, and then to think through the implications of future change on the relative importance of each within that organization. As the proportions of each of the four types of work change, so will the demand for the different kinds of office layout. In this way, future demand can be anticipated and measured and provision made for the inevitable transition from one mix of office space to another. This technique makes possible systematic planning to accommodate change and is the basis for 'future proofing' office buildings.

In this way business planners can explore, and even determine, appropriate directions for change at the same time as the designers of the physical working environment are stimulated to investigate wider ranges of design solutions. In other words office design and strategic business planning can be integrated to the benefit of both. In this way it is also possible to predict the overall shape of the demand for office space in cities of different economic circumstances.

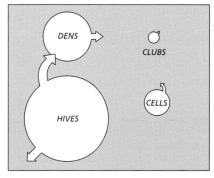

The likely proportion of the four types of office towards the end of the 1990s.

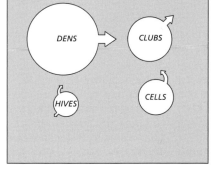

A prediction of how the proportion of the four types of office might change.

25
Exhibition Design as Metaphor of a New Modernity

Andrea Branzi

Source: *Lotus International*, no. 115, 2002

The sector of fitting out interiors and designing displays is considered a recent discipline, one which emerged in the twentieth century in relation to the growth in commercial and exhibition events. As such it is seen as a sort of minor category of architecture, an activity not endowed with the necessary attributes of curability and permanence, and thus close to the world of temporary installations or theatrical settings, wholly superstructural and transitory. Precisely because it is superstructural and transitory, however, the sector is not a subcategory of architecture but on the contrary today plays a new and central disciplinary role in urban transformations. In other words, when an exhibition, a stand or a showroom is prepared, or when work or living spaces are fitted out, when a play or an opera or a ballot is staged, what is constructed is a piece of city. A piece of city that can be regarded as belonging to its most highly evolved fringe, one responding to the logic of reversibility, adaptation and re-functionalization of the constructed world. This evolutionary space, which can also be seasonal or promotional, is the one that most precisely differentiates the city of the twenty-first century from the city of the twentieth. In the category of the design of displays, and its technological characteristics, there are in fact all the genetic elements typical of a new modernity, which we shall call "light" and "diffuse" to distinguish it from the "heavy" and "concentrated" one of the last century. Interior design, fitting out architecture of interiors, interior decoration, preparation of displays or other names of this kind provide very unsatisfactory descriptions of a design activity that is concerned with the transformation of internal spaces, as a response to new functional, production or advertising needs.

In fact these definitions often fail to give due emphasis to the role that system of objects and their display plays in today's city, as an element of its continual functional re-adjustment to cope with the phenomenon of the metabolism of the systems of use and retirement under way. What we need to do is focus on the central role that ambient technologies (elements of furnishing, components, instrumentation, technical plant, advertising) play in the urban system today, guaranteeing its function and above all permitting it to absorb the continual changes in modes of production and living, thrown into crisis by the advent of new technologies and new ways of using the city itself. It is necessary, in fact, to start out from the recognition that contemporary cities seem to be going through a period characterized solely by a process of adaptation of their infrastructures and services. But on close examination, we become aware instead of the existence of a vast phenomenon of functional up-rootedness in the contemporary city with respect to the predictions of use and the functional plans of just a few years ago.

There is no urban function, allocation or zoning that has not been contradicted in the last ten years. The phenomenon of industrial retirement is only the first and most conspicuous aspect of a process that involves other urban functions, from commerce to housing and from the tertiary sector to services. People work at home, live in the office, sell things in houses and study in factories. Services are provided in warehouses, museums set up in gasholders: this revolution does not produce conspicuous phenomena from the viewpoint of the urban landscape, but corresponds to deep tectonic processes, to continual shifts and tremors within the entire engine of the city. All postindustrial cities are undergoing this silent revolution.

Something similar, although on a much smaller scale, had happened in the nineteenth century during the Napoleonic campaigns, with the suppression of the religious orders and the alienation of ecclesiastical property. This brought onto the urban market a large number of monasteries, abbeys and charterhouses, which were subsequently converted into barracks, prisons, hotels and schools. It took more than a hundred years for this vast and difficult patrimony to be absorbed, and many of those retirements in the past served to re-functionalize our historic cities.

At the time the urban scenario did not appear to have been altered, and yet the cities functioned better. In fact the retirements often created new opportunities and lowered the values of the market, favoring a sort of updating of the city with respect to its new functions, and a greater freedom in the use of its existing structures.

These profound, invisible and dynamic phenomena pertain to what is called "light" modernity, that is a modernity which produces widespread transformations that are not very obvious and reversible, but of great structural significance. A modernity characterized by the design of flexible or temporary environmental micro-systems, architectural sub-systems. This urban metabolism, which produces a continuous evolution of functional codes, is spontaneously handled and absorbed today by the presence of the fluid and pliable system of furnishing components in the urban territory. This system of objects and technologies allows the city to adapt itself continually to new functions, rehabilitating abandoned buildings and transforming large and small containers, redefining their internal functions; taking over entire urban territories and adapting them to new markets. So this new dimension of design plays a leading part in the functioning of contemporary cities, in the age of continual retirements, changing functions and the new structural role of the micro-economies of scale. In other words interior design and the preparation of displays, precisely because they are provisional and interstitial, constitute one of the most important activities today in the phenomenology of the liquefaction of the solid bodies of the contemporary city. In an attempt to explain this change in the overall picture in the twenty-first century, the sociologist Zygmunt Bauman has published *Liquid Modernity*, an essay in which he traces a long analysis of the processes of transformation in the concept of modernity at the beginning of the third millennium.

For Bauman the term "liquid" is a positive way of representing the idea of a state of matter that does not possess a form of its own (but only that of its container) and tends to follow a temporal flow of transformations. These conditions serve to describe "the nature of the current and in many ways new phase in the history of modernity."

The concept of liquefaction belongs to the primitive processes of modernity, as a movement of liberation from the structural nodes of history, of dissolution of the academic blocks of the discipline, of dispersion of the character structures of repression (Wilhelm Reich). It needs to be remembered, however, that the "liquefaction of solid bodies" that the first modernity offered did not at all presuppose the formation of a permanent liquid state, but on the contrary represented a transitory phase, a necessary premise for the construction of new and more resistant solid bodies. In today's highly complex societies these containers, these solid bodies, have become extremely rigid organisms, owing to the enormous normative effort that has to be made in order to coordinate the multiplicity of reality, to the point of turning into obsolete and fragile structures, wholly unusable and remote from any efficient procedure. For Bauman the operational void that has resulted from this is filled today by the spontaneity of individual modes of behavior and local initiatives, by constant reform of the regulations and by the elimination of constraints. To the point where the flexibility of the system "is the product and the sediment of the freedom expressed by human agents."

Taken as a whole, deregulation, liberalization of enterprises and of spaces, flexibility of use and social fluidity, free access to financial markets and freedom from topologies represent the inverse process to what the modern solid had created as a container for the liquid state of the modern. In this sense the end of the age of revolutions, as producers of normative mega-containers, derives from the definitive (and apparent) identification between free enterprise and society, between economy and superstructures, between spontaneous action and politics; between the fluidity of institutions and the fluidity of the market. The functional crisis of the modern city is resolved through the modern use of the environmental instruments (interior design).

Modernity becomes the only judge of modernity itself. It falls back on itself and proceeds with its own modernization. The powers of coercion have passed from the system to life, have descended from the macro- to the micro-scale, from architecture to interior design. So Bauman concludes "ours is a type of individualized, privatized modernity, in which the burdens of weaving its fabric and the responsibility for failure fall principally on the shoulders of the individual." Thus individual freedom appears to coincide today with the freedom of the system's liquefaction, given that in the age of mass entrepreneurship there no longer exists any apparent distance between the whole and a small part of it, between private interests and collective interests. Between the design of permanent structures and the design of temporary structures. The current political tendency to operate on the basis not of plans and manifestos, but of micro-enterprises and the world of products, of domestic economies and the subsystems of the market, does not modify the structures of society but produces a slow energy of evolution, a perpetual mutation, an incessant reform. These are weak and imperfect instruments, but the only ones capable of avoiding dangerous crises in the system, and the only systems of planning suited to the paradigms of our definitive society of uncertainties, where transitory conditions are the only lasting realities and liquid structures are the definitive state of modern bodies. Modifying the space inherited from previous processes of retirement to meet its own residential, productive, commercial or promotional needs produces a sort of urban metabolism that is hard to predict and govern, as it is linked to the discontinuous flows of this new relational economy. However, the regulations in force do not always prove suitable for this sort of creeping revolution, and city authorities have serious problems in deciding today whether a building is used as a habitation or an office. In both cases it contains chairs, tables, shelves, couches, computers, bathrooms. In some cities in the United States a new approach to building regulation is being studied which no longer sets out to determine the ambiguous activities that are carried out in a district – a district that may be made up of docklands transformed into incubators of various activities – but to define bands of energy instead. A space is no longer assigned a particular function, but classified on the basis of its consumption of energy, allowing any activity whatsoever to be carried out there so long as it is limited to a determinate number of computers. In this way sufficiently elastic ranges of use are created that, while guaranteeing an overall control of urban standards, leave a great deal of freedom in the purpose to which the premises are put. This new internal functioning of the city goes beyond typologies and resolves everything through the use of computers and elements of furnishing. This universe of micro-structures deals with the process of retirement and substitution of the functions case by case, permitting cities to adapt rapidly to changing needs. The result is an extraordinarily pliable plankton that makes it possible to renew the form and the function of interior spaces inside the immobile containers of architecture. And also to make use of constructions from a thousand or two thousand years ago without difficulties. A sort of lubricant that prevents the city from seizing up, and allows it to adapt itself continually to the new.

26
The Hotel Lobby

Siegfried Kracauer

Source: *The Mass Ornament: Weimar Essays*. Translated by Thomas Y. Levin. Harvard University Press, 1995

. . . In the *house of God*, which presupposes an already extant community, the congregation accomplishes the task of making connections. Once the members of the congregation have abandoned the relation on which the place is founded, the house of God retains only a decorative significance. Even if it sinks into oblivion, civilized society at the height of its development still maintains privileged sites that testify to its own non-existence, just as the house of God testifies to the existence of the community united in reality. Admittedly society is unaware of this, for it cannot see beyond its own sphere; only the aesthetic construct, whose form renders the manifold as a projection, makes it possible to demonstrate this correspondence. The typical characteristics of the *hotel lobby*, which appears repeatedly in detective novels, indicate that it is conceived as the inverted image of the house of God. It is a negative church, and can be transformed into a church so long as one observes the conditions that govern the different spheres.

In both places people appear there *as guests*. But whereas the house of God is dedicated to the service of the one whom people have gone there to encounter, the hotel lobby accommodates all who go there to meet no one. It is the setting for those who neither seek nor find the one who is always sought, and who are therefore guests in space as such – a space that encompasses them and has no function other than to encompass them. The impersonal nothing represented by the hotel manager here occupies the position of the unknown one in whose name the church congregation gathers. And whereas the congregation invokes the name and dedicates itself to the service in order to fulfil the relation, the people dispersed in the lobby accept their host's incognito without question. Lacking any and all relation, they drip down into the vacuum with the same necessity that compels those striving in and for reality to lift themselves out of the nowhere toward their destination.

The congregation, which gathers in the house of God for prayer and worship, outgrows the imperfection of communal life in order not to overcome it but to bear it in mind and to reinsert it constantly into the tension. Its gathering is a *collectedness* and a unification of this directed life of the community, which belongs to two realms: the realm covered by law and the realm beyond law. At the site of the church – but of course not only here – these separate currents encounter each other; the law is broached here without being breached, and the paradoxical split is accorded legitimacy by the sporadic suspension of its languid continuity. Through the edification of the congregation, the community is always reconstructing itself, and this elevation above the everyday prevents the everyday itself from going under. The fact that such a returning of the community to its point of origin must submit to spatial and temporal limitations, that it steers away from worldly community, and that it is brought about through special celebrations – this is only a sign of man's dubious position between above and below, one that constantly forces him to establish on his own what is given or what has been conquered in the tension.

Since the determining characteristic of the lower region is its lack of tension, the togetherness in the hotel lobby has no meaning. While here, too, people certainly do become detached from everyday life, this detachment does not lead the community to assure itself of its existence as a congregation. Instead it merely displaces people from the unreality of the daily hustle and bustle to a place where they would encounter the void only if they were more than just reference points. The lobby, in which people find themselves *vis-à-vis de rien*, is a mere gap that does not even serve a purpose dictated by *Ratio* (like the conference room of a corporation), a purpose which at the very least could mask the directive that had been perceived in the relation. But if a sojourn in a hotel offers neither a perspective on nor an escape from the everyday, it does provide a groundless distance from it which can be exploited, if at all, aesthetically – the aesthetic being understood here as a category of the non-existent type of person, the residue of that positive aesthetic which makes it possible to put this non-existence into relief in the detective novel. The person sitting around idly is overcome by a disinterested satisfaction in the contemplation of a world creating itself, whose purposiveness is felt without being associated with any representation of a purpose. The Kantian definition of the beautiful is instantiated here in a way that takes seriously its isolation of the aesthetic and its lack of content. For in the emptied-out individuals of the detective novel – who, as rationally constructed complexes, are comparable to the transcendental subject – the aesthetic faculty is indeed detached from the existential stream of the total person. It is reduced to an unreal, purely formal relation that manifests the same indifference to the self as it does to matter. Kant himself was able to overlook this horrible last-minute sprint of the transcendental subject, since he still believed there was a seamless transition from the transcendental to the preformed subject-object world. The fact that he does not completely give up the total person even in the aesthetic realm is confirmed by his definition of the 'sublime', which takes the ethical into account and thereby attempts to reassemble the remaining pieces of the fractured whole. In the hotel lobby, admittedly, the aesthetic – lacking all qualities of sublimity – is presented without any regard for these upward-striving intentions, and the formula 'purposiveness without purpose'[1] also exhausts its content. Just as the lobby is the space that does not refer beyond itself, the aesthetic condition corresponding to it constitutes itself as its own limit. It is forbidden to go beyond this limit, so long as the tension that would propel the breakthrough is repressed and the marionettes of *Ratio* – who are not human beings – isolate themselves from their bustling activity. But the aesthetic that has become an end in itself pulls up its own roots; it obscures the higher level toward which it should refer and signifies only its own emptiness, which, according to the literal meaning of the Kantian definition, is a mere relation of faculties. It rises above a meaningless formal harmony only when it is in the service of something when instead of making claims to autonomy it inserts itself into the tension that does not concern it in particular. If human beings orient themselves beyond the form, then a kind of beauty may also mature that is a fulfilled beauty, because

it is the consequence and not the aim – but where beauty is chosen as an aim without further consequences, all that remains is its empty shell. Both the hotel lobby and the house of God respond to the aesthetic sense that articulates its legitimate demands in them. But whereas in the latter the beautiful employs a language with which it also testifies against itself, in the former it is involuted in its muteness, incapable of finding the other. In tasteful lounge chairs a civilization intent on rationalization comes to an end, whereas the decorations of the church pews are born from the tension that accords them a revelatory meaning. As a result, the chorales that are the expression of the divine service turn into medleys whose strains encourage pure triviality, and devotion congeals into erotic desire that roams about without an object.

The *equality* of those who pray is likewise reflected in distorted form in the hotel lobby. When a congregation forms, the differences between people disappear, because these beings all have one and the same destiny, and because, in the encounter with the spirit that determines this destiny, anything that does not determine that spirit simply ceases to exist – namely, the limit of necessity, posited by man, and the separation, which is the work of nature. The provisional status of communal life is experienced as such in the house of God, and so the sinner enters into the 'we' in the same way as does the upright person whose assurance is here disturbed. This – the fact that everything human is oriented toward its own contingency – is what creates the equality of the contingent. The great pales next to the small, and good and evil remain suspended when the congregation relates itself to that which no scale can measure. Such a relativization of qualities does not lead to their confusion but instead elevates them to the status of reality, since the relation to the last things demands that the penultimate things be convulsed without being destroyed. This equality is positive and essential, not a reduction and foreground; it is the fulfilment of what has been differentiated, which must renounce its independent singular existence in order to save what is most singular. This singularity is awaited and sought in the house of God. Relegated to the shadows so long as merely human limits are imposed, it throws its own shadow over those distinctions when man approaches the absolute limit.

In the hotel lobby, equality is based not on a relation to God but on a relation to the nothing. Here, in the space of unrelatedness, the change of environments does not leave purposive activity behind, but brackets it for the sake of a freedom that can refer only to itself and therefore sinks into relaxation and indifference. In the house of God, human differences diminish in the face of their provisionality, exposed by a seriousness that dissipates the certainty of all that is definitive. By contrast, an aimless lounging, to which no call is addressed, leads to the mere play that elevates the unserious everyday to the level of the serious. Simmel's definition of society as a 'play form of sociation' is entirely legitimate, but does not get beyond mere description. What is presented in the hotel lobby is the formal similarity of the figures, an equivalence that signifies not fulfilment but evacuation. Removed from the hustle and bustle, one does gain some distance from the distinctions of 'actual' life, but without being subjected to a new determination that would circumscribe from above the sphere of validity for these determinations. And it is in this way that a person can vanish into an undetermined void, helplessly reduced to a 'member of society as such' who stands superfluously off to the side and, when playing, intoxicates himself. This invalidation of togetherness, itself already unreal, thus does not lead up toward reality but is more of a sliding down into the doubly unreal mixture of the undifferentiated atoms from which the world of appearance is constructed. Whereas in the house of God a creature emerges which sees itself as a supporter of the community, in the hotel lobby what emerges is the inessential foundation at the basis of rational socialization. It approaches the nothing and takes shape by analogy with the abstract and formal *universal concepts* through which thinking that has escaped from the tension believes it can grasp the world. These abstractions are inverted images of the universal concepts conceived within the relation; they rob the ungraspable given of its possible content, instead of raising it to the level of reality by relating it to the higher determinations. They are irrelevant to the oriented and total person who, the world in hand, meets them halfway; rather, they are posited by the transcendental subject, which allows them to become part of the powerlessness into which that transcendental subject degenerates as a result of its claim to be creator of the world. Even if free-floating *Ratio* – dimly aware of its limitation – does acknowledge the concepts of God, freedom and immortality, what it discovers are not the homonymic existential concepts, and the categorical imperative is surely no substitute for a commandment that arises out of an ethical resolution. Nevertheless, the weaving of these concepts into a system confirms that people do not

want to abandon the reality that has been lost; yet, of course, they will not get hold of it precisely because they are seeking it by means of a kind of thinking which has repudiated all attachment to that reality. The desolation of *Ratio* is complete only when it removes its mask and hurls itself into the void of random abstractions that no longer mimic higher determinations, and when it renounces seductive consonances and desires itself even as a concept. The only immediacy it then retains is the now openly acknowledged nothing, in which, grasping upward from below, it tries to ground the reality to which it no longer has access. Just as God becomes, for the person situated in the tension, the beginning and end of all creation, so too does the intellect that has become totally self-absorbed create the appearance of a plenitude of figures from zero. It thinks it can wrench the world from this meaningless universal, which is situated closest to that zero and distinguishes itself from it only to the extent necessary in order to deduct a something. But the world is world only when it is interpreted by a universal that has been really experienced. The intellect reduces the relations that permeate the manifold to the common denominator of the concept of energy, which is separated merely by a thin layer from the zero. Or it robs historical events of their paradoxical nature and, having levelled them out, grasps them as progress in one-dimensional time. Or, seemingly betraying itself, it elevates irrational 'life' to the dignified status of an entity in order to recover itself, in its delimitation, from the now liberated residue of the totality of human being, and in order to traverse the realms across their entire expanse. If one takes as one's basis these extreme reductions of the real, then (as Simmel's philosophy of life confirms) one can obtain a distorted image of the discoveries made in the upper spheres – an image that is no less comprehensive than the one provided by the insistence of the words 'God' and 'spirit'. But even less ambiguously than the abusive employment of categories that have become incomprehensible, it is the deployment of empty abstractions that announces the actual position of a thinking that has slipped out of the tension. The visitors in the hotel lobby who allow the individual to disappear behind the peripheral equality of social masks, correspond to the exhausted terms that coerce differences out of the uniformity of the zero. Here, the visitors suspend the undetermined special being – which, in the house of God, gives way to that invisible equality of beings standing before God (out of which it both renews and determines itself) – by devolving into tuxedos. And the triviality of their conversation haphazardly aimed at utterly insignificant objects so that one might encounter oneself in their exteriority, is only the obverse of prayer, directing downward what they idly circumvent.

The observance of *silence,* no less obligatory in the hotel lobby than in the house of God, indicates that in both places people consider themselves essentially as equals. In *Death in Venice* Thomas Mann formulates this as follows: 'A solemn stillness reigned in the room, of the sort that is the pride of all large hotels. The attentive waiters moved about on noiseless feet. A rattling of the tea service, a half-whispered word was all that one could hear.' The contentless solemnity of this conventionally imposed silence does not arise out of mutual courtesy, of the sort one encounters everywhere, but rather serves to eliminate differences. It is a silence that abstracts from the differentiating word and compels one downward into the equality of the encounter with the nothing, an equality that a voice resounding through space would disturb. In the house of God, by contrast, silence signifies the individual collecting himself as firmly directed self, and the word addressed to human beings is effaced solely in order to release another word, which, whether uttered or not, sits in judgment over human beings.

Since what counts here is not the dialogue of those who speak, the members of the congregation are anonymous. They outgrow their names because the very empirical being which these names designate disappears in prayer; thus, they do not know one another as particular beings whose multiple determined existences enmesh them in the world. If the proper name reveals its bearer, it also separates him from those whose names have been called; it simultaneously discloses and obscures, and it is with good reason that lovers want to destroy it, as if it were the final wall separating them. It is only the relinquishing of the name – which abolishes the semi-solidarity of the intermediate spheres – that allows for the extensive solidarity of those who step out of the bright obscurity of reciprocal contact and into the night and the light of the higher mystery. Now that they do not know who the person closest to them is, their neighbour becomes the closest, for out of his disintegrating appearance arises a creation whose traits are also theirs. It is true that only those who stand before God are sufficiently estranged from one another to discover they are brothers; only they are exposed to such an extent that they can love one another without knowing one another and without using names. At the limit

of the human they rid themselves of their naming, so that the word might be bestowed upon them – a word that strikes them more directly than any human law. And in the seclusion to which such a relativization of form generally pushes them, they inquire about their form. Having been initiated into the mystery that provides the name, and having become transparent to one another in their relation to God, they enter into the 'we' signifying a commonality of creatures that suspends and grounds all those distinctions and associations adhering to the proper name.

This limit case 'we' of those who have dispossessed themselves of themselves – a 'we' that is realized vicariously in the house of God due to human limitations – is transformed in the hotel lobby into the isolation of anonymous atoms. Here profession is detached from the person and the name gets lost in the space, since only the still unnamed crowd can serve *Ratio* as a point of attack. It reduces to the level of the nothing – out of which it wants to produce the world – even those pseudo-individuals it has deprived of individuality, since their anonymity no longer serves any purpose other than meaningless movement along the paths of convention. But if the meaning of this anonymity becomes nothing more than the representation of the insignificance of this beginning, the depiction of formal regularities, then it does not foster the solidarity of those liberated from the constraints of the name; instead, it deprives those encountering one another of the possibility of association that the name could have offered them. Remnants of individuals slip into the nirvana of relaxation, faces disappear behind newspapers, and the artificial continuous light illuminates nothing but mannequins. It is the coming and going of unfamiliar people who have become empty forms because they have lost their password, and who now file by as ungraspable flat ghosts. If they possessed an interior, it would have no windows at all, and they would perish aware of their endless abandonment, instead of knowing of their homeland as the congregation does. But as pure exterior, they escape themselves and express their non-being through the false aesthetic affirmation of the estrangement that has been installed between them. The presentation of the surface strikes them as an attraction; the tinge of exoticism gives them a pleasurable shudder. Indeed, in order to confirm the distance whose definitive character attracts them, they allow themselves to be bounced off a proximity that they themselves have conjured up: their monological fantasy attaches designations to the masks, designations that use the person facing them as a toy. And the fleeting exchange of glances which creates the possibility of exchange is acknowledged only because the illusion of that possibility confirms the reality of the distance. Just as in the house of God, here too namelessness unveils the meaning of naming; but whereas in the house of God it is an awaiting within the tension that reveals the preliminariness of names, in the hotel lobby it is a retreat into the unquestioned groundlessness that the intellect transforms into the names' site of origin. But where the call that unifies into the 'we' is not heard, those that have fled the form are irrevocably isolated.

In the congregation the entire community comes into being, for the immediate relation to the supralegal *mystery* inaugurates the paradox of the law that can be suspended in the actuality of the relation to God. That law is a penultimate term that withdraws when the connection occurs that humbles the self-assured and comforts those in danger. The tensionless people in the hotel lobby also represent the entire society, but not because transcendence here raises them up to its level; rather, this is because the hustle and bustle of immanence is still hidden. Instead of guiding people beyond themselves, the mystery slips between the masks; instead of penetrating the shells of the human, it is the veil that surrounds everything human; instead of confronting man with the question of the provisional, it paralyses the questioning that gives access to the realm of provisionality. In his all-too contemplative detective novel *Der Tod kehrt im Hotel ein* (Death Enters the Hotel), Sven Elvestad writes:

> Once again it is confirmed that a large hotel is a world unto itself and that this world is like the rest of the large world. The guests here roam about in their light-hearted, careless summer existence without suspecting anything of the strange mysteries circulating among them.

'Strange mysteries': the phrase is ironically ambiguous. On the one hand, it refers quite generally to the disguised quality of lived existence as such; on the other, it refers to the higher mystery that finds distorted expression in the illegal activities that threaten safety. The clandestine character of all legal and illegal activities – to which the expression initially and immediately refers – indicates that in the hotel lobby the pseudo-life that is unfolding in pure immanence is being pushed back toward its undifferentiated origin. Were the mystery to come out of its shell, mere possibility would disappear in the fact: by detaching the illegal from the nothing, the Something would have appeared. The hotel management therefore thoughtfully conceals from its guests the real events which could put an end to the false aesthetic situation shrouding that nothing. Just as the formerly experienced higher mystery pushes those oriented toward it across the midpoint, whose limit is defined by the law, so does the mystery – which is the distortion of the higher ground and as such the utmost abstraction of the dangers that disrupt immanent life – relegate one to the lapsed neutrality of the meaningless beginning from which the pseudo-middle arises. It hinders the outbreak of differentiations in the service of emancipated *Ratio*, which strengthens its victory over the Something in the hotel lobby by helping the conventions take the upper hand. These are so worn out that the activity taking place in their name is at the same time an activity of dissimulation – an activity that serves as protection for legal life just as much as for illegal life, because as the empty form of all possible societies it is not oriented toward any particular thing but remains content with itself in its insignificance . . ..

NOTE

1   This hallmark phrase from Kant's *Critique of Judgement* is put in quotation marks in the later republication of the essay.

27
Pattern of Town Houses

Johan Van De Beek

Source: *Raumplan Versus Plan Libre, Adolf Loos and Le Corbusier 1919-1930*. Edited by Max Risselda. Rizzoli International, 1988

Raumplan

Adolf Loos' particular contribution to architecture is usually summarized under the heading of "Raumplan", a term introduced by Kulka, one of Loos' pupils.[1] Raumplan was not precisely defined, as more aspects of Loos' work were described, the concept of Raumplan grew accordingly, it is a container concept. Since "Raumplan" is only used in connection with Loos' work, it has played no part in developing a theory, the word has a chiefly polemical function.

Translating "Raumplan" as "space plan", I supplement it with what I regard as necessary, complementary plans the "living plan" and the "material plan". I group the "patterns" round these three plans (space, living and material).

1. "Raumplan" – "spaceplan" – the manner in which a sort of 3 dimensional or vertical space is ordered.
   In which is compounded:
2. "Living plan" – the way the ground plan, a sort of 2 dimensional or horizontal space is ordered.
3. "Material plan" – the way the various building and surfacing materials are employed, to give texture and thus sensation and atmosphere.

N.B. the qualification "a sort of 2 dimensional space" recognises that any groundplan has a 3 dimensional constituent.

I start by describing a group of "patterns" pertinent to the work Loos produced around the period of the Great War, but without tracing their evolution. At that time Loos had already converted about forty apartments and had built several private houses. I go on to show how new solutions in Loos' work were influenced by a re-orientation towards the "classics". Finally I describe the fruits of this re-orientation as exemplified by one of his last three villas: the Villa Müller.

A SURVEY OF PATTERNS DEVELOPED BEFORE THE GREAT WAR

Living Plan

Compact living

The most general statement which can be made about habitation concerns the degree and the nature of the distribution of various living activities. Adolf Loos' dwellings are marked by a maximum of three-dimensional compactness and a concentration of length, width and height. The opposite is demonstrated by, say, Frank Lloyd Wright's prairie houses, or the traditional Japanese dwellings which attracted architects' attention in Loos' day. In European stone-built villas, compactness is the rule rather than the exception, Loos avoids wings, annexes and separate outhouses.

Movement: A consequence of compact living is that internal contacts are maximized and external contacts minimized, another consequence is the approach to the house as an object. There is no gradual external preparation (e.g. lodge, forecourt, gate, courtyard, passage, front door). Loos shifts this gradual introduction to the inside, compact living places maximum emphasis on entering and leaving.

The difference between up and down (gradient of vertical privacy)

The vertical structure of Adolf Loos' town houses consists of four functional levels. The top and bottom levels – attic and basement respectively – accommodate the secondary functions amply represented in the villa's programme. These are mainly service areas (storage, heating, garage, washing, ironing, staff quarters, etc.). The living programme is implemented on the two middle levels. The lower of the two contains the common living rooms, the upper one the various bedrooms and related facilities such as bathrooms and dressing-rooms.

The living layer leads directly outside (entrance, veranda), and is hence the most public of the four levels. The sleeping level is only accessible from the living level, privacy is thus ensured.

Movements: Vertical differentiation of the living programme generates vertical movement in the house. This movement takes place via staircases, occasionally a small service elevator and in a later house (Müller) via a passenger elevator.

The difference between front and back (gradient of axial privacy)

The town houses relate directly to the street, the street-front is the most public and contains the entrance. The principal living rooms are at the back, facing away from the street towards the private outside-area, the side with the greatest privacy.

This pattern distinguishes these houses from the traditional town house, which is orientated towards the street, although working-class and middle-class dwellings by Loos are street-oriented.

The difference between front and back is only significant on the living level. The bedroom level, being higher, shows less difference in this respect.

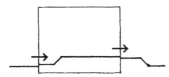

Figure 27.1

Movement: The front-back difference introduced movement from the front towards the rear (Figure 27.1). The difference between street level and living level is bridged just beyond the front door, movement towards the main living space is always upward. The difference between the living level and the garden is bridged just outside the back door.

The difference between left and right (gradient of lateral privacy)

A distinctive feature of Loos' houses is the pronounced difference between left and right. Movement from front to back is no longer, as in classical architecture, via the central axis. Loos re-routes the movement along one of the sides, where he places a cloakroom with an outside view.

Whether the cloakroom is on the left or right depends on the situation and hence on whether the movement has a left or right bias (from front to side and rear). Combined with stair-climbing, this generates a spiral movement.

The side with the cloakroom is the living side of the house. The opposite side contains the service area, often including the kitchen. This provides kitchen staff with a short cut to the front door.

The centrifugal use of space

Adolf Loos furnishes his rooms in a way conducive to a centrifugal use of the space. Activities shift to the sides of the rooms, leaving the middle free.[2] This means that couches and dining-room furniture are no longer in their traditional position in the middle of the room, but along the walls,[3] activity areas are now oriented towards the empty space in the middle.

In Loos' work this seating pattern nearly always works out. He used it for the dining area in his own house, though not always in his other projects, where the dining table often still occupies the middle of the room.

Space Plan

The simple exterior

In Loos' houses, compact living is packed into a simple, basic cubic shape, seen from outside, the centripetal character dominates.[4]

Loos' white-plastered, unadorned cubic exteriors (notably the Steiner house) label him as a forerunner of Functionalism, but more recently it has been pointed out that he was inspired by the simple bourgeois architecture of around 1800.

The difference between top and bottom

Where required by local regulations, the roof is pitched, but the chosen form – a cradle or mansard roof – emphasizes the space-enclosing aspect and the terrace in front of the living space provides a link with the ground.

The difference between front and back

Seen from the front, the house has an object-like character and from the back more of a space-shaping character. This space-creating character was later expressed increasingly by a terraced construction.

The difference between left and right

On the outside the difference between left and right is played down as much as possible.

The compound interior

The interior is composed of cubic spaces, some early works display the odd exception of a round space. Space on the sleeping level is defined by bedrooms which are individually accessible from the circulation area. The living rooms are related in a variety of ways; we shall therefore concentrate on the living level.

Sleeping and living levels are separate. Even when Loos did design double-height rooms, they do not exceed the living layer and never form a link between the living and sleeping levels, unlike the traditional "hall" in English country houses and the double-height rooms in Le Corbusier's houses.

Recesses

The centrifugal pattern often generates alcove-like appendages to rooms.[5] The commonest of these is the fireplace, and also the window recess, often fitted with a built-in seat commanding a view of the room; the window recess is also often used as a flower window. Various types of storage unit can be built into these recesses, such as sideboards and bookshelves, and these recesses have lower ceilings than the main area of a room.

Open staircases

Stairs on the living level have open access to the living rooms[6] and the space under staircases is sometimes used for a fireplace. These recesses and open stairs have a theatrical effect, highlighting the difference between "audience" and "actor".

Eccentric circulation (asymmetrical experience of symmetry)

Doors to rooms are positioned off-centre, which gives an improved view of the room. Circulation through the room avoids the centre and the route leaves the room by another door which is also eccentrically placed. In this way circulation routes are kept to the perimeter of the room and away from the centre which can then become a "place". This "place" on the symmetrical axis may then be given extra focus when a recessed space, an alcove, is added to the main space.

This "spiral" circulation pattern, in "horizontal plan" (Living Plan) is matched by a spiral circulation pattern in section, the "vertical plan" (Space Plan). By contrast, symmetrical movement can occur at the front door and the doors to the terrace.

Material Plan

Supporting construction

External walls are invariably load-bearing and of brick, with brick, load-bearing partition walls or a single column, accommodating the flue (Rufer, Moller). Floors are of timber with larger floor areas and supporting joists of concrete. Partition walls are of timber or thin brick, or are formed by cupboards.

The supporting construction is a necessity which does not play an architectonic role in Loos' work. In that sense a greater difference between him and the Functionalist architects is barely conceivable, so-called "constructional honesty" meant nothing to him.

Exterior cladding

On the town houses around 1920 this is always plain plaster, frequently with a stone plinth and topped by a cornice: (this combination is used hardly at all in the preceding period and is abandoned again in later projects).

This plaster is in the tradition of undecorated plaster, its lack of ornament contrasting with the nineteenth-century predilection for eclectic decoration. Plaster like this has the value of maximum neutrality, like that of a man's gray three-piece suit on the social plane.

Interior cladding

The inside surfaces always differ from one room to the next, the choice of material, determining a room's mood or character, was important to Loos.[7] Material was chosen mainly for its affective value.

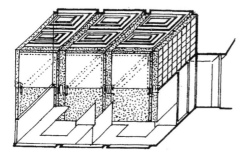

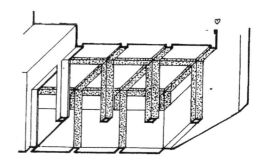

Figure 27.2

Natural stone and hardwood were treated so as to show off the natural qualities of the material to their best advantage, but simpler material was also used, and softwood was painted. Traditional patterns such as dado panelling, parquet and beamed ceilings were adhered to. Both the choice of distinctively marked materials and their plastic treatment tend to play down their object-like character and create a suggestion of spaciousness.

Framing elements such as columns, pilasters and beams delineate space by standing out from the wall as separate elements. The infill panels (panelling and coffered ceilings) act as space modulators. A composition may exploit the interaction of both aspects but variation is liable to occur in the details, for example the regular S-shaped moulding of pilasters, or between the square panels and framing of the wallpanelling construction.

Interior surfaces in early designs do not treat frames and panels systematically, meaning that they are interchangeable on both walls and ceilings. In his apartments Loos made frequent use of stone frames in the dining-room and timber panels in the drawing-room.

In public spaces surfaces are often totally systematized. A complete frame system is created: piers, beams and joists, filled with panels. The frame is dominant, enclosing the space like a cage (Kärtnerbar, Goldman & Salatsch, Figure 27.2).

Reorientation

In the previous section the patterns used by Adolf Loos were described as static. Between about 1905 and 1923, however, his work underwent a development which can only be comprehended fully by examining a number of projects in their proper order. We are chiefly interested here in the residences and since this period of Loos' work is distinguished by a marked increase in classical

elements, it is also necessary to look briefly at projects with a public, urban, orientation.

Increase in spatial contrasts

In Loos' many apartment conversions, all the rooms are on one level and one of the means by which spatial differentiation was achieved was to lower the ceiling in recessed areas. In new villas, too (Steiner 1910, Stoessl 1911, Horner 1912, Scheu 1912), Loos worked with uninterrupted floor levels, as was also the case with the Duschnitz house of 1915. Movement from one room to the next was still a progress through rooms but from 1916 on, movement in a house was dramatized by intensified spatial contrasts. The device of the split-level provided a good introduction: the front door and a low cloakroom at street level, and an extra-high reception hall on the living level. Above the cloakroom there might be a second, low room belonging to the living level (Figure 27.3).

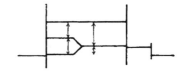

Figure 27.3

Movement from the cloakroom to the reception hall proceeds by way of a short, closed flight of stairs with a turn and without a door, achieving the maximum element of surprise. Movement from the hall to the second room, on the other hand, is by way of open stair in the hall, which heightens the contrast in the movement pattern.

The problem which Loos now had to solve was how to give form to the open connection, including the split level, between the hall and the second room. The first design to exploit the pattern of spatial contrasts is the Mandl conversion (1916). It features a relatively high reception hall from which a staircase winds its way up to the sleeping quarters. The stairs also serve a separate extra room above the entrance, leading to another small room overlooking the hall, rather like a stage-box. The idea seems to be inspired jointly by an English country-house hall and the Theatre.

The Strasser house (1918/19), too, has a closed room (the library) above the cloakroom, but on the same level is another room which opens up like a kind of concert stage onto a sitting-room (Figure 27.4). The connection is still additive here, as if a wall had been omitted.

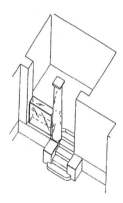

Figure 27.4

The Rufer house (1922) was the first completely new building to display this spatial pattern (Figure 27.5). Here, it is no longer a case of two rooms added together, but of interpenetrating dining and living rooms.

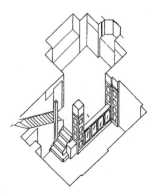

Figure 27.5

The designing of split levels

The gallery in the Mandl house has the effect of a theatre box overlooking the large reception hall,

Loos subsequently sought a more direct and open form for connecting the smaller room with the large one. The split is diminished, there is a direct staircase connection and balustrades and banisters are avoided.

In the case of the dais in the Strasser house, Loos solved the transition problem by placing a stone pillar and a glass case, almost as independent objects on the periphery, near the short flight of stairs (Figure 27.4). The same three elements – stairs, pillar, glass case – occur in the Rufer house, where they are, however, an integral part of the architecture and interior decoration of the house (Figure 27.5). In both houses the three transitional elements are designed in a manner intended to accentuate the transition in different, but equivalent ways. At the place where the level actually changes, the material is given a more active plastic effect because it is no longer flush with the wall.

Increased visual quality

The facades of the prewar houses are characterized by the struggle against superfluous decoration. Old schemes had been abandoned, but no new organization was yet apparent. The various elements of the living programme could be expressed more liberally. Restrictions imposed by municipal authorities with regard to gutter-height had a strong influence on the idea of mass, leading to highly original residences which however failed to indicate an architectural programme (in contrast to the programmatic use later made of the illustration of the Steiner residence).

The process of reorientation is also expressed in the architecture of the facade. An enhanced visual quality is first perceived in the horizontal-vertical contrast in the Duschnitz house (1915), besides the strongly horizontal extension with its large hall, there is the vertical addition of a square tower. A similar tower was added to the Mandl house (1916), with its horizontal loggia and balcony. The designs of these towers derive from neo-classical examples from Germany, and perhaps even from Schinkel (Schloss Tegel in Berlin). It is easy to see why Loos did not feature this type of tower in his other work, there being no grounds for it in the living programme.

A horizontal-vertical contrast can already be observed in Loos' early sketches. It is also confirmed in such projects as the Gartenbaugrunde (1917) and others in which Loos integrated high with more horizontal, low buildings.

The horizontal-vertical contrast recurs later in a flatter form in the facade of the Bronner villa (1921).

Loos also experimented with another kind of visual contrast: the plastic contrast between part and whole, effected by small extensions. In the Strasser conversion it looks like a strange pimple on the front of the house while the design from the Konstandt villa (1919) has an extension on each of the four walls. Plastic accents are a feature of each of the three villas to be discussed later on in this article.

The Greek Revival

In the Strasser conversion (1918/19) Loos used a classical column in the living area for the first time. Up to then he had only used such columns in the Karma villa (1903/06), in a "Serlio-passage" leading to the "Roman bathroom". Classical elements had never been entirely absent from his previous buildings, public buildings in particular.

After Strasser, Loos' residential designs featured more and more columns, both as a transition from one room to another and in loggias giving onto the garden. The columns act as a classicistic framework for the spatial picture.

The cornice, too, as in the Duschnitz and Mandl towers, was given a more pronounced function. In the Reitler conversion (1922) and the new Rufer house (1922), a cornice finishes off the whole house at the top and there is even a copy of a fragment of a frieze from the Parthenon on the facade of the Rufer house.

The use of classical elements to enhance the visual effect appears too in unexecuted projects: the Konstandt villa (1919), the Bronner villa (1921), a palace in Vienna (1921), the Stross house (1922) and the villa for Dr. von Simon (1924).

The Greek revival culminated in the design for the Tribune Tower competition, which also marked its end. Henceforth, apart from the odd sketch, Loos made no further use of classical elements.

While Aldo Rossi regards the tower as the highlight of Loos' oeuvre, and his subsequent work as part of the architect's daily grind, we are concerned here with the question of what architectonic approach replaced the Greek revival.

The surface-column relationship

The single column in the Strasser house has the effect of an objet trouvé. It should however be seen in context with the profuse use of marble panelling of the adjacent dining room. The relationship between the column and the wall, here still far apart, is the pre-eminent problem of neo-classicism. In the un-executed designs mentioned above, this relationship is conceived in a traditional manner. The Tribune Tower is of course a fairly unorthodox solution of the problem.

Examples of untraditional column integration in Loos' earlier work are the H & A Spitz facade (1918, Figure 27.6) and the entrance to the Loos House on the Michaelerplatz (1909–11, Figure 27.7). In neither case does the desired size of the column correspond with the height of the stone base. Loos extends the column at the top by a square section of column in the same material, topped by a cornice with a simple molding. This breaks down the traditional tectonic relationship between carrier and carried, introducing a visual structure which emphasizes still further the reciprocity of part (column) and whole (wall-surface).

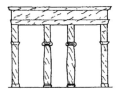

Figure 27.6

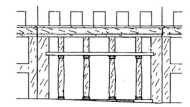

Figure 27.7

Differentiation of wall and column

Another neo-classical problem is how to provide an architectural conclusion at the top. This problem occurs frequently in some projects designed by Loos in the winter of 1922/23, which he spent on the Côte d'Azur: the Babylon Hotel (Figure 27.8),

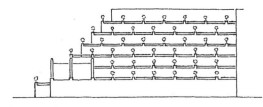

Figure 27.8

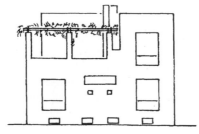

Figure 27.9

a group of twenty villas and the Moissi house in Venice (Figure 27.9). These are all terraced projects overlooking the sea.

Two aspects are important in the design for these terraces: the flower-boxes in Babylon and the columns in the other projects, which are not treated separately but "grow" from the walls. I call this "wall-column differentiation".

The columns are not topped by heavy cornices, but by light lattice-work, another break with the traditional tectonic pattern. Any vegetation, like the orange trees, enhances the ethereal transition to the sky. The material has a serial structure from bottom to top: columns-lattice-twigs-sky . . .

Loos probably borrowed the idea of square columns ending in lattice-work from Schinkel (the casino at Schloss Klein Glienicke, near Berlin). Schinkel, however, used such columns as independent elements.

The blank wall

In Loos' early work the wall is a passive actor in the architectural image. It forms a background for the pattern of window apertures and is upstaged by the columns and cornices. This all changed in 1922. In the design for the Moissi villa (1923) a large section of wall at the top of the facade is left undivided for the first time: a blank surface. In a scale model made for the Salon d'Automne, the wall-surface had a pronounced texture which stood out in the light and there is a lovely water-colour of the Verdier villa (1923), an expressive rendering of the play of light and colours on the building mass. The treatment of the outside wall of the Spanner house (built in 1923/24) produces a distinctive pattern, as was later the case, but with different results, in Josephine Baker's house (1927). Perspectives of projects for Prince Sangusko's stables (1924) and an exhibition palace in Tientsin (1925) show the variegated light on the facade surfaces and in the sky in an almost expressionistic manner. In the blank wall Loos discovered a canvas

for changing daylight and the texture of the material, and used it as an architectonic tool, a quality presaged in the facade of the Karma villa of 1904.

Inside-outside relation

To Loos, the external wall forms an emphatic division between inside and outside. There are of course such necessary transitional elements such as entrance, windows, terrace doors and balconies. These elements are placed on the outside in a more or less compelling visual arrangement: symmetry, horizontal zones, vertical window axes. The rather curious facade of the Strasser house (1918/19) qualifies, in my opinion, as the first example of a facade organized in analogy to the spatial organization of the living level: plastic extension = large hall, the extrusion below, with two windows = the raised level with library and music dais, the two large openings one above the other at the right = the dining and music rooms.

This attempt to invest the facade with the expression of what lies beyond it is linked with the house's urban setting on the street. The rear aspect is quite a different matter, this is where the architectural contrast between front and back is developed.

Subsequent projects have fewer parallels. This might be due to the freer situation, to greater focusing on the development of other visual aspects, or dissatisfaction with this first result.

However, in the three villas to be discussed, this pattern returns explicitly, but now in combination with the plain wall.

The material-space relation

Loos' seaside sojourn apparently provided new impulses. In the terraced projects, living moves outside, to be confronted with the sky, sun and vegetation. A year later, Loos bade farewell to Vienna and moved to Paris. His stay in France engendered a new sense of space in his interiors, he started to design a new kind of room which I refer to as "the salon".

The quality of the outside terrace is brought into the salon, as much light as possible enters through windows on the long wall, a new design for the white plaster ceiling creates a sense of openness at the top, the contiguous surround invests the ceiling area with a more active architectonic meaning because field and frame are united. Ceiling and salon space enter into a material-space relationship.

The design of the wall-covering often echoes the wall-column differentiation pattern. Stone or wood forge a link with the earthly sphere.

The older influence of the English living pattern was now joined by a French one, manifest in the form of the salon. As well as spatial contrasts, the space-material contrasts now become important. Once this relationship had acquired a form of its own, Loos abandoned classical elements. Having performed its function as a catalyst, the Greek revival was played out.

The Müller House (1928–30)

This house was built in Prague for Dr. Frantisek Müller, a building contractor. Because of the success of the collaboration between client and architect, the very differentiated brief resulted in Adolf Loos' most sophisticated "Raumplan". The particular site had a crucial influence on the plan.

The situation

The site lies on the northern slope of the hills above Prague (Figure 27.10). The northern aspect commands a panoramic view, but faces away from the sun. The site is steep (Figure 27.11), and is bordered at the top by a quiet road serving an older residential area. The house stands free on one side, where public steps skirt the site. One of Prague's major approach roads runs past the lower end of the terrain.

The site is thus surrounded on three sides by public space, only the east side bordering on private terrain. The house is developed depthwise and as far west as possible, yielding a closed

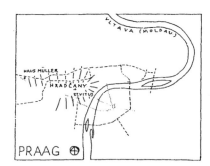

Figure 27.10

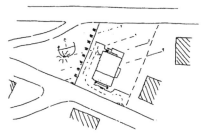

Figure 27.11

garden on the east side. For maximum privacy the garden area was levelled and a retaining wall built on the side bordered by the road.

The living level

A large salon occupies the entire width of the back of the house (Figure 27.12). Due to the sloping site it has a high situation, which gives adequate privacy. A terrace is not feasible here, and would in any case face north. The salon therefore leads out onto a small balcony with a closed parapet and no relationship to the garden. Compensation for this is achieved on the top floor (reached by an elevator) in the form of a large roof-garden leading off the breakfast room.

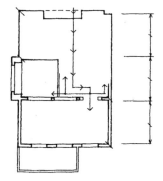

Figure 27.12

As in the Tzara house, there is no room for the dining room at the back of the house, but there is room at the side. The east side, overlooking the closed garden and hence the most private side, is the obvious place for it. The dining-room window, however, is plainly visible from the access road, a problem which was solved by adding a bay window.

Due to the situation of the dining room and the adjacent pantry and kitchen at the side of the house, there is plenty of room on the other side for the introduction. The cloakroom at the side looks out onto an open space. Above the lobby and cloakroom there is room for a library and a room reserved for the lady of the house. This room faces side-ways while the library is oriented towards the access road.

The position of the living area offers little scope for a living hall served by the route past the stairs. Nor is a completely separate staircase, as in the Tzara house, here a feasible option for the Raumplan. For the first time, Loos combines a French salon-like room with an open staircase, so doing by opening up the salon wall and placing the stairs along the periphery.

The stairs to the bedrooms are behind the dining room, in the centre of the house, and receive daylight from a skylight in the roof. The stairs command outside views in three directions, through the salon, dining room and roof skylight. This development makes for a more gradual separation between living and sleeping than in previous projects.

The dining room opens off the salon and has a higher floor, as in earlier projects, a displacement of more than a metre this time (Figure 27.13). The gap is bridged by the through-route upstairs, behind the salon wall. Two axes, at right angles to one another, determine the orientation of the dining room: via the bay window on the side and via the salon at the back, the square plan of the dining room is a reaction to this situation.

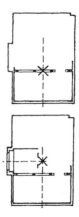

Figure 27.13

Surprising effects result from relationship between the dining room and salon due to the open walls of the salon. As usual, the salon is divided longwise into three, the dining room lying on the secondary axis. The dining room is wider than one bay of the salon, so that the corner of the dining room does not coincide with a salon post. This produces an open corner in the dining room – Loos' first open corner. It relates the dining room diagonally to the salon; moreover, this oblique line of slight is echoed further down by a

stepped stringer, reminiscent of the outside steps of the Moller house.

The relationship between living level and ground level

The oblique line of sight from the dining room to the salon continues outside, having passed through the salon window (Figure 27.14). This downward-slanting line is possible because there is no balcony in front of this window. The line of sight appears to run parallel to the sloping site, this is because the difference in level between the dining room and salon is parallel to the difference in ground level both longitudinally and laterally.

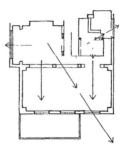

Figure 27.14

The ensuing parallel course of nature and culture replaces an actual outward extension of the living level.

The introduction

As in the Moller house, access to the living area is via an alcove approached by a short flight of stairs and a turn – a theatrical entrance (Figure 27.15). The alcove lies on the secondary axis of the salon. On entering the room one's first sight is the

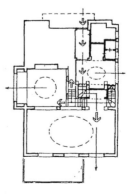

Figure 27.15

panorama that is visible through the same window that frames the diagonal view from the dining room. A number of routes intersect directly in front of this alcove and immediately behind, the open wall of the salon acts as a monumental gateway.

The cloakroom, that precedes the large salon, is classically divided into three along its length, and again is approached along a secondary axis. The cloakroom is on the same level as the front door, to which it is linked by a short, passage-like vestibule.

The front door is set in a shallow recess topped by a flat, open porch. The front door is at one side of the recess, a built-in bench in the middle (this is the south side) and a hatch to the coal-cellar chute on the other side. This is the most effective example of Loos' front-door treatment, which always relates subtly to its surrounding spaces and functions. The almost straight line of approach from the front door to the salon maintains a secondary axis, but the primary axis moves to and fro. Never before was symmetry so dynamic.

Closer inspection, however, shows that the axis of the façade does not coincide with that of the salon (Figure 27.16) but is staggered by half the width of the stairs. The main practical advantage of this staggered axis is that the entrance recess is then able to develop fully, thus having the same width and arrangement as the cloakroom. On the outside the staggered axis is compensated for by a recessed corner of the building. I do not consider it too far-fetched to associate this recessed corner with the open corner in the dining room; the recessed corner faces a side-road nearly opposite the house.

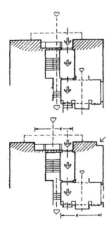

Figure 27.16

The floor levels

Determining the floor levels with regard to the street is problematical, because of the steeply sloping terrain. Loos keeps to the pattern of ascending to the salon. The displacement of the salon floor is reduced by having the front door lower than street level (Figure 27.17) so the salon ends up at almost the same level as the street. Consequently, in order to reach the garage under the salon, a car must descend a whole storey, passing along a long driveway in front of the house and along the side. This lower entrance makes it easier to fit in the library and a room for the mistress of the house, nonetheless, the plan results for the first time in different levels on the bedroom storey; a difference which contributes to a less abrupt transition between the living and sleeping levels. Both the library and mistress's room take up the theme of different levels, each in its own manner. The mistress's room adopts the diagonal line of sight down the stairs almost literally. In the library the theatrical entrance predominates.

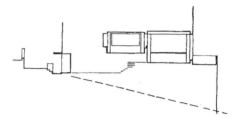

Figure 27.17

Characterization of the space plan

The salon is the dominant space. The central axis does not connect up with any other room, but with the staircase leading to the bedrooms (Figure 27.18). The main axis accommodates the extremes of mobile and stationary activity.

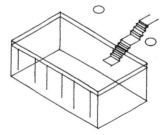

Figure 27.18

The other rooms on the living level are oriented towards the salon to a diminishing degree: dining room, the mistress's room, the library; there is no break, no constriction.

The spatial characteristics and the site

The site is characterized by being open practically the whole way round, the only interruption being on the garden side. Inside there are no continuous axes or lines of sight except for the line between the dining-room window over-looking the garden and the salon window nearly opposite. The stair-case in the middle of the house has a centrifugal effect on the various living rooms.

The difference between front and back

Both the front and back walls face roads. Each duly displays a mainly closed surface with the almost graphic rendering of the window openings that determine the house's appearance. Due to the fall in the ground and the flat roof-garden, the back wall is one storey lower than the facade. A lateral shift is particularly in evidence at the rear, where the driveway turns into a terraced extension for the automobile. The garage entrance is set in a low recess. Recess and terrace give the basement a strong sideways orientation, towards open space. This orientation is reinforced by means of the closed parapet of the terrace at the back and open railings at the side. This is the first time that Loos gives spatial meaning to the basement.

The relation with the city centre

The roof-garden is partly-enclosed by two side-walls that link the chimneys with the roof construc-tion (Figure 27.19). A large window pierces the east end wall. One's first sight, on arriving at the roof-garden, is of Prague Castle and St. Vitus' Cathedral, framed in this window and this is the first time that Loos makes an explicit relationship with the city. Because of the view and because of the breakfast room giving onto the roof-garden, the roof-garden acquires a social meaning, as well

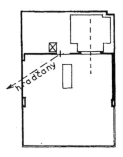

Figure 27.19

as a relationship with the sky: social aspect and the spatial aspect merge.

The plasticity of the facade

The house is close to the road and this proximity is matched by a subdued plasticity (Figure 27.20): a semi-recessed porch and a subtly-projecting porch. Because of the sunken area in front of the house a semi-open area is generated between the facade and the road. The peripheral character of this area is echoed by the shallow plasticity of the recessed entrance, which has a detailed fill-in and a traver-tine lining. For a brief moment, the living area is extended outside.

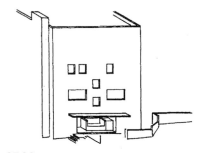

Figure 27.20

The articulation of the facade

In this house the plastered facade is without plinth (Figure 27.21). To the cursory glance, there is not a square in sight, until one notices the yellow brick retaining wall between drive and entrance, which is now seen to assume the character of a separate plinth. The dividing line corresponds with the level of the salon floor.

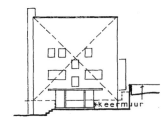

Figure 27.21

Above the entrance is an arrangement of small and large windows. The middle windows overlooking the service stairs, are displaced by a half-storey. This makes the blank space above the windows appear to spread out fan-wise down-wards, between the windows – an effect which the added surround to the Moller house windows deliberately avoids.

An asymmetrically placed window is added above. This of course corresponds with the asymmetrical disposition of the house behind the facade, the centre point of the top windows, corresponds however, with the central axis of the salon and rear wall.

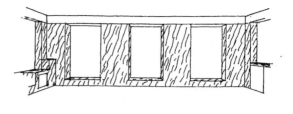

The facade and spatial characteristics

The entrance recess is the spatially dominant element of the facade, separated from a cluster of windows by an overhang. An analogy is provided by the separation of the salon from a cluster of rooms by the autonomous rear wall. The centre of the facade is marked by the windows which are shifted because of the staircase, analogous to the central position of the stairs inside the house.

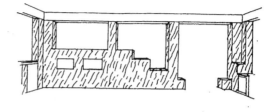

Articulation of the rear aspect

The rear facade has no evident base. (Figure 27.22). The projecting balcony and garage terrace follow the gradient of the terrain, thus enhancing lateral orientation towards open space. The garage terrace is formally involved in the whole.

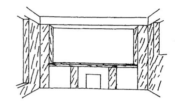

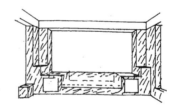

Figure 27.23

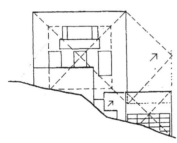

Figure 27.22

The articulation of the rear facade is arranged inside a square, the image is reinforced in order to compensate for the missing base.

Only if one is familiar with the plan inside can the special position of one particular window in the salon be appreciated: this window now marks the centre of the rear facade together with the open space of the garage terrace.

The interior surfaces: the salon

This is the most opulently decorated salon of all the houses described here (Figure 27.23). The

ceiling and its surround are white, this is enhanced by four matt-white spherical lamps on secondary axes. Columns are expressed as separate from walls with free-standing columns in the rear wall, the corners are indented. By contrast, the seating area opposite is incorporated into the mass of the wall, the indented corners are transformed into projecting ones. This doubles the column zone between which the seating is fitted.

The open rear wall makes it undesirable to limit the marble cladding to the interior of the salon and it duly continues to the back of this wall, in the dining room and traffic zone. The other side of the peripheral traffic zone, round the entrance recess below the mistress's room, is clad with the same Cipollino marble, thus reinforcing the character of the peripheral circulation zone.

Interior surfaces: dining room

The open corner in the dining room makes it impossible for the space to be defined either by projecting corner columns or by indented panelling. The room is therefore primarily determined by the fixed-table in the middle, its granite surface supported by an octagonal pillar (Figure 27.24). A round lamp of matt plate-glass is suspended above the table and the room is further defined by a coffered mahogany ceiling. The horizontal planes of the room are primary, and enclose the space like ice-cream wafers.

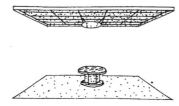

Figure 27.24

In none of the rooms so far described does Loos open up the walls to such an extent as in this dining room (Figure 27.25). The treatment of the wall adjoining the salon has already been indicated: the

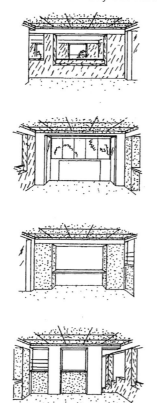

Figure 27.25

green-veined Cipollino marble of the autonomous rear wall. However, the dining room needed a character of its own, independent of the salon. The salon is light, so the dining room for contrast, is dark. This means that the marble has to stop and each wall is consequently different, the differences meeting abruptly at the corners. White plaster; mahogany cupboards. Due to the variation in the wall finishes we observe for the first time a centrifugal force emanating from the centre, unchecked by the centripetal force of the wall-order.

The mistress's room

The seating area in the room reserved for the lady of the house is panelled in lemon-wood, including its ceiling, which gives the room a box-like character. The texture of the wood contrasts with the openness of the dining room, in view of the symmetrical position of the two rooms (Figure 27.26c).

Proportions

As in the Tzara house, the salon is nearly twice as long as it is wide (Figure 27.26). Like Tzara again, the depth of the dining room, including the column zone, equals the depth in the salon of the space between the columns. The entire house is based on these proportions, within the walls, the whole house is in a ratio of 2:3. The dining room, including the column zone, is one-sixth of this arrangement, but turns out to have been moved the thickness of one column, in order to connect it with the secondary axis of the salon and to create the space needed in the centre of the house for the stairs. This one-column shift also occurs elsewhere.

The column thickness is the same as ceiling panel in the dining room, the salon is 22k × 12k, and the total inside is 24k × 36k. The dining-room lamp and the lamp in the mistress's room appear to form together the double centre of the house.

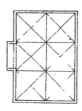 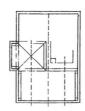 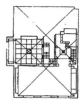

Figure 27.26

SUMMARY AND CONCLUSION

This article describes the "Raumplan" of private urban residences designed by Adolf Loos. In describing the "Raumplan" the author subdivides the term to distinguish between living plan, space plan and material plan.

In turn, each of these is formed by a complex of patterns.

The article starts with a survey of the patterns characterizing Loos' houses up to World War One. This was followed by a process of reorientation towards classical architecture in Loos' work of the first postwar years. This reorientation eventually led to the emergence of classical elements (column, cornice), and to the development of a method focussing on relationships (between material and space, interior and exterior). This new method evolved into its definitive form in the last three town houses to be built by Loos. The Müller is described in detail.

The living plan of these houses plan displays no innovations. As far as the living plan is concerned, Loos was conservative. Each living plan was realized in a different, concrete situation. The author shows how each situation generated a specific space plan.

Given the plan and situation, this space plan emerges as a (functional) necessity.

The material plan confirms the specific structure of the space plan. This confirmation is caused by the kind, place and size of the surface materials. The relationships between material and space are seen to develop increasingly into a serial organization.

This deprives the space plan of its character of necessity, its uniqueness emerging as a differentiated whole.

In this differentiation of space and material, Adolf Loos was revolutionary.

NOTES

1   Where we spoke of the floor plan hitherto, since Loos we can speak of a space plan. Kulka p. 14.
2   The plan of the room under the current Japanese influence is centrifugal. The furniture is in the corners (not at a slant, however, but straight). The centre is free (space for movement). Artificial light belongs where it is needed. The middle is not accentuated. Kulka p. 28.
3   The walls of a house belong to the architect. There he rules at will. As with the walls so with any furniture that is not movable, such as built-in cupboards and so forth. They are part of the wall, and do not lead the independent life of ostentatious unmodern cabinets. The manufacture of mobile furniture (brass bedstead, iron bedstead, table, chair, armchair, desk, etc.) should be left to craftsmen. Everybody should collect these objects according to his own desire, taste and inclination. Kulka p. 24.
4   The house should be withdrawn on the outside, revealing all its riches inside. Adolf Loos: *Sämtliche Schriften*, ed. Franz Glück, vol. 1, Vienna, Munich 1962 p. 339.
5   The theatre has tiered, storey-high galleries or annexes (boxes), in open connection with a main space which occupies several floors. Loos realized that the cramped box would be unbearable without a view of the main space, and thus that by connecting a higher main space with a lower annex he could save space; he made use of this discovery in his residential buildings. Kulka p. 13.
6   As in all Loos houses, the stairs are in the living room (hall), rendering it more spacious. There is only any point in having a separate staircase in an apartment building shared by several parties. Inside stairs make a one-family house more spacious and comfortable. Rooms on different floors are easily reached from the landings. Kulka p. 33 (on Strasser).
7   As Richard Neutra has remarked, in that period Loos had transplanted to Vienna "the characteristics of H.H. Richardson, that is, false beams in light oak placed for their beauty and fireplaces of unplastered bricks". Benedetto Gravagnuolo: *Adolf Loos: Theory and Work*, New York 1982 p. 97.

PART 3

INTERIOR ARCHITECTURE

Introduction

Interior architecture is a discipline that is generally concerned with the remodelling of existing buildings, although it is also a subject that will address the design of interiors from an architectural viewpoint and will often deal large-scale interior projects. The subject has a direct relationship both with interior design and with architecture, because it often deals with complex spatial, functional, structural, environmental and servicing problems, while also understanding the impact that these will have upon the quality of the interior space.

Throughout history, buildings have been reused and adapted, buildings survive as culture and civilizations change. The already built provides a direct link with the past; it is a connection with the very building bricks of our society. The existing tells the tale or story of how a particular culture evolved. A simple building may depict a certain moment in time; it may relate the particular sensibility of specific era. A more complex structure may have a much more elaborate story to tell. Jorge Silvetti describes this direct link with the past as part of our "fundamental urban condition". He links the physical survival of particular elements of the city with the spiritual survival of our civilisation, and it is this visibility and durability of the physical man-made environment that is testimony to the societies that produced them. "At the risk of sounding too partisan and biased, I would say that even in historic times documents were not always available, and buildings (monuments, vernacular constructions, and public works) are themselves important texts, often providing the first and most lasting impression of a culture".[1]

One of the most pressing concerns for our twenty-first century society is the challenge of the huge stock of existing buildings that have outlived the function for which they were built. Their worth is well recognised, and the importance of retaining them has been long debated, but if they are to be saved, what is to be done with these redundant buildings? Whether these are edifice of character and worth, or ordinary straightforward structures that have simply outlived their purpose, demolition and rebuild is no longer seen as the obvious solution to the continuous use of the specific site. It is now a commonplace architectural approach to reuse, adapt and add-to, rather than the building being razed and a new structure erected in its place.

Issues of heritage and sustainability are at the forefront of many discussions about architecture today. Adaptation offers the opportunity to reinforce the particular character of an area. Issues of collective memory and identity combined with ideas of tradition, history and culture mean that it is important to retain a sense of continuity with the past as a way of creating the future.

The reuse of an existing building to accommodate new use is a very environmentally friendly approach to the creation of new space. By adapting the existing building, the amount of natural resources required to build a structure is greatly reduced. Reuse is obviously a sustainable act; many of the essential services are already in place and the amount of new materials and elements is necessarily limited. This sustainable approach to the reuse of existing buildings can lead to a particular identity for a building and the interior. When remodelling a building, the architect or designer has the opportunity to select elements and materials that reflect the character of place while also being environmentally friendly, and of course the designer can also create an interior that is to be occupied in a sustainable manner. The discovery and re-discovery of methods of reducing energy use are one of the contemporary society's foremost preoccupations, and the attitude taken by the designer can contribute to this debate.

This chapter is divided into three sections, and each will focus upon a particular aspect of the discipline. Interior architecture is possibly the most site-specific of all the architectural and design disciplines. The building that is to be adapted is bound to its situation, it cannot be moved; it can be changed, however, and this is the starting point for the process. It is almost impossible to remodel an existing building without taking the context into consideration, and even if this is little more than the position of the front door! The opening section is entitled **The Understanding of the Context**; this collection of texts and essays discusses the problems and opportunities offered by this connection with site and debates the ideal approach to the practice.

The Process of Remodelling collects together essays that discuss both historical and contemporary attitudes towards the practice of remodelling. The approach that the designer will take towards the character and nature of the existing building will inevitably affect the relationship between the original structure and the new additions. All these essays discuss the search for that theoretical underpinning.

The architect or designer has to come to some conclusion about the worth of the existing building; if it is important, for say historical or political reasons, then in what way should it be preserved: as a monument or should it be allowed to evolve into a building that is appropriate for twentieth century life? This collection of essays, called **Approaches to Conservation**, considers the changing attitudes towards the conservation of buildings and also includes key documents in the establishment of a set of principles for conservation.

Sally Stone

Reference

1 Silvetti, Jorge. "Interactive Realms", in Alexander von Hoffman (Ed.), *Form Modernism and History*. University Press 1996.

Andrea Bruno (1931–)

Andrea Bruno is recognised for his design approach to adaptive reuse and the design of contemporary additions to historic buildings. His most celebrated works include the museums in the Rivoli Castle, Madama Palace and Carignano Palace in Italy, and the Corsica Museum, the Conservatoire des Arts et Métiers de Paris, the University in Fort Vauban in Nîmes, the Castel of Lichtenberg and the Clamecy Museum in France.

His approach is to fully restore the existing building, before making any new interventions upon it. This process involves the selection of a particular point within the building's history, and then restoring the building to that moment in time. So, for example, the Castello di Rivoli is a former residence of the Royal House of Savoy and Bruno's aim was to re-establish the building to its early eighteenth century form. This acts to distance the original from the new additions and thus underscore the separation of the contemporary from the antique.

Bruno is the Professor of Restoration at Milan Polytechnic, but also lectures in Louvain, Belgium, and Rome. Bruno serves as a consultant for the Italian Foreign Ministry and UNESCO.

SECTION 3.1
THE UNDERSTANDING OF THE CONTEXT

Introduction

Interior architecture and the remodelling of an existing building is possibly the most site-specific of all architectural and design activities. The particular situation is completely prescribed, because of course the contextual conditions are dictated by the original structure. The location, position, orientation, structure, materiality and form of the existing building are, needless to say, already in place. The interior architect will respond to these givens in a manner of their own choosing.

There are a number of factors, both within and beyond the existing building, that will have a profound influence upon the adaptation of the building and the design of the interior. These vary from direct relationships with the immediate surroundings to more ephemeral connections with things further away, and all of the texts within this section examine the sense of discovery and recognition that can be uncovered through an investigation of these elements.

The environment around the building can be an important and influential consideration. There are many site-specific conditions that influence the shape and form of a building and subsequently have an effect upon the remodelling. Such contextual factors can include: aspect, orientation, topography, the patterns of street and roads, urban density, and the relationship with a significant landmark. The particular climatic conditions that a building is situated within will also influence the adaptation. The weather needs to be mediated; extremes of heat and cold, too much or too little sun, rain and wind all need to be accommodated. The prevailing environmental conditions around a building are generally predictable and therefore can be worked with.

The building that is to be designed or remodelled is also part of its own context. The three-dimensional relationships within the building, the quality of the individual spaces, the relationship of one room with another and of each floor with the one below or above, the positions of the doors, the windows and the circulation areas can all contribute to the intricate composition of the existing building.

The four essays in this section all discuss the important contribution that context makes towards the consideration or approach to the design of both remodelled and new interiors of buildings. Each argues that it is through the understanding of the given characteristics of a particular environment that an attitude towards the proposal for the design can be formulated. But each essay is from a different angle or point of view.

Sébastien Marot, in what is the first chapter of his book, *Sub-Urbanism and the Art of Memory*, presents the idea of the subversion of urbanism; the idea is that place becomes the over-riding principle of any project and that emphasis is redirected from programme to site. He argues that when the architect considers the design of the urban environment (and with that, the building or the interior), the most important consideration is not the function, but the relationship of the design proposal with its context. He uses four principles to expand upon this, and although these have their basis in the culture of garden design, all are equally applicable to the design of the interior. The four attitudes that characterise his approach are: memory, process rather than product, in-depth reading of the site, and fields of relations. He refers to the works of Francis Yates and her seminal book, *The Art of Memory*, and how mnemonic aids can reinforce the sense of urban and collective memory that for so many urban environments has the potential to be lost.

The design, maintenance and ownership of public space within buildings is a controversial subject. The sheer amount of it has been steadily increasing; covered shopping malls have become a regular feature of the urban environment, and who owns it, how are people allowed to behave within it and the qualities and character of it are much debated. The nature and extent of public space was first explored in an incredible map of Rome constructed by Nolli in 1748. This drawing was much more than a simple map of the city, it depicted all the public spaces, both inside and out. The interior plan of every public building was shown, and thus public space was shown to continue beyond the threshold and into the interior of the building.

Denise Scott Brown in conversation with Maurice Harteveld explores the concept of interior public space, especially the arcade or covered street, in the essay "Interior Space". These spaces always have a direct relationship with the exterior; they often act as links or shortcuts and as such have an intrinsic link with the exterior environment. Maurice Harteveld describes the need to closely study the surrounding urban patterns to ensure that an architecture is designed that fits in with these and therefore encourages communication. These are spaces on a grand architectural scale that although very much part of the interior of the building, need to be addressed in a manner that is normally applied to the urban environment.

The artist has the luxury of not having to take into consideration function, so an installation artist can use the same intellectual process as the architect or designer, but then doesn't have to consider the end user. Many artists have created thought provoking and influential works on an architectural scale that deal with many of the same issues of context and site that the architect or designer is also grappling with. One of the most influential was Gordon Matta-Clark. He literally cut holes and slices into existing buildings. He described this practice as "Undoing" the building. He would, through this process of removal, expose the very character of the place. Rachel Whiteread is an artist who also works with existing buildings to create powerful pieces. Her most controversial was simply called "House". She sprayed the interior of a terrace house in London with concrete, and then removed the containing walls. What was left was a representation of the space with the property; she had literally made solid the interior void. For this in 1993, she won the prestigious Turner Prize.

Robert Irwin, in his essay "Being and Circumstance: Notes Towards a Confidential Art", outlines the four different working categories of public art. Each class or grouping is classified by the sheer amount of interaction with the public space. He then expands upon the final category: "Site Conditioned/Determined". This is where he would place his own work, and he describes it as: "Here the sculptural response draws all its cues (reasons for being) from its surroundings." This is a process of conducting an intimate and hands-on reading of the site, before embarking upon the process of creating an artwork that is integral to the site. Once created, it cannot then be separated; it couldn't exist without its situation.

Beatriz Colomina in an extract from her essay "Interior" investigates the nature of the space within the houses of Adolf Loos. Loos famously once said that: "A cultivated man does not look out of the window; his window is of ground glass; it is there only to let light in, not to let the gaze pass through." And thus, Loos designed buildings that allowed the gaze to travel through the three-dimensional spaces of the interior of the house, rather than from the interior to the outside. Colomina describes the way in which the position of both the furniture and the windows in these houses controlled the manner in which the inhabitants occupied them. A couch, which is placed with its back to a window, is intrinsically linked to the glass. The window provides natural light for the occupant to read by, while the couch is given security by virtue of the sitter becoming silhouetted against the glass. However, it is uncomfortable for the sitter to turn around to look out of the window, so the gaze is always through the long interior space of the house. Loos explores the private three-dimensional interior relationships, and although the forms of the insides of the building are explicitly rendered upon the exterior facades of the building, it is the interiors that are rich, complex and at a scale perfectly suited to human occupation.

This section introduces the notion of the site and how the exploitation of the particular attributes can influence and inform the design of the interior. An interior is bound to its site and it is through the resolution of the factors of building and site, of space and environment, and of place, that an understanding between inside and outside can be reached.

Sally Stone

Gordon Matta-Clark (1943–1978)

Gordon Matta-Clark was a pivotal figure in the Soho art community in New York during the mid-1970s. It was a time when artists were actively seeking new ways of creating art and attempting to move art out of the rarefied atmosphere of the gallery into the public domain. His artwork was completely site-specific and he used houses, warehouses, old office spaces and dock buildings that were abandoned or about to be demolished. He would intervene directly with these buildings by using a chainsaw to literally slice them open. He cut holes in them and score the very fabric of the building to reveal the previously unmade connections between floors, ceilings and walls, the exterior and the interior. His work was much respected at the time and for the 1975 Paris Biennale he constructed "Conical Intersect", a large cone-shaped void cut through buildings in the Les Halles area of the city.

  Matta-Clark came from an artistic dynasty; his parents, Anne Clark and Roberto Matta, were artists, his twin brother was also an artist, and his godfather was Marcel Duchamp.

Building Study: Church of Christ Scientist

Manchester, UK
1998
OMI Architects

When a building is to be remodelled, the architect or designer will make a thorough analysis of the context; this will include an examination of the orientation, aspect, neighbouring buildings, light and space. The building that is to be remodelled is also part of its own context. The quality of the individual spaces, the relationship of one room with another and of each floor with the one below or above, the positions of the doors, the windows and the circulation areas all contribute to the intricate composition of the existing building.

This examination led OMI Architects to carve, from deep within the lower floors of a disused office block, a triple height chapel. This large room or volume is surrounded by circulation space, through which shines natural light, and so this atmospheric room is subtly lit from these large west-facing windows. The long evening sun glows through the circulation areas to provide the congregation with secondary yet evocative light. This is reinforced by artificial light secreted behind structural openings, and thus the chapel is radiant with hidden luminosity.

At ground floor level, at the front of the building, the designers have manipulated the barely double height space to accommodate a reception and bookshop with a tiny reading room. This clever little structure contains bookshelves and a service desk at the lower level and a quiet retreat above.

The architects have exploited the three-dimensional qualities of the building and combined these with the long northern evening light, to create an interior of great consequence.

28
Memory

Sébastien Marot

Source: *Sub-Urbanism and the Art of Memory*. AA Publications, 2003, pp. 6–16

The great question in the field once known as urban design is no longer that of Alberti's day – how to choose the site where a city or a given programme will be built – but how to accommodate sites that have now all been subsumed, in one way or another, by the *suburban condition.*

This new situation entails a complete role reversal between the two major categories of reasoning involved in any given project: *site* and *programme*. While the methods and routines of urban design have traditionally mimicked those of architecture, thereby perpetuating the dominance of programme (and of an approach that goes from programme to site), the suburban condition calls for an inversion of this hierarchy, in which site becomes the regulatory idea of the project.

For this alternative approach and its critical concerns, which today come most clearly into view in the realm of landscape architecture, I propose the name *'sub-urbanism'*.[1]

While this neologism may lack grace, it undoubtedly has several advantages. First, it directs attention to the third territorial estate, found between city and country, where most of us experience the unfolding of daily life, and where architects and designers are most likely to be called upon to intervene. Second, it brings into question the concept of urbanism (itself a neologism, a century ago), which has remained almost etymologically tied to models of the centred city. Third, sub-urbanism recognizes *suburbia* as the historical hotbed of garden design – its concrete Utopia, the very place from which landscape architecture has envisioned the world and locally undertaken its transformation – thereby reclaiming a whole alternative tradition of design and thinking which has seldom been revisited up till now. And finally – and most importantly – sub-urbanism points at the substrate of our practices of territorial development and improvement, revealing site, setting or landscape as the ultimate *infra-structure* whose meaning is put into play in every project.

It should thus be clear that by sub-urbanism I do not mean a regional kind of urban design but, literally, a subversion of urbanism, redirecting emphasis from programme to site – site as the matrix of design, and programme as a tool to explore, read, reveal, invent and ultimately *represent* the site.

There are four attitudes firmly rooted in the culture of garden design that in my view characterize this alternative approach: an active regard for the *memory* of the site; a vision of site and design as processes rather than products; an *in-depth* rather than merely planar reading of open spaces; and a conception of site and design as *fields of relations* rather than as arrangements of objects.[2]

I regard these four principles not as inflexible rules of ethics but rather as the precepts (themselves essentially relative) of a preliminary and therefore imperfect code of conduct that, to borrow from Descartes, 'can be followed by way of provision, so long as one does not yet know any better'.[3] The situation of an architect who embarks upon a new project can often be compared to that of a man dropped by parachute into the middle of a thick forest. In the absence of a map or other devices likely to orient him with certitude, a few plausible principles (such as always moving in as straight a line as possible) may help him find a way out of his predicament.

This is how these four heuristic principles may be considered. They form a travel kit to aid navigation through the tangle of a project's beginnings, but at the same time they act as a critical instrument for a retrospective analysis of the way a project relates to the site – the way it translates and *represents* it.

The idea of memory in architecture – architecture as an instrument of memory, memory as a material or as a dimension of architecture – is a fairly commonplace theme. What instigates me to revisit it here is the idea that, by positioning it in the context of the suburban condition, this old concept may be given new depth.

The concept of sub-urbanism is not planted here as just another flag for just another missionary groping behind the spirit of the times, but as a critical tool to help reflect on what a lot of architects, landscape architects and urban designers actually do, and on the historical context in which they do it.

The essential features of our current knowledge about the art of memory as it was practised by the ancients, and about its evolving status in the history of western culture up to the seventeenth century, were exposed by Frances Yates in a book that remains the major reference on the subject.

SPACE AND MEMORY: THE REDISCOVERY OF A FORGOTTEN ART

'Few people know that the Greeks, who invented many arts, invented an art of memory which, like their other arts, was passed on to Rome whence it descended in the European tradition. This art seeks to memorize through a technique of impressing "places" and "images" on memory. It has usually been classed as "mnemotechnics", which in modern times seems a rather unimportant branch of human activity. But in the ages before printing a trained memory was vitally important; and the manipulation of images in memory must always to some extent involve the psyche as a whole.'[4]

Yates's book reveals the degree to which the art of memory, far from being merely an annexe to the edifice of classical culture, played a crucial structural role, interrelated with all the other major divisions of rhetoric. As a practice, it was so pervasive that its importance tended to go unstated in the texts, with the result that it can be easily overlooked by the contemporary reader, who no longer makes use of it. In our day, the philosophy student will no doubt consider it a curiosity that certain of Plato's works depict individuals capable of reciting, from beginning to end, a dialogue overheard and then memorized. While the references are rare and their interpretation is not always crystal-clear, we do have a few relatively concordant sources that allow us to reconstruct the mechanism of the *ars memorativa* as it was transmitted from Greece to Rome. The major ones are the anonymous treatise *Ad Herennium*, Cicero's

De Oratore and Quintilian's *Institutio Oratoria*. By analysing these treatises, and comparing them to other canonical texts from the history of philosophy – whose interpretation she thereby clarifies – Yates is able to describe the general principles of the art of memory:

'The first step was to imprint on the memory a series of *loci* or places. The commonest, though not the only, type of mnemonic place system used was the architectural type. The clearest description of the process is that given by Quintilian. In order to form a series of places in memory, he says, a building is to be remembered, as spacious and varied a one as possible, the forecourt, the living room, bedrooms, and parlours, not omitting statues and other ornaments with which the rooms are decorated. The images by which the speech is to be remembered . . . are then placed in the imagination on the places which have been memorized in the building. This done, as soon as the memory of the facts requires to be revived, all these places are visited in turn and the various deposits are demanded of their custodians. We have to think of the ancient orator as moving in imagination through his memory building *whilst* he is making his speech, drawing from the memorized places the images he has placed on them. The method ensures that the points are remembered in the right order, since the order is fixed by the sequence of places in the building.'[5]

The sources give similar recommendations on the rules to be observed for the formation of the places (their number, proportions, lighting, etc.) and for the fabrication of the images (size, expression, etc.). They differentiate between images according to whether they involve the memorization of things (notions or arguments of the speech) or the memorization of words (expressions or even sentences that will be used to evoke the things). One after another, they outline the framework of a mnemotechnics founded on a spatial and figurative metaphor of speech (describing its movement, its moments). Yates has demonstrated the consistency between this metaphor and certain major assumptions of ancient philosophy, such as the primacy given to the sense of sight – perceptible in the very etymology of *idea*, which in Plato designates the essence of things, or in the Aristotelian thesis holding that 'the soul never thinks without a mental picture'. Indeed, classical rhetoric and syllogistics, as codified by Aristotle, seem to be profoundly governed by this assimilation of *logos*, or speech, into a space that has been structured into places (*topoi*) that represent so many 'problems' or 'common' debates, whose identification and description is the concern of *topics*. Stretching the metaphor to insist on the coherence of ancient thought in this regard, one could say that topics, the theory of the commonplaces of discourse, provides a map of this mental space where the orators construct their edifices of memory, each according to his own will.

FROM ARCHITECTURE TO THE ARS MEMORATIVA, AND BACK AGAIN

Concerning the nature and operations of these memory places, the reading of the sources yields as many questions as answers.

1. – First of all, as we have seen, the most common systems of mnemonic places are systems of architectural places, i.e., groups of spaces constructed or planned by man.[6] The example most often given is that of a house, with its articulation of open or closed rooms, but there are also references to public buildings (baths, for example), building complexes (an abbey), urban sequences

or cities. Quintilian even speaks of a long road. Crucially, the configurations and relations between the places are in each case established and governed by one or several fixed itineraries. This seems from the outset to eliminate less structured spaces – spaces man is less likely to have organized – where the relations between places are not determined in advance. In short, artificial memory calls for a landscape that itself is relatively artificial.

2. – On the other hand, the memory of places precedes that of images, for which it serves as a framework and a support medium. It is a memory that 'helps another memory'. As a syntactic schema of structure and order, the articulation of places therefore must be easily distinguishable from the furnishings of images or figures that will be lodged there according to the orator's needs. Even if a place of memory is not just a 'void' defined by structural limits, but rather a place that decorative elements can help to identify (statues, for example), one can still suppose that the principle of convenience again tends to

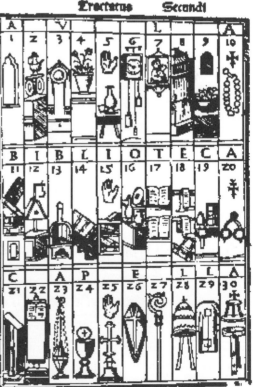

An abbey memory system and the vocabulary of images to be used in it, from Johannes Romberch, *Congestorium Artificiose Memorie*, Venice, 1563.

Serlio's Design for the Comic Scene (1545).

Serlio's tragic, comic and satiric scenes: the distinct connotations of city, town and suburb.

eliminate nonarchitectural spaces, where the distinction between structure and object (place and image) cannot be clearly assigned.

A question arises, however, as to the possible correspondence between mnemonic systems of places and mnemonic series of images: could affinities be established between kinds of places and kinds of speeches? We are told that orators could make use of several systems of memory places, and this permits several hypotheses. Did they do so to memorize a number of speeches simultaneously? Did one need more or less expansive and complex buildings, adapted to speeches of differing length and sophistication? Could a building become too small and be saturated by overuse? Did the orators feel the need to store certain series of images inside the buildings to which they had initially been confided, and to distinguish the new ones by the choice of other places?

All these hypotheses are no doubt simultaneously plausible.[7] But it is equally possible that the possession and mental manipulation of several systems of places may have gradually answered the need to assign different types of speech to different spaces, and that an affinity of theme or genre may have governed this division. One can then imagine that forms of correspondence, administered by conventional rules, may have been sought between the places and their furnishings of symbolic figures, opening the door to a differential semanticization of places according to their nature (house, public building, district of a city, outskirts, countryside), and reciprocally to a contamination of the figures by their frames. This hypothesis would lead us to examine the role that the art of memory may have played in distinguishing *scenes* (tragic, comic, satirical) and *genres* (pictorial, literary, etc.) by their appropriate decor. In any case, one clearly sees how the common practice of the *ars memorativa* must have led to a form of *encrustation* of the images in the memory places.

3. – Additionally, the mnemonic places could, according to the sources, be either real or imaginary: either articulations of existing spaces that the

orator has first chosen, then patiently observed and memorized, or fictional articulations that he has mentally conceived and constructed at his convenience, following the rules that the authors recommend concerning the number, proportions, distances and lighting of these places. Most plausible is the idea that the systems of mnemonic places would have been a little of both, and most often would have consisted of real arrangements revised and corrected by the imagination – enlarged, simplified, connected – in order to satisfy the orator's needs. Thus one can picture the built reality of the cities of antiquity being continually rebuilt, recomposed in the imagination of their inhabitants and repopulated with symbolic figures and landmarks of memory. This daydream opens up important questions: what relations did these analogous cities and buildings entertain among each other and with the real city? One can indeed wonder what influence this practice of artificial memory, which makes the orator not only an imaginary stroller but also an imaginary architect or urbanist, may have had on the reading and conception of real places. To ask such questions is to reflect on the reciprocal borrowings between classical rhetoric and classical architecture.

4. – Finally, this artificial memory is principally described as a technique that individuals exploit at will, choosing their own places and shaping their own images. Yet one can easily imagine how the generalization of this practice and the diffusion of its teaching through scholarly exercises, recommendations and examples must have led to the gradual constitution and transmission of a stock of conventional images and places. This form of standardization or partial collectivization of mnemotechnic tools, which obliges us to enquire into the relations between the art of memory and the descriptions and productions of art in the strict sense (literature, painting, sculpture, architecture), is in any case a major feature of what Yates calls 'the medieval transformation of the classical art of memory'. Christian culture, as she explains, brings about a profound mutation in the *ars memorativa*, shifting it from the domain of rhetoric to that of ethics. The Christianization of the art of memory can be seen at work in the texts of thinkers from St Augustine to Albertus Magnus and St Thomas, who elevated memory from the rank of a faculty to that of a virtue (a subdivision of Prudence). The result was to transform a *technique* used by the orator to recall that which he *wished* to remember into a *didactics* designed to impress upon the soul of the

faithful that which they *ought* to remember. Artificial memory, whose classical rules are revived and readjusted to this end, is mobilized in the service of the contemplation, meditation and observation of Christian doctrine. Hence the places and images, referring as they do to the discourse of revealed truth that forms the communal tie, now take on the status of shared symbolism ('a system of images') and almost of a language serving to commune in this truth, and to impress upon the souls the notions or *intentions* that are to govern their conduct in this world. The conception and fabrication of the mnemonic devices no longer simply appeals to the secret recipes of an orator, but becomes part and parcel of the representation and communication of speech itself. In this way, all the conditions are present for these mnemonic places and images to begin existing concretely – to be described, painted, sculpted and finally constructed.

'And though one must be extremely careful to distinguish between art proper and the art of memory, which is an invisible art, yet their frontiers must surely have overlapped. For when people were being taught to practise the formation of images for remembering, it is difficult to suppose that such inner images might not sometimes have found their way into outer expression. Or, conversely, when the "things" which they were to remember through inner images were of the same kind as the "things" which Christian didactic art taught through images, that the places and images of that art might themselves have been reflected in memory, and so have become "artificial memory."'[8]

As Yates herself demonstrates, in several examples, this hypothesis of an overlapping of the art of memory and the art, architecture and imagery of the Middle Ages proves fruitful for enlarging and renewing our understanding of the period. Yates thus casts new light on the supposed predilection of the Middle Ages for the grotesque and the bizarre in painting, statuary and manuscript illumination, which may only be an effect of the classical mnemotechnic rules recommending the use of expressive images, because they are easy to remember.[9]

She completely renews the interpretation of literary monuments such as *The Divine Comedy*, inviting us to read the spatial arrangements they describe (Hell, Paradise) as mnemonic systems.[10] Finally, and most importantly, she offers new frameworks for appreciating the structure and decoration of constructed edifices, extending Erwin Panofsky's hypothesis of a point-by-point correspondence between Gothic architecture and scholastic philosophy (basilica of St Denis = *Summa Theologica*),[11] and thereby lending new pertinence to Victor Hugo's famous phrase, *'Ceci tuera cela'* ('the one will kill the other'), which designated the printed book as the gravedigger of the built book, i.e., the cathedral.[12]

NOTES

1   Cf. 'Sub-urbanisms et paysage', programme of the l996–7 series of the Tribune d'histoire et d'actualité de l'architecture, Societé française des architectes, November 1996, where I proposed the following definition for a future encyclopedia of the twenty-first century:

'Sub-urbanism: n. derived from suburban (cf. *suburbia)* and distinguished from urbanism.

1.   Corpus of experiments and techniques of territorial development (involving landscaping, architecture, infrastructure and geotechnies) specifically developed in the suburbs, whereby the latter have given shape to their particular spaces and physiognomies.
2.   Discipline of architecture initially inspired by suburban situations, and where the hierarchy that urbanism has established between programme and site (imitating the programme-oriented approach that is more genuine to architecture) is overturned, such that the site becomes the regulatory idea or the project. Cf. *landscape design.*
3.   Theoretical and critical hypothesis, not necessarily exclusive of its opposite, which reads territorial development as a movement 'from the outside inward', from the outlying areas towards the city. By extension: historiographic approach that considers these suburban experiments, their landscape techniques and in particular their gardens as veritable laboratories for urbanism and for territorial development.'

2   Cf. 'L'alternative du paysage', in *Le Visiteur* 1, Autumn 1995. A first version of this article appeared previously in English as 'Landscape as Alternative' in *Het Landschap/The Landscape* (ed, K. Vandermarliere, Antwerp:

deSingel, 1995, pp. 9–36). I also came back to these ideas in 'The Return of the Landscape', preface to *Desvigne/Dalnoky* (Motta Editore: Milan, 1996; English edition, Whitney Library of Design, New York, 1997), and in the 'Reclaiming of Sites', in *Recovering Landscapes: Essays in Contemporary Landscape Architecture* (ed. James Corner, New York: Princeton Architectural Press, 1999, pp. 44–57).

3   Descartes beautifully names it a 'morale provisoire', principles de la philosophie, preface. Cf. Discours de la méthode part III.

4   Frances Yates, *The Art of Memory* (London: Routledge and Kegan Paul, 1966), p. xi. A few years before, in 1960, Paolo Rossi published his *Clavis Universalis*, focusing on the history of the arts of memory in the sixteenth and seventeenth centuries. The second edition of his book in 1988 owed a great deal to the research of Frances Yates, and was dedicated to her memory. Paolo Rossi, *Clavis Universalis, Logic and the Art of Memory: The Quest for a Universal Language,* trans. Stephen Clucas (Chicago: University of Chicago Press, 2000). In two lectures given at the AA, Yates herself addressed the possible relevance of her research to contemporary architects: 'So I leave you with the thought that buildings may be less solid than they seem, existing invisibly in the mind of the architect before they are born; remembered invisibly down the ages in the memories of the generations.' F. Yates, 'Architecture and the Art of Memory', *AA Quarterly* 12:4, 1980.

5   *The Art of Memory*, op. cit. p. 3.

6   Among the other systems of memory places, research by Mary Carruthers has revealed the importance of books themselves, particularly for the Middle Ages. Mary Carruthers, *The Book of Memory: A Study of Memory in Medieval Culture* (Cambridge University Press, 1990).

7   St Teresa of Avila uses a similar approach in *The Interior Castle* to describe the soul's successive movements to increasingly large edifices, corresponding to heightened degrees of spirituality. In *L'Age de l'éloquence* (Paris: Albin Michel, 1994), p. 421, Marc Fumaroll has also shown that Loyola's spiritual exercises make use of techniques derived from the *ars memorativa.*

8   *The Art of Memory*, op. cit. p. 81.

9   Ibid. p. 104: 'This inner art which encouraged the use of the imagination as a duty must

surely have been a major factor in the evocation of images. Can memory be one possible explanation of the mediaeval love of the grotesque, the idiosyncratic? Are the strange figures to be seen on the pages of manuscripts and in all forms of mediaeval art not so much the revelation of a tortured psychology as evidence that the Middle Ages, when man had to remember, followed classical rules for making memorable images?'

10   Ibid. p. 96: 'The Divine Comedy would thus become the supreme example of the conversion of an abstract summa of similitudes and examples, with Memory as the converging power, the bridge between the abstraction and the image.'

11   Ibid. p. 79, referring to Panofsky's Gothic Architecture and Scholasticism (Latrobe, PA: Archabbey, 1951).

12   Ibid. p. 124. Readers desiring to better grasp the influence of the ars memorativa on the architecture and religious painting of the Middle Ages can usefully consult the 1996 special issue of the Cahiers de la Villa Gillet, 'Lieux ou espaces de mémoire?', ed. Jean-Philippe Antoine (Paris: Editions Circé, 1997), and particularly the articles by Mary Carruthers, 'Locus Tabernaculi, mémoire et lieu dans la méditation monastique' and Jean-Philippe Antoine, 'Invention spacieuse et scène de la parole: les fresques monumentales en Italie au tournant du Duecento et du Trecento'.

Figure 1.1.1 Court Essington, David Archer Architects
The Garden Room is flooded with natural light and is decorated with pale shades that encourage a direct relationship with the exterior. [©David Archer Architects]

Figure 1.1.2 Court Essington, David Archer Architects
Many of the original features of the building were retained, which, when combined with the new elements creates a timeless environment, one which no longer belongs to the era when the building was constructed, but one which is more suited to a contemporary lifestyle. [©David Archer Architects]

Figure 1.1.3 Court Essington, David Archer Architects
The dining hall is situated at the heart of the building and is decorated in a warm and intense manner. It is a room built for cold winter evenings, when the large fireplace and big radiators can provide warmth and comfort. [©David Archer Architects]

Figure 1.1.4 Court Essington, David Archer Architects
The simple decoration of the vertical circulation area is complemented by the natural light from the large north-facing windows. [©David Archer Architects]

Figure 1.2.1 St Mary of Furness, E. W. Pugin, restored by Francis Roberts Architects
The decoration within the polygonal apse is more intense at the base, becoming simpler as it rises
through the space. [Credit: ©Dominic Roberts]

Figure 1.2.2 St Mary of Furness, E. W. Pugin, restored by Francis Roberts Architects
The new decoration is based upon an interpretation of the ornate capitals present within
the building. The stencils were made from full-size patterns and are painted with authentic colours.
[Credit: ©Dominic Roberts]

Figure 1.2.3 St Mary of Furness, E. W. Pugin, restored by Francis Roberts Architects
The capitals are deliberately decorated in a simple fashion, thus ensuring that the delicate articulation of
the carved forms is apparent. [Credit: ©Dominic Roberts]

Figure 1.2.4 St Mary of Furness, E. W. Pugin, restored by Francis Roberts Architects
The austere treatment of the nave is in sharp contrast to the highly decorated chancel. This reflects
E. W. Pugin's intentions, as can be seen in the original more elaborate windows of the east end.
[Credit: ©Dominic Roberts]

Figure 1.3.1 Teatro Olimpico, Palladio
The stage is a permanently fixed classical street scene. The proscenium, which is constructed from wood
and plaster, is decorated in an elaborate manner. [©David Cox]

Figure 1.3.2 Teatro Olimpico, Palladio
The streets, which are clearly visible behind the central arch of the proscenium, contain an exaggerated perspective, and so they appear to recede much further into the depths of the stage than they actually do. [©David Cox]

Figure 1.3.3 Teatro Olimpico, Palladio
The smaller doorway to the right of the central arched opening shows the foreshortened street scene. [©David Cox]

Figure 1.3.4 Teatro Olimpico, Palladio
The ceiling is painted to resemble an open sky above the theatre, increasing the illusion of the classical world. [Photomontage credit: ©David Cox]

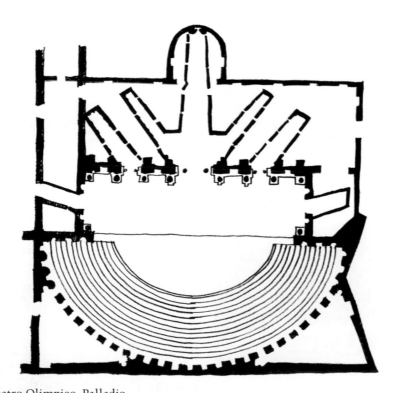

Figure 1.3.5 Teatro Olimpico, Palladio
The plan of the theatre shows the intense relationship between the semicircular seating and the fixed stage. The dramatic perspective contained within the fixed street behind the proscenium is clearly visible. [©Sally Stone]

Figure 2.1.1 St Martin's Lane Hotel, Philippe Starck
The tall thin leaning post tables of the
bar contrast with the more traditional dining seating in
the different zones of the main restaurant interior.
[©Credit: Richard Davies. Image supplied courtesy of
Philippe Starck]

Figure 2.1.2 St Martin's Lane Hotel, Philippe Starck
The stage set lobby is populated with a range of unusual
furniture such as the "molar teeth" stools. [©Credit:
Richard Davies. Image supplied courtesy of Philippe
Starck]

Figure 2.1.3 St Martin's Lane Hotel, Philippe Starck
The light bar colourfully illuminates the interior space.
[©Credit: Richard Davies. Image supplied courtesy of
Philippe Starck]

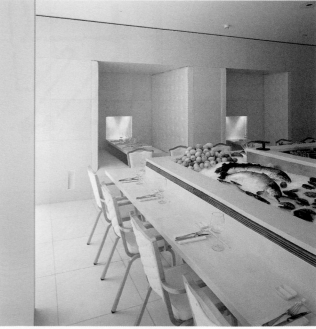

Figure 2.1.4 St Martin's Lane Hotel, Philippe Starck
The fish restaurant is a clean and clinical white space, in
sharp contrast to the adjacent bars and restaurants on the
ground floor [©Credit: Richard Davies. Image supplied
courtesy of Philippe Starck]

Figure 2.2.1 Apartment, George Ranalli
The two-storey furniture element provides space for a range of functions, such as dining and reading on the steps that lead to an upper-level sleeping platform. [©George Ranalli]

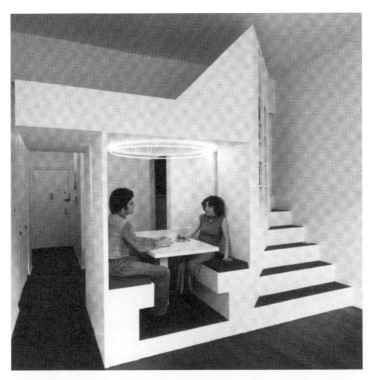

Figure 2.2.2 Apartment, George Ranalli
The compact free-standing object is inserted into the small main room of the apartment. [©George Ranalli]

Figure 2.2.3 Apartment, George Ranalli
The element frames the views through the room. The neutral tones of its painted white timber
construction reinforce the light qualities of the space. [©George Ranalli]

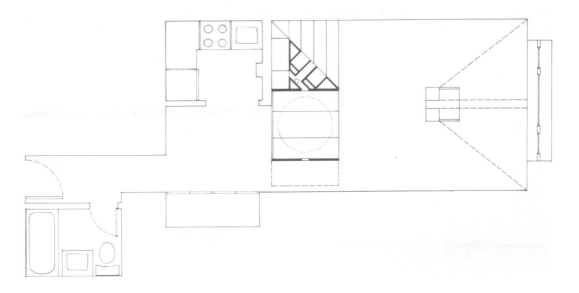

Figure 2.2.4 Apartment, George Ranalli
The new addition to the small apartment is meticulously ordered and enables the occupants to comfortably inhabit the room. [©George Ranalli]

Figure 2.3.1 Haçienda, Ben Kelly Design
Once the clubber had passed through the entrance sequence the main hall of the ex-yacht showroom was reused to house the dancefloor, bars and the stage. [©Ben Kelly Design]

Figure 2.3.2 (Top Left) Haçienda, Ben Kelly Design
The design language of the interior consisted of a mixture
of everyday materials and symbols such as chevrons and
strong graphic colours. [©Ben Kelly Design]

Figure 2.3.3 (Top Right) Haçienda, Ben Kelly Design
Urban elements such as traffic bollards and cats eyes were
taken from their original context and used in the interior
in order to denote the edge of the dance-floor.
[©Ben Kelly Design]

Figure 3.1.1 (Left) Church of Christ Scientist,
OMI Architects
The architects' own conceptual drawing that shows the
secondary natural light shining through the circulation
and mezzanine areas and into the chapel.
[Credit: OMI Architects]

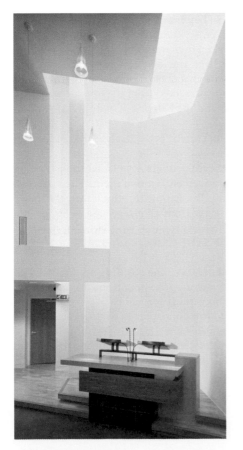

Figure 3.1.2 (Top Left) Church of Christ Scientist,
OMI Architects
The architects have made use of a simple, difficult to
access space to provide a dramatic and symbolic naturally
lit, ground level alcove. [Credit: OMI Architects]

Figure 3.1.3 (Top Right) Church of Christ Scientist,
OMI Architects
It was necessary to retain a certain amount of structure to
provide stability and support within the carved-out space
of the chapel. These exposed elements are back-lit to create
a dramatic backdrop. [Credit: OMI Architects]

Figure 3.1.4 (Left) Church of Christ Scientist,
OMI Architects
The chapel walls are simple and unadorned, and thus
encourage a focus upon the double lectern.
[Credit: OMI Architects]

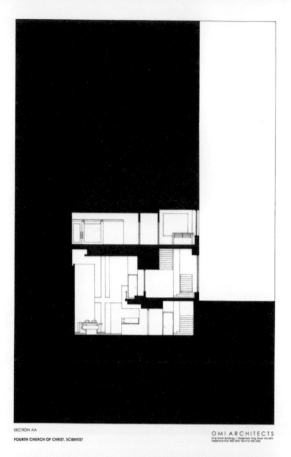

SECTION AA

FOURTH CHURCH OF CHRIST, SCIENTIST

OMI ARCHITECTS
King Street Buildings, 1 Ridgefield, King Street M2 6EG
Telephone 0161 832 5345 Fax 0161 832 5420

Figure 3.1.5 (Top Left) Church of Christ Scientist, OMI Architects
The architects' own drawing that shows how the church was carved from the lower floors of the office block. The double-height chapel is situated deep within the confines of the building, protected from the outside world by the circulation and the balcony. [Credit: OMI Architects]

Figure 3.2.1 (Top Right) Castelvecchio Museum, Carlo Scarpa
The exhibits are deliberately placed slightly off axis to encourage movement around them. The visitor is obliged to walk around this sculpture, which is in the upper gallery, and thus view it from all sides. [©Sally Stone]

Figure 3.2.2 (Left) Castelvecchio Museum, Carlo Scarpa
The new elements of the building are carefully positioned so that they do not quite touch the original structure. A small gap or gutter is formed between the floor and the walls and so the floor appears to float or glide from room to room. the statues are generally lit from the side, this encourages the visitor to move around the artwork and also accentuates the act of separation between the sculpture and the building. [©Sally Stone]

Figure 3.2.3 (Top Left) Castelvecchio Museum,
Carlo Scarpa
Scarpa placed the Cangrande Sculpture at the pivotal point
where the city walls and the tower meet the castle
buildings. It was here that he removed a substantial
amount of structure to expose this moment of collision and
provide a shelter for this symbol of Verona. [©Sally Stone]

Figure 3.3.1 (Top Right) Sackler Galleries, Julian Harrap
Architects and Foster Associates
The new circulation route allows the visitor to view
elements of the existing building that were originally
intended to be seen from distance. [©Sally Stone]

Figure 3.3.2 (Left) Sackler Galleries, Julian Harrap
Architects and Foster Associates
The reception area, the cornice of the main galleries, forms
a low plinth for Gibson's sculptures. [©Sally Stone]

Figure 3.3.3 Sackler Galleries, Julian Harrap Architects and Foster Associates
The underside of the reception area. Natural light streams around the new platform highlighting the texture of the original building. [©Sally Stone]

Figure 3.3.4 Sackler Galleries, Julian Harrap Architects and Foster Associates
The white glass, which surrounds the reception lobby at the top of the building, encourages an inward focus towards the original building. [©Sally Stone]

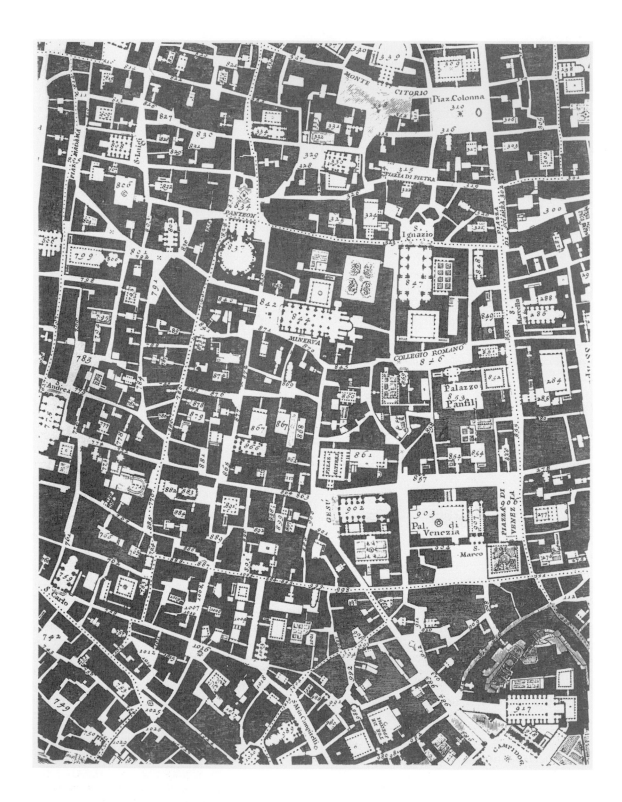

29
Interior Space

Denise Scott Brown

Source: *AA Files 56*. AA Publications, 2010, pp. 64–73

In the city today, we meet in public atria and shop in malls, we move along covered walkways and go from street to street by taking shortcuts through the buildings of a city block. In recent decades, the amount and proportion of public space within urban buildings has steadily increased, with much of it forming part of a larger interior and exterior pedestrian network. Yet, although interior public space has become an important constituent of the contemporary city and of our urban experience, it is rarely designed as such. Prompted by this disconnection, Maurice Harteveld has followed different leads to examine contemporary urban design in relation to public interiors. Through this research, he has documented in particular the urban analyses and architectural designs of Robert Venturi and Denise Scott Brown, in which interior public space is accorded significant and multiple roles. Ideas pioneered by Venturi and Scott Brown have become absorbed within architectural practice, notably their use of the Nolli Map introduced in their 1972 study of Las Vegas. Similarly, the concept of the 'rue interieur' seen in their earliest projects, has matured in their later work to include an internal street imbedded in a network of urban public spaces and pathways, both interior and exterior. However, although they refer to interior public space frequently in their writing, Venturi and Scott Brown have yet to describe their views on it in any great detail; a more focused examination that the following dialogue between Maurice Harteveld and Denise Scott Brown seeks to provide.

MH: 'The street through the building' is a recurring theme in your design work. In your recent book, *Architecture as Signs and Systems: For a Mannerist Time*, I learned that this street always ties into the exterior pathway system leading to the building. With this approach, the internal street can be designed to support the urban circulation system while at a smaller scale it forms the spine, as you call it, of the public sector of your building. To make appropriate public interiors you closely study the surrounding urban patterns then design the architecture to fit with these and to encourage communication. This seems to bring the two of you together: the urbanist and the architect.

DSB: I am happy that you have found the book useful. It attempts to broaden our grasp, as architects, by applying urban ideas to architectural design, in and out of buildings. But it's perhaps an over-simplification to call Bob an architect and me an urbanist. We are each both. The dichotomy is within us as well as between us. It's a four-way dichotomy.

MH: In looking at these internal streets, there seems to be significant variations between projects – in both their public nature and how they are designed. For example, the street between the Life Sciences Institute and the Commons Building in your University of Michigan complex, is more accessible than the one between the two wings of the regional governmental complex in Toulouse. In both designs, the major street is internal to the project but outdoors, and it is aligned with surrounding pathways. But in Toulouse it can be closed off by gates, therefore it is perhaps more private. In the Trabant Student Center of the University of Delaware the route is interior; it is both a street and the major public area of the building. And within the existing Princeton building that you converted to the Frist Campus Center the streets are low and narrow. They are the least open in the series, and are also set at right-angles to the outdoor path. Could you explain how these differences in publicity are affected by the design assignment and the urban analysis? In what sense are they all public?

DSB: It would take a book to answer these questions. But first, a linguistic issue: in English, 'publicity' commonly means 'communication for the purpose of making certain information: better known'. This, I think, is different from what you intended. How such publicity is achieved through architecture and urbanism interests Bob and me very much: however, weren't you referring in your question to a more general and abstract idea of 'public quality'?

MH: When I use the term 'publicity' I'm referring to sociologists who categorise interiors public if they are part of the so-called public realm. In the 1950s, through writers such as Hannah Arendt, this realm was defined as the sphere of action and speech. So, in its origin, the notion is closely related to communication. I would say that interiors are public when they open themselves to the knowledge of a community. A shopping mall, for example, unlike a home or private club, issues an invitation to the general public. Therefore, to continue this reasoning, it is open to general regulations similar to those for an outdoor street. But you are right that, in design, the state of being publicly known is only one aspect of a much broader quality of being public. Others might include being inviting to the public, and being part of a network of public spaces and pathways. In considering these broader aspects, the emphasis on the public quality of the space becomes most important.

DSB: The difference between 'public' and 'civic' should be noted too. And you're right: our various internal streets and spaces have very different public qualities – as different as those of a city. As we design them, we find metaphors in a range of urban prototypes, from medieval market routes to expressways, and we bear in mind the issues of location and capacity that transportation planners consider. We develop our categories and hierarchies of street types from, among others, transportation engineering, from Lou Kahn's famous plan for Philadelphia's streets, from our 1960s analyses of Las Vegas, and from David Crane's 'four faces of movement'. Crane was one of the few members of the University of Pennsylvania planning faculty during my time there who tried to maintain a link between architecture and social-sciences-based, 'non-physical' (as they called it) urban planning. It was Crane who set me to study regional science, and whose interest in urban change and unpredictability has been an influence on my work ever since. These, then, are the underpinnings of our ideas on the design of the public sector, or street, in building. But this is half the story. The other half concerns specifics of the brief or programme, which give the basis for the project. In the client's intended activities, the relation between them and the spaces required to accommodate them lies the first definition of the public realm. And the first role of the 'street through the building' is circulation. It forms part of the movement system, along which the building's spaces are located, and from which access to and among users' activities is obtained. Urbanists study urban economics and transportation engineering to understand how patterns of circulation affect urban development and how land use and movement are interrelated in the city. And Crane includes 'giving access' as one of his four faces of movement, pointing out that this quality defines the street as a 'city builder', because giving access to land enables its development. In the same way, we consider the street-through-the-building as an access-giver and try to combine activity patterns and circulation in designing buildings as we would in planning a city. This forms the basis of our claim that we do land use and transportation planning *inside* buildings. Yet, as 'interior urbanists', we find we must work with categories of function beyond those of the brief. These relate to the building's role in the community, and may concern the size and volume of movement or activity. Particularly important are categories that differentiate between public and private activities or spaces, and help to define the character of each and the relations between them. In considering public–private relationships in architecture, we have learned from a comparison of Nolli's map of Rome and our Nolli map of the Las Vegas Strip, and from Crane's idea of the 'Capital Web', which he describes as the infrastructure of all public facilities in a city.

MH: So understanding public space means understanding its relation to private space, and especially so as we consider public interiors, I am reminded of a discussion that was at the centre of the discourse on urbanism in the late nineteenth century. The pioneering urban theorist Josef Stübben pleaded for a clear division of public and private space, while Camillo Sitte argued in support of an interwoven relationship because a great part of public life took place within buildings. Not only public squares but also enclosed spaces were, he claimed, used publicly. This is what we see in the city today, but many designers seem to have forgotten the complex symbiosis that exists between public and private.

DSB: A beach is public and a town hall is civic. In the first we all share a common good but don't join together to do so. In the second we are part of a community. But public and civic functions may also be served by the interiors of some private and institutional buildings. Shopping malls are to some extent public today, and Las Vegas simulates the public sector both indoors and out. The combination of public and private has a long and varied history. An auspicious early twentieth-century example is the much loved interior of the John Wanamaker department store (now Macy's) in Philadelphia. It's a large atrium inside a private building, but people arrange to rendezvous there as if it were a public square. It feels civic and it has a role, both retail and ritual, in the communal Christmas celebrations of the city.

In Toulouse, the client saw our diagonal street across the site as highly civic but in addition to its civic functions it provides a pedestrian shortcut between two existing commercial areas. I had hoped it could contain a street market as do other Toulouse streets; however, the client would not countenance a commercial use and although this street is the public access to all government offices it is shut off at night for security. There is also a small civic *place* before the *Salle de l'Assemblée* that is lined with trees and benches like the square of a traditional French *mairie*. Unfortunately this has been closed to the public again for reasons of security. But children walk to school along our street and the local community gathers there for events. And some internal spaces have developed ancillary uses. The assembly hall complex is used for important public announcements and conferences, and a market for fruit and vegetables has appeared, unofficially, underground in the parking structure along the route to the elevator.

At our University of Michigan Life Sciences complex, a series of pedestrian paths, bridges and public spaces connect the academic sciences, a life sciences research facility and the medical centre. These routes are more like medieval streets than a civic plaza. They take users directly where they need to go, via relatively narrow pathways that widen to give access to doorways or to allow eddy space in which people can congregate. Encouraging serendipitous meetings between scholars of different disciplines is a major aim in the planning of our academic streets. We therefore locate informal stopping places at points of encounter where important pathways cross. In lab buildings, we place coffee lounges off the main corridor near the elevator. In exterior spaces around intensely used buildings we provide informal seating, sometimes café chairs, often just steps, parapets and ledges. Here in good weather students can study or workers eat lunch. These informal opportunities along the way reveal rather than demonstrate their function. People, especially students, seem happy to discover and define uses for themselves. Give students a bench to sit on and they will lie on it or dance on it, but provide a parapet or ledge and they will treat it as an engaging opportunity.

The major route that passes through the Trabant Center lies on a direct path between the college dormitories and the lecture halls. It serves the two primary functions of all streets – to join points longitudinally and to provide access to activities and structures bordering it. Sitting spaces along it purvey the feeling of a combination seminar room and sidewalk cafe. It is therefore much more than a food court. The narrow streets of the Frist Campus Center emerge directly from the heavy basement structure of the existing building. Bob managed to draw from this picturesque but uncompromising heritage a needed interplay between the Center's tight, low spaces and its high, expansive ones. The right-angle turn that concerns you at the main entry to the building must be seen in the context of the circulation plan in that part of the campus. A pathway does indeed traverse the front of the Frist Building, and it widens to form a patio at the entrance; but it's less used for access to the Center than is McCosh Walk, which runs parallel to it, to the north. The entry arcade added to the Frist exterior is designed to draw from this larger crowd of pedestrians, bringing them from several directions into the building via a series of new doorways, created from what were originally basement windows. People walk across the pathway and into the basement. Once there, they move between the heavy supports, through tight, low ways, past campus centre facilities in a Las Vegas-like setting, then on to the vast, light spaces of the cafeteria and student offices above. This sequence converts what was once a building serving one academic department into a facility for the whole community. Although the original front door still admits students and faculty to classrooms and a library above, a more civic entry and access pattern has been added for the campus centre. But 'civic' for undergraduates can be funky and a little (but only a little) like Las Vegas.

MH: In all these designs the internal street is used as a connector and communicator between the private and the public domains, linking pathways, interweaving the public sector, and using communication-graffiti (signs and symbols).

DSB: Streets can play many roles. Crane's 'four faces of movement' suggest that they function as channels for the circulation of people, goods and vehicles; city builders, in that they give access to places for settlement; rooms for activities, especially in mild climates and in developing areas, where much of life takes place outdoors and on streets; and information givers, telling travellers where they are in the city, providing the locus for communication between individuals and purveying messages, communal and commercial. This is the publicity function, whose iconography we studied in Las Vegas.

In all its roles the street is a link between the public and the private, at scales that range from the sidewalk access of a row house to the movement networks that serve major facilities and urban areas. And this applies to interior streets too. Yet if interior public space is to contribute to urban circulation, careful study of its context is required. For this reason we analyse activity and movement systems around the project site and document the quality of nearby public space, exterior and interior. And we consider trends within these systems and demands on them. This gives a framework for the planning of relationships both within the project and beyond it. And from these planning studies of the broader surroundings our designs frequently spring. In evolving designs from context, we've found the transportation planning concept of 'desire lines' to be useful. These lines are drawn directly between where people are and where they want to be, regardless of whether direct routes exist. Many VSBA project *partis* stem from desire lines. Sometimes the building or complex encloses a portion of the area-wide movement system and is literally built around the desire lines.

MH: The internal street seems very much akin to the model of the Parisian arcade. These covered streets are part of the network of public space, giving access to shops and theatres, and they also display signs. But more important to this comparison, arcades also function as systems of shortcuts that have survived over time.

DSB: Yes, it's important that interior streets take people where they want to go and, just as the market place sits at the crossroads in a town, so the more public functions must be located at major access and crossing points, where most people pass. And yes, arcades that run within buildings make an interesting comparison with the street. Your research reminds me of the two-level main street of Chester, England. Here interconnected pedestrian ways are set one above the other. They face the street on one side and are lined by shops on the other. This building section occurs in all the private buildings along the length of the street. It has been maintained by successive builders over hundreds of years, so valuable is it to the retail uses of the city. We also experienced the longevity of shortcuts in Toulouse. The site, when we first saw it, had already been cleared and we planned our diagonal across it to serve as a shortcut between two nodes in the city. But only when our project was well into construction did we discover from an old map that we had sited our route exactly where a street had once run.

MH: Although a comparison could be made between urban internal arcades and the internal streets in your designs, the urban contexts are quite different. VSBA buildings are mostly free-standing, while in general the arcades are embedded within a city block. Your buildings are surrounded by public open areas while arcades have backs which are private. How, then, in your designs do these open spaces keep or achieve their public meaning without contradicting the objectives of the internal street? How, through architectural and urban design, do you prevent rear areas and anonymous outdoor space from flanking the building?

DSB: The internal arcades are lined on either side by private (mainly retail) uses. They are connected, as well, with service and loading areas at the back. In our work as urban planners we sometimes collaborate with retail economists who help us define the commercial nature of the street and set up the relationships you are discussing. They choreograph the various retail uses to achieve the most profitable selling environments for individual stores and the community. We must also plan carefully for service functions. Though these may lack beauty, they can't be evaded but must be adequately sized and well located. We wax lyrical on the subject of service planning. If we don't, trucks and maintenance vehicles will invade the public places of Main Street and the pedestrian paths of the campus.

MH: There is a more extreme version of the internal street in the form of the suburban mall. Architects who design them seem to focus only on the inside. Their building complexes are introverted; blind outdoor facades form a blank box surrounded by parking lots. But recently there has been development towards a more outdoor-oriented typology. Competition with renewed city centres and with other retail areas has forced some malls to be abandoned. Others are being redesigned to introduce outdoor pedestrian spaces, which surround parts of the complex and open up the facades of the buildings. It seems that interior public space needs outdoor space and more important, needs to be part of a differentiated and hierarchic system of public space.

DSB: This is a major finding of both your work and ours. From it, further questions derive.

For example, how should the advantages of a lively indoor street be weighed against the need for vitality on the exterior? We made a study of the Republic Square district in Austin, Texas, where our client was planning to build office buildings and hoped to achieve vital retail activity on the street. We analysed ways in which building entrance and access patterns could be designed to support and enliven ground floor, street-facing retail. If the entrances to the office building are located too near the road intersection, then mid-block retail uses may suffer because fewer people will go by them. But mid-block entrances draw people past storefronts as they head toward building lobbies and elevators.

As you have noted, mall developers are seeking ways to open up shopping malls and give them some of the interest of Main Street. When we plan for small main streets, we try to help storekeepers to differentiate themselves from the malls by using the fact that they have the great open sky, not a mall roof, over them, and by imaginatively adapting their historical buildings to create unique outdoor and indoor shopping spaces. For this work we must find economists who love old buildings and understand their possibilities. We have also tried to apply concepts of retail planning to the major thoroughfares that pass through and around our institutional buildings. Meeting places, which could be lounges, cafes, community buildings, or outdoor congregating spots, belong where routes cross. The 'hundred per cent area' of urban economics is at or near the busiest crossing. Here should be the most intense group activities, physical or mental, of a city – and also, we suggest, of a building. Large-volume lecture halls require wide corridor access space. This is congested only every hour, when classes change, but as students wait there they can meet and chat. We try to provide seating and a glass wall facing the campus, so this corridor can augment the sparse common-room space that is all most universities can afford. As it continues to other parts of the building, this way may widen or narrow to serve its access functions. It may give information via notice boards and provide convenient locations for telephones and electronic communication systems. Off it, indoors or out, we like to provide eddy places with a coffee machine nearby, so that fruitful discussions, initiated as students walk out of lectures can continue informally.

MH: You could also refer to the unique Las Vegas Strip of the 1960s. It showed that a vast system of public interiors could exist that, as you explained in *Learning from Las Vegas*, was disconnected from the outside in order to keep patrons disorientated in time and space so they would lose count of the hours and remain at the gambling tables. Nowadays along what was once the Strip, the outdoor space is more established and more part of the whole system. Outdoor piazzas and open areas between buildings and on what is now Las Vegas Boulevard are introduced. So both Las Vegas and the malls have transformed or evolved. Do you think these transformations share a similar logic concerning the differentiation of the public system and the elimination of anonymous outdoor space?

DSB: On Las Vegas Boulevard today hardly anything is public and probably in the malls it never was, but both try to imitate a public sector. Malls encourage semi-civic and political events to take place on their parking lots or in their interior courts and 'community halls', which are usually tucked-away spaces unsuitable for retail use and with little public presence. Las Vegas has created a private–public sector. The Boulevard is so different from the Strip we studied in the 1960s. Highly pedestrianised, it seems like an elongated Piazza Navona. The 'public' plazas that lie between the Boulevard and the casinos imitate the public sectors of historic European cities. Where strident signs, *a porte-cochère* and a reassuring view of parking once beckoned the automobile, now, famous plazas of Europe are jammed together to beguile the pedestrian on the boulevard. Why go to Venice, Italy, they seem to ask, when you can experience Venice, Nevada? But the more the casino front yards have been made to resemble old civic places, the more private they've become. There is almost no public sidewalk left. Everything that looks like a civic plaza is private to within half a metre of the street. And 'private–public' is not really public, as would-be protesters discovered when they tried to assert their right to public assembly on Boulevard sidewalks.

Both Las Vegas and the malls must think hard-headedly about systems for service and parking, especially customer parking. On the Boulevard, parking has graduated to structures behind the casino hotels, leaving the front yards available for a pseudo civic townscape. But vast parking lots remain the prevalent and reassuring first view of the shopping mall. In both cases, the store service system is out of view and anonymous.

Now Las Vegas is changing once again. Like contemporary architecture it is moving away from architectural allusion and the aim to communicate and toward architectural abstraction and the projection of luxury and quality service. It is hard to imagine a Las Vegas hotel that no longer romances you off the boulevard but purveys, instead, an air of privacy and high-class exclusiveness. What will be the nature of the public realm in such a complex? I suspect that landscaping will provide the primary image, and that it will be used to shield the view, while disclosing discreet but fascinating hints of the facilities reserved for just a few inside. Perhaps this will work. Perhaps by the laws of contrast, abstract neo-modern architecture will present an irresistible attraction to a public jaded by the old Las Vegas. But how soon will people of the 2010s tire of architectural abstraction, as their grandparents did in the 1960s?

MH: It seems that for you mapping is the single most important element in understanding interior public space. It helps to depict the public interior as a segment of a pedestrian path system or part of a bigger network of public space. In the past you have explained your use of different techniques of analysis. I would argue that interiors contribute to the city if they have an urban use and an urban location. It seems, therefore, that analyses should be made of the numbers and patterns of users. Do you recognise these themes in your analysis?

DSB: In deciding what kinds of analysis and analytic mapping to do we face a dilemma: the range of possible investigations is vast and the tasks could go on forever but funds are limited. So we consider how to focus from the start. We try to avoid what one of my professors called the 'whale method' of urban research. The whale opens its mouth as it swims, and whatever flows in is what it eats. This is not effective. Therefore, as urban researchers, we must devise techniques to discover, early, the most relevant research variables for a given topic. We may do this by conducting a brief, once-over-lightly overview of the project, before delving into detail. We have also learned to introduce a first attempt at design deliberately too early in the process to help structure the next rounds of research. So design can serve as a research tool – as a heuristic for further research – as well as vice versa. But generally we examine patterns of activities and movement, and differentiate these by type and intensity, preferably over time. We also consider natural patterns and systems and those of built structures; and we distinguish between activities and the structures that hold them. The age of structures is an important variable, and there are many others, particularly those to do with capacity and location. Mapping the raw data of use and structure is just a first step. Beyond that, we may want to break our information down further. The computer allows us to disaggregate one variable, for example, the distribution of all sciences on campus, and to study the pattern it makes. And our analysis includes synthesis (we are after all architects). We may juxtapose two variables. For example, for Tsinghua University in Beijing one of our most cogent maps superimposed densities of people on a map of campus green space. It showed that there was little match between where people and landscape were. At Michigan, we derived the location and the conceptual design of our Life Sciences complex from juxtaposing mapped distributions – of campus sciences, theatres (on campus and in downtown Ann Arbor), museums, topography and pedestrian pathways. For the Las Vegas Strip, we mapped signs and lighting by intensity, location and purpose. The maps that resulted portrayed the feel of the place better than could traditional urban land use maps or the orthogonal plans of architecture.

These analyses and syntheses provided information, but they were also design tools. They helped us move seamlessly, into the process of synthesis architects call design. And they had a heuristic value, in that some early syntheses of variables led to astonishing insights and in many cases to

the *parti*. For us, design and analysis proceed in tandem throughout the design process. In sum, what you analyse and how you do it depends on your problem. You hope that your once-over-lightly study and your successive cycles of analysis and synthesis will give you a good sense of where to go.

MH: Either intense activities or a good urban location can make interiors appear more urban. Beside this, public interiors, for a casino, campus centre or church, require high-quality space where urban discomfort is eliminated. This brings me back to Nolli's plan. In their ability to clearly reveal the urbanistic network – the mazes of public space – these maps clarify the urban designer's role in forming interior spaces. In this sense, they redefine the dichotomy between the city planner and the architect. As you once wrote, Nolli's map reveals the sensitive and complex connections between public and private space.

DSB: The relationship between public and private has always been very important in our work. This topic has perhaps different ramifications in American urban planning from those in Europe, because American culture tends to avoid the use of government support or action in favour of the private sector. This brings up questions for urbanists and architects regarding the relation between the public and private sectors, the opportunities for action within each and, for activists in the public sector, the public leverage possible on private-sector decisions. All of this would still have been important without the notion of mapping; however, Nolli's map is influential and relevant in our work because it provides a method of showing physical relations between the public and the private city. In campus planning, in particular, we rely on the Nolli system, adapted for today (there were few grassy areas and no parking lots in his Rome). We map Nolli's variables, showing the *poché* of all public buildings and of major public spaces in private buildings. On these we juxtapose the system of pedestrian pathways that cross the campus. It forms a nervous pattern of movement, resembling macramé, and running continuously between exterior and interior spaces. This pattern subtends the campus open spaces, which we differentiate by type giving special prominence to those we feel are highly symbolic. A Nolli map for a university campus, in this way, portrays its overall public system and the relation between its public and private uses. It shows where the capacity of pedestrian ways is not related to the demand on them, and where gaps exist because new buildings were erected but the pathway system was not adapted to them.

The Nolli map has taught us a great deal about the character of public architecture, including the architecture of the street through the building. The map is all about the processional. Why wouldn't it be? It was conceived as an information system for religious pilgrims. Rome's winding and sinuous street pattern stands out in marked contrast to its formal piazzas, for example the Piazza Navona. But the buildings, with their strong black plans, are particularly suggestive of the difference between the public architecture of streets and institutions and the private tissue of the city. The fact that the plans are baroque does not indicate that public space should be baroque. The plans of modern architects, particularly Alvar Aalto, lend themselves to a similar analysis. But we have certainly learned from Nolli to think of the street through the building as if it were an exterior street. Therefore in our National Gallery Sainsbury Wing the main lobby and stairway spaces are clad in rusticated stone, as are the facades of buildings on an Italian Renaissance street. The entry area and main lobby are sinuous, taking the shape of the crowd that uses them. We planned a widened sidewalk and sheltered portico where visitors could wait for the museum to open, before proceeding through a narrow door into a larger space beyond. Here a crowd of people might all stop at once, while deciding where to go next. Our entryway is therefore pretzel-shaped. Similarly, in our lab and classroom buildings, seating occurs in eddy areas off the main circulation. These are designed as widenings of corridors, not rooms. Sitting beside the continuing space of the street should feel like a pause not a commitment. It should be possible, while moving, to glance in and make a quick decision to enter for a chat or to pass by. But sometimes the safety requirements for fire doors

on major corridors are a restraint. Then we must specify hinge mechanisms to allow these doors to remain open unless there is a fire. So urban design concerns a door hinge as well as a region.

MH: Today's design guidelines cover accessibility and various public qualities, but designers could still learn from Nolli: the churches he mapped were seen as both a retreat from daily life and a centre of the society, and designing their interiors was considered a privilege. Taking such an approach to our more secular interiors could change the discourse on future public space.

DSB: Of course, the churches shown by Nolli weren't public. Today we might call them NGOs (non-governmental organisations), but the streets and plazas *were* public, and we consider the churches as stand-ins for the public buildings that we study in our urban analyses. The churches could also represent a private sector that 'feels' public. We tried using other mapping techniques as well to suggest different types of public–private relationship, particularly kinetic ones – for example, to show how an investment by government in urban development could lead to a reaction by the private sector. The opportunities lie in both sectors.

MH: In learning from Beijing, Newark, Philadelphia or Toulouse you began by studying Rome and Las Vegas. It is generally known that you first travelled to Las Vegas in 1965, but when and where did you discover the Nolli Plan? Was it perhaps when you visited Frutaz's exhibition in 1962 in Rome, or did you simply come across the catalogue?

DSB: Bob believes he came across Nolli's map in Rome at the American Academy in the mid 1950s, when he was a Fellow there. I think I first saw it in the early 1960s at the University of Pennsylvania where it was much in evidence around the school of architecture. Perhaps some faculty member there, possibly Aldo Giurgola, had visited Rome in 1962. David Crane had been in Rome in the mid 1950s and in his studio we applied the idea of the capital web to the design of a new city. Our maps resembled Nolli's in that they showed the buildings, open spaces and circulation systems of the public sector differently from those of the private sector, but in making them I don't remember using Nolli as a guide. In planning school we learned to pore over maps and aerial photographs, trying to discern in them what was happening in the city. It was great to discover in a land-use map or photograph that something you were considering recommending was already happening. Later, when we studied aerial photographs of the Las Vegas Strip, the parallels between it and Nolli's map of Rome were obvious.

MH: You begin *Architecture as Signs and Systems* with an acknowledgment of evolution as well as revolution. 'Viva pragmatic/evolutionary over heroic/revolutionary!' Bob writes in the introduction, echoing sentiments you had expressed in Las Vegas in 1968. But given our growing recognition today that interior public space can be a constituent part of the public city, where would you place what you wrote in 1968? As evolution or revolution? Perhaps your formulations on Las Vegas and Le Piante di Roma were not, in themselves, revolutionary, but did bringing them together cause a revolution?

DSB: Perhaps. We like the paradox that juxtaposing evolutions can cause revolution. The 1960s was an era of paradox, when revolution was stood on its head for good reason and anti-revolution became the new revolution. At that time, the real revolutionaries were those who embraced the paradox and stood for evolution in architecture and against the stultified revolution of late modernism. Today, architects and urbanists are similarly challenged by the conundrum of public spaces within private buildings. But this, too, is a paradox that we can embrace. History shows how richly the public interiors of private buildings can extend and enhance the city's public offering.

30
Being and Circumstance

Robert Irwin

Source: *Being and Circumstance: Notes Toward a Conditional Art*. Lapis Press, 1985, pp. 9–29

To help sort out some of the confusion of ambitions and practices, let me rough out some general working categories for public/site art, in terms of how we generally process (recognize, understand) them. (Note: there are no value judgments intended here, only distinctions.) Put simply, we can say that any given work falls into one of the following four categories:

1. *Site dominant*. This work embodies the classical tenets of permanence, transcendent and historical content, meaning, purpose; the art-object either rises out of, or is the occasion for, its "ordinary" circumstances— monuments, historical figures, murals, etc. These "works of art" are recognized, understood, and evaluated by referencing their content, purpose, placement, familiar form, materials, techniques, skills, etc. A Henry Moore would be an example of site-dominant art.
2. *Site adjusted*. Such work compensates for the modern development of the levels of meaning-content having been reduced to terrestrial dimensions (even abstraction). Here consideration is given to adjustments of scale, appropriateness, placement, etc. But the "work of art" is still either made or conceived in the studio and transported to, or assembled on, the site. These works are, sometimes, still referenced by the familiarity of "content and placement" (centered, or on a pedestal, etc.), but there is now a developing emphasis on referencing the oeuvre of the individual artist. Here, a Mark di Suvero would be an example.
3. *Site specific*. Here the "sculpture" is conceived with the site in mind; the site sets the parameters and is, in part, the reason for the sculpture. This process takes the initial step towards sculpture's being integrated into its surroundings. But our process of recognition and understanding of the "work of art" is still keyed (referenced) to the oeuvre of the artist. Familiarity with his or her history, lineage, art intent, style, materials, techniques, etc., are presupposed; thus, for example, a Richard Serra is always recognizable as, first and foremost, a Richard Serra.
4. *Site conditioned/determined*. Here the sculptural response draws all of its cues (reasons for being) from its surroundings. This requires the process *to begin* with an intimate, hands-on reading of the site. This means sitting, watching, and walking through the site, the surrounding areas (where you will enter from and exit to), the city at large or the countryside. Here there are numerous things to consider; what is the site's relation to applied and implied schemes of organization and systems of order, relation, architecture, uses, distances, sense of scale? For example, are we dealing with New York verticals or big sky Montana? What kinds of natural events affect the site—snow, wind, sun angles, sunrise, water, etc.? What is the physical and people density? the sound and visual density (quiet, next-to-quiet, or busy)? What are the qualities of surface, sound, movement, light, etc.? What are the qualities of detail, levels of finish, craft? What are the histories of prior and current uses, present desires, etc.? A quiet distillation of all of this—while directly experiencing the site—determines all the facets of the "sculptural response": aesthetic sensibility, levels and kinds of physicality, gesture, dimensions, materials, kind and level of finish, details, etc.; whether the response should be monumental or ephemeral, aggressive or gentle, useful or useless, sculptural, architectural, or simply the planting of a tree, or maybe even doing nothing at all.

Here, with this fourth category of site-conditioned art, the process of recognition and understanding breaks with the conventions of abstract referencing of content, historical lineage, oeuvre of the artist, style, etc., implicit in the other three categories, and crosses the conventional boundaries of art vis-à-vis architecture, landscape, city planning, utility, and so forth, reducing *such quantitative* recognitions (measures and categories) to a secondary importance. We now propose to follow the principles of phenomenal, conditional, and responsive art by placing the individual observer in context, at the crux of the determining process, insisting that he or she use all the same (immediate) cues the artist used in forming the art-response to form his or her operative-response (judgments): "Does this 'piece,' 'situation,' or 'space,' make sense? Is it more interesting, more beautiful? How do I feel about it? And what does it mean to me?" Earlier, I made the point that you cannot correctly call anything either free or creative if the individual does not, at least in part, determine his or her own meaning. What applied to the artist now applies to the observer. And in this responsibility of the individual observer we can see the first social implication of a phenomenal art.

Being and Circumstance, then, constitute the operative frame of reference for an extended (phenomenal) art activity, which becomes a process of reasoning between our mediated culture (being) and our immediate presence (circumstance). *Being* embodies in you the observer, participant, or user, your complete genetic, cultural, and personal histories as "subsidiary" cues bearing on your "focal" attending (experiencing) of your circumstances, again in a "from-to relation." *Circumstance*, of course, encompasses all of the conditions, qualities, and consequences making up the real context of your being *in* the world. There is embedded in any set of circumstances and your being in them the dynamic of a past and future, what was, how it came to be, what it is, and what it may come to be.

If all of this seems a bit familiar, it should. No one "invents" a new perceptual consciousness. This process of being and circumstance is our most basic perceptual (experiencing) action, something we already do at every moment in simply coming to know the nature of our presence, and we almost always do so without giving the wonder of it a second thought. Once again this "oversight" speaks not of its insignificance; on the contrary, it speaks of its extraordinary sophistication. What I am advocating is simply elevating this process, this reasoning, to a role of importance that matches its innate sophistication. It should be noted that it is upon this "reasoning" process that all of our subsequent logics (systems) are instinctively patterned—although this generally goes unacknowledged. But with one modification (gain and loss): to cut the world down to a manageable size, our logics hold their components to act as a kind of truth, locking them in as a matter of style into a form of *permanence*. Conversely, the process of reasoning, our being and circumstance (which I am here proposing), is free of such abstraction and can account for that most basic condition (physic) of the universe—*change*. . . .

The wonder of it all is that what looked for all the world like a diminishing horizon—the art-object's becoming so ephemeral as to threaten to disappear altogether—has, like some marvelous philosophical riddle, turned itself inside out to reveal its opposite. What appeared to be a question of object/non-object has turned out to be a question of seeing and not seeing, of how it is we actually perceive or fail to perceive "things" in their real contexts. Now we are presented and challenged with the infinite, everyday richness of "phenomenal" perception (and the potential for a corresponding "phenomenal art," with none of the customary abstract limitations as to form, place, materials, and so forth)—one which seeks to discover and value the potential for experiencing beauty in everything.

31
Interior

Beatriz Colomina

Source: *Privacy and Publicity*. The MIT Press, 1994, pp. 232–252

"To live is to leave traces," writes Walter Benjamin, discussing the birth of the interior. "In the interior these are emphasized. An abundance of covers and protectors, liners and cases is devised, on which the traces of objects of everyday use are imprinted. The traces of the occupant also leave their impression on the interior. The detective story that follows these traces comes into being. . . . The criminals of the first detective novels are neither gentlemen nor apaches, but private members of the bourgeoisie."[1]

There is an interior in the detective novel. But can there be a detective story of the interior itself, of the hidden mechanisms by which space is constructed as interior? Which may be to say, a detective story of detection itself, of the controlling look, the look of control, the controlled look. But where would the traces of the look be imprinted? What do we have to go on? What clues?

There is an unknown passage of a well-known book, Le Corbusier's *Urbanisme* (1925), that reads: "Loos told me one day: 'A cultivated man does not look out of the window; his window is a ground glass; it is there only to let the light in, not to let the gaze pass through.' "[2] It points to a conspicuous yet conspicuously ignored feature of Loos's houses: not only are the windows either opaque or covered with sheer curtains, but the organization of the spaces and the disposition of the built-in furniture (the *immeuble*) seem to hinder access to them. A sofa is often placed at the foot of a window so as to position the occupants with their back to it, facing the room, as in the bedroom of the Hans Brummel apartment (Pilsen, 1929). This even happens with the windows that look into other interior spaces—as in the sitting area of the ladies' lounge of the Müller house (Prague, 1930). Or, more dramatically, in the houses for the Vienna Werkbundsiedlung (Vienna, 1930–1932), a late project where Loos has finally brought himself to make a thoroughly modern, double-height window; not only is this opening still veiled with a

curtain, but a couch in the sitting nook of the upper-level gallery places the occupants with their back to the window, hovering dangerously over the space. (Symptomatically, and we must return to this point, when the sitting nook in an identical house is used as a man's study, the seat faces the window.) Moreover, upon entering a Loos interior one's body is continually turned around to face the space one has just moved through, rather than the upcoming space or the space outside. With each turn, each return look, the body is arrested. Looking at the photographs, it is easy to imagine oneself in these precise, static positions, usually indicated by the unoccupied furniture. The photographs suggest that it is intended that these spaces be comprehended by occupation, by using this furniture, by "entering" the photograph, by inhabiting it.[3]

In the Moller house (Vienna, 1928) there is a raised sitting area off the living room with a sofa set against the window. Although one cannot see out the window, its presence is strongly felt. The bookshelves surrounding the sofa and the light coming from behind it suggest a comfortable nook for reading. But comfort in this space is more than just sensual, for there is also a psychological dimension. A sense of security is produced by the position of the couch, the placement of its occupants against the light. Anyone who, ascending the stairs from the entrance (itself a rather dark passage), enters the living room, would take a few moments to recognize a person sitting on the couch. Conversely, any intrusion would soon be detected by a person occupying this area, just as an actor entering the stage is immediately seen by a spectator in a theater box.

Loos refers to this idea in noting that "the smallness of a theater box would be unbearable if one could not look out into the large space beyond."[4] While Kulka, and later Münz, read this comment in terms of the economy of space provided by the *Raumplan*, they overlook its psychological dimension. For Loos, the theater box exists at the intersection between claustrophobia and agoraphobia.[5] This spatial-psychological device could also be read in terms of power, regimes of control inside the house. The raised sitting area of the Moller house provides the occupant with a vantage point overlooking the interior. Comfort in this space is related to both intimacy and control.

This area is the most intimate of the sequence of living spaces, yet, paradoxically, rather than being at the heart of the house, it is placed at the periphery, pushing a volume out of the street facade, just above the front entrance. Moreover, it corresponds with the largest window on this elevation (almost a horizontal window). The occupant of this space can both detect anyone crossing-trespassing the threshold of the house (while screened by the curtain) and monitor any movement in the interior (while "screened" by the backlighting).

In this space, the window is only a source of light, not a frame for a view. The eye is turned toward the interior. The only exterior view that would be possible from this position requires that the gaze travel the whole depth of the house, from the alcove to the living room to the music room, which opens onto the back garden. Thus, the exterior view depends upon a view of the interior.

The look folded inward upon itself can be traced in other Loos interiors. In the Müller house, for instance, the sequence of spaces, articulated around the staircase, follows an increasing sense of privacy from the drawing room to the dining room and study to the "lady's room" (*Zimmer der Dame*) with its raised sitting area, which occupies the center or "heart" of the house.[6] But the window of this space looks onto the living space. Here, too, the most intimate room is like a theater box, placed just over the entrance to the social spaces in this house, so that any intruder could easily be seen. Likewise, the view of the exterior, toward the city, from this "theater box" is contained within a view of the interior. Suspended in the middle of the house, this space assumes the character both of a "sacred" space and of a point of control. Comfort is produced by two seemingly opposing conditions, intimacy and control.

This is hardly the idea of comfort that is associated with the nineteenth-century interior as described by Walter Benjamin in "Louis-Phillippe, or the Interior."[7] In Loos's interiors the sense of security is not achieved by simply turning one's back on the exterior and immersing oneself in a private universe—"a box in the world theater," to use Benjamin's metaphor. It is no longer the house that is a theater box; there is a theater box inside

the house, overlooking the internal social spaces. The inhabitants of Loos's houses are both actors in and spectators of the family scene—involved in, yet detached from, their own space.[8] The classical distinction between inside and outside, private and public, object and subject, becomes convoluted.

Traditionally, the theater box provided for the privileged a private space within the dangerous public realm, by reestablishing the boundaries between inside and outside. It is significant that when Loos designed a theater in 1898 (an unrealized project), he omitted the boxes, arguing they "didn't suit a modern auditorium."[9] Thus he removes the box from the public theater, only to insert it into the "private theater" of the house. The public has entered the private house by way of the social spaces,[10] but there is a last site of resistance to this intrusion in the domestic "theater box."

The theater boxes in the Moller and Müller houses are spaces marked as "female," the domestic character of the furniture contrasting with that of the adjacent "male" space, the library. In these, the leather sofas, the desks, the chimney, the mirrors represent a "public space" within the house—the office and the club invading the interior. But it is an invasion that is confined to an enclosed room—a space that belongs to the sequence of social spaces within the house, yet does not engage with them. As Münz notes, the library is a "reservoir of quietness," "set apart from the household traffic." The raised alcove of the Moller house and the *Zimmer der Dame* of the Müller house, on the other hand, not only overlook the social spaces but are exactly positioned at the end of the sequence, on the threshold of the private, the secret, the upper rooms where sexuality is hidden away. At the intersection of the visible and the invisible, women are placed as the guardians of the unspeakable.[11]

But the theater box is a device that both provides protection and draws attention to itself. Thus, when Münz describes the entrance to the social spaces of the Moller house, he writes: "Within, entering from one side, one's gaze travels in the opposite direction till it rests in the light, pleasant alcove, raised above the living room floor. *Now we are really inside the house.*"[12] So, where were we before? we may ask, when we crossed the threshold of the house and occupied the entrance hall and the cloakroom in the ground floor or while we ascended the stairs to the reception rooms on the second or elevated ground floor. The intruder is "inside," has penetrated the house, only when his/

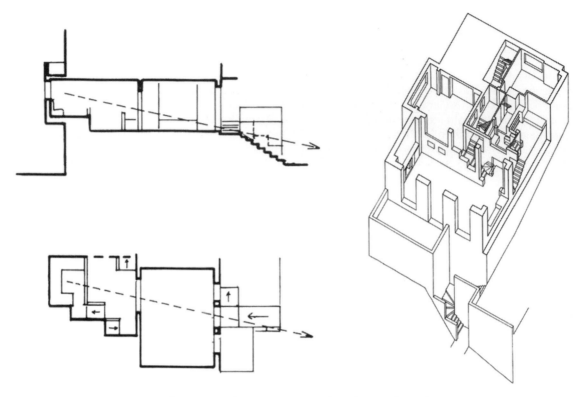

Figure 31.1 Image courtesy of Beatriz Colomina. Drawing by John van de Beek

her gaze strikes this most intimate space, turning the occupant into a silhouette against the light. The "voyeur" in the "theater box" has become the object of another's gaze; she is caught in the act of seeing, entrapped in the very moment of control. In framing a view, the theater box also frames the viewer. It is impossible to abandon the space, let alone leave the house, without being seen by those over whom control is being exerted. Object and subject exchange places. Whether there is actually a person behind either gaze is irrelevant:

> I can feel myself under the gaze of someone whose eyes I do not even see, not even discern. All that is necessary is for something to signify to me that there may be others there. The window if it gets a bit dark and if I have reasons for thinking that there is some-one behind it, is straight-way a gaze. From the moment this gaze exists, I am already something other, in that I feel myself becoming an object for the gaze of others. But in this position, which is a reciprocal one, others also know that I am an object who knows himself to be seen.[13]

Architecture is not simply a platform that accom-modates the viewing subject. It is a viewing mech-anism that produces the subject. It precedes and frames its occupant.

The theatricality of Loos's interiors is constructed by many forms of representation (of which built space is not necessarily the most important). Many of the photographs, for instance, tend to give the impression that someone is just about to enter the room, that a piece of domestic drama is about to be enacted. The characters absent from the stage, from the scenery and from its props—the conspic-uously placed pieces of furniture—are conjured up.[14] The only published photograph of a Loos domestic interior that includes a human figure is a view of the entrance to the drawing room of the Rufer house (Vienna, 1922). A male figure, barely visible, is about to cross the threshold through a peculiar opening in the wall.[15] But it is precisely at this threshold, slightly off stage, that the actor/intruder is most vulnerable, for a small window in the reading room looks down onto the back of his or her neck. This house, traditionally considered to be the prototype of the *Raumplan*, also contains the prototype of the theater box.

Figure 31.2 Image courtesy of Beatriz Colomina. Image from Der Architect, no 22 (1922)

NOTES

1 Walter Benjamin, "Paris, Capital of the Nineteenth Century," in *Reflections*, trans. Edmund Jephcott (New York: Schocken Books, 1986), pp. 155–156.

2 "Loos m'affirmait un jour: 'Un homme cultivé ne regarde pas par la fenêtre; sa fenêtre est en verre dépoli; elle n'est là que pour donner de la lumière, non pour laisser passer le regard.'" Le Corbusier, *Urbanisme* (Paris, 1925), p. 174. When this book was published in English under the title *The City of To-morrow and Its Planning*, translated by Frederick Etchells (New York, 1929), the sentence read: "A friend once said to me: 'No intelligent man ever looks out of his window; his window is made of ground glass; its only function is to let in light, not to look out of'" (pp. 185–186). In this translation, Loos's name has been replaced by "a friend." Was Loos "nobody" for Etchells, or is this just another example of the kind of misunderstanding that led to the mistranslation of the title of the book? Perhaps it was Le Corbusier himself who decided to erase Loos's name. Of a different order, but no less symptomatic, is the mistranslation of "laisser passer le regard" (to let the gaze pass through) as "to look out of," as if to resist the idea that the gaze might take on, as it were, a life of its own, independent of the beholder.

3 The perception of space is produced by its representations; in this sense, built space has no more authority than do drawings, photographs, or descriptions.

4 Ludwig Münz and Gustav Künstler, *Der Architekt Adolf Loos* (Vienna and Munich, 1964), pp. 130–131. English translation: *Adolf Loos, Pioneer of Modern Architecture* (London, 1966), p. 148: "We may call to mind an observation by Adolf Loos, handed down to us by Heinrich Kulka, that the smallness of a theatre box would be unbearable if one could not look out into the large space beyond; hence it was possible to save space, even in the design of small houses, by linking a high main room with a low annexe."

5 Georges Teyssot has noted that "The Bergsonian ideas of the room as a refuge from the world are meant to be conceived as the 'juxtaposition' between claustrophobia and agoraphobia. This dialectic is already found in Rilke." G. Teyssot, "The Disease of the Domicile," *Assemblage* 6 (1988), p. 95.

6 There is also a more direct and more private route to the sitting area, a staircase rising from the entrance of the drawing room

7 "Under Louis-Philippe the private citizen enters the stage of history. . . . For the private person, living space becomes, for the first time, antithetical to the place of work. The former is constituted by the interior; the office is its complement. The private person who squares his account with reality in his office demands that the interior be maintained in his illusions. This need is all the more pressing since he has no intention of extending his commercial considerations into social ones. In shaping his private environment he represses both. From this spring the phantasmagorias of the interior. For the private individual the private environment represents the universe. In it he gathers remote places and the past. His drawing room is a *"box in the world theater."* Walter Benjamin, "Paris, Capital of the Nineteenth Century," in *Reflections*, p. 154. Emphasis added.

8 This calls to mind Freud's paper "A Child Is Being Beaten" (1919), where, as Victor Burgin has written, "the subject is positioned both in the audience *and* on stage—where it is both aggressor *and* aggressed." Victor Burgin, "Geometry and Abjection," *AA Files*, no. 15 (Summer 1987), p. 38. *The mise-en-scène* of Loos's interiors appears to coincide with that of Freud's unconscious. Sigmund Freud, "A Child Is Being Beaten: A Contribution to the Study of the Origin of Sexual Perversions," in *Standard Edition of the Complete Psychological Works of Sigmund Freud* (London: Hogarth Press, 1953–1974), vol. 17, pp. 175–204. In relation to Freud's paper, see also Jacqueline Rose, *Sexuality in the Field of Vision* (London, 1986), pp. 209–210.

9 Münz and Künstler, *Adolf Loos*, p. 36.

10 See note 7 above. There are no social spaces in the Benjaminian interior. He writes: "In shaping his private environment he [the private person] represses both [commercial and social considerations]." Benjamin's interior is established in opposition to the office. But as Laura Mulvey has noted, "The workplace is no threat to the home. The two maintain each other in a safe, mutually dependent polarisation. The threat comes from elsewhere: . . . the city." Laura Mulvey, "Melodrama Inside and Outside the Home" (1986), in *Visual and Other Pleasures* (London: Macmillan, 1989), p. 70

11 In a criticism of Benjamin's account of the bourgeois interior, Laura Mulvey writes: "Benjamin does not mention the fact that the private sphere, the domestic, is an essential adjunct to the bourgeois marriage and is thus associated with woman, not simply as female, but as wife and mother. It is the mother who guarantees the privacy of the home by maintaining its respectability, as essential a defence against incursion or curiosity as the encompassing walls of the home itself." Laura Mulvey, "Melodrama Inside and Outside the Home."

12 Münz and Künstler, *Adolf Loos*, p.149.

13 Jacques Lacan, *The Seminar of Jacques Lacan: Book I, Freud's Papers on Technique 1953–1954*, ed. Jacques-Alain Miller, trans. John Forrester (New York and London: Norton, 1988), p. 215. In this passage Lacan is referring to Jean-Paul Sartre's *Being and Nothingness*.

14 There is an instance of such personification of furniture in one of Loos's most autobiographical texts, "Interiors in the Rotunda" (1898), where he writes: "Every piece of furniture, every thing, every object had a story to tell, a family history." *Spoken into the Void: Collected Essays 1897–1900*, trans. Jane O. Newman and John H. Smith (Cambridge: MIT Press, 1982), p. 24.

15 This photograph has only recently been published. Kulka's monograph (a work in which Loos was involved) presents exactly the same view, the same photograph, but without a human figure. The strange opening in the wall pulls the viewer toward the void, toward the missing actor (a tension that the photographer no doubt felt the need to cover by literally inserting a figure). This tension constructs the subject, as it does in the built-in couch of the raised area of the Moller house, or the window of the *Zimmer der Dame* overlooking the drawing room of the Müller house.

SECTION 3.2
THE PROCESS OF REMODELLING

Introduction

The adaptation of existing buildings and structures for new uses is probably as old as construction itself is. Economic, social and expedience are all factors that have historically contributed towards the rationale behind reuse. As a society changed, so did the way in which the buildings were occupied, and often the most convenient and practical approach was to simply reuse what was available, rather than starting afresh. Building reuse is now a most widespread architectural practice, something that engages most architectural and interior design practices, and yet there is little theoretical underpinning to it.

The most successful adaptations occur when a sound relationship between the old and the new is established. The architect or designer will generally embark upon a comprehensive reading of the building that is to be remodelled. This will include the history, context, structure and materials, and it is this understanding, combined with a thorough knowledge of the needs of the new users, that will form the basis of the remodelling. Issues of sustainability, economics, structure and culture can all contribute towards the design proposal, but given the intrinsic link between the site and the new elements of the proposal, the approach is generally based upon finding a formal link or connection between the two. The form or three-dimensional shape of the remodelled building will inevitably be based upon that of the original building.

Another crucial factor within the remodelling process is that of the culture that implements the adaptation. Our perception of the past is determined by our present. That is, the manner in which the past is perceived is not solely dependent upon the available information about the past, but it is also influenced by the interpretation of that information by the contemporary individual or society. Contemporary society imposes modern values, morals or culture upon this interpretation; after all it is impossible to place oneself in the position of the occupant of a mediaeval building.

All of the essays in this chapter discuss the theory that underpins the process of adaptation, from changing historical attitudes towards reuse through to contemporary thinking about the subject. It is interesting to note that attitudes towards reuse have not really changed and it does seem that the key questions of, Will the new function fit into the existing building? and Is it appropriate for it to do so?, have always been asked.

Dora Crouch, in her essay "Early Christian Architecture: Adaptive Reuse", discusses the manner in which pre-Christian buildings were remodelled to accommodate a new use. In the very early Christian period, worshippers were not clear about what a church should look like, and Crouch describes the evolution of the building type from the Roman Temple, through the reuse of shrines, tombs and catacombs (especially when Christian worship was frowned upon). Eventually, the nature and form of the Basilica was settled upon. Basilica is a Latin word and was a general Roman expression for a public building, which was usually located in the forum of a town. It has become a Christian term, and now specifically refers to a large and important church that has been given special ceremonial rites, and so the word has both ecclesiastical and architectural meaning. Although Crouch limits her exploration to southern Europe, it was very common for Christians to reuse important and strategically placed buildings and sites for their own structures. They wanted the church to be given a place of authority within the heart of the community, but Crouch also cites other economic reasons for this choice.

Emphasis upon the importance of the contrast between the old and new was laid out in the guidelines of the Athens Charter, CIAM 1931. This document was written in reaction to the sometimes overzealous restoration of many monuments and other important buildings. The committee felt that too many buildings were suffering from such passionate repair, that it had become impossible to understand or read the history of the place; it appeared to have all been constructed at the same time and had survived in a pristine condition. **Crimson** argue in this essay, "Re-Arch: New Designs for Old Buildings" from *Too Blessed to be Depressed*, that this demand for a contrast between the original building and the adaptation led to a position where additions and extensions have become either insensitive and overpowering, or conversely, in an attempt to respond to the existing, "the new building became little more than a museum of the old one". Crimson quote Nietzsche's essay "On the Use and Abuse of History", when he discusses the need to take not the magnificent or universal, but the everyday and the incidental. They conclude with the somewhat controversial argument that the search for some fragment of history can sometimes be so strong that there is maybe a futility in it, and there is actually some importance in forgetting.

"Old Buildings as Palimpsest" by **Rodolfo Machado**, published in 1976, was written as the Contextual movement was beginning to emerge as a powerful and influential voice. In a reaction to modernism, architects and theorists such as Colin Rowe, Fred Koetter, Jane Jacobs and Aldo Rossi were espousing the need for the preservation of the urban environment, the conservation of existing buildings and the sensitive integration of new and appropriate elements. Machado's highly influential essay was one of the first to suggest a theory of adaptation, based upon an interpretation of the history and nature of the building. He argues "in remodeling, the past takes on a value far different from that in the usual design process" . . . "because it, itself, is the material to be altered and reshaped". The use of the word palimpsest creates an interesting analogy, because its original meaning was that of an inscribed surface from which the text has been scraped away so that the space could be used again for another, but traces of the original text remain and inevitably have an influence upon the reading of the next inscription. A term that is obviously very apt for the use and reuse of a building. Machado concludes with a discussion that questions the well-known modernist maxim: "Form follows function", instead preferring: "Form follows form".

Ignasi de Sola-Morales Rubió in his essay "From Contrast to Analogy: Developments in the Concept of Architectural Intervention" argues against the implementation of a permanent doctrine that governs the manner in which adaptation can take place. He maintains that there is a relationship between the culture of those who constructed the original building and those who are to make the new interventions and that it is the consideration of the two cultures that should determine the design.

There is a fundamental difference between the monumental value of an existing building and its documentary value. Simply being old, de Sola-Morales argues, has novelty value, but a noteworthy structure contains significant information. He discusses the work of the Viennese Art Historian, Alois Riegl, who in 1903 analysed attitudes towards heritage. Riegl claimed that there is value attached to the ancient, and thus contrast between old and new within a project projected an authority. Meaning in architecture and design is discovered through the accumulation of references; within building adaptation, these belong both to the new and to the old.

The approach to the remodelling of a building can be based upon a discriminating reading of the existing, rather than trying to directly impose a function upon it. This analysis can inform the architect or designer of the best course of action. The character and qualities of the original can suggest the best spatial of formal organisation. The designer can then decide upon how best to integrate the old and new. **Graeme Brooker** and **Sally Stone**, in what is the introduction to the Strategy section of their book *Rereadings: Interior Architecture and the Design Principles of Remodelling Existing Buildings*, categorise the different levels of interaction between old and new. They argue that the taxonomy of adaptation can be ordered through the sheer amount of integration. This they catalogue into three sections: Intervention, Insertion and Installation. Intervention is the practice of the old and new becoming completely integrated; such is the level of work to the original building, that once the work is complete, the two could not viably exist independently. If a new element is designed to fit exactly within the confines of an existing building, then the category is Insertion; it is almost as if the new component is just conceptually lowered into place. Installation is the process of the new sitting among the old; they may have a spatial relationship, but it would be possible to remove the additions without affecting the integrity of the original building. Of course, as with many taxonomy processes, there are exceptions to these categories, but it is surprising how few these are.

Philippe Robert uses the analogy of "Architecture as a Palimpsest" as the introductory title in his book *Adaptations*. This was one of the first books specifically about the remodelling of existing buildings to be published. He lists a series of projects, not by function or use, but by the level of interaction between the old and the new. So the first few categories are: building within, building over, building around and building alongside. He regards this "inventory as a reminder of the way in which conversion brings into play memory of place with future use, at the same time and within the same place". He argues that, for a conversion to be successful, there should be some symbolic memory of the original. The essay ends with the claim that the naïve attitude of architects towards remodelling is "astonishing". This declaration was written in 1989, which pre-empts much of the twenty-first century debate about the appropriation of adaptation work by architects as their more traditional new build works dry up.

The remodelling process is a long arduous journey in pursuit of coincidence. Intersections and points of congruence between the original building and the new function are sought as a means of negotiating a fit between the old and the new. **Fred Scott**, in the chapter "Some Resolutions" from the book *On Altering Architecture*, argues that the designer needs "an acute eye for the poetry of the everyday" if the qualities of the existing building are to be best amalgamated with a new function. However, he warns against an approach that is too meek or inconsequential, arguing that adaptation is a work of savagery that needs a brave spirit and a lack of reverence. It is also the quest for uncertainty that provides the remodelled building with its authenticity.

Scott seeks to reopen the old argument between Ruskin and Viollet-le-Duc about the best way in which to approach restoration. Interestingly he comes down on both sides. At first he concedes that modernist buildings need to be restored as if brand new; they need the same treatment as the classic car, restored to a condition more pristine, more clean, more perfect than when constructed, but then he ruminates upon the possible misdirection of that attitude. Pre-modernist buildings, however, should be allowed to show their age and history if they are to have any authenticity.

Sally Stone

Carlo Scarpa (1906–1978)

Carlo Scarpa was born in Venice, Northern Italy, and his work is mainly within the Veneto area. His approach to architecture was influenced by the contextual qualities and character of the area combined with an earnest belief in modernism. Water, time, movement, the beauty of materials and truth were design principles that he strove to adhere to. He completed very few new buildings, preferring to work with existing buildings. His masterpiece was the restoration and remodelling of the Castelvecchio in Verona, although his works at the Fondazione Querini Stampalia, the Olivetti Shop and the Brion Cemetery are all extremely highly regarded. Scarpa is regarded as the greatest exponent of the remodelling process.

Building Study: Castelvecchio Museum

Verona, Italy
1957–64
Carlo Scarpa

Carlo Scarpa developed a progressive and at the time controversial attitude towards the remodelling of existing buildings. His approach to the subject was based upon an interpretation of the meaning of the original building. He endeavoured to understand the historical and contextual qualities of the place and then to apply a new contemporary layer of value and consequence to the building. This was in direct violation of the Athens Charter, which dictated that contrast between old and new was the most important approach to adaptation. However, Scarpa regarded himself as belonging to the Italian tradition of working with existing buildings, often citing the example of Brunelleschi, whose masterpiece, the dome of the Duomo in Florence, was an addition to an existing building.

The Castelvecchio Museum is possibly Scarpa's greatest work. The museum in Verona is composed of the complex of buildings, courtyards, gardens and the tower of the Scaliger castle. It is situated by a bridge over the river Adige, which runs through the centre of Verona. In response to the three main periods of the castle's history, the layers of building were scraped away or exposed until the junctions where time was most obvious were revealed. A new layer of small, beautifully composed additions were then imposed upon the building, a layer that expressed the contemporary nature of their design but which was totally appropriate and sympathetic to the original building.

Scarpa felt that for reasons of clarity it was important to introduce gaps or shadows between the historical strata of the building; therefore, the junction between the west wing of the building and the bridge over the Adige was excavated, the false Napoleonic windows were recessed and new elements were held lightly away from the original building. Into the gap between the bridge and the castle, Scarpa placed the Cangrande I della Scala statue. The residents of Verona held this artwork in special affection, and its location, high in the pivotal position between the city and the river, sheltered under the new roof, is a fitting tribute to the old gentleman.

32
Early Christian Architecture
Adaptive Re-use

Dora Crouch

Source: *History of Architecture: Stonehenge to Skyscrapers*. McGraw-Hill, 1985, pp. 114–124

Reuse is a word often heard in architecture today. Cities have always been rebuilt: it is their nature to change. In the past 200 years the pace of such change has been accelerated. In previous periods change was slower since new ways had to be found to use what was there before. Starting with a city from the late Roman period, we can see how buildings were adapted over time to suit new uses, and the fabric of the city was subtly changed. Some of the major early Christian buildings are other examples of reuse as a result of adaptation to different needs.

DURA-EUROPOS

Dura-Europos, an ancient town of Mesopotamia, was located on the right bank of the Euphrates River in what is today Iraq. When the soldiers of Alexander the Great settled down to rule what had been the Persian Empire, they founded cities like this one all across the Middle East and gave them European names—hence Dura (the old Semitic name) plus Europos (the Greek name). The town is an example of gradual renewal of a settlement by an evolving culture.

As can be expected in a Greek town, there was an agora at the center surrounded on three sides of the rectangle by stoa-like buildings. Through intermarriage the population became less and less Greek and more and more Mesopotamian, and the open space filled up with irregular structures; thus by 100 A.D. the open market resembled an oriental bazaar. The new population used the space in ways that matched the developing orientalism of the society.

In the original plan, the Greek grid was surrounded by a wall rather loosely flung around the city on the hilly sides, advantage being taken of the terrain for defense, but with an almost straight wall along the flat desert side. There were changes through time in how this wall and its towers were used. For over 200 years, until the third quarter of the second century, when peace prevailed, there was little need for a defensive wall. The flat-roofed tower at the north extremity of the wall became a sanctuary. A major reason for this reuse of the tower had to do with the local tradition of worshiping on a high place. The gods honored in the northern tower were Palmyrene gods from the nearby capital Palmyra. (Palmyrenes frequently hired themselves out as mercenaries; while garrisoning Dura-Europos, they set up this temple to their own gods.)

The wall of Dura-Europos is important for us today because it has preserved two additional sanctuaries of major importance. During the third century, the Persians invaded this area several times. Their favorite types of warfare were raids, or sieges, in which they undermined the walls of the city they were attacking. To prevent the Persians from marching in through the holes created in their desert wall, the people of Dura-Europos reinforced the wall with a huge earthen embankment that was fairly shallow on the desert side but 35 meters deep on the inside. If the Persians tried to dig a tunnel under so much dirt, there was no collapse. The houses of the blocks nearest the wall were filled up with dirt and became part of the embankment.

It is fortunate for our study that Dura-Europos was threatened in this way, because two of the houses immured had already been reused for religious buildings. Both were small Mediterranean courtyard houses built probably in the first century. About the middle of the second century, perhaps in 165, one was turned into a Christian church. The house was changed very little, except for wall decorations, which are in the museum at Yale University. Though modest, this house church at

Dura-Europos is one of the very earliest churches that has come down to us.

More unusual is the other house at Dura-Europos that was made into a religious building—a synagogue. The main meeting room of the Dura-Europos synagogue was painted in bands of pictures of Old Testament stories. Until this synagogue was found, it was not known that Jews of the ancient world used visual representations of human figures in their synagogues. Here in this provincial town, then, significant artifacts have been preserved through having been accidentally covered up in the embankment.

ADAPTIVE REUSE OF OLDER STRUCTURES: ADDITIONAL EXAMPLES

In Rome, some early structures have survived by being incorporated in later buildings. For instance, under the church of Saints Giovanni and Paolo lie the remains of an early apartment building. Originally it had shops along the sloping street and apartments above, in the usual pattern. Within that pattern, a Christian church was built, one which became later the titular church of a bishop. Inserted as it was within the crowded residential framework, Saints Giovanni and Paolo resembled the house church at Dura-Europos.

Early Christian building types grew out of the adaptive reuse of older structures for reasons having to do with the general history of the period. In the late Roman era, a variety of cultural strains made up the society of the empire, many of which contributed to the development of Christianity. For instance, Jewish and Persian forms of worship were adopted, and Christian theological ideas were represented with both Old Testament and Mithraic symbols. Because Jews and half-assimilated pagans—potential converts to Christianity—lived in cities, the major cities of the imperial network became in turn important centers for the church's expanding network. Church organization was patterned after imperial government, with both titles and costumes being carried over into the new community. As the population became Christian, the old pagan buildings no longer had a religious use. They became houses, stores, and other public structures, as excavation has shown. Parts of the old buildings were used again to decorate new ones.

In the first, second, and third centuries, the Christian religion was officially outlawed. At that time, worship of the emperor as a god was a unifying political and religious concept. Christians who would not worship the emperor were considered traitors and were therefore persecuted.

In the early fourth century, Emperor Constantine the Great had a vision which changed the status of Christianity. As he was sleeping before an important battle for control of the empire, he saw a cross in the sky. Next morning he ordered his soldiers to put a cross on their shields. When Constantine's forces won the battle, he decided to stop the official persecution of Christians. Meetings of the sect for worship were made legal. After a while Constantine and his family became Christians. They are responsible for some important Christian buildings of the second quarter of the fourth century. The early Christian period begins with this legalization and extends until the beginning of the Dark Ages in the second half of the sixth century, overlapping somewhat with the Byzantine era.

In the fourth century, it was not clear in people's minds what a church should look like. Until the time of Constantine, Christian worship had taken place in borrowed structures. Traditional religious buildings had a negative association with pagan worship that prevented their adoption for Christian use. It took a while to work through this question of what images or forms would be proper for a religious building in the new Christian sense of religion. Both in building types and in decoration, it was well into the fourth century before the iconography (meaning of forms) and the content of the religion were compatible. (See *The Age of Spirituality*, and Panofsky's *Renaissance and Renascences*.)

TOMBS AND CATACOMBS

One possible alternative was to use an imperial tomb as a church building—a satisfactory combination of iconography and building, stating the Christian message of resurrection after death. The church of St. George at Salonika in Greece was originally an imperial tomb. It is a massive round building, rather like a coarse version of the Pantheon. The church of Santa Costanza in Rome is of the same type. Following the imperial tradition going back through Hadrian and Augustus to the Etruscans, Costanza, the daughter of Constantine, built a fine circular tomb for herself. Santa Costanza also adopted the plan and section of the Pantheon, with a lower space that introduces one to the high central domed space. This tomb was also later used as a church.

Another tomb type associated with the death and hence the resurrection of Christ, is the catacomb, which was not a new concept. Even in pagan times, it had been prudent to excavate underground corridors in stone to inter people in slits in the walls rather than use up precious agricultural land around a city. Mixed Christian and pagan catacombs, purely pagan ones, and even Jewish ones, are known to have existed in several cities of the empire, such as Syracuse, Antioch, and Alexandria. The Christians made something more meaningful of their catacombs than did others who used them.

Among the Romans it was customary to form burial societies, in which members could count on the group burying them and caring for their widows and orphans. At the same time, it was illegal to have political meetings or to belong to religions that the state proscribed. The Christians therefore called themselves a burial society. Among the burial corridors were occasional rooms where an important person could be honored by a free-standing coffin at one end or in the center. The Christians gathered in such a room around the remains of one of their martyrs, using the coffin as the table for their sacrificial meal.

When Christianity became legal, among the very first churches that were built out in the open air were shrines to favorite martyrs buried in the catacomb areas. The combined function of tomb and place of celebration of the martyr became the theme for a special type of shrine. Here the people came to honor not only the martyr but also the dead from their own families who were buried in the catacombs and to have memorial services for them. The building was then a special-event church, where people went at stated intervals after a death. A typical church of this kind was St. Agnese in Rome, a simple truss-roofed basilica with an apse at one end. It was built after 330, of brick-faced concrete, a favorite Roman combination that persisted in Italy into the early sixth century. Looking at the interior, we can see that the altar table in the shape of a tomb has become universal. The columns are of different materials, because they have been reused from different earlier buildings.

Reuse of buildings and their elements was common among the Romans. Most famous is the case of a public latrine at Ostia, where the seats are of marble slabs that had previously been gravestones. The sides carved with names, dates, and so on, were placed downward for their new use as seats. This reuse took place during the second century.

Not merely gravestones but a whole cemetery site could be reused—and was in the two famous examples we will now discuss. The Church of the Holy Sepulcher in Jerusalem (345) and the basilica in Rome dedicated to St. Peter (about a decade earlier).

CHURCH OF THE HOLY SEPULCHER

Constantine and his family were patrons of the two structures. Helena, mother of Constantine, became a Christian long before her son. She made a pious journey to Jerusalem, hoping to find the True Cross on which Jesus had been crucified. (You can read an interesting account of this in Evelyn Waugh's novel *Helena*.) The Christian community in Jerusalem preserved knowledge of where the events of Good Friday and Easter had taken place and were able to guide her to that area. She arranged to build a church at the site of these events, which had happened very close together. The cross had been set up on a hill, and Jesus's body was then taken down across a small valley and placed in a new tomb of a row cut in the rock opposite.

When Helena and her architects attempted to build the new church, it became apparent that the ancient geography was a problem They therefore cut out the hill site where the cross was supposed to have stood, leaving an outcropping of stone but otherwise leveling off the hill, as was the Roman practice. They thus obtained a level site that extended over the small valley to the tomb, whereon they put up a compound structure that ultimately had several uses. This particular church had to cope with three problems: a meeting place for the congregation, preserving the Rock of Calvary and access to it, and preserving the tomb and access to it. A separate solution was found for each problem.

Like Roman houses, and the earlier Pantheon, the Church of the Holy Sepulcher had an atrium in front where people who perhaps did not belong to the faith could gather because they were curious and interested. The congregation assembled for the Eucharistic service was accommodated in an interior space. At the far end of that space were doors leading to the courtyards in back. Individuals or processions could go to the Rock of Calvary and to the tomb and then back into the church. Later than the fourth century, a rotunda was built over the tomb area. Many churches throughout the next 1200 years copied the style of this rotunda—that is, some of the features, such as the use of twelve columns were the same. Medieval churches reused some but not all of the architectural ideas of the Church of the Holy Sepulcher.

As a solution for a congregational meeting place, early Christian architects adopted the Roman basilica, a law-court building—a type that was appealing because it could handle large numbers of people and had some relation to the law, for Christians considered themselves to be living under the new law given by Christ.

Among the Romans, the basilica was actually a function rather than a type of building. In theory it could be round or elliptical, but it was generally a narrow rectangle with either a wooden truss roof or vaulting. The Christians opted for the wooden roofs, perhaps because of poverty. However, the social and architectural organization that had made great vaulted structures possible no longer existed in the west, where the truss-roofed basilica became dominant. Adapted from Roman models was division of space into a high central nave with lower side aisles. Galleries were frequently placed over the side aisles. At least one short end was an apse, a curved space where the image was set up that legalized the proceeding in the building. In the Roman basilica, it was an image of the emperor, without which nothing that took place in the court was valid. In the Christian basilica, the image was of Christ. Christ was then thought of as judge and ruler.

The other basilica associated with Constantine is St. Peter's in Rome. To make clear the connection between this structure and his sovereignty, Constantine directed that it be built (after 330) with a ground plan in the form of a cross, the sign under which he had conquered. Like St. Agnese, this basilica was built in a cemetery area—in fact, over the cemetery in which St. Peter was buried.

In the first century, Nero built a circus in this area outside the built-up city. The area was used for a long time as the site of horse races and chariot races. To add a little zest to the chariot racing, the Romans would sometimes crucify criminals or rebellious slaves along the spine of the circus. St. Peter was crucified here and then buried in the adjacent cemetery. The cemetery continued to be used for another 250 years, until Constantine decided to build his great memorial church there in honor of Peter.

Already in the second century (ca. 160) a shrine had been built over Peter's grave. Excavations under the present building began in 1965 and physical evidence has confirmed many of the traditional explanations of the location and form of the church. Some fragments such as columns match early depictions of Peter's shrine. The bones of a man of about 65, found just where Peter's bones ought to have been, are at least suggestive. Thus, a strong tradition and physical evidence connect Peter with this particular site. The evidence helps to explain the compelling religious reasons for building old St. Peter's here, even though the area was not physically satisfactory as a site for a very large church. The slope of the land down to the river and the interfering preexistence of the cemetery that had to be preserved meant that site was difficult and troublesome to prepare. Tons of fill dirt were needed, for instance, to make a level platform for the church. The cracking and sagging that finally caused old Saint Peter's to be torn down and replaced was probably caused by the church's having been built on filled land.

Like the Church of the Holy Sepulcher in Jerusalem, the basilica of St. Peter's was planned to include the spot of the martyr's death, on the spine of the circus, as well as the site of his tomb. The final form is what we think of as the traditional early Christian basilica form: an atrium out in front; a big porch, called a narthex, with three sets of doors; the church, which was limited to the baptized Christians; and the ceremonial area across the back, called a *bema*, or (later) transept. Old St. Peter's incorporated both an association with the legal structure of Rome and the moral authority of the martyr.

The obelisk of the circus went on standing at the side of the new church. Today it stands in the great ceremonial plaza of St. Peter's, reused for the fourth time: once to proclaim an Egyptian pharaoh, once to mark the spine of a Roman circus, once to commemorate the death of a martyr, and now as a focus for crowds that gather in the plaza for ceremonial occasions.

The form that reached its epitome at St. Peter's was seldom copied in its own time. St. Paul's outside the walls at Rome, built during the same decade by the same patron, was of the same pattern. But already in the fifth century in Santa Sabina a simplified form without a bema and with single instead of double side aisles was used. Even with imperial patronage, the church of Sant' Apollinare in Classe in Ravenna—built in the second quarter of the sixth century—retained the simpler fifth-century form. It was not until Charlemagne in the eighth century attempted to revive the Christian days of Rome that more basilicas of the Constantinian type were built. (See W. Sanderson, "The Sources and Significance of the Ottonian Church of St. Pantaleon at Cologne.") Charlemagne's needs to legitimize his regime with imperial Roman associations were so similar to

Constantine's that the imperial basilica was suitable to both.

In the early Christian period, shrinking imperial resources made the need to conserve a factor in architectural design. At the same time, the forms of new buildings reused associations which gave authority to innovative building types designed for the new social order. This set of circumstances would again give special energy to the adaptation of traditional structures and designs in the period of Charlemagne and after the French Revolution, just as they did in the early Christian era.

BIBLIOGRAPHY

Kraeling, C. H., *The Christian Building*, J. J. Augustin, Locust Valley, N.Y., 1967. An account of the discovery and significance of this early house-church, which you may visit at the Yale University Art Gallery.

Krautheimer, R., *Early Christian and Byzantine Architecture*, Penguin, Baltimore, 1965. The first half of this book deals with the origin and development of architectural forms to serve the newly Christian society of Europe.

Krautheimer, R., "Introduction to an Iconography of Medieval Architecture," *Journal of the Warburg & Courtauld Institute*, vol. 5 (1942) pp. 1–33. What copying meant and other questions of meaning in early medieval architecture.

Lewis, S., "Function and Symbolic Form in the Basilica Apostolorum at Milan," *Journal of the Society of Art Historians*, vol. XXVIII –2 (May 1969) pp. 83–98. Together with the same author's, "San Lorenzo Revisited: A Theodorian Palace Church at Milan," *Journal of the Society of Art Historians*, vol. XXXII –3 (Oct. 1973) pp. 197–222, an important study in the adaptation of imperial architectural forms to new Christian meanings.

Panofsky, E. *Renaissance and Renascences*, Harper & Row, New York, 1972. This and other writings by Panofsky on iconography make us aware of the many layers of meaning a work of art can have.

Van der Meer, F., and C. Mohrmann, *Atlas of the Early Christian World*, translated by M. F. Hedlund and H. H. Rowley. Nelson, London, 1958. Not only maps, but photographs of monuments and important persons as well as interpretive essays.

Ward-Perkins, J. B., "Constantine and the Origins of the Christian Basilica," *Papers of the British School at Rome*, vol. 22 (1954) pp. 68–89. Should be read together with the next two articles: G. T. Armstrong, "Constantine's Churches: Symbol and Structure," *Journal of the Society of Art Historians*, vol. XXXIII –1 (March 1974) pp. 5–16 and T. C. Bannister, "The Constantinian Basilica of St. Peter at Rome," *Journal of the Society of Art Historians*, vol. XXVII –1 (March 1968) pp. 3–32.

Weitzmann, K. (ed.), *Age of Spirituality*, Metropolitan Museum and Princeton University Press, 1979. Scholarly articles of the highest caliber, copious illustrations—a fine record of the definitive exhibition about the transition from the ancient to the medieval world.

33
Re-Arch

Crimson

Source: *1994–2002 Crimson Architectural Historians. Too Blessed to be Depressed.* 010 Publishers, 2002, pp. 65–76

NEW DESIGNS FOR OLD BUILDINGS

What do architects mean when they talk about history? If we regard 'history' solely as an idea and as a science we can quickly dispose of this question. Indeed, from an intellectual point of view, history has scant connections with Dutch architecture. We are posing this question here, however, out of an interest in the history that is concretized in the old building and in dealing with this history when that building once again is the subject of an architectural design: when it is converted, extended, facelifted or revamped. Such architectural tasks we would like to term Re-Architecture, *Re-Arch* for short.

What attitude do Dutch architects adopt when making a new design for an old building? 'Individuality plus respect for the original state' is the standard wish of clients and the standard design statement among architects. Old and new must be 'in equilibrium', one works to achieve 'harmony without pastiche', a 'dialogue with the historical state' or an image that is 'historical though not back-to-the-classics'. This essay sets out to put the zip back into these euphemisms and clichés and inject habitual concepts with a new lease of life.

The fact is, the real content of the projects for old buildings resides less in the polite phrases used to explain them than in the architecture as a physical intervention in the existing. The intense one-to-one relationship that a new design enters into with history, and all the paradoxes and ambiguity this brings, is, *Re-Arch*.

For the present we must conclude that there is no consistent approach to *Re-Arch*. Historical architecture is just too multifaceted in nature, status and meaning. An additional factor is that the relationship between old and new architecture is subject to changing cultural ideas about the significance of listed buildings and that of new-build. A 'scholarly definition' of architectural intervention would consist merely of frictions and paradoxes. But this is precisely where its essence lies. By analysing in every individual case the idea contained in a new design, it is possible to discover which characteristics inform the relationship between old and new at a given moment.

USE AND ABUSE

Now the multiformity of Re-Arch issues on the one hand from the multiformity of present-day architectural culture, and on the other from a shift in attitude that we, along with the Spanish architectural historian Ignasi de Solà-Morales, can describe as 'from contrast to analogy'.[1] In the attitude of *contrast*, emphasis is on the singularity and contemporariness of the design; on its own identity with regard to the former state. This attitude derives from the presupposition that contrast intensifies and visualizes the meaning of old and new. In that of *analogy*, the design springs from the oscillation between old and new, whereby the interference between the two generates a new thing. Accordingly, the identity of the new is *connected* with history rather than being confronted with it.

The distinction between contrast and analogy thus exists in a formal architectural sense, but also occurs as a concept in more general texts on the dialectics between old and new. Of these the most probing is Friedrich Nietzsche's *On the Use and Abuse of History for Life*. Here he describes in ruthless terms the dilemmas and paradoxes, the dos and don'ts of dealing with history. This book was published in 1874, just as historic preservation in the Netherlands as advocated by the likes of Victor de Stuers and Alberdingk Thijm was beginning to gain a foothold. Nietzsche points to the dangers of history: too much can have a numbing effect and prevents a culture from managing to convert its creative powers into deeds: 'There is a degree of insomnia, of rumination, of the historical sense, through which living comes to harm and finally is destroyed, whether it is a person or a people or a culture.' He calls for 'forgetting', for 'the capacity to sense things unhistorically', and for an artistic, operative history that 'stands in the service of life'.[2]

Nietzsche formulated the thought, still relevant today, that in most cases history only requires renewing or rejecting. But he leaves us with more questions than answers: where exactly is the border between man the memory-less animal and a numbed being with a stomachful of undigested historical rocks; in other words, what is too much history and what too little? How can we equate history, placed in independence by the historian, with the ability of that history to produce effects?

CONTRAST

De Solà-Morales explains the complexity of the attitude of contrast using canonical designs by Mies van der Rohe, Hilberseimer and Le Corbusier. The skyscrapers on Friedrichstrasse (1921) and the Plan Voisin for Paris (1925) have been interpreted by other historians as the death knell for the existing city. But according to De Solà-Morales even this architecture could do nothing other than give its own reading of the material presented to it by the city and by history, defining along paradigmatic lines a relationship marked by the emphasis on the effect of contrast above every other type of formal category.[3] He sees contrast and presenting projects as photomontages merely as a way of dealing with the existing and not necessarily as destructive acts.

In 1931, two years before CIAM, the Dutch professional organizations for historical preservation themselves published a document entitled 'The Athens Charter'. They propagated that all restoration should exhibit a visible contrast between old and new. This faction, traditionally regarded as hostile to designers, therefore contributed to the unchecked rise of contrast. Contrast was seen as a didactic principle and a striving to achieve clarity, not as a Marinetti-style exhortation to burn down the museums and churches.

For those who wish to see the 20th century not just in terms of an overhaul (dialectic or otherwise) of the history of architecture, modern architecture does prove to carry within itself the stance of analogy. Indeed, this holds particularly for a handful of pre-eminently modern architects, whose designs are geared to creating formal and semantic complexity instead of distinction and certainty.

The extension J.B. van Loghem (modernist of the first generation and hardcore communist) made in 1928 for an ironmongery in Amsterdam – 'the palimpsest of the century' according to Joseph Buch – is characteristic of the search to find a way of making distinctions without polarity, of showing difference and similarity simultaneously. In van Loghem's first version the warehouse and office are fronted by a taut concrete facade with narrow vertical strips of fenestration. After this design was rejected by the beauty commission he made a second version. Van Loghem designed – in concrete – window 'order' that mediated between ribbon windows and those of an Amsterdam canal house. On the office level the full-width window betrays the non-loadbearing function of the facade, a theme known to us as much from the Golden Age as from Le Corbusier's Oeuvre Complète. With its 'modified' facade and slanting roof supporting three enormous dormer windows the new-build leans as a colossal volume on, alongside and behind the old building. The old warehouse has been unceremoniously tucked into the new volume with not a shred of respect.

POST-WAR MODERNISM

In the decades after the war most architects of modern signature and their clients took a hard and unequivocal line: the contemporariness of new-build was of such importance that the historicity of the old building has no initiating role to play in creating the new design. The strategy of contrast was endowed with a cartoonesque banality it did not have in pre-war modernism. The architect Vegter designed the extension to the neo-classical town hall in Groningen (1949–1962), with old and new strictly distinguishable in terms of volume, material, building method and style. The reason in this case was that Vegter was searching for a modern equivalent of the 18th century town hall. His marble geometry represented a new monumentality and a new dignity. The Goudkantoor – a 17th century listed building – was drawn as a third object into the new order by linking it to an elevated glass walkway. This loose configuration issued from the Department of Preservation's resistance to extending the old town hall. Even so, the point of contact was later read as a deliberate and unfortunate break with history. The building, with all its aspirations as a hopeful and proud contemporary architecture, was demolished in 1994.

Around 1960 a new wind blew through international architectural theory that left its traces in

Dutch architectural practice. In 1959 the new generation of modernists united in Team X pitted its version of modernism against the 'old' brand. Their seminal contribution on the Re-Arch front was to counter the generalizing concepts adhered to by the 'generation of 1930' with the notion of 'unicity'. Whereas in the Heroic Period existing buildings and cities were replaced by universal concepts, Team X chose the 'time-conscious techniques of renewal and extension derived from the recognition of the positive ecological trends to be found in every particular situation'.[4] This 'metabolic' conception of history as a process of growth became a window opened to the site's specificity as the foodstuffs of the design.

Herman Hertzberger's unrealized 1975 proposal to convert a 19th-century church (Broerkerk) in Groningen into a university library is emblematic of the ideas on the existing city as upheld by the 'Team X subsidiary' Forum, most particularly of the influence psychology and sociology had on those ideas. This design was the logical sequel to a 1972 policy document on government objectives (Doelstellingennota), which drew attention to the value of a fine-meshed, small-scale urban morphology. Clearly, preserving the historic Broerkerk was not the prime objective of this scheme; the building is used as an on-site container for a humming throng which can give full rein to its urge to create and digest literature. The building dissolves in the 'urban fabric': it disappears below ground to emerge in a wash of semicircular roofs. In secularizing the 19th-century church, the Neo-Gothic chancel would have become little more than an element of mystery in an otherwise 'open and inviting' library.

The site-specific, the concern with transformation and growth espoused by Team X on the one hand, and the historical research by the Italians (Aldo Rossi, Giorgio Grassi, Saverio Muratori) and later by French architects and historians (Bruno Fortier, André Chastel) on the other, paved the way in architectural thinking for a complex and layered – analogous – attitude towards Re-Arch, in which history is conceived of as a storehouse of form and knowledge. Dutch theory first encountered this foreign train of thought via Ungers's design for the TU Twente (1967) and Rossi's proposals for Kop van Zuid and the attendant research done by Donald van Dansik, Jan de Graaf and Wim Nijenhuis (1983). There were, additionally, the unremitting arguments of the architectural historian Ed Taverne for giving a serious role to historical research in architecture.

An authentic Dutch contribution to the debates on historical context made its entrance with urban renewal. Aldo van Eyck and Theo Bosch reintroduced a small-scale urban morphology in Amsterdam in the Nieuwmarkt area; a redevelopment strategy which became the icon of seventies architecture and planning. The heroic deeds of 1970 – reasserting architecture's socio-critical position – have since fallen into disrepute due to the disappointing architectural offerings it went on to spawn. Concern for the built history of cities remained skin-deep. 'Building for the neighbourhood' and the allied 'contextualism' did, however, mean a turning point for the public at large, the authorities and the institutional clients and drove home the fact that preserving the historical city was worthy of respect and contributed to providing 'approved living conditions'. Housing associations, municipal bodies and architects adapted their ideas, working methods and organization to the new 'culture', which made a world of difference with the housing output in the sixties. The many recycling projects of the eighties and nineties were able to profit from the expertise gained in the seventies.

1980

In retrospect, two projects mark a major hitch in the relationship between history and architecture: the fault line lies somewhere around 1980 and the projects are the Lower House competition and the design for the Koepel Prison by OMA. The design for extensions to Parliament was an issue of national interest, full of drama and chaos. The prime meat of the matter was the relationship between old and new, in this case between the existing Binnenhof complex and the new addition.

The proposal submitted by OMA was rejected because of the incursion it made on the Binnenhof (Inner Court) with a volume that penetrated the complex from the side. Issuing from a paranoid-critical analysis of Dutch society, it gave our democratic system the same treatment as Rem Koolhaas's book *Delirious New York* had done for the Manhattan of the twenties. The scheme was a montage of the attributes and excesses of the Dutch democracy, including a 'smoke-filled room' and a sunken sitting area for discussions with the public.

Many ideas seem to have been buried along with the Lower House competition: the small-scale as symbolic of adapting to history, 'building for the neighbourhood' as a social foundation for architecture and lastly contrast as the exclusive means of dealing with the existing.

OMA's design of 1980 for the Koepel Prison in Arnhem marked less an end than the onset of a new concept. The relationship with the historical state was no longer described exclusively as a formal problem; the design attaches to the meaning and idea of the old building. This prompted the critic Hans van Dijk to describe the project as a kind of conceptual conservation: 'a strategy of respecting the existing not so much to the letter as in spirit'.[5]

The original panopticon designed by J.F. and W.C. Metzelaar in 1880 was an interior world controlled (and its occupants spiritually administered) from a central 'eye'. In the course of a century its panoptic principle had been turned inside-out: lack of space had meant housing numerous functions in sheds in the prison grounds, and the guards had been dispersed from their original central position. OMA accommodated the new use of this 'purely theoretical building' by totally overhauling the grounds within the prison walls. The rigid configuration of the old building prompted them to draw a cross of two sunken streets off which are new spaces for facilities. This Suprematist composition leaves the panopticon largely intact along with its principle of imprisonment and surveillance, 'saving the new the embarrassment of having either to ignore or express the idea of incarceration, which is incompatible with its aspirations. After the intervention, the dome represents the dismantled past, its former center crossed out, resting on a podium of modernity, which is concerned only with improving the prisoners' conditions'.[6] Proceeding from the required programmatic improvements, the image of the panopticon is used as an object alienated from the present, towering above the programmatic platform. The unrelenting geometrical and inward-looking form has been undermined by a not quite symmetrical cross, sweeping the core from the old building and taking it over formally and programmatically.

THE RECENT PAST

A question that sets the heart of Dutch architecture culture all aflutter, is that of modern monuments. The old age of Modern Movement buildings now makes even young architects, given their almost paranormal affinity with the famous modern exemplars, set to work as restoration architects. Thus, the twin poles of invention and conservation are suddenly in hair-raisingly close proximity. This gives rise to the philosophical problem of how to preserve for eternity along honest lines, buildings whose designers certainly did not build them to last for ever, such as Sanatorium Zonnestraal and the Kiefhoek and Witte Dorp housing. Strictly speaking, respect for the ideas underlying this architecture sits uncomfortably with the need to protect it. However, we seem to have managed to leave our fear of a fetishistic response to these buildings behind and let the desire to preserve them prevail. The upshot is that it is in precisely these monuments of modernism that we now encounter the most extreme form of historic preservation, namely reconstruction. The 'white' work of J.J.P. Oud would seem to exert a particular attraction in this respect: Café de Unie and the Witte Dorp works office building were rebuilt (not at the original sites; there are even two examples of the works hut these days) as was the entire Kiefhoek housing estate, also in Rotterdam. That these icons of modernism have been resurrected is entirely thanks to their visual quality. A monument, it transpires, can simply be made anew. We express disdain when it comes to historical illusion of the likes of the Dutch Village in Nagasaki, yet the reconstruction of Kiefhoek itself amounts to an attraction for architectural tourists. We can only conclude that simulation is sometimes more fun than the real thing, the way Rotterdam's Tropicana 'swimming paradise' with all its features and without salt is more fun than the sea.

THE HISTORICAL EXPERIENCE

We have seen that today the notion of contrast is losing ground; architects and clients regard adding a new portion to an old building more as an analogous operation exhibiting continuity with the past. Seen thus, experience of the proximity of history is a quality that is aspired to. Accordingly, old and new are not set in dialectic opposition, but are brought into alignment, in time and value as well as place.

The historical material at once becomes the backdrop against which the new architecture is enacted; a strategy taken to extremes by Aldo Rossi and Ignazio Gardella in their reconstruction of the theatre at Genoa (1982–1990), where new 'old' facades act as an 'urban' stage set in the main auditorium. We see this displaying of history again, though now eschewing theatricalities, in Giorgio Grassi's project for the ruins of a Roman theatre in the Spanish town of Sagunto. Grassi reconstructed the architectural space, turning it into a theatre in modern working order. In the project there is no attempt made to imitate a historical unity, so that the outcome resembles the method of restoring sculptures and paintings where missing pieces or areas are filled in with 'blank' patches.

Archaeological finds on site, parts of a frieze, columns, before then carted off to a museum, now have a place in the wall at the back of the stage. Here they are put on show rather than serving as decor. Thus the new building has become the museum of the old one.

This idea of exhibiting is present in a pedagogic sense in the Limburg Public Records Office in Maastricht, converted and expanded by Marc van Roosmalen in 1989–1996, where the foundations of a Gothic church have been excavated and can be viewed from the new promenade. The old town walls dug up in the courtyard, are back in view and a hole in the facade shows – also to passers-by – how the wall resumes its course across the street. In the chancel of the church, meetings are held underground beneath a glass roof bearing a bizarre exhibition of mediaeval tombstones.

These modes of displaying, of the mise-en-scène of old and new, result in an unpredictable moment of intimacy with the past, which the historian Frank Ankersmit calls 'the historical experience'; an uncontrollable moment in which history is sensed and undergone.[7] The value of this idea for Re-Arch lies in the call to conserve the paradox; in allowing buildings, building parts and ideas that clash, to coexist. There is no overarching principle that covers this; indeed a generalizing concept has a contrary effect. Letting contradictory ideas act upon one another can contribute to the unpredictable emergence of something truly new.

TODAY

Apart from being an intellectual issue Re-Arch is also a question of technique and material. There is a tendency to drop universal theories in the case of Re-Arch and seek out a unique and particular stepping-off point in the old building: at times colour, detailing or material, at others the surroundings or the landscape. Designers scour the old building for latent architectural qualities. In such cases the new design does not begin with an overarching concept but perhaps with the smallest detail. Nietzsche hoped that history would seek its significance not in universal laws, but that 'its worth is directly one which indicates a known, perhaps a habitual theme, a daily melody, in an elegant way, elevates it, intensifies it to an inclusive symbol, and thus allows one to make out in the original theme an entire world of profundity, power and beauty'.[8] This sounds like a manifesto for a design stance which we might term hyper-empirical.

What can recycling mean in an age where temporary, unstable aspects of architecture are central to the avant-garde and the economic lifespan of buildings is decreasing? The Dutch government however, now in the throes of calculating environmental expenses so that replacing buildings will become less lucrative, is pointing things in exactly the opposite direction. Reversibility – the new magic word in the marketplace – sounds like temporariness translated to the task of interventions: the new intervention can always be reversed because it does not essentially alter the old building. However, this argument seems to have been drummed up more to soften extreme proposals than to actually address their temporary quality.

The connection with recent developments in architecture is sooner found in the idea of layeredness, multiformity and the demise of generalistic and normative design principles. Layeredness and juxtaposition can surely be linked to the notion of historical experience. By placing objects in unmediated adjacency or wrapping them in translucent materials unpredictable frictions and paradoxes can arise. These do not necessarily need to be resolved and brought to synthesis, but proffer as they are a new definition of harmony. Re-Arch's aim, then, is to make something new at all costs, something that rises above what it was that was there first. When history is not restricted by a logic of politeness it can present itself unexpectedly, the way the historical experience does: as a thing that is new.

NOTES

1 Ignasi de Solà-Morales, 'From contrast to analogy. Developments in the concept of architectural intervention', *Lotus* no. 46 (Interpretation of the past), 37–45.
2 Friedrich Nietzsche, *On the Use and Abuse of History for Life*, 1873, trans. Ian C. Johnston, Nanaimo, 1998.
3 Ignasi de Solà-Morales, op.cit., 39.
4 John Voelker, quoted in Joan Ockman (ed.), *Architecture Culture, 1943–1968. A Documentary Anthology*, New York: Columbia Books of Architecture/Rizzoli, 1993, 19.
5 Hans van Dijk, 'Het bezwijken van tegenstellingen', *Wonen TA/BK*, 1982, no. 13/14,12–49.
6 Rem Koolhaas. 'Project for the renovation of a panopticon prison', *Art Forum*, Sept. 1981, 41.
7 Frank Ankersmit, *De historische ervaring*, Groningen: Historische Uitgeverij, 1993.
8 Friedrich Nietzsche, op. cit.

34
Old Buildings as Palimpsest: Towards a Theory of Remodeling

Rodolfo Machado

Source: Progressive Architecture, 11: 76, pp. 46–49

These 'thoughts on remodeling' present some pre-theoretical, 'suggestive material' that could be developed as concepts to consider what is specific to remodeling, how it differs from architecture in general, how it can be dealt with on a theoretical level, and what its most important potential critical, cultural, and educational values might be.

There is a superabundance of freshly-coined and almost synonymous terms referring to the type of architectural work traditionally called "remodeling." Terms such as "architectural recycling," "environmental retrieval," "adaptive reuse," and lately, "retrofitting," should be rejected because they are superficial, empty labels that do not represent any conceptual change with respect to previous stages of remodeling activity (reuse and improved technical performance, for instance, have always figured among the remodeler's goals).

This extravagant use of euphemisms denies the specific nature of remodeling, which is characterized by formal intervention upon existing form, and it also denies the tradition and history of remodeling practice, which is as old as the practice of architecture itself. (If one were to think of the churches of Santa Maria Novella in Florence and San Francesco in Rimini, both of which were "remodeled" by Alberti, and then add to this Le Corbusier's remodeling of the Beistegui apartment in Paris, one can see how intrinsically related the origins and great moments of architecture and remodeling are.)

Other terms used by architects who are fully aware of recent developments concerning the formal and systematic nature of remodeling are almost interchangeable word-clusters, such as "subtraction/addition/transformation," "reproduction/derivation/invention," or "deletion/addition/insertion." Even though these words belong to technical vocabularies that are properly used for referring to matters of form generally, they represent early attempts to form architectural concepts of a structuralist type—which are goals that have not yet been fully achieved.

Instead of any of these terms, it might be more appropriate simply to use the word "remodeling" since, as already noted, its meaning clearly includes the concept of formal intervention on existing form.

THE BUILDING AS PALIMPSEST

In order to build a theory of remodeling it would be useful to consider a series of metaphors, including the one used in the title to this article, which may suggest ways of thinking about remodeling once they are clarified and interrelated. These metaphors are borrowed from literary criticism, which is a discipline with a well-developed tradition for discussing matters of sense, such as architecture, at a general level.

The Encyclopedia Britannica defines palimpsest as "scraped again; a term referring to any inscribed surface from which one text has been removed so that the space could be used again for another. In antiquity the word was applied loosely to any writing material that had been cleared and reused. . . . In late classical and medieval times the scarcity and costliness of vellum were so great that it was quite frequently salvaged after the text, which had been inscribed thereon, fell into neglect. . . . Rarely a book might be doubly palimpsest, i.e., exhibit two erased texts with a third one overlying them."

Some architectural drawings could be regarded as the equivalent of a palimpsest. In Jappelli's remodeling of a garden at Castelqomberto, for instance, the original drawings were drawn over; some elements of the composition that were due to remain were redrawn, some to be torn down were erased. In pursuing this metaphor, it is not only the architectural drawings that can be regarded as palimpsest, but also the remodeled architectural work itself, since it can be seen as a text of a special kind that is characterized by the juxtaposition and co-presence of other texts. If an original building is considered as a first discourse that conditions future formal discourses to be inscribed upon it, then remodeling can be conceived of as rewriting.

REMODELING AS REWRITING

From a formal point of view, it is possible to discuss remodeling as rewriting, that is, as work altering the formal features of a building without attempting to alter its basic content (function). In this fashion, and in expanding on the previously established metaphors, remodeling can be seen as writing over, as underlining, as partially erasing, as interstitial writing (writing between the lines), as a way of qualifying, accentuating, quoting, commenting upon, as digression, interlude, or interval, as a way of writing parenthetically, of setting off by punctuation, as a new form for an old story. (The uses of metaphor are thick and richly layered because they expand the awareness of possibilities; let them explode, and with them liberating images of exhausted vocabularies and uncommon rhetorical manners will appear, and perhaps some invention.)

On another level, it is possible to discuss remodeling as rewriting when the alterations in the building's content (the re-semanticization) are of such a type that the building's original or latest function is changed; then the building is refunctionalized, a different story is born, a new plot is composed out of the old words, a new interpretation has taken place.

REMODELING AS INTERPRETATION

It is also possible to consider the already-built, the building to be remodeled, as a script or written indication upon which each designer will draw his or her own interpretation of the given "piece." But just as in theater, for instance, where the interpretive markings are clearly detailed, a wide range of interpretations is still possible. Remodeling thus becomes a technique of formal interpretation, a special design technique for which very little prescriptive information has been established. And that which is interpreted is always a product of the past.

THE PAST IN REMODELING

In remodeling, the past takes on a value far different from that in the usual design process, where form is generated "from scratch." In the traditional design process, the influence of the past is felt through its effect both as a repository and as a moral force. As a repository, the past is seen as a complex package of interrelated repertories, of things already built, drawn, and written. This repository is there to learn from, to copy, to transform. Being almost impossible to forget, its "presence" or "weight," its importance, has different values at different moments in the development of architecture. As a moral force the past behaves as a repressive mechanism. The already-built (the "real world"), by means of its own existence and as a result of the mythical value the old takes in our culture, becomes institutionalized as "true" and "normal," as "common sense." As an "example to be followed," the old acquires a moral power that in turn limits, in a rather complex way, the process of production of form.

In the process of remodeling, however, the past takes on a greater significance because it, itself, is the material to be altered and reshaped. The past provides the already-written, the marked "canvas" on which each successive remodeling will find its own place. Thus, the past becomes a "package of sense," of built-up meaning to be accepted (maintained), transformed, or suppressed (refused).

If one quickly reviews what is being remodeled today, some common characteristics show up. The object that survives, the cherished one that is kept, belongs generally to two classes: the monuments and buildings of the rich, and those buildings which, as objects of a process of mythification, have acquired new meanings, such as the Connecticut barn or the New York loft. The ordinary buildings that are neither monumental nor mythically loaded are rarely objects of much concern. But, since monuments grow rather easily and mythical species change fast, things which are today inconceivable as objects of remodeling might be seen in a wholly different light in the future. In this respect, the remodeler might soon face some interesting problems. For instance, with buildings that are not conceived as "Architecture," such as most roadside-strip buildings, which are produced through a different set of criteria from that for architecture, a future question could be whether and how to "architecturalize" them, or to keep them within the original "genre." The remodeler will go beyond the question of the juxtaposition of vocabularies, which commonly characterizes a remodeled building, and into an area where the different modes of *conceiving* a building could be manifested and be juxtaposed. Then we will reach a level of deeply eclectic buildings.

THE CONTEXT IN REMODELING

In remodeling, then, the past is represented by the old object itself. But this object is also the most immediate context of the work of remodeling; the past pervades the building and the building itself becomes the primary level of the context of intervention. This temporal/spatial coexistence of past, content, and building accounts for the remarkable characteristic that the notion of cultural context takes in remodeling. The ways in which an existing building has or has not acknowledged the requirements of its cultural context over time becomes the most important feature of the context for the remodeler.

THEORETICAL INTEREST AND CRITICAL POWER

From a theoretical point of view, remodeling has always been a kind of minor, neglected area, conceptually close to the "negative pole" of decoration. But, for several reasons, it is necessary to consider a theory of remodeling, as a branch of architectural theory, having as its object of study the description of the interrelations and design operations that exist between old and new form.

Since the form/form relationship is the primary consideration of remodeling activity, it is naturally there where the critical potential of the activity lies. Because remodeling is implemented through a series of design operations, including those affected by the designer's view of the world, the effect of the remodeled object can be either of a critical or non-critical nature. In architecture, certain critical effects are characterized by the presence of what has been defined as a quality of "formal opacity" or "estrangement," of a formal condition of an uncommon or "unnatural" type, which leads the beholder to reflect upon the nature of formal vocabularies, their rules, and the arbitrary quality of their conventions. The juxtaposition of different formal vocabularies in a remodeled building produces a natural "estrangement" that can enormously facilitate the criticism, the exposure, of architectural languages as cultural conventions. It

can also facilitate the manifestation of a designer's own critical intentions.

This coexistence of vocabularies provides very rich grounds for the design of complex buildings that allow a multiplicity of levels of reading, as opposed to buildings where the only sense can easily be "consumed" at first sight. Another element that can increase the potential for criticism is the notion of "type" in architecture. Through it, one can easily conceive of a remodeling activity (when dealing with clearly defined building types) that deals with the notion of type transformation. This could be the most critical function remodeling could offer, considering the antithesis toward the notion of type in the premises of the Modern movement.

EDUCATIONAL AND CULTURAL VALUE OF REMODELING

The value of remodeling exercises in architectural education is high. In dealing with such problems, the student must concentrate on form/form problems rather than on form/function aspects. This in itself is useful because it seriously questions the arbitrary nature of the form/function relationship. In addition, the student is encouraged to think of generating form from considerations of the complex tri-dimensionality of the building itself, or at least from its façades and vertical planes in general, instead of from plan considerations. The educational value of this displacement lies in the fact that issues of meaning and character are immediately addressed at the beginning of the design process, which is not common in the usual design process.

Contact with the already-built expands the students' awareness of the multiplicity and availability of formal languages in architecture; and, in turn, a lively, intelligent use of history can be taught in the context of remodeling exercises. Other important aspects can also be dealt with if desired, such as the notion of formal, serial transformations which encourage a practical understanding of the semantic changes a small, formal modification might bring about. Such ideas can form a good introduction to the uses of rhetorical devices that can increase future architects' knowledge of their techniques.

The valuable service remodeling can provide in helping to preserve cultural heritage is well known, but more important is that it can take on more active roles to prevent undesirable environments in the first place.

35

From Contrast to Analogy

Developments in the Concept of Architectural Intervention

Ignasi de Sola-Morales Rubió

Source: *Lotus International,* no. 46, 1985, pp. 37–45

The relationship between a new architectural intervention and already existing architecture is a phenomenon that changes in relation to the cultural values attributed both to the meaning of historic architecture and to the intentions of the new intervention.

Hence it is an enormous mistake to think that one can lay down a permanent doctrine or still less a scientific definition of architectural intervention. On the contrary, it is only by understanding in each case the conceptions on the basis of which action has been taken that it is possible to make out the different characteristics which this relationship has assumed over the course of time. The design of a new work of architecture not only comes physically close to the existing one, entering into visual and spatial rapport with it, but it also produces a genuine interpretation of the historical material with which it has to contend, so that this material is the object of a true interpretation which explicitly or implicitly accompanies the new intervention in its overall significance.

When Mies van der Rohe presented his project for sky-scrapers on Friederichstrasse to the authorities in Berlin, in 1918, the form of the new buildings in Alexanderplatz in 1921, and the other ones by Ludwig Hilberseimer for the centre of Berlin in 1927 or by Le Corbusier for the central zone of Paris in 1936, just to mention the best-known examples, have in common not only the same technique of representation but also the same sensitivity in the definition of a particular type of relationship between existing architecture and what is projected as new.

The technique of photomontage, or analogous perspective drawings, is particularly suited to emphasizing the *contrast* between old and new architecture. But this contrast which reveals differences in texture, materials and geometry, as well as in the density of the urban grid, makes no pretence of being a negative judgement, a repudiation of historic architecture. On the contrary, as Le Corbusier commented on his project, "the new modern dimensions and the showing to advantage of historic treasures produce a delightful effect."[1]

It is often claimed that the avant-garde architecture of the Modern Movement completely ignored the architecture of the past, and that this lack of interest was the sign of a purely negative evaluation of it. It is true that the architecture of that time was the product of a formal system which claimed to be self-sufficient, at least in its programmatic expressions, based on the abstract geometry of form and simple three-dimensional shapes. But even this kind of attitude could not help but make its own interpretation of the material presented to it by the city and by history, defining in paradigmatic fashion a type of relationship that is characterized by preponderance of the effect of *contrast* over any other type of formal category.

At the beginning of the century, Alois Riegl had analyzed the modern attitude to the problems of the monumental heritage in a series of penetrating and illuminating articles. In one written in 1903, Riegl described a typical category of the new sensitivity with regard to historical monuments.[2]

Alteswert, the quality of antiquity, is different from *Denk-malswert,* monumental value or monumentality, and from *kunsthistorisches Wert*, the historic-artistic value of buildings as it had been expressed in pre-20th-century culture. Since the Renaissance European culture has developed a system of evaluation based not only on the current value that works of art might have, but also on their exemplary value as prior models of the good art of the past. From the 19th century onwards an additional value came into play, the historical value of the building or monument as a record of a positive and documented situation. The dichotomy between monumental value and documentary value emerged with the positivistic culture of the 19th century. But for Riegl, who started out from the crisis in positivism and in the objectivity of the new culture's language at the end of the century, the beginning of the 20th century would be characterized by another situation. It was a question, to some extent, not only of a new relationship but also a more radical one between historical and monumental material and the cultural value assigned to it. Antiquity or the value of oldness, giving this term the ambiguity and lack of precision that it itself inspires, is a novelty typical of contemporary sensibility, in an attitude which makes the establishment of any kind of artistic standard relative and which ignores the positive significance of the information contained within a work of art.

Antiquity is a subjective quality that produces a purely psychological satisfaction derived from a view of the old as a manifestation of the passing of historical time.

Riegl, from the perspective of mass psychology, realized that the modern citizen is not interested in erudite information that can be decoded in the detail of an ornament or the arrangement of a colonnade, but in a more sweeping view. What attracts him is the testimony to a certain age offered by the monument. Precisely because the prime value of urban culture was, and still is, the finished perfection of new building, and given that new buildings have value only to the extent that they present a challenge to the passing of time, an image of intangibility to the erosion of history and a permanence in their form, colour and finishing, this same subjective and mass sensitivity, little inclined towards rational cognition, finds in antiquity the all-embracing value in terms of which it can interpret historical architecture. It is in the necessary alternation between new and ancient architecture that fundamental aesthetic satisfaction is produced.

What typifies the new sensitivity, the new *Kunstwollen* or will to art of the 20th century is the contrast between *Neuheitswert* or novelty value and *Alteswert*, or oldness as value. That is to say, the *contrast* between newness and oldness.

But this value attributed to what is ancient has a psychological key which Riegl explains in the same text with great precision. It is a purely perceptual satisfaction, which seeks no precise gain in knowledge, expressing itself as pure feeling of a subjective, vague and comforting character.

Comparison with the late classical attitude and with the religious subjectivism that characterized early Imperial culture served Riegl to define, in greater detail, the type of perceptibiliy to which he

was referring. A more than tactile viewpoint and one that is more interested in the condition of life expressed by the monument than in this concrete specifications, the search for antiquity represents a certain renunciation of knowledge, but also the affirmation of a collective and synthetic sensitivity which characterizes metropolitan man en masse.

Riegl's accurate description serves to explain what type of sensitivity it is that is revealed in the examples cited at the start of this article and in the special way in which the *contrast* between old and new architectural materials is established, as happens in those avant-garde projects that have to contend with the architecture of the past.

In order to back up the theory of *contrast* at the level of perception, as it is formulated by Riegl, it would not be difficult to draw too on the theoretical models utilized by intellectuals of the day when they were piecing together the history of architecture or looking for its psychological foundations in the *Gestalttheorie* that theoreticians and protagonists of the new art used as a basis for their own aesthetic experiences.

In the case of historiography it is clear that beginning with Riegl and at least up until Giedion, but significantly in the works of Platz and Kurt Behrendt as well, the history of the architecture of the past is analyzed as a product of the past, bringing out its *novelties* and *differences* with respect to the architecture of the present.[3] Not only did they get over the reluctance about using the past in order to experience the more immediate and contemporary present, but they realized that this explanation served above all to show up the radical opposition, the contrast, between the ancient and the new, between history and current events.

In the treatises on the psychology of form by Köller in 1929 and by Koffka in 1935, one finds a systematic organization of the more general principles of a conception in which the notions of *ground-form* and of *contrast* are fundamental to an explanation of perception and of its significance.[4]

In fact in the same years the teachings of Kandinsky, Albers, Moholy-Nagy and even Paul Klee during the early phase of the Bauhaus made use of just the same psychological categories for the training of draughtsmen and designers. Not only was architecture described – by Moholy-Nagy – as a phenomenon that is perceived three-dimensionally on the basis of a geometry and texture, thereby making a clean sweep of any kind of meaning, but it was even asserted that the phenomenon of meaning in any field of the visual arts is produced through juxtaposition, interrelation and contrast of fundamentally heterogeneous shapes, textures or materials.

Just as *collage* and *photomontage* develop techniques of extracting new and specific meanings from the confrontation of autonomous fragments, architecture, by contrasting ancient with new structures, finds the ground and the form in which the past and the present recognize each other.

But if there is a clear relationship between Riegl's diagnosis, the positions of historiography and the psychology of aesthetics and the work of the architects of the Modern Movement when confronted with historical materials, it is also worth calling attention to the connections with a field that would seem to have little to do with avant-garde debate. This is that of the conservators and professional restorers who were developing a conception of the restoration of monuments in their specialized publications and debates that in its way had something in common with the idea of *contrast* as a fundamental category of the relationship between old and new architecture.

If ever since the end of the 19th century the theoretical literature produced by experts in restoration, such as Camillo Boito, defended a criterion of clear-cut differentiation in those interventions of restoration that involved an element of construction, it is this very idea that became one of the fundamental principles laid down in the 1931 Athens charter of restorers. More than once in the ten fundamental points into which this charter is divided, the clear conception of the *contrast* that must be produced between the protected historical building and new interventions is defended. Not just by recommending that modern materials should be used on certain occasions, but above all by the repeatedly expressed criterion according to which difference is noted in the different arrangement of added elements, in the use of different materials and in the absence of decorations in new constructions, in their geometrical and technological simplicity. Thus it can be said that the Athens charter accepted in a generalized and standardized fashion the criteria and approaches already elaborated in that period by architects. Architects who, whether they belonged to the world of avant-garde experimentation or the academic one of restoration, were subject to an identical historical sensibility. When the other Athens charter, that of the men of the CIAM in 1933, also insisted on the impossibility of accepting the historical pastiche and appealed to the *Zeitgeist* to justify their demand that new interventions in historical zones

be made in the language of present-day architecture, this was not in reality so far from what had been asserted two years earlier by other professionals with whom they appeared to have very few things in common. Indeed, the two bodies were distinguished by the militant and progressive character of one and the historicist and conservative interests of the other.

But at a distance of fifty years, the differences between the two professional categories were not of such an absolute nature as it was in the interest of the protagonists to have people believe at the time.

Beneath the obvious differences there was a common attitude towards historical material and its interpretation. In both cases their guiding principle was formed by the late Romantic taste for rough textures and for the patina left by time on old buildings, without precise ornamental or stylistic distinctions, in overall contrast with the limpid, precise and abstract geometry of the new works of architecture. In this way, the *contrast* between old and new was transformed not just in the outcome of radically opposing approaches, but also the perceptual procedure through which each kind of architecture established, reciprocally, its dialectical significance in the metropolitan city, was changed.

The predominance of the category of *contrast* as a fundamental principle of aesthetics in problems of intervention already belongs to the past. At least one cannot speak today of its privileged position. The effects of *contrast* remain in work of recent intervention, both as vestiges of the poetics of the Modern Movement in a few of today's architects and, in any case, as one of the many rhetorical figures that are used in the new and more complex relationship that current sensibility has established with the architecture of the past.

Let us take a number of examples that we find expressive of the new situation. Examples which, even though they are not all recent, seem to typify the new sensitivity with regard to this problem.

The project that Asplund worked on over a long period, from 1913 to 1937, for the extension to the Göteborg town hall cannot be explained on the basis of a simple notion of *contrast*. On the contrary, what seems to characterize the line taken by the Swedish architect over the course of five successive projects is his interpretation of dominant features in the old building in order that they should find an echo in the part that was to be added on.

As much in the organization of the plan, extending the system of arcades, as in the lay-out of the facade, prolonging the pattern of empty spaces and pillars, in one case and in the other by extending the horizontal tripartite division as a dominant formal structure, in all the successive versions the approach to a satisfactory solution was developed through similarity between what were considered to be outstanding elements in the old structure and the forms that were proposed for the new extension. Difference and repetition were seen simultaneously through a controlled handling of the relations between similarity and diversity that are proper to any *analogical* operation.

When Carlo Scarpa turned Castelvecchio in Verona into a museum of the city he too had to deal with the prestige of the mediaeval building and the need to adapt it to requirements of a modern museum. Not so much through a comprehensive analysis of its composition as by means of a narrative and fragmentary development, Scarpa's intervention introduces historicist figures into the historical authenticity of the existing building. Through a display of a cinematographic kind, he accumulates redesigned images of architectural works of the past, both from the Middle Ages and from other periods perhaps with far-off mediaeval origins but conjuring up more recent European experiences, such as those of the turn of the century in Glasgow or Vienna.

Here the *analogical* procedure is not based on the visible synchronism of interdependent orders of form, but on the association made by the observer over the course of time. By this means situations of affinity are produced and, thanks to the connotative capacity of the languages evoked in the intervention, relations or links are established between the historic building – real and/or imaginary – and the elements of design that serve to make the building effectively dependent.

Some of Giorgio Grassi's finest theoretical writing sets out to explain his approach to the restoration of the castle of Abbiategrasso, in 1970.[5] Basing himself on writings by Ambrogio Annoni and on the most cultivated tradition of restoration and the highest level of professionalism, Grassi found that the methodological key to organization of the intervention lay in the very architecture of the existing building. This was a correction of the kind of idealism practised by Viollet-le-Duc, who tried to find the basis for intervention in the *idea* hidden within the building. Grassi transformed this into a realism completely bound up with the spatial, physical and geographical materiality of the artefact on which he was operating.

Drawing from typological analysis a first approximation to its internal laws, the project turns out as a compromise between the modes proper to the modern tradition based on the independence of new and old structure, and the dimensional, typological and figurative correspondence between old and new parts in an attempt to create a mutual correlation that would unify the totality of the complex. Again it is a dialectical way of expressing the synchronism of similarity and difference.

Rafael Moneo's 1980 project for expansion of the Banco de España building in Madrid lies almost at the opposite extreme. Like Grassi, Moneo follows in the narrow track marked out by the laws of the building itself, by the logic of its composition and by the existing organization of structure and space. Leaving almost no room for irony and without any kind of separation to delimit the characteristics of each aesthetic operation, Moneo's project completes the existing building while effacing itself to the utmost and emphasizing to just what extent the existing building imposed its own exigencies. Here *analogy* becomes tenuous, almost imperceptible, turning into mere tautology.

The four examples analyzed so far have a series of characteristic traits in common. The cultural crisis is a crisis of universal models. The difference between the present situation and that of academic culture or modern orthodoxy lies in the fact that it is not possible today to formulate an aesthetic system with sufficient validity to make it applicable beyond the individual circumstances.

Nietzsche's critique of metaphysics and Wittgenstein's critique of language have stripped away all pretence of generality or permanence in the processes of culture. It is the same radically historical situation that post-Foucaultian knowledge acknowledges in itself. While academic culture has been able to create universally applicable procedures of intervention through the notion of style and modern culture has been able to create an interwoven system of fragments by means of psychological subjectivism, it is difficult in the present situation to recognize anything but the factual nature, on the one hand, of the concrete work with which one has to deal and on which one has to operate and, on the other, the infinite system of referents with which the collective imagery of architecture is studded.

The liberal optimism of Colin Rowe may still have faith in the effectiveness of collage when he thinks that a fragmentary dismemberment does not conflict with a certain kind of comprehensive strategy that allows some measure of control over the city and its architecture.[6] But what happens to

Colin Rowe with the collage is the same as happened to the terrified Pandora, Epimetheus' wife, when she let all the evils that afflict humanity out of her golden box and was left with nothing in her hands but the container in which she still counted on keeping hope.

But the hope of collage rests solely, as a technique, on a *Gestalt* composition of which today's barbarous artists of *frottage* and *dripping* have given a good account. The current reality is, in a sense, more reductive in that it is more critical. But for the very same reason it is more precise at the moment of acting, with an acute awareness of what the building is telling us and what the history of architecture teaches us.

In recent years knowledge of the intimate structures of buildings has led to the development of techniques and tools that are as sophisticated as they are accurate.

The typo-morphological analysis championed by Aldo Rossi in his writings of the sixties has resulted, on the one hand, in a genuinely encyclopaedic culture of representation, dimensional comparison and structural awareness of all the problems of form presented by existing buildings. Since the sixties architectural culture has been imbued with an authentic obsession with analysis, making use of cartographic, planimetric and three-dimensional instruments of extraordinary effectiveness.

But it is no less true that we are today in a position to know just how little this analytical mechanism has to do with creating a sufficient condition for the project. While the analytical protocols of the project have been refined to limits virtually impossible to achieve in other historical eras, this very precision has revealed that creativity of design represents a level of operation completely untrammeled by and independent of the need for analysis.

Instrumental knowledge of the object does not allow us to evade the risk of the project and, in this case, the risk of the representation and new linguistic structures which the intervention will have to introduce.

But in this situation history is not, as it once was, *magistra vitae*. Nor is it a logical instrument for tendentious explanation of the present. On the contrary, running parallel to the drastic historicizing of the present there is a polycentric dispersion of historical awareness.

Since the sixties we have seen an unmasking of the illusions of an ideological history that tended not only to dispel the anxiety of the present, but also to justify its choices. That history can no longer hang on to a pretence of veracity. There is no guiding thread leading from the past to the present. Manfredo Tafuri, the most decisive thinker with regard to the holistic nature of the cycle of architectural history in the modern era, has constructed a model that is as effective for criticism as it is tautological for representation of the passing of historical time. If on the one hand, the idea of the origin of modernity has been pushed back ad infinitum, no longer stopping in the last century or at the Enlightenment but reaching back to the well-springs of modern culture in the Renaissance, on the other the problems that are raised in Brunelleschi turn up in Mannerism and in the culture of the Counter-Reformation, as well as in the crisis in enlightened thought or the decline of the avant-garde.

The idea that architecture and architects give birth at one and the same time to their affirmation and their negation, and therefore to the meaning and the contradiction of their logic, represents not only a central hypothesis of his work, but also the dominant paradigm in the majority of recent architectural historiography.

Historical awareness, like the analytic techniques of the project, is caught in the contradiction between the sophisticated development of its areas of knowledge and the most absolute impoverishment of methodology. Microhistory, anthropological history or the history of mentality are, at bottom, private, reductive and fragmentary responses to the impossibility of defending interpretative models of a wider range.[7]

In his book *Lo bello y lo siniestro*, Eugenio Trias discusses the meaning and scope of contemporary aesthetic production.[8] If the whole of European aesthetics after Kant is experienced from the barriers which Kant himself placed on the aesthetic object, in the sense that only the dreadful had to be estranged from the field of creation, in the present, post-Freudian era, creation appears, instead, to be the clear confrontation between the dreadful and its artistic expression.

The disorder that contemporary thought finds in reality lies at the origin of the experience of the dreadful. The task of art is that of the veil of Maya, a chaste covering that wraps the horror of Chaos in transparent material and displays it at the same time as covering it.

The linguistic comprehension of artistic phenomena, which originates in formalistic linguistics, has made it possible to understand with greater precision the conditions in which the meaning can shift, be transformed and undergo metamorphosis through structural relationship. This linguistic structure which, recognized in the tissue of objects, permits their liberation and play, is also the one which in the field of architectural intervention defines the situation of the present day.

The meanings suggested to us by the works that we discussed at the beginning of this article are not explicable without the greatest liberty in the manipulation of the sense, and at the same time the structures of meaning that the concrete building displays exist only as a support for this manipulation. To this must be added the accumulation of historical references that replace the ancient systematic and efficient knowledge of history with a multiple stock of imagery.

As an aesthetic operation, the intervention is the imaginative, arbitrary and free proposal by which one seeks not only to recognize the significant structures of the existing historical material but also to use them as *analogical* marks of the new construction.

Comparison, as difference and similarity, from within the only possible system, that particular system defined by the existing object, is the foundation of every *analogy*. On this *analogy* is constructed every possible and unpredictable meaning.

NOTES

1 Le Corbusier, *Oeuvre Complète, 1934–1939*, Zurich 1946.
2 A. Riegl, *Der moderne Denkmalkultus, sein Wesen, seine Entstehung (Enleitung zum Denkmalschutzgesetz)*, Vienna 1903.
3 Analysis of the early historiography linked to the fortunes of the Modern Movement has been carried out recently by M.L. Scalvini and M. Gaudi in *L'immagine storiografica dell'architettura contemporanea. Da Platz a Giedion*, Rome 1984.
4 W. Köller, *Gestalt Psychology*, New York 1929; K. Koffka, *Principles of Gestált Psychology*, New York 1935.
5 G. Grassi, "Il progetto di intervento sul castello di Abbiategrasso e la questione del restauro", in *Edilizia Popolare*, no. 113, Milan 1973. Now in the book *La arquitectura como oficio y otros escritos*, Barcelona 1980.
6 C. Rowe, *Collage City*, Cambridge, Mass. 1979.
7 J. Le Goff, *La nouvelle histoire*, Paris 1979.
8 E. Trias, *Lo bello y lo siniestro*, Barcelona 1982.

36
Rereadings

Graeme Brooker and Sally Stone

Source: *Rereadings: Interior Architecture and the Design Principles of Remodelling Existing Buildings*. RIBA Enterprises, 2004

STRATEGY

When designing a new building the architect, whether consciously or not, will employ an architectural strategy, that is, a device that will inform and order the building. This controlling device is often the basis of the theoretical issues that drive the design of the building. This strategy can manifest itself in many different ways, whether it is the controlling grid and ultimate freedom of Le Corbusier's plan libre used for example in the Villa Savoye or the spatial qualities of Adolf Loos's Raumplan as shown in the Muller or the Moller Houses, the complex contextual issues of Hans Hollein's Gallery in Munchengladbach or the prominent symbolic imagery of Smirke's British Museum.

These strategic moves are of course supplemented a complex combination of different factors, such as site conditions, structural systems, programmatic requirements, the era in which the building was constructed or the pursuit of the individual architect. These all combine to produce a building of rich complexity driven by an often-simple strategy.

But when a building is reused, the most important and influential factor in the design is, of course, the original building and it is the establishment of a relationship between the old and the new that is the most influential device in the design. The new could not exist without the original. The method by which the relationship is established is the key to the strategic analysis of building reuse. Of course those other factors intrinsic in the design of new building play an important part in the redesign of a building, but they really are overshadowed by the association of the new programme with the original building.

It is the understanding of how the two fit together, of their affinity or otherwise, of their complete integration or their standing apart that provides the categories for the analysis of types of building reuse.

The three categories of building reuse are based upon the sheer extent of the integration between the host building and the new elements. If the original building wholeheartedly accepts and establishes an intimate relationship with the new design, that is the two become one, the category is intervention. When the host building allows and accommodates new elements, which are built to fit the exact dimensions of the existing, to be introduced in or around it yet remains very much unchanged then the category is insertion and if the old and the new exist together but very little rapport between them is established, then the category is installation.

INTERVENTION

Intervention is a procedure that activates the potential or repressed meaning of a specific place. It only truly works when the architectural response of the modifications draw all their cues from the existing building. The architect will regard the building as a narrative, as a story to be discovered and retold and through a process of uncovering, clarification and interpretation will reveal and reactivate the place.

The original building provides the impetus for change; the architect's localised and highly specific reading of the place will dictate the appropriate moves. In order to impose a degree of control or order the building may need to be simplified thus producing a new way of looking or understanding it. The analysis and reading of the original building can often be as destructive as it is constructive, the architect will strip away, remove, clarify, UNDO in order to reveal new or hidden meanings.

Carlo Scarpa was the architect responsible for the restoration and remodelling of the Castelvecchio Museum in Verona. By the use of creative demolition he uncovered the various historic strata of the building. The castle was a complicated confusion of many eras of construction and Scarpa strove to explore and isolate the various phases of building to reveal the complex and rich beauty of the place.

> Scarpa achieved three things with his adaptive reuse project. First he accepted and presented parts of the building complex as historically preexisting, therefore maintaining their original integrity. Second he lay bare through conceptual surgery all the genuine survivals of the Castelvecchio. Finally, he added new parts, which would bind together the entire complex and fill in the gaps without destroying the patina or even the mishaps or wounds of time.[1]

The modifications to the building can act in an extremely intrusive manner with new elements imposing themselves directly upon the existing structure. The new elements, which are often many small changes, alterations, additions and subtractions are, of course, related completely to the original building as they are inspired by it, but the language used is usually completely at odds with the host although the character may be balanced.

When converting Giles Gilbert Scott's Bankside Power Station in London into the Tate Modern, Herzog and de Meuron strove not to obliterate the qualities of the industrial building but to heighten them. They aimed to integrate the everyday life and the cityscape with the urban fabric of the building. The transformation of now defunct industrial areas into places of high cultural interest is to be found in every Western country, the impact that Frank Gehry's Guggenheim Museum in Bilbao has had makes it a fantastic example. The position of the old power station, which was designed as a counterpoint to St. Paul's Cathedral, directly opposite it on the south bank of the Thames gave it the prime conditions for regeneration. Herzog and de Meuron describe their strategy as one that unleashes the hidden depths of the building:

> It is exciting to deal with existing structures, because the constraints demand a very different kind of creative energy. When you don't start from scratch you need architectural strategies that are not primarily motivated by taste or stylistic preferences. Our strategy was to accept the physical power of Bankside's massive mountain-like brick building and even to enhance it rather than breaking it up or trying to diminish it. This a kind of Aikido strategy where you use your enemy's strategy for your own purposes. Instead of fighting it you take all the energy and shape it in an unexpected and new way.[2]

The majority of the spaces in the conversion are dictated by the original building, the huge former turbine hall provides a massive street or public space, which penetrates the entire length and height of the building, and from this the galleries and other activities are accessed. The gallery spaces themselves vary in proportions, scale and size and their use of natural or artificial light, all of which is of course dependent on their position within the building. But the modification that is the most obvious and has the greatest impact is the creation of a huge body of light hovering above the main bulk of the massive brick structure of the building. This functions as a light well during the day and as a beacon at night. Most importantly, this intervention has the symbolic quality of representing the sheer quantity of energy once physically generated in the building and it now appears to hum with the stored latent energy.

Interventions are rarely function led. The form of the new building is dictated by the form of the original building. Form follows form! The building determines how it is to be reused, the position of the new spaces, how they are to relate to one another and their size and scale is already imbued within it. The distinctive qualities of the building are explored, the story is read, and it is altered, reshaped and retold and often irretrievably changed. New or hidden meanings are revealed, the building becomes endowed with significance often greater than the value of the new use: intervention can be seen as the activation of the place.

INSERTION

Insertion is a practice that establishes an intense relationship between the original building and the remodelling and yet allows the character of each to exist in an incredibly strong and independent manner.

Insertion as its title suggests, is the introduction of a new element into, between or beside an existing structure. The inserted object can often be seen as independent and confrontational, a single large powerful element that establishes surprising dialogues between itself and the existing structure or volume. It is at its best when the clearest possible distinction between the crisp new contemporary work and the crumbling antiquity of the existing is established and therefore the style, the

Figure 36.1 Installation: Basis Wien Arts Information Centre, Vienna, propeller z, 1997. The vertical plane is a single element that contains many of the activities that support the office environment. The storage, digital technology and signage are all contained within this simple and dynamic wall that also provides a link between the exterior with the interior. [©Sally Stone]

Figure 36.2 Insertion: The Royal Exchange Theatre Manchester, Levitt Bernstein, 1976. The dramatic theatre is situated within the old Exchange building. The new element is built to fit within the ample confines of the original building. [©Graeme Brooker]

language, the materials and the character of each are different.

Although the inserted element is independent, particular qualities are derived from the original building. This is inevitable because the insertion always has a direct architectural relationship with the absolute physical properties of the existing space. It is built to fit. Factors such as the scale and the dimensions, the proportions, the rhythm and the structural composition of the existing building influence the design of the insertion. At times perhaps, the insertion can be seen as some sort of interpretation of the past.

It is necessary for the form of the host building to be sufficiently powerful in order to accommodate the addition of a new and autonomous object, that it is not overawed. It is also important that the host building is relatively physically unaltered, that it retains its original integrity. Often it is

necessary for the architect to do little more than address any structural or environmental problems, although sometimes the complete restoration of the building to its original majesty may be required but the recognition of the distinction between the original building and the insertion is important. Equally, the insertion must be sufficiently strong to sit easily within or around it, a counterpoint or balance must be realised. For a successful dialogue to be established the two components must be speaking with a similar magnitude of language.

The tension and the ambiguities in the relationship between the two can also strengthen and reinvigorate the existing building, it can be considered and examined in a new way, it is looked at afresh and it is almost as if new life has been drawn into it.

At the Royal Exchange Theatre in Manchester, the theatre was inserted as an alien element into

Figure 36.3 Insertion: The Royal Exchange Theatre, Manchester, Levitt Bernstein 1976. All of the structural support for the theatre is taken by the huge columns of the original building, and so the new structure just floats above the ground floor of the Exchange building. [©Graeme Brooker]

Figure 36.4 Intervention: Tate Modern, London, Herzog and de Meuron, 2000. The architects have designed a series of small elements to populate the interior of the Turbine Hall; these directly reflect the industrial qualities of the original building. [©Sally Stone]

the original exchange building. Levitt Bernstein designed the steel and glass "space ship" in direct contrast to the formidable classical marble and stone of the existing building. It provides a focus for the space. The open hall of the Exchange building is so huge that the theatre can comfortably sit within it, as a sculptural object and can be accessed from all sides. There is no confusion about what and where the theatre is. The original building and the insertion both have strong independent characters and yet the theatre depends upon the exchange for such measures as scale, proportion, size and support. The floor of the exchange wasn't structurally capable of supporting the new structure, so the weight of the theatre is loaded onto long legs, which actually raise the theatre from the ground and the columns of the original building then take the load. The insertion of this new object reinvigorates the original building. A symbiotic relationship between the two elements is established based upon juxtaposition, counterpoint and contrast, and this relationship heightens the quality of both.

The insertion of a new functioning element not only provides a use for an often redundant or neglected space but also serves to heighten and intensify the building itself. The strong relationship of attracting opposites, each complementing and enhancing the other generates a building of a new and greater worth.

INSTALLATION

Installation is the placement of a series or group of related elements within the context of an existing building. This is a process that whilst recognising the oeuvre of an architect will heighten the awareness of an existing building and successfully combine the two without compromising or interfering with either.

The character of the objects or elements that constitute the installation is usually dictated by the style or the passion of the commissioned architect or artist. There are generally a number of related imported objects, concepts and ideas that embody the character of the creator and are positioned in groups or in series. The objects are usually of a limited size and often have a limited lifespan, perhaps an exhibition.

The objects are not necessarily without a relationship with the host building, they can be grouped together or placed in positioned to give maximum impact, both to the building and to themselves. They can be used to organize and delineate space or to create order in a confusion of buildings and volumes. Considerations such as adjustments of scale and appropriateness can be dictated by the building itself. The site can set up the parameters and be part of the reason for the installation. It can inspire the installation; the existing materials, structure, quality of space, history, context all may directly provide the impetus or generate the design of the new installed elements.

The host building generally needs few physical modifications, the architect will repair or even restore it but these changes have generally have nothing to do with the installation.

Sometimes the host building is little more than a stage for the performance of the objects but the best installations actually expose and reveal the beauty and qualities of it, allowing it to be read and understood in its own condition. The installation will enliven and reveal the true, possibly hidden or lost character of the building.

Christo and Jean Claude created an installation within an old gasometer in Oberhausen, Germany. This huge structure was a very unusual host building; circular with a diameter of over 50 metres, the empty space was 25 storeys high, that is, about 100 metres. The artists constructed a high wall made from oil barrels in the middle of the space, the coloured barrels, which were stacked 10 deep and reached to about half the height of the building, were intended to provoke reflections upon the scale of the space and its former function. The barrels were imported objects intended to enliven the space, they were neither built to fit, they were collected and placed within the space, nor did they alter the building in any way. At the end of the exhibition, the installation was dismantled and removed, the two elements returning to their original state.

Installation can be seen as the generation of a symbiotic relationship between a building and the series of elements placed within it. The two often have quite different characters and it is their juxtaposition that provides life and vitality for both.

NOTES

1. John Kurtich and Garret Eakin. *Interior Architecture*. 1993, p.26.
2. Rowan Moore and Raymond Ryan. *Building the Tate Modern*. 2000, p.215.

37
Adaptations

Architecture as a Palimpsest

Philippe Robert

Source: *Adaptations: New Uses for Old Buildings.* Princeton Architectural Press, 1989, pp. 6–11

Our aim is to analyse conversion as a *conceptual instrument* in architectural creation. Thanks to new economic realities and changing public attitudes towards the national heritage, we now consider conversion a "normal" architectural practice. The formal vocabulary, building techniques, and architectural design of certain buildings represent outstanding creative potential; today, there is a renewed awareness that the history of architecture is also the history of buildings which have been altered, re-arranged, extended — in short, *re-created.*

The term *palimpsest*, which refers to any written surface that has been erased and used for a new text (e.g. medieval parchments), can be applied metaphorically to recycled architecture.

The architect who modifies the drawing of an elevation on one or several superimposed sheets of tracing paper creates a palimpsest. And, by extension, an existing façade made up of elements built over several centuries is a kind of palimpsest.

There are various types of palimpsest — notably in literature, music, and painting. Medieval *Chansons de gestes,* French classical tragedies derived from Greek tragedies, the compositions of J.-S. Bach inspired by those of Vivaldi, and above all, "repainted paintings" are all types of palimpsest.

To mention only a few painters, works by Goya, Rembrandt, Fouquet, Picasso, Picabia and Max Ernst spring to mind: re-interpretations painted over canvases which had been previously painted by themselves or by other artists.

MEMORY AND ANTICIPATION

"Places we remember and places we anticipate are mingled in present time. Memory and anticipation, in fact, constitute the real perspective of space, giving it depth." This quote from Aldo Van Eyck neatly describes the relationship between time and space in converted architecture.

The history of architecture also includes buildings that underwent alterations, transference of function, additions, or had their materials recycled. One should also add those buildings that were merely used for a different purpose without undergoing any fundamental alteration.

A brief historical survey will serve as a compendium of examples of such changes.

BUILDING WITHIN

- The amphitheatres at Aries and Nîmes which became medieval villages.
- The church inserted in the Great Mosque of Cordova.
- The Museum of Architecture in the envelope of a 19th century town house in Frankfurt by Oswald Mathias Lingers.

BUILDING OVER

- The Pan Am Building by Walter Gropius above Grand Central Station, New York.
- The raising of the Berliner Tageblatt building by Erich Mendelsohn and Richard Neutra.

BUILDING AROUND

- The Vicenza Basilica — the concentric extension of the Palazzo della Ragione by Andrea Palladio.

BUILDING ALONGSIDE

- The extension to the Göteborg Law Courts by Gunnar Asplund.

- Thomas Jefferson's duplication of his neoclassical house at Monticello, Virginia.
- The Frankfurt Museum of Decorative Arts by Richard Meier — an extension of an 18th century house.
- Projects for extensions to New York museums: Guggenheim Museum by Gwathmey/Siegel, and Whitney Museum by Michael Graves.
- The Tate Gallery extension by James Stirling.

RECYCLING MATERIALS OR VESTIGES

- The town of Split, integrated into the ruins of Diocletian's Palace (Yugoslavia).
- Turkish villages built with stonework from ancient cities.
- The re-utilisation of pavilions from the 1889 Universal Exhibition (La Ruche in Paris and the Gare du Sud in Nice).

ADAPTING TO A NEW FUNCTION

- Roman temples converted into churches by Leone Battista Alberti.
- The Baths of Diocletian converted into a church by Michelangelo (Santa Maria degli Angeli in Rome).
- The museum in the Castelvecchio in Verona, by Carlo Scarpa.
- The Mausoleum of Augustus in Rome, converted into a fortress, gardens, an amphitheatre, and then into a concert hall.
- The Panorama on the Champs-Élysées, converted into a skating rink and then a theatre.

BUILDING IN THE STYLE OF

- The arcade, column, tympanum, rustication, and the classical vocabulary employed by the post-modernists, from Hans Hollein to Kohn-Pedersen-Fox, and from Charles Moore to Ricardo Bofill.

This inventory — limited to outstanding examples — illustrates the variety of such interventions, which span every period of history and which cover the whole range of architectural forms.

It includes no work of the modern movement; although Le Corbusier, Mies van der Rohe, Alvar Aalto and Frank Lloyd Wright often made reference to the past, they never proposed integrating their projects with existing buildings. The return to historicism, and the "contextual", approach which typifies today's architectural production, perhaps constitute a reaction against the way in which the modern movement envisaged cohabitation with the existing built fabric or even the destruction of the latter.

Finally, the inventory is a reminder of the way in which conversion brings into play memory of place and future use, at the same time and within the same space. It is this relationship which has inspired so many architects and which, today, has once more emerged as a particularly fertile field of intervention.

FORM-FUNCTION

Function creates form, but what is to be done with the form once the function has disappeared? Can the existing form accommodate the new function? The whole business of working with existing buildings turns upon the form/function dialectic: a conversion only succeeds when there is a good match between new function and existing form. It is therefore necessary to analyse the nature of the existing built fabric before one can suggest a new use, because "out of the encounter between old envelope and new requirements and means, a unique object will be born — one which is no mere juxtaposition, but a synthesis from the point of view of both construction and architecture" (Claude Soucy).

There may exist a symbolic affiliation as when, for example, a church is built within a pagan temple. The use to which any building is converted ought to feature a symbolic content at least equivalent to that found in the original.

VOLUMES AND SPACES

Historic monuments, public edifices, and industrial buildings represent large volumes — often too large for a future use.

Architects thus have at their disposal over-sized spaces from which to draw advantage for new uses (as, for example, spinning mills converted into low-cost housing).

They can also, however, intervene in a "negative" manner by altering the silhouette of a building or by creating hollow spaces (internal courtyards, set backs).

This involves reducing a volume rather than — as is the case with a new building — increasing it.

It should also be kept in mind that a large building can accommodate several functions and that this allows a reconstitution of the multiple amenities found in towns: shops on the ground level, offices and/or housing on the upper floors, collective facilities in specific places (boiler room, Head Executive residence, etc.).

In addition to the volume of old buildings, there is the size of their structural elements: thick walls, ashlar wall bases and arcades, large areas of floor and framework. One is thus confronted with a "macrostructure" which is built to last, and is capable of accommodating more limited internal layouts which can be adapted to variable functions. Very fine results have thus been achieved with the interaction of two architectural vocabularies, as in the case of apartments laid out in medieval palaces in Italy.

OLD STRUCTURES AND ORNAMENT

Conversion work brings the architect face to face with history, and this contact can generate novel architectural solutions which feature an ideal combination of past and present. The conceptual attitudes of architects vary according to the nature of the dialectical relationships they develop between new functional elements and the existing built fabric. Some architects underline the contrast between elements, perhaps employing strong colours, whereas others seek to ensure visual continuity by subtly relating architectural components while at the same time distinguishing the specific nature of each.

Moreover, the re-utilisation of existing architectures allows for work with ornament, and for arrangement of certain architectural details, the existence of which would be inconceivable in a new building. 19th century metal architecture or Art Deco buildings are, in this respect, particularly interesting owing to their wealth of ornamentation. Their architectural vocabulary can provide the basis for a stylistic rewriting of the building, either by highlighting certain architectural features or by giving them new effect. This method of working from a detail in order to achieve an overall conception is typical of conversion work, based on the existing building.

INTERIOR ARCHITECTURE

Large converted buildings, by definition, require work on their interior, and this therefore involves an architecture of interior space rather than of external volume. Staircases, mezzanines, the interplay of light and shade, contact with load-bearing structures and the frame — large buildings provide the designer with architectural "effects" which would be difficult to obtain in a new building.

Architects are required to practice an "interior" architecture in which space, movement, and light figure more prominently. The large size of industrial buildings and the frequent presence of courtyards between buildings, allow a different relationship between inside and outside to be envisaged: erecting a building within another — as in the case of the Frankfurt Museum of Architecture — or covering a courtyard with a glazed roof, create new spatial and functional situations.

"This movement from interior to exterior in the opposite direction, that is to say entering one space and finding oneself outside the next one, opens up the possibility of a conscious perception of space" (Oswald Mathias Ungers).

RECYCLING: A CHALLENGE

In Europe today, in the building industry, the conversion of towns and buildings has become a major challenge, and this has caused profound changes in architectural practice.

The naive attitude of the majority of architects is astonishing; they are unaware of the various aspects of conversion and design their buildings for a single function, a single environment, and a single period. Perhaps a new way of thinking ought to be fostered, one which considers that towns are never completed and that the buildings which are erected are always complements or additions to what already exists. Michael Graves has proposed a similar attitude when he suggests that an existing building can be thought of as an unfinished fragment of a larger edifice.

Historic buildings, industrial buildings, and obsolete public buildings provide exceptional opportunities to those architects who can "understand" them. And, over and above the economic advantages which conversion offers, recycling "can create a 'magical effect' in towns — something they would never have possessed had they been mummified like historic monuments" (Pierre Schneider, speaking of Rome).

38
On Altering Architecture: Some Resolutions

Fred Scott

Source: *On Altering Architecture*. Routledge, 2008, pp. 167–183

To demolish and build something better is the legitimate purpose of architecture, in perpetuity, but this presupposes an assumption that not everyone can manage. On the other hand, the symbiotic or dependent nature, the feeling of subservience that infuses alteration, regularly provokes a sense of claustrophobia in many architects. It is possible that two contrary imaginations are involved. The paradox of architecture is that the adored city must in part be destroyed to allow for the new. The enigma of intervention is that one sets out to alter, but at the same time to be the advocate for a building.

All buildings are in an imperfect state, they are made of reflections of a model, which has generic status, and of particularities, or peculiarities. A purpose of alteration is to move the building in the direction of its model as discerned through the processes of stripping back. The outcome will properly have temporal qualities, from the overlay of changes on the original, but also will have, through the interest in archetype, timeless qualities. The work is a mediation between the processes of accretion and purification.

Two taboos of alteration are rendered obsolete by the realization of the lack of difference between restoration and conservation. They are the taboos against improvement and against copying.

All works to existing buildings related to their original condition are restorative, including those that are now generally considered to be conservation. As the original condition of the building is lost from the moment of its inception, works of restoration are imaginative, or a matter of judgement if a more sober description is required. The aims of restoration have been historically uncertain in most cases; it has been usual to assume that such work has been carried forward with some extraneous goal in mind, some precise knowledge regarding the original condition. At what exact moment was this certainty supposed to have occurred, when the last workman withdrew from the site, when the building was handed over to the client, or the Tuesday after that? It is illusory.

Intervention must aim to be always equal to the host building in some respect, and better in others, or else it is a failure. It is incontrovertible that the interventionist may be more talented than the original builders, as it is equally true that the opposite will also occur. Their effort in resuscitation[1] of the host building is akin to transcription in poetry and music.[2] The designer has it within his or her scope to clarify the intentions of the original builders through their intervention; this is a question of licence, and as with all creative undertakings, there can be no preordained promise of the excellence of the outcome.

Copying was ever present if unrecognized in the practice of altering buildings, and it needs now to be raised up, and considered paradoxically as a true component of alteration.[3] Restorative work is imitative and interpretive;[4] of course all 'conservation' work involves imitative work, but this somehow is considered the realm of the workmen or craftsmen, and so is relegated to beneath critical consideration. However, when considered critically, the impossibility of an exact copy opens the discussion onto the realm of imitation and parody and works *in the manner of* in the composing of new work and the existing.[5] Imitative work is an important project within the art or conscious craft of intervention, which requires awareness throughout of the dangers of mimicry and its potential for destabilization.[6] It should be considered as not of equivalence, but rather as an attempt at interpretation. Imitation is concerned with what is possible today; and imitative work, and its associate, variation, constitute a central project of intervention.

These two taboos are in actuality reflections of the same issue: the key to both is the status of the copy. As it is impossible to make an exact copy, both in terms of physicality and in undertaking, and as an equivalence is a misty destination, does the copy set out to be inferior to or an improvement on the original? What is set out here might through a proper reticence lead to nothing being attempted, but if the work of alteration is to go forward, and the client will usually have a view about this, then a programme of improvement may begin to be defined from the status of the imitative work.

Because of this, one may question if every intervention needs to be in a contemporary style, as suggested by William Morris. The argument today would surely be the same as the situation in the second half of the nineteenth century, which was as stricken with idiosyncrasy in matters of style as the beginning of this new millennium. The admonition relies on there being a single contemporaneous style, established beyond counter, and it falters in the absence of such a condition. In addition, as Modernist belief has space-making matched to specific uses, the fitting of new uses into existing spaces would seem to preclude this deeper motive for the implementation of Modernist form.[7]

The universality of Modernist work,[8] as suggested by Mondrian's work to his Paris studio,[9] might more properly be seen as an aspect, and confirmation, of a commitment to the abstract, and in particular geometric abstraction. Geometry, with its close correspondence between the ideal and the actual, the point without dimension, the line without width, it is an apt component of interventional work. Being without style, it stands outside of time and so can act as a trans-temporal medium for composition.[10] As Colin Rowe set out to explain in the 'Mathematics of the Ideal Villa',[11] there may be geometric correspondences between very different styles of building, and so geometry may also act as a medium for the blending of the new with the existing.

To an altered building and the time-lapse camera, the occupants are like spirits, transitory and passing magically through what had once been floors and walls.[12] For the occupants, the new circulation of the altered interior may be like a journey through ruins, taking previously impossible routes, and having new, almost aberrant viewpoints as a result. An altered building explains itself; it is in this way an inhabited ruin. The ruin may, however, be neither accidental nor imprecise, as is made evident by the work of Gordon Matta-Clark. The altered condition may have qualities of exposure that previously one thought of as confined to drawings, such as sectional perspectives.

Alteration is breaking and entry, the precise cut, the strategic section exposed. It makes absences as well as additions. An over-reverent and potentially tiresome regard for every aspect of the existing can clog the creative mind. A clear diagram of intention, however radical, is more likely to lead to an effusive absorption of a new occupation into the host building.

The two conflicting types of spatial articulation, which seem destructive one of the other, need to be conflated in the work of alteration. Symmetry assumes completeness, and asymmetry suggests incompleteness, with the chance of addition and subtraction. This marriage of opposite styles requires that the remains of a symmetrical plan imply the complete; this need not be too restricting, for as noted elsewhere, half a symmetrical building can describe the whole. The use of transparency to unify and to integrate the new programme with the host building can be worked through geometry and transparency, which are together the strongest tool for the work of intervention.[13]

Change of use[14] almost always requires spatial and physical changes. Unlike Ise and the Villa Savoye, most alteration occurs as a result of change of use; this is the source of the new life of the building. The new use is one usually derived from expediency, from needs that may be outside of formal considerations. Unlike the making of a new building, the question of fit is different and more complex in re-use than in pure architecture. This disjuncture has its value.[15]

The aptness of the new occupation within the existing is derived from coincidence; such intersects are often not clear at the outset, and the search for them is commonly the longest phase of the design process. The process of insinuating new use into the given building is coloured throughout with reappraisal and reinterpretation. The fitting of the new into the existing is ever a negotiation, and so the fit is likely to become less clear than the more explicit requirements that can be made of a new building, and of course the new identity often needs to be made explicit within the old context. The work will always provoke divided loyalties in this way. The designer needs an acute eye for the poetry of the everyday, of the play between the fleeting and the fixed, as this is how the success of the new colonization can best be appreciated or judged. The play between the new occupation and original use contains meaning for the overall work; use, re-use and seeming misuse are rife with significance, which may be other than spatial. The terminology of the plan contains an encounter between the past and the present, a contrast of form and function, a play of temporal differences, the salon and the boardroom, the inspection pit and the sacristy. Encounter is the essence of surrealism, and composition in interventional design is fired by unexpected encounters.

New life is made manifest through new materials and new techniques of building; this is how a tenet of Modernism becomes a part of intervention, the strength of the new materials, as image and actuality. James Gowan has written that when it comes to details,[16] time is meaningless, the purposes of detailing remaining the same regardless of the age, whether for instance to cast off water or to ensure an enclosure or to give adequate support. While this is true, the choice of new materials will give it a temporal twist. This will apply to any age, as with the Adam brothers' insertion of the stone staircase in the Elizabethan wood-panelled Great Hall at Hatfield House. The designer is more inclined than the architect to experiment with new materials[17].

The programme of intervention has the same aim as that of certain contemporary painters: to quote Sean Scully, the proposition that 'things must fit together'.

Regarding composition, allegiance to a particular style is usually the source of cohesion, consistency and coherence in architecture, and in other things. Such an allegiance can be almost religious in its intensity, and to stand outside of it might be considered heretical. One might reasonably claim that the great developments of architecture and design in the last century were manifestations of just such allegiances.[18] Such purity of production is unavailable to the interventional designer. She or he must seek other paths to composition, among which is collage, a means to engage confrontation and contradiction in composition.[19] This is a territory of real difficulty. The usual reliance on purity of style for coherence is familiar to all, but the results of its absence are far less certain. Alteration is best considered as a postmodern project, in that 'post-modernism acknowledges and ascribes importance to content, context, and to eclecticism, and considers appropriation one of its fundamental strategies'.[20] It is difficult on the other hand for the pure architect to celebrate eclecticism in other than words, as Robert Venturi was to find out, in contrast to working with the found or given as in interventional work.

An altered building is a complex thing, a set of co-habitations, where one style may emulate, parody or paraphrase another. It is the outcome of an encumbered struggle towards a norm, having regard for both the idea of paradigm and for the otherwise vernacular qualities of the host building or buildings. It will therefore contain comparative elements. If even through the most conscientious analysis some aspect of the host building remains unfathomable, whether in planning or in detail, abstract or material, such a feature then needs treating with special circumspection. The old push and pull between what Christopher Wren described as the two ideas of beauty[21] is the designer's constant companion in the difficult work of alteration.[22]

The ideal in alteration is the same as how Dr Kinsey[23] considered the normal in his work: it exists only as an idea, and as such it is suited to only allusion and is inimical to realization.

The existing needs to be broken in a manner to allow for a resolved intervention; greater dangers may lurk in doing too little. The work of intervention requires a certain savagery, otherwise a confused mélange of petty changes will result from a too reverent approach to the host building, and this will surely ultimately destroy it.[24] An altered building is not old fashioned, that is in the sense of being in Lionel Trilling's phrase 'inauthentic for the present time'.[25] There is necessarily something speculative in the nature of an altered building, that is a sense of the tentative, which eschews preclusion and false certainty.[26] Restoration aims to complete a building, and it has other purposes. Alteration is progressive and is not an attempted recuperation, such as a pure restoration sets out to achieve. It is in part like a rehearsal for a completed building. Restoration is an important component of alteration, but alteration is the agent of re-occupation rather than emptying buildings.

The approach to alteration requires that the designer strives to know everything, and then to improvise,[27] ever alert to the appearance of coincidence, the exquisite affirmation between the existing and the imposed. As ever, improvisation and repetition are twinned.[28]

That an old building should show its age would seem to have the ring of truth about it, which would in addition seem to support the far-flung crusades for authenticity. However, here is another seeming certainty that after a while begins to lose its firm footing in the mind. Modernist buildings seem to need to be restored as if brand new; look at the restoration of the Villa Savoye, or Duiker's Zonnestraal Sanatorium buildings near Hilversum, or any other examples of restored Modernist monuments. This would appear to be accepted wisdom, or at least convention, or the code of practice. One might be led to think that here is an odd confirmation of Le Corbusier's edict that the house is a machine, and so needs the same treatment as, for instance, a classic car. But in all these matters, time is still the architect to a certain extent. I remember, on my first visit to America, stopping in a high car park somewhere in the Sierra Nevada in California to watch the sunset. Similarly occupied, if occupation it was, were an elegant elderly couple with an equally elegant and elderly Chrysler Imperial. Both car and owners were venerable. The Chrysler was undeniably old, as were the owners, but because of the inevitable deterioration of the fittings – the worn leather seats, despite repeated treatment with saddle-soap or the like, the pitted chrome on the fenders – the original inspiration of the designers seemed all the more evident, because the temporal context was legible: one could see, without the distraction of illusion that restoration imparts, that this was an old car, better at transmitting the energy and elegance of the times when it was conceived and then mass produced.[29]

What are the consequences of making a three-hundred-year-old building appear new? Should a building not show its age? One might answer that a building may indicate its age in two distinct modes: it may be maintained, as is the Villa Savoye, as eternally new in order to give clear expression of a style; or it may, as Ruskin believed, gain its architectural status through the wear of time.[30] To maintain a building as seemingly new is a particular form of illusion. Equally, the condition in which the Parthenon is maintained is the result of judgement, as much as of its age. Savoye and the Parthenon are the same in being monuments preserved in a particular chosen condition, in a version that stands to represent authenticity.[31]

The differences between the aims of preservation and those of alteration are made more evident through cases such as these,[32] in contrast to alteration. Formally, for instance, restoration may reinstate symmetry, but alteration causes asymmetry. What is true of both Viollet-le-Duc and the restoration of the Villa Savoye is that the treatment of the built structure is intended as a completion and therefore also a curtailment. But this work is addressed to something other, to a building altered in order to remain in use, occupied and not removed from the transactions of the everyday, a building that has been altered to this end, to accommodate a new use or uses.

What is transient? What is considered ephemeral is a result of judgement. Is dust sacrosanct? One thinks of Man Ray's photograph of dust on Duchamp's *Great Glass*[33] and may be persuaded to consider it.[34] The fading painted advertisements

on buildings, particularly those in France, a surviving spectacular neon sign,[35] a building might show its experience as well as its age. Are these contributions to authenticity or digressions?

A surviving piece of the original[36] should, I suppose, be treated generally as sacrosanct, but there is ever the danger of *fetishism*. Does the authentic reside in the surface?[37] How then can it ever survive? The worn element, or surface, is a given. How a chosen material ages has a validity, even if it is not as comprehensive and exclusive as suggested by Ruskin.[38] If one accepts that the qualities imparted by time, through scuffing, wearing and the like, have an authenticity, this contrasts with the authentic upon which copying relies, the exercise that aims to ascertain original aspects of the host building.

The quest for the authentic is in part an attempt to curtail speculation or any other form of questioning, but even after admitting this, the itch remains. One might conclude that only the original impulse of the builders, to which they themselves may have been partly blind, is authentic. The physical remains are merely material evidence of that thought, realized in different cases with various degrees of success. The idea of the model, archetype or paradigm is one that is accompanied by the copy, or by work *in the manner of,* derived from an ideal that can be known with precision in part. But one needs to remember that the worn is a given.

Authenticity, patina and the copy can be seen to constitute a triplet of ordinates, which allows the host building to be treated as the scientific object, as Damisch says of Viollet-le-Duc's method.[39] Stripping back then may proceed by the accepted sequence of hypotheses that must be supported by evidence found within the subject in order to stand. Within this too is the understanding that, as with all scientific truths, it is always interim, awaiting contradiction in its turn. This is the reason for the combination of restoration, the original and an uncertainty, all three present in any correct alteration.

NOTES

1 This term was first suggested to me by my friend Stephen Donald, who taught with me for many years, and was and continues to be a constant source of information, energy and inspiration.
2 Arnold Schoenberg, who made transcriptions of J. S. Bach, among others, said that it was the

duty of the transcriber to set a piece free from weaknesses in the original in carrying out the work.

3 The French of course have been engaged for some time in the reinstatement of the legitimacy of copying. 'Plagiarism is necessary, progress implies it. It tightly squeezes an author's phrase, serves his expression, erases a false idea, replaces it with a just notion.' From Centre de Lautréamont, *Poesies*, vol. II (Paris: Librairie Gabrie Questroy et Cie, 1870), brought to my attention by Calum Storrie.

4 Unlike the rebuildings of Ise, this work is not necessarily ritualized, except in an informal manner through the under-praised processes of craftsmanship. One can imagine, however, work *in the manner of* might over time become a canon, amassed through the recognition of the generally accepted excellence of certain examples, probably from diverse projects.

5 One of the most valuable writings on the subject of imitation and related issues is Gerd Neumann, 'Like Yonder Cloud that is Very Like a Whale, On Eclecticism and the Meaning of Conservation', in *Daidalos* 8 (June 1983), p. 87: '"Electio", in the meaning thus attributed to it, is intimately connected by way of the concepts "imitatio" and "mimesis", with the problems of beauty and ideality, and the problems of establishing rules and standards for them. The existence of exemplars and exemplarity presupposes their perception and selection.'

6 Although reference has been made earlier (Chapter 5) to fine art practices regarding transcription and copying, certain contemporary artists, such as the Berliner Thomas Demand, deserve special mention.

> Known for his photographs of meticulously constructed environments of cardboard and paper, Thomas Demand uses source material from historical, political and media images. The resultant work enables an eerie merging of the boundaries between the imagined and real. His meticulous craftsmanship means that the photographs often look at first glance like real places. Critic Neville Wakefield observed Demand 'proposes architecture as silent witness to the pathologies of social disturbance'.
>
> (Parveen Adams, *AA Events List*, 3 February 2006)

7 This will further confirm the requirement of interventional training to contain the study without prejudice of architectural style. Such work has long been abandoned in schools of architecture everywhere, apart from a few trivial exercises in reactionary private institutions in the UK.

8 The universality of Modernism depends, as Cézanne recognized, upon the idea that everything is infrastructurally made up of combinations of pure forms. The true experimental proof of this in alteration is in the insertion of spaces that are the evacuated presences of pure form, the cube, the sphere, the cylinder, the cone, as with Matta-Clark's work at rue Beaubourg. Such operations may be as enabling work and as a bridge or mediation between existing and the new work.

9 Frans Postma, *26, Rue du Depart Mondrian's Studio Paris 1921–1936* (Berlin: Ernst & Sohn, 1995).

10 The designer's absorption in the power of line, point and arc should match that of the geometer. In addition to the work of Preston Scott Cohen discussed in Chapter 7, Peter Beard teaching at the Architectural Association in London has done exemplary work with respect to the role geometry plays in buildings. In 'San Carlino and the Cultivated Wild', *AA Files* 31 (1996), pp. 31–38, he describes an excellent project set in the school working with Borromini's San Carlino church in Rome. In introducing the work, the Unit Master writes:

> Brutta e deforma. Gotico ignorantissimo et corruttore dell 'Architeturra, infamia del nostro secolo.' Borromini was described by his contemporaries as 'a most ignorant "gotico" and a corruptor of architecture'. Using the work of this 'corrupt' figure and his 'ugly and deformed' church of San Carlino in Rome as a starting point, the project described in the following pages approaches themes of Baroque space principally through geometry. Anamorphic and other geometric projections, cupping, splaying and torsional distortion are used as elements of a complex synthesis. The church is read as a space of controlled savagery.

11 Colin Rowe, *The Mathematics of the Ideal Villa and Other Essays* (Cambridge, Mass.: MIT Press, 1976).

12 See Michael Wesely's book of long-exposure photographs of the rebuilding of MOMA in Manhattan, the Potsdamer and Pariser platzes in Berlin and other sites (Sarah Hermanson

Meister, *Michael Wesely Open Shutter,* New York: The Museum of Modern Art, 2004).

13 One might note a similar conflict between the ornamented surface and the pure surface of Modernism. In this regard, the recent experiments by Herzog and de Meuron, in particular, in architectural decoration should be noted. These would suggest that there is now available a wider licence for the treatment of surfaces.

14 Probably at the outset I intended to write more extensively on the difficulties of fitting new uses into existing buildings. I now think this is best done by case studies, of some depth and intensity, and that has not fallen within the scope of this present enquiry. I have tried to deal more generally with the issue. It is obviously another two-part problem, the first dealing with dimensional fit, how and how much the existing might be changed to accommodate the new set of uses, or simply is the building big enough? I'm sure there are examples also where the programme of the new occupation has been brilliantly altered to allow accommodation between building and use. The second part is the more elusive correspondence between the new and the previous uses, the new occupation and the original purpose of the building. This touches on what might be called appropriateness or its opposite, of questions of propriety. A building, unlike a ship, will not die of shame. However if such judgements are applied, I have tried to show how much of the poetic might be lost or obscured by such preconceptions. The contrasts and coincidences between the new and the usurped occupation are the cause of much wonder, and a source for the designer in their work. It may be possible and possibly useful to devise a taxonomy of occupancy, an anthropometries of occupancy as a tool for the designer, that is morally neutral, being concerned with spatial compatibility, and so avoiding or ignoring charges of impropriety. This would be less inhibiting. The old chestnut of 'fit' bobs to the surface here, a cause of much debate in an earlier age. Stemming from functionalism, there was the belief, which was almost a Modernist credo, that there was a tight fit between built form and occupation. This was first challenged in the 1960s with the motto 'Long life, loose fit', which was generally considered at the time to be a reactionary assertion.

15 Regarding recent works, if the great Hawksmoor church, Christchurch at Spitalfields in London, had been deconsecrated, and had consequently undergone a change of use, it may have been more immune to the Ruskian destruction it has recently suffered.

16 See the essay 'Details' in his *Style and Configuration* (London: Academy Editions; Berlin: Ernst & Sohn, 1994, pp. 40–42). This piece may be the best demonstration in print of an elegant architectural intelligence:

> The bridge is a first year project on timber construction in the late 50s . . . At the time I did it in a rush, made the model one weekend and photographed it. I thought the bridge was elementary in every respect. Just timber scantlings – four-by-twos and six-by-twos – and based on triangulation – underneath and at the first posts. Some twenty years later one looks more closely at Palladio and sees, if not the inverted ties, rather nice unmannered bridges in the same theme, the point being that the gap of 400 years has no meaning at all if one is building in a basic manner. Fashion is absolutely irrelevant and it does not matter whether you are classical, modern or extremely with-it. At root, when one gets down to detailing, the language becomes shared.

17 As mentioned in a previous note on the use of colour, Ben Kelly Design has always adopted an 'art school' approach to intervention in its bold use of new materials and finishes, as well as colour. See *Plans and Elevations: Ben Kelly Design,* ed. Catherine McDermott (London: ADT Design File, 1990).

18 The adoption in the latter part of the twentieth century in certain quarters of computer-generated forms for buildings has perhaps moved the condition from one of belief to one of immersion, from which a total and suffocating aesthetic has emerged, a product of technique outside of any didactic framework, immune therefore to criticism, and freed of the sense of morality which attached to the earlier crusades of Modernism.

19 Picasso's famous 'Still Life with Chair Caning' united oil paint with pasted-on oil cloth, while the first *papiers collés* were undoubtedly done by Braque. As a technique of picture-making, the term 'collage' comes from the French verb *coller,* to paste, stick, glue; and *papier colié* is the more restricted expression referring only to paper. Collage

itself is now an accepted art form, making a direct contribution towards creative expression . . . As many artists have admitted in their commentaries, it was the only way out of an impasse that they had reached at some difficult stage of artistic expression, and it has brought to them a new liberation of vision and form.

(Helen Hutton, *The Technique of Collage,* New York: Watson-Guptill Publications, 1968, p. 9).

20 Roni Feinstein, *Robert Rauschenberg: The Silkscreen Paintings 1962–64* (Boston, Toronto, London: Whitney Museum/Bullfinch Press, Little, Brown), p. 92.

21 'There are two causes of beauty – natural and customary. Natural is from geometry consisting in uniformity, that is equality and proportion. Customary beauty is begotten by the use, as familiarity breeds a love to things not in themselves lovely.' Sir Christopher Wren, quoted by Colin Rowe at the beginning of his essay on 'The Mathematics of the Ideal Villa' – see note 11, above.

22 At the risk of being obvious, the study of architectural style and its history, as well as the study of projective geometry, are to be twinned cardinal interests in any teaching concerned with the art and practice of alteration.

23 Alfred C. Kinsey, author with others of the two *Kinsey Reports on Sexual Behavior: in the Male* (1948) and *in the Female* (1953).

24 This comment may be addressed to the work on Christchurch, Spitalfields, also referred to elsewhere.

25 Lionel Trilling, *Sincerity and Authenticity* (Cambridge, Mass.: Harvard University Press, 1971).

26 One may consider all total restorations, such as the recent work at Christchurch, Spitalfields, as acts of this type. I was, however, first struck by the debilitating and stifling quality of preclusion by the video work recently acquired by MOMA in New York (Eve Sussman, *89 Seconds at Alcazar,* 2004), which purports to show like a scene from a larger film the goings-on in the room as *Las Meninas* was being painted. It is difficult to think of a more potent means of diminishing the original.

27 Improvisation: the art of improvising, to fabricate with what is to hand, combining disparate parts to create a whole; working with the accidental and the coincidental. In jazz, a soloist playing a classic American song, something

by Cole Porter perhaps, is an exercise in extending the given musical bases so as to test recognition of the source, a game of explanation and obscuration, dependent always on a spirit of love and reverence for the original tune. In truth, Charlie Parker, the greatest of the be-bop improvisers, would sometimes play a tune quite straight, as with 'How Deep is the Ocean' or 'The Gypsy', almost devoid of improvisation. However, at other times, as with three versions of 'Embraceable You', he would from the first note play such an abstracted line that only slowly does one come to suspect what the song is. (All Dial recordings.)

28 As with, for instance in music, John Coltrane repeatedly playing 'These Are a Few of My Favourite Things' by Rodgers and Hammerstein. This may stand as a metaphor for the richness that can be drawn from imitative and interpretative work. It may be considered one day that the Modernist expedition into originality was a strange anomaly; however, it indicates more than anything else Modernity's utopian programme, to leave everything else behind. One should note the increasing number of fine artists working in the realm of copying and imitation, so much so that one thinks that they might begin to constitute an important general project for our time, for designers and architects as well as artists. It will be obvious by these references and others elsewhere that the author thinks of these activities as central to the education of the interventional designer. As I completed these notes, an exhibition of Thomas Demand's cardboard facsimiles had opened at the Serpentine Gallery in London. The *Tavern* series in particular seems to give substance to a connection between event and place.

29 Original pieces, prototypes of Modernist furniture, especially those emanating from the Bauhaus, have such a touching quality of aspiration, which the consequent mass-produced item always lacks. It is embodied in creative attempts to avoid certain inabilities and inadequacies at the outset, which will be later solved in production. Such precious pieces are like items from a cargo cult, harbingers of an intensely desired future.

30 John Ruskin, 'The Lamp of Memory' in *The Seven Lamps of Architecture* (London, 1849), p. 202:

But so far as it can be rendered consistent with the inherent character, the picturesque or extraneous sublimity of architecture has just this of nobler function in it than that of any other object whatsoever, that it is an exponent of age, of that in which, it has been said, the greatest glory of the building consists; and therefore, the external signs of this glory, having power and purpose greater than any belonging to their mere sensible beauty, may be considered as taking rank among pure and essential characters; so essential to my mind, that I think a building cannot be considered as in its prime until four or five centuries have passed over it; and the entire choice and arrangement of its details should have reference to their appearance after that period, so that none should be admitted which would suffer material injury either by the weather staining, or the mechanical degradation which the lapse of such a period would necessitate.

31 In this respect, one might understand the contrary positions of Ruskin and Viollet-le-Duc as being between two different notions of authenticity.

32 The Villa Savoye may be compared with the Acropolis and its buildings, with regard to the decisions taken to ascertain the condition in which each monument was to be maintained. One might consider that one emphasizes a view of dimensional authenticity, a quality of a newly completed building which can be re-captured, and the other a conviction in the physical remains alone as authentic. It will be seen that the first will emphasize spatiality, and the other will focus upon surface.

33 Man Ray and Marcel Duchamp, *Dust Breeding* (1920).

34 In many museums, the ephemeral production of certain times, of the 1960s for instance, is a cause of many conservational quandaries. The conservation of the inflatable plastic furniture from that era is a case in point, to which the Victoria and Albert Museum in London has given much effort. See *The V&A Conservation Journal,* October 1996.

35 Much of this is the territory of architectural salvage, but where the borderline in between retention and salvage seems very difficult to delineate exactly. Of course in practice the designer comes upon the building with much that was considered of value having been removed.

36 In the confusion between actual and authentic, isn't the authentic also always a result of judgement, by an authenticating authority, an individual or a group? The actual is quite different. In the arguments that derive from Ruskin, those which perhaps come closer to forming a convention than any other set of arguments, a convention of assumed conservation and pretended non-alteration is clearly based upon the physical remains of the original building. The remains are revered as much for their being worn down by age as for their being authentic. There is nowhere suggested that the wear of time dilutes the piece's authenticity. In fact, for Ruskin in *The Seven Lamps of Architecture,* the opposite would seem to apply. Because of this lack of a clear central idea, these arguments are prone to deteriorate quickly into picturesque and sentimental considerations.

37 Ruskin, 'The Lamp of Memory'.

38 *Ibid.*

39 Hubert Damisch, 'The Space between: A Structuralist Approach to the Dictionary', *Architectural Design* 3/4 (1980), p. 88.

SECTION 3.3
APPROACHES TO CONSERVATION

Introduction

Existing buildings provide a sense of connection with the previous ages. They reinforce the relationship that those who dwell in a place have with it and they can become part of the collective memory of a society. The conservation of such buildings is a complex process that combines the need to preserve as much of the existing structure as possible with a new, and often conflicting, function. Our perception of the past is very much based upon our reading of these buildings.

Many western cities are now an eclectic mix of historic, modern and contemporary buildings, all of which combine within the urban environment to create a vibrant and highly functional place to live and work in. It is well-known that these architecturally mixed locations attract creative people, thus also pulling in further innovative and service industries. Cultural regeneration is seen an extremely viable method of revitalising a run-down area.

Temple Bar, a neglected district next to the River Liffy in Dublin, is a fine example of such a practice. The architects, Team 8, proposed that the neighbourhood should remain relatively untouched, apart from the insertion of a series key cultural buildings; these were a mixture of new build and reuse, but importantly they all paid great respect to the grain and patterns of the area. This meant that the small scale and slightly random quality of the environment was not lost. These museums and cinemas attracted visitors, which in turn attracted service industries, such as bars, cafes and small independent shops. These, in their own way, acted as a draw to yet more visitors, and so an area that was once considered ripe for whole scale demolition has become a thriving destination in the city. This area consisted of a large number of ordinary buildings, admittedly a few important landmarks, but most of the neighbourhood consisted of modest inconsequential structures. These were typical of the locality, important elements in the evolution of the city and thus key components of the collective memory of the place. But retaining these buildings was not a simple process of repair or even rebuild; the character and qualities also had to be kept hold of. Conservation is not really that straightforward and it has an eventful history.

There are a number of different methods of conservation. All of them deal directly with the existing building, but the sheer amount of intervention differs with each approach. Conservation is the general term that covers the process.

Preservation is a method that maintains the building in its found state, whether ruinous or not. Sufficient work is carried out to ensure that further decay does not take place, but improvements are not generally made. The damaged and weathered quality is important to the understanding of the historical quality of the place.

Restoration is the process of returning the building to its original condition. This often involves the use of techniques and materials from the original period with the aim of ensuring that the building looks as it was when originally constructed. This can be a fairly controversial approach, not just because the building itself may have gone through a series of different forms and identities, so it is difficult to know which one to select, but also, restoration can be a process that contests history; it can actively deny the life of the building. It is, however, relatively common; the owners and the users of the building want a pristine building.

Renovation is the practice of repairing and updating a building to make it suitable for contemporary use. The function does not change, just the method in which the building is used.

Adaptation is the process of making large-scale changes to a building. These may be structural as well as aesthetic and often are made to facilitate a new function.

Of course, a number of different methods can be used together to facilitate the conservation of the building. For example, within the tiny slot of what was once exterior space, Julian Harrap Architects carried out careful and painstaking restoration work upon the facades of the original buildings of the Royal Academy in London. Foster Associates then embarked upon the remodelling or adaptation of the space, for it to become the entrance to the Sackler Gallery.

All of the essays in this chapter were written in reaction to the whole scale destruction that has been wreaked upon the western world over the last two hundred years, whether this was the casual destruction of the early industrial age, the havoc of the Second World War or the almost callous disregard for the historic elements of the urban fabric by the modernist society.

Active conservation is actually a relatively recent subject, modern really. In previous eras, there were two basic approaches to conservation. Buildings that were considered to be of value were either simply added to in the style of the day, or restored in a manner that paid no respect to the age or weathering. Reuse often took place without regard for the history or culture of the society that constructed it; for example, the amphitheatre in Luca, Italy, when no longer required, the structure was simply absorbed into the fabric of the city. Another example of the first approach is Rufford Old Hall in Lancashire, UK, which was constructed in the late fifteenth century and is a fine example of English mediaeval architecture. It has an additional wing dating from 1662 and a further extension dating to 1821. Although some attention has been paid to the picturesque, little was done to integrate the styles of architecture; the different eras simply exist next to each other. This method actively appreciates history and embraces the values of each society that contributed to the evolution of the building.

The second method of conservation was much more vexing to nineteenth century aesthetes. Up until about the middle of the century, the prevailing attitude was for the weathered or worn areas of the building to be simply rebuilt in the original style. This style of conservation was advocated by the French architect Eugene Viollet-le-Duc, who felt that he was fully authorised to *fill-in-the-blanks* of damaged buildings. For him, the building could (and indeed *should*) be restored to as good a state as possible. His ambition was for the building to be restored to a condition that was "pristine", which may indeed be a condition that might never have actually existed

This type of restoration began to be regarded as a false description of the thing destroyed. **John Ruskin**, who was deeply saddened by the level of casual neglect and destruction, especially such as he encountered in Venice, was a vociferous critic of this practice. He argued that "simple copying is palpably impossible". The workers of the nineteenth century could not understand the attitude and thinking of the mediaeval craftsmen and therefore were not in a position to make the replacement. Restoration destroyed the spirit of the previous age and was merely a false description of the thing that was replaced. He called for care and maintenance, arguing that the "buildings belong partly to the generation that constructed it and partly to those who have subsequently occupied them, but the present generation has no right to tear it down or damage it, just care for it".

William Morris, building upon the work of Ruskin, founded **SPAB** (the Society for the Protection of Ancient Buildings) in 1877. They continued the fight against the zealous restoration practices that were causing too much of the historic fabric of ancient buildings to be removed. Within their manifesto they "call upon those who have to deal with them, to put Protection in the place of Restoration".

Of course, Viollet-le-Duc, Ruskin and Morris were not the only theorists who offered opinions upon the correct approach to conservation. The Italian architect Camillo Boito was a bold defender of the idea of the monument-as-document, while Gustavo Giovannoni and Luca Beltrami tried to find a middle ground between the extreme approaches. A consequence of these differing approaches was the formation of the **Athens Charter** in 1931, which attempted to set down a definitive approach to the subject. The **Venice Charter** followed this in 1972. The texts by **Alberto Grimoldi**, "Architecture as Reparation", and **James Strike**, "The Field of Study", are both good surveys of the historical attitudes towards conservation, Grimoldi from the Italian perspective and Strike from the British.

The destruction of a number of much loved and respected buildings, including Euston Arch, Penn Station and Les Halles, became important moments in the rise of the popularity of the conservation movement. A number of important books were also published that reinforced the plea for respect for the historic and eclectic nature of the city. Jane Jacobs in her influential book *The Death and Life of the American Cities* (1916) declared that "cities need old buildings so badly it is probably impossible for vigorous streets and districts to grow without them".[1] Colin Rowe and Fred Koetter in their seminal book of 1978, *Collage City*, declared that "the city is a didactic instrument",[2] and Aldo Rossi attributed the soul of the city to memory. These, and of course many more, discuss how important it is to retain existing buildings, although not always agreeing upon the best method to go about this.

Modernist buildings are still not necessarily valued and are rarely considered for reuse. Just as we regret the unenlightened destruction of pre-modernist structures, so we will rue the loss of many creditable twentieth century constructions. One such building is the Bus Station in Preston, Lancashire, UK. It is a magnificently heroic concrete structure, incredibly long with upward curving linear edges and spiralling entrances, and is reputably the biggest Bus Station in Europe. Attitudes toward public transport have radically changed since it was constructed, and in the digital age, a small city no longer needs 86 bus-bays, so it is due to be demolished. Adaptation is not an option that the city council are prepared to consider, so it is doomed to go, to be replaced with an uninspiring clone town shopping centre. It is a loss equal to the destruction of many eighteenth and nineteenth century buildings, which future generations will look on with great sadness and disappointment.

The heritage industry in all western societies now places great emphasis upon the preservation and reuse of existing structures. Often this approach is more akin to that of Viollet-le-Duc: the existing building is repaired, parts of it replaced, cleaned and the whole thing repainted, so that often, these structures do indeed look more new, more pristine than when originally constructed.

Conservation is a controversial subject, not just in the manner in which it is carried out, but also the selection of the buildings to be conserved. Attitudes towards the subject are continuously changing and it promises to become more difficult as the need for sustainable redevelopment becomes greater and our attitude towards the past is reassessed.

Sally Stone

References

1. Jacobs, Jane. *The Death and Life of the Great American Cities*. Random House, 1961.
2. Rowe, Colin and Koetter, Fred. *Collage City*. The MIT Press, 1984.

John Ruskin (1819–1900)

John Ruskin was a British art critic and social thinker. His ideas inspired the Arts and Crafts Movement and the foundation of the National Trust, the Society for the Protection of Ancient Buildings, and the Labour Movement. He fiercely attacked the worst aspects of industrialisation and actively promoted art education and museum access for the working classes. Throughout his life he undertook extensive tours of Britain and the Continent, providing material for literary works such as *The Poetry of Architecture*, *The Seven Lamps of Architecture*, *The Stones of Venice*, *Mornings in Florence* and *The Bible of Amiens*.

The Industrial Revolution and the advent of mass-produced cheap goods greatly troubled him; he saw within both architecture and society the replacement of strong moral elements with cheap badly made imitations. The following quote, which sums this up this attitude, is attributed to him:

"There is scarcely anything in the world that some man cannot make a little worse, and sell a little more cheaply. The person who buys on price alone is this man's lawful prey."

Building Study: Sackler Galleries, Royal Academy

London, UK
1991
Julian Harrap Architects, Foster Associates

Foster Associates with Julian Harrap Architects were commissioned to design the Sackler Galleries in an unused attic space at the Royal Academy in London. This was a complex process of conservation and adaptation; Harraps conducted the sensitive restoration of the existing building while Fosters designed new elements to facilitate the circulation and the new galleries.

The Royal Academy itself is an extremely complicated set of buildings and extensions. Sir John Denham designed the front section, Burlington House, as a family home in 1665, a Palladian facade by Colen Campbell was added in 1715 and Sydney Smirke completed the Garden House in 1867. These are the major changes to a set of buildings that have been extended or adapted fourteen times.

The Sackler Galleries are accessed through what was once a narrow gap between the rear of the original building and the Garden House extension. Into this fine and slender slot of space was inserted a contrasting steel and glass circulation route. However, before these new elements were added, the facades of the original buildings were completely restored by Julian Harrap Architects. The quality of the conservation is superb and it has to be because the past is directly encountered; the new glass stairs mean that the visitors are in very close contact with an area of the building that would normally be seen from a distance, from the ground below.

The project involved the removal of drainpipes and other extraneous items, repair to heavily damaged walls, the blocking up of non-original windows, the restoration or replacement of the original windows and the re-rendering and painting of the facades. This project follows the theories of Viollet-le-Duc; the restoration has brought the buildings to a condition as if just constructed, possibly more faultless and immaculate than then. The facades of the buildings now look more new than when constructed, as pristine as the contemporary circulation and gallery spaces.

39
The Lamp of Memory

John Ruskin

Source: *The Seven Lamps of Architecture*, Dover, 1989, pp. 353–360. Published with permission of Dover Publications Inc.

Neither by the public, nor by those who have the care of public monuments, is the true meaning of the word *restoration* understood. It means the most total destruction which a building can suffer: a destruction out of which no remnants can be gathered: a destruction accompanied with false description of the thing destroyed.[1] Do not let us deceive ourselves in this important matter; it is *impossible*, as impossible as to raise the dead, to restore anything that has ever been great or beautiful in architecture. That which I have above insisted upon as the life of the whole, that spirit which is given only by the hand and eye of the workman, can never be recalled. Another spirit may be given by another time, and it is then a new building; but the spirit of the dead workman cannot be summoned up, and commanded to direct other hands, and other thoughts. And as for direct and simple copying, it is palpably impossible. What copying can there be of surfaces that have been worn half an inch down? The whole finish of the work was in the half inch that is gone; if you attempt to restore that finish, you do it conjectur-ally; if you copy what is left, granting fidelity to be possible, (and what care, or watchfulness, or cost can secure it,) how is the new work better than the old? There was yet in the old *some* life, some mysterious suggestion of what it had been, and of what it had lost; some sweetness in the gentle lines which rain and sun had wrought. There can be none in the brute hardness of the new carving. Look at the animals as an instance of living work, and suppose the markings of the scales and hair once worn away, or the wrinkles of the brows, and who shall ever restore them? The first step to restoration, (I have seen it, and that again and again—seen it on the Baptistery of Pisa, seen it on the Casa d'Oro at Venice, seen it on the Cathedral of Lisieux,) is to dash the old work to pieces; the second is usually to put up the cheapest and basest imitation which can escape detection, but in all cases, however careful, and however laboured, an imitation still, a cold model of such parts as *can* be modelled, with conjectural supplements; and my experience has as yet furnished me with only one instance, that of the Palais de Justice at Rouen, in which even this, the utmost degree of fidelity which is possible, has been attained, or even attempted.

XIX. Do not let us talk then of restoration. The thing is a Lie from beginning to end. You may make a model of a building as you may of a corpse, and your model may have the shell of the old walls within it as your cast might have the skeleton, with what advantage I neither see nor care: but the old building is destroyed, and that more totally and mercilessly than if it had sunk into a heap of dust, or melted into a mass of clay: more has been gleaned out of desolated Nineveh than ever will be out of re-built Milan. But, it is said, there may come a necessity for restoration! Granted. Look the necessity full in the face, and understand it on its own terms. It is a necessity for destruction. Accept it as such, pull the building down, throw its stones into neglected corners, make ballast of them, or mortar, if you will; but do it honestly, and do not set up a Lie in their place. And look that necessity in the face before it comes, and you may prevent it. The principle of modern times (a principle which, I believe, at least in France, to be *systematically acted on by the masons*, in order to find them-selves work, as the abbey of St. Ouen was pulled down by the magistrates of the town by way of giving work to some vagrants,) is to neglect buildings first, and restore them afterwards. Take proper care of your monuments, and you will not need to restore them. A few sheets of lead put in time upon a roof, a few dead leaves and sticks swept in time out of a water-course, will save both roof and walls from ruin. Watch an old building with an anxious care; guard it as best you may, and at *any* cost, from every influence of dilapidation. Count its stones as you would jewels of a crown; set watches about it as if at the gates of a besieged city; bind it together with iron where it loosens; stay it with timber where it declines; do not care about the unsightliness of the aid: better a crutch than a lost limb; and do this tenderly, and reverently, and continually, and many a generation will still be born and pass away beneath its shadow. Its evil day must come at last; but let it come declaredly and openly, and let no dishonouring and false substitute deprive it of the funeral offices of memory.

XX. Of more wanton or ignorant ravage it is vain to speak; my words will not reach those who commit them,[2] and yet, be it heard or not, I must not leave the truth unstated, that it is again no question of expediency or feeling whether we shall preserve the buildings of past times or not. *We have no right whatever to touch them.* They are not ours. They belong partly to those who built them, and partly to all the generations of mankind who are to follow us. The dead have still their right in them: that which they laboured for, the praise of achievement of the expression of religious feeling, or whatsoever else it might be which in those buildings they intended to be permanent, we have no right to obliterate. What we have ourselves built, we are at liberty to throw down; but what other men gave their strength and wealth and life to accomplish, their right over does not pass away with their death; still less is the right to the use of what they have left vested in us only. It belongs to all their successors. It may hereafter be a subject of sorrow, or a cause of injury, to millions, that we have consulted our present convenience by casting down such buildings as we choose to dispense with. That sorrow, that loss, we have no right to inflict. Did the cathedral of Avranches belong to the mob who destroyed it, any more than it did to us, who walk in sorrow to and fro over its foundation? Neither does any building whatever belong to those mobs who do violence to it. For a mob it is, and must be always; it matters not whether enraged, or in deliberate folly; whether countless, or sitting in committees; the people who destroy anything causelessly are a mob, and Architecture is always destroyed causelessly. A fair building is necessarily worth the ground it stands upon, and will be so until Central Africa and America shall have become as populous as Middlesex: nor is any cause whatever valid as a ground for its destruction. If ever valid, certainly not now, when the place both of the past and future is too much usurped in our minds by the restless and discontented present. The very quietness of nature is gradually withdrawn from us; thousands who once in their necessarily prolonged travel were subjected to an influence, from the silent sky and slumbering fields, more effectual than known or confessed, now bear with them even there the ceaseless fever of their life; and along the iron veins that traverse the frame of our country, beat and flow the fiery pulses of its exertion, hotter and faster every hour. All vitality is concentrated through those throbbing arteries into the central cities; the country is passed over like a green sea by narrow bridges, and we are thrown back in continually closer crowds upon the city gates. The only influence which can in any wise *there* take the place of that of the woods and fields, is the power of ancient Architecture. Do not part with it for the sake of the formal square, or of the fenced and planted walk, nor of the goodly street nor opened quay. The pride of a city is not in these. Leave them to the crowd; but remember that there will surely be some within the circuit of the disquieted walls who would ask for some other spots than these wherein to walk; for some other forms to meet their sight familiarly: like him who sat so often where the sun struck from the west, to watch the lines of the dome of Florence drawn on the deep sky, or like those, his Hosts, who could bear daily to behold, from their palace chambers, the places where their fathers lay at rest, at the meeting of the dark streets of Verona.

NOTES

1   False, also, in the manner of parody,—the most loathsome manner of falsehood.
2   No, indeed!—any more wasted words than mine throughout life, or bread cast on more bitter waters, I never heard of. This closing paragraph of the sixth chapter is the best, I think, in the book,—and the vainest.

40
The SPAB Manifesto

Source: www.spab.org.uk

The manifesto of the SPAB was written by William Morris and other founder members and issued in 1877. Although produced in response to the conservation problems of the 19th century, the manifesto extends protection to "all times and styles" and remains to this day the philosophical basis for the Society's work. Applicants for SPAB membership must sign to say that they agree with the manifesto's conservation principles.

"A society coming before the public with such a name as that above written must needs explain how, and why, it proposes to protect those ancient buildings which, to most people doubtless, seem to have so many and such excellent protectors. This, then, is the explanation we offer.

No doubt within the last fifty years a new interest, almost like another sense, has arisen in these ancient monuments of art; and they have become the subject of one of the most interesting of studies, and of an enthusiasm, religious, historical, artistic, which is one of the undoubted gains of our time; yet we think that if the present treatment of them be continued, our descendants will find them useless for study and chilling to enthusiasm. We think that those last fifty years of knowledge and attention have done more for their destruction than all the foregoing centuries of revolution, violence and contempt.

For Architecture, long decaying, died out, as a popular art at least, just as the knowledge of mediaeval art was born. So that the civilised world of the nineteenth century has no style of its own amidst its wide knowledge of the styles of other centuries. From this lack and this gain arose in men's minds the strange idea of the Restoration of ancient buildings; and a strange and most fatal idea, which by its very name implies that it is possible to strip from a building this, that, and the other part of its history – of its life that is – and then to stay the hand at some arbitrary point, and leave it still historical, living, and even as it once was.

In early times this kind of forgery was impossible, because knowledge failed the builders, or

perhaps because instinct held them back. If repairs were needed, if ambition or piety pricked on to change, that change was of necessity wrought in the unmistakable fashion of the time; a church of the eleventh century might be added to or altered in the twelfth, thirteenth, fourteenth, fifteenth, sixteenth, or even the seventeenth or eighteenth centuries; but every change, whatever history it destroyed, left history in the gap, and was alive with the spirit of the deeds done midst its fashioning. The result of all this was often a building in which the many changes, though harsh and visible enough, were, by their very contrast, interesting and instructive and could by no possibility mislead. But those who make the changes wrought in our day under the name of Restoration, while professing to bring back a building to the best time of its history, have no guide but each his own individual whim to point out to them what is admirable and what contemptible; while the very nature of their task compels them to destroy something and to supply the gap by imagining what the earlier builders should or might have done. Moreover, in the course of this double process of destruction and addition, the whole surface of the building is necessarily tampered with; so that the appearance of antiquity is taken away from such old parts of the fabric as are left, and there is no laying to rest in the spectator the suspicion of what may have been lost; and in short, a feeble and lifeless forgery is the final result of all the wasted labour. It is sad to say, that in this manner most of the bigger Minsters, and a vast number of more humble buildings, both in England and on the Continent, have been dealt with by men of talent often, and worthy of better employment, but deaf to the claims of poetry and history in the highest sense of the words.

For what is left we plead before our architects themselves, before the official guardians of buildings, and before the public generally, and we pray them to remember how much is gone of the religion, thought and manners of time past, never by almost universal consent, to be Restored; and to consider whether it be possible to Restore those buildings, the living spirit of which, it cannot be too often repeated, was an inseparable part of that religion and thought, and those past manners. For our part we assure them fearlessly, that of all the Restorations yet undertaken, the worst have meant the reckless stripping a building of some of its most interesting material features; whilst the best have their exact analogy in the Restoration of an old picture, where the partly-perished work of the ancient craftsmaster has been made neat and smooth by the tricky hand of some unoriginal and thoughtless hack of today. If, for the rest, it be asked us to specify what kind of amount of art, style, or other interest in a building makes it worth protecting, we answer, anything which can be looked on as artistic, picturesque, historical, antique, or substantial: any work, in short, over which educated, artistic people would think it worth while to argue at all.

It is for all these buildings, therefore, of all times and styles, that we plead, and call upon those who have to deal with them, to put Protection in the place of Restoration, to stave off decay by daily care, to prop a perilous wall or mend a leaky roof by such means as are obviously meant for support or covering, and show no pretence of other art, and otherwise to resist all tampering with either the fabric or ornament of the building as it stands; if it has become inconvenient for its present use, to raise another building rather than alter or enlarge the old one; in fine to treat our ancient buildings as monuments of a bygone art, created by bygone manners, that modern art cannot meddle with without destroying.

Thus, and thus only, shall we escape the reproach of our learning being turned into a snare to us; thus, and thus only can we protect our ancient buildings, and hand them down instructive and venerable to those that come after us."

41
The Athens Charter for the Restoration of Historic Monuments

Adopted at the First International Congress of Architects and Technicians of Historic Monuments, Athens 1931

Source: www.icomos.org/en/component/content/article/179-articles-en-francais/ressources/charters-and-standards/167-the-athens-charter-for-the-restoration-of-historic-monuments

At the Congress in Athens the following seven main resolutions were made and called "Carta del Restauro":

1. International organizations for Restoration on operational and advisory levels are to be established.
2. Proposed Restoration projects are to be subjected to knowledgeable criticism to prevent mistakes which will cause loss of character and historical values to the structures.
3. Problems of preservation of historic sites are to be solved by legislation at national level for all countries.
4. Excavated sites which are not subject to immediate restoration should be reburied for protection.
5. Modern techniques and materials may be used in restoration work.
6. Historical sites are to be given strict custodial protection.
7. Attention should be given to the protection of areas surrounding historic sites.

GENERAL CONCLUSIONS OF THE ATHENS CONFERENCE

I. Doctrines. General Principles

The Conference heard the statement of the general principles and doctrines relating to the protection of monuments.

Whatever may be the variety of concrete cases, each of which are open to a different solution, the Conference noted that there predominates in the different countries represented a general tendency to abandon restorations *in toto* and to avoid the attendant dangers by initiating a system of regular and permanent maintenance calculated to ensure the preservation of the buildings.

When, as the result of decay or destruction, restoration appears to be indispensable, it recommends that the historic and artistic work of the past should be respected, without excluding the style of any given period.

The Conference recommends that the occupation of buildings, which ensures the continuity of their life, should be maintained but that they should be used for a purpose which respects their historic or artistic character.

II. Administrative and Legislative Measures Regarding Historical Monuments

The Conference heard the statement of legislative measures devised to protect monuments of artistic, historic or scientific interest and belonging to the different countries.

It unanimously approved the general tendency which, in this connection, recognises a certain right of the community in regard to private ownership.

It noted that the differences existing between these legislative measures were due to the difficulty of reconciling public law with the rights of individuals.

Consequently, while approving the general tendency of these measures, the Conference is of opinion that they should be in keeping with local circumstances and with the trend of public opinion, so that the least possible opposition may be encountered, due allowance being made for the sacrifices which the owners of property may be called upon to make in the general interest.

It recommends that the public authorities in each country be empowered to take conservatory measures in cases of emergency.

It earnestly hopes that the International Museums Office will publish a repertory and a comparative table of the legislative measures in force in the different countries and that this information will be kept up to date.

III. Aesthetic Enhancement of Ancient Monuments

The Conference recommends that, in the construction of buildings, the character and external aspect of the cities in which they are to be erected should be respected, especially in the neighbourhood of ancient monuments, where the surroundings should be given special consideration. Even certain groupings and certain particularly picturesque perspective treatment should be preserved.

A study should also be made of the ornamental vegetation most suited to certain monuments or groups of monuments from the point of view of preserving their ancient character. It specially recommends the suppression of all forms of publicity, of the erection of unsightly telegraph poles and the exclusion of all noisy factories and even of tall shafts in the neighbourhood of artistic and historic monuments.

IV. Restoration of Monuments

The experts heard various communications concerning the use of modern materials for the consolidation of ancient monuments. They approved the judicious use of all the resources at the disposal of modern technique and more especially of reinforced concrete.

They specified that this work of consolidation should whenever possible be concealed in order that the aspect and character of the restored monument may be preserved.

They recommended their adoption more particularly in cases where their use makes it possible to avoid the dangers of dismantling and reinstating the portions to be preserved.

V. The Deterioration of Ancient Monuments

The Conference noted that, in the conditions of present day life, monuments throughout the world were being threatened to an ever-increasing degree by atmospheric agents.

Apart from the customary precautions and the methods successfully applied in the preservation of monumental statuary in current practice, it was impossible, in view of the complexity of cases and with the knowledge at present available, to formulate any general rules.

The Conference recommends:

1. That, in each country, the architects and curators of monuments should collaborate with specialists in the physical, chemical, and natural sciences with a view to determining the methods to be adopted in specific cases;
2. That the International Museums Office should keep itself informed of the work being done in each country in this field and that mention should be made thereof in the publications of the Office.

With regard to the preservation of monumental sculpture, the Conference is of opinion that the removal of works of art from the surroundings for which they were designed is, *in principle*, to be discouraged. It recommends, by way of precaution, the preservation of original models whenever these still exist or if this proves impossible, the taking of casts.

VI. The Technique of Conservation

The Conference is gratified to note that the principles and technical considerations set forth in the different detailed communications are inspired by the same idea, namely:

In the case of ruins, scrupulous conservation is necessary, and steps should be taken to reinstate any original fragments that may be recovered (anastylosis), whenever this is possible; the new materials used for this purpose should in all cases be recognisable. When the preservation of ruins brought to light in the course of excavations is found to be impossible, the Conference recommends that they be buried, accurate records being of course taken before filling-in operations are undertaken.

It should be unnecessary to mention that the technical work undertaken in connection with the excavation and preservation of ancient monuments calls for close collaboration between the archaeologist and the architect.

With regard to other monuments, the experts unanimously agreed that, before any consolidation or partial restoration is undertaken, a thorough analysis should be made of the defects and the nature of the decay of these monuments. They recognised that each case needed to be treated individually.

VII. The Conservation of Monuments and International Collaboration

a) Technical and moral co-operation

The Conference, convinced that the question of the conservation of the artistic and archaeological property of mankind is one that interests the community of the States, which are wardens of civilisation,

Hopes that the States, acting in the spirit of the Covenant of the League of Nations, will collaborate with each other on an ever-increasing scale and in a more concrete manner with a view to furthering the preservation of artistic and historic monuments;

Considers it highly desirable that qualified institutions and associations should, without in any manner whatsoever prejudicing international public law, be given an opportunity of manifesting their interest in the protection of works of art in which civilisation has been expressed to the highest degree and which would seem to be threatened with destruction;

Expresses the wish that requests to attain this end, submitted to the Intellectual Co-operation Organisation of the League of Nations, be recommended to the earnest attention of the States.

It will be for the International Committee on Intellectual Co-operation, after an enquiry conducted by the International Museums Office and after having collected all relevant information, more particularly from the National Committee on Intellectual Co-operation concerned, to express an opinion on the expediency of the steps to be taken and on the procedure to be followed in each individual case.

The members of the Conference, after having visited in the course of their deliberations and during the study cruise which they were able to make on this occasion, a number of excavation sites and ancient Greek monuments, unanimously paid a tribute to the Greek Government, which, for many years past, has been itself responsible for extensive works and, at the same time, has accepted the collaboration of archaeologists and experts from every country.

The members of the Conference there saw an example of activity which can but contribute to the realisation of the aims of intellectual co-operation, the need for which manifested itself during their work.

b) The role of education in the respect of monuments

The Conference, firmly convinced that the best guarantee in the matter of the preservation of monuments and works of art derives from the respect and attachment of the peoples themselves;

Considering that these feelings can very largely be promoted by appropriate action on the part of public authorities;

Recommends that educators should urge children and young people to abstain from disfiguring monuments of every description and that they should teach them to take a greater and more general interest in the protection of these concrete testimonies of all ages of civilisation.

c) Value of international documentation

The Conference expresses the wish that:

1. Each country, or the institutions created or recognised competent for this purpose, publish an inventory of ancient monuments, with photographs and explanatory notes;
2. Each country constitute official records which shall contain all documents relating to its historic monuments;
3. Each country deposit copies of its publications on artistic and historic monuments with the International Museums Office;
4. The Office devote a portion of its publications to articles on the general processes and methods employed in the preservation of historic monuments;
5. The Office study the best means of utilising the information so centralised.

42
The Venice Charter

International Charter for the Conservation and Restoration of Monuments and Sites

Source: www.icomos.org/en/component/content/article/179-articles-en-francais/ressources/charters-and-standards/157-the-venice-charter

[Preamble]

Imbued with a message from the past, the historic monuments of generations of people remain to the present day as living witnesses of their age-old traditions. People are becoming more and more conscious of the unity of human values and regard ancient monuments as a common heritage. The common responsibility to safeguard them for future generations is recognized. It is our duty to hand them on in the full richness of their authenticity.

It is essential that the principles guiding the preservation and restoration of ancient buildings should be agreed and be laid down on an international basis, with each country being responsible for applying the plan within the framework of its own culture and traditions.

By defining these basic principles for the first time, the Athens Charter of 1931 contributed towards the development of an extensive international movement which has assumed concrete form in national documents, in the work of ICOM and UNESCO and in the establishment by the latter of the International Centre for the Study of the Preservation and the Restoration of Cultural Property. Increasing awareness and critical study have been brought to bear on problems which have continually become more complex and varied; now the time has come to examine the Charter afresh in order to make a thorough study of the principles involved and to enlarge its scope in a new document.

Accordingly, the IInd International Congress of Architects and Technicians of Historic Monuments, which met in Venice from May 25th to 31st 1964, approved the following text:

DEFINITIONS

ARTICLE 1. The concept of an historic monument embraces not only the single architectural work but also the urban or rural setting in which is found the evidence of a particular civilization, a significant development or an historic event. This applies not only to great works of art but also to more modest works of the past which have acquired cultural significance with the passing of time.

ARTICLE 2. The conservation and restoration of monuments must have recourse to all the sciences and techniques which can contribute to the study and safeguarding of the architectural heritage.

AIM

ARTICLE 3. The intention in conserving and restoring monuments is to safeguard them no less as works of art than as historical evidence.

CONSERVATION

ARTICLE 4. It is essential to the conservation of monuments that they be maintained on a permanent basis.

ARTICLE 5. The conservation of monuments is always facilitated by making use of them for some socially useful purpose. Such use is therefore desirable but it must not change the layout or decoration of the building. It is within these limits only that modifications demanded by a change of function should be envisaged and may be permitted.

ARTICLE 6. The conservation of a monument implies preserving a setting which is not out of scale. Wherever the traditional setting exists, it must be kept. No new construction, demolition or modification which would alter the relations of mass and color must be allowed.

ARTICLE 7. A monument is inseparable from the history to which it bears witness and from the setting in which it occurs. The moving of all or part of a monument cannot be allowed except where the safeguarding of that monument demands it or where it is justified by national or international interest of paramount importance.

ARTICLE 8. Items of sculpture, painting or decoration which form an integral part of a monument may only be removed from it if this is the sole means of ensuring their preservation.

RESTORATION

ARTICLE 9. The process of restoration is a highly specialized operation. Its aim is to preserve and reveal the aesthetic and historic value of the monument and is based on respect for original material and authentic documents. It must stop at the point where conjecture begins, and in this case moreover any extra work which is indispensable must be distinct from the architectural composition and must bear a contemporary stamp. The restoration in any case must be preceded and followed by an archaeological and historical study of the monument.

ARTICLE 10. Where traditional techniques prove inadequate, the consolidation of a monument can be achieved by the use of any modern technique for conservation and construction, the efficacy of which has been shown by scientific data and proved by experience.

ARTICLE 11. The valid contributions of all periods to the building of a monument must be respected, since unity of style is not the aim of a restoration. When a building includes the superimposed work of different periods, the revealing of the underlying state can only be justified in exceptional circumstances and when what is removed is of little interest and the material which is brought to light is of great historical, archaeological or aesthetic value, and its state of preservation good enough to justify the action. Evaluation of the importance of the elements involved and the decision as to what may be destroyed cannot rest solely on the individual in charge of the work.

ARTICLE 12. Replacements of missing parts must integrate harmoniously with the whole, but at the same time must be distinguishable from the original so that restoration does not falsify the artistic or historic evidence.

ARTICLE 13. Additions cannot be allowed except in so far as they do not detract from the interesting parts of the building, its traditional setting, the balance of its composition and its relation with its surroundings.

HISTORIC SITES

ARTICLE 14. The sites of monuments must be the object of special care in order to safeguard their integrity and ensure that they are cleared and presented in a seemly manner. The work of conservation and restoration carried out in such places should be inspired by the principles set forth in the foregoing articles.

EXCAVATIONS

ARTICLE 15. Excavations should be carried out in accordance with scientific standards and the recommendation defining international principles to be applied in the case of archaeological excavation adopted by UNESCO in 1956.

Ruins must be maintained and measures necessary for the permanent conservation and protection of architectural features and of objects discovered must be taken. Furthermore, every means must be taken to facilitate the understanding of the monument and to reveal it without ever distorting its meaning.

All reconstruction work should however be ruled out *"a priori."* Only anastylosis, that is to say, the reassembling of existing but dismembered parts can be permitted. The material used for integration should always be recognizable and its use should be the least that will ensure the conservation of a monument and the reinstatement of its form.

PUBLICATION

ARTICLE 16. In all works of preservation, restoration or excavation, there should always be precise documentation in the form of analytical and critical reports, illustrated with drawings and photographs. Every stage of the work of clearing, consolidation, rearrangement and integration, as well as technical and formal features identified during the course of the work, should be included. This record should be placed in the archives of a public institution and made available to research workers. It is recommended that the report should be published.

The following persons took part in the work of the Committee for drafting the International

Charter for the Conservation and Restoration of Monuments:

Piero Gazzola (Italy), Chairman
Raymond Lemaire (Belgium), Reporter
Jose Bassegoda-Nonell (Spain)
Luis Benavente (Portugal)
Djurdje Boskovic (Yugoslavia)
Hiroshi Daifuku (UNESCO)
P.L. de Vrieze (Netherlands)
Harald Langberg (Demmark)
Mario Matteucci (Italy)
Jean Merlet (France)

Carlos Flores Marini (Mexico)
Roberto Pane (Italy)
S.C.J. Pavel (Czechoslovakia)
Paul Philippot (ICCROM)
Victor Pimentel (Peru)
Harold Plenderleith (ICCROM)
Deoclecio Redig de Campos (Vatican)
Jean Sonnier (France)
Francois Sorlin (France)
Eustathios Stikas (Greece)
Mrs. Gertrud Tripp (Austria)
Jan Zachwatovicz (Poland)
Mustafa S. Zbiss (Tunisia)

43
Architecture as Reparation
Notes on Restoration in Architecture

Alberto Grimoldi

Source: *Lotus International,* no. 46, 1985, pp. 117–122

From "old towns and new building" to "fitting into the existing environment" and "analogue cities,"[1] just to stick to the Italian scene, the theme of the relationship between "old" or "ancient" and "new" has enjoyed seventy years of incessant and highly comprehensible limelight. A vast audience of public administrators, businessmen, landlords and "technicians" (surveyors, engineers, architects) were seeking reliable and scientifically neutral advice on how to do away with the existing cities and replace them with living conditions and structures of worse and worse quality. A "science of destructions" has flowered in response to this demand, a whole set of attempts, sometimes naive, sometimes more learned and sophisticated, to reformulate the most appropriate chapters of architectural literature on the basis of substitution, of destruction as incontrovertible premise. This attempt at re-use of verbal pre-existences followed two major trends. The first harks back to the greatest Italian theorist of the 19th century, Camillo Boito and his popular theory concerning the differentiation of adjuncts.[2] The entire output of "modern" Italian museums since the war can be traced back to this. When Carlo Scarpa was given the task of organizing the National Gallery of Sicily in 1954, its future home, Palazzo Abatellis, incorporated in the Monastery of the Pietà for centuries, had already been reconstructed as an unlikely Gothic-Aragonese residence.[3] Against this background the architect used elements of finishing and decoration in such a way that the figurative culture of the "historical avant-garde movements" could be recognized in the building's interior. He achieved this result thanks to his ability to make use of the most sophisticated traditional building techniques, detached from the design to which they customarily gave rise. Highly accurate craftsmanship and the most traditional materials play an ever greater part in Scarpa's work, but he adopts

glossy stucco without its customary compartments, the seminato without its background painting or flourishes. In this logic of design it is indispensable to have a term of comparison against which the differences can be measured. A past revised by eclectic architects, especially late eclectic ones, lends itself well to this: a hypertrophic, scenographic past, answering more to what ordinary (and illustrious) people consider specific to a far-off age.

The materials called on to serve as a go-between, to ensure the "rapport," the "dialectic," are either traditional ones used to shape new forms or "new" ones (usually that very old material iron) used according to a design that harks back (in simplified fashion) to patterns and styles of the era on which one wishes to comment. Others opt for literal quotation, but taken out of the context of its usual spaces and references. In Genoa's Palazzo Bianco, partially reconstructed by Franco Albini,[4] the octagons of black slate and white Carrara marble spread out from the staircases and porches, to which they were limited in the 17th and 18th century, to the halls, where they define a basic grid against which to gauge the order (and the highly studied disorder) of the pedestals. The quality and the meaning of these interventions can only be grasped in the new parts, in the additions and substitutions, in which the architect believes his task to be over. So restoration means the superimpositon of a design, the "project," on a ground, walls and finishings, whose fate is wholly subordinate to the requirements of the project itself, to the intention of making a contemporary "mark."

These more or less subtle games played with assonances and differentiations go beyond the parts of a building to involve the parts of a city. On this scale especially, they become a code for evoking the densest periods of culture and capacity for progress in individual urban contexts, periods which in Italy rarely coincide with the heroic years of the "historical avantgarde movements."[5] The result has been the exceptional liveliness of Italian design and construction in the fifties. And yet the individual solutions, the details, have been put forward by an apologetic journalism, as words of a repeatable language. Hence the formation of genuine regional schools, and the fact that these aging vocabularies, managed by the disciples or schools of dead or retired masters, are still rampant today. Even the authorities in charge of preservation have got used to them and, now that they have been superseded, accept these languages as alternatives to a more or less clumsy form of mimetism. For the public and those involved in the work, a good restoration is still a matter of coming up with a more or less shrewd and erudite harmony of fittings and colours, and above all new finishings (floors, walls, fixtures) in order to carry off prodigious feats of transformation: converting an underground stable into a bridge club, the crypt of a tomb into furniture stores, a slaughter-house into a library. This is a skill which wins admiration (and suggests, for those who wish to see them, the "magnificent opportunities and roads" of man). On the level of method it extends and radicalizes the experience of converting a fortress, monastery or palace into a museum. Today fashion demands a certain amount of bibliographical work, the display of learned or curious references. It is no longer possible to rely on intuition or taste; a diversified and apparently cultured system of allusions is necessary. The most shrewd and well-informed clients – which means private ones – are no longer content with red drapes and double T-irons. And yet a knowledge of what already exists, of its peculiar traits, its basis and its deterioration, still seems to be a wholly secondary part of the stock in trade of architects.

Another tendency which was already trying to respond to the glaring deficiencies of the "dominant taste" at the end of the fifties goes back to the concept of type. Two sorts of appeal to type exist, generally in conflict with one another. The first, more literal and prescriptive one, limits its field of application to individual buildings, and has enjoyed great success in town-planning regulation and legislation.[6] This typology, underlying the "conservative reconstructions" and "typological restoration" of Brescia and Bologna, consists in the identification of a number of superficial recurrences of forms, finishings, materials and dimensions in the building patterns of individual cities, with a view to defining widely applicable and easily verifiable parameters around which to

organize substitutions. A second more precise and wide-ranging appeal to typology goes beyond the relationship between the old and the new to construct an entire theory of architecture. The concept of type is the key to seeing what has been built as a reality from which to extrapolate laws analogous to those which a positivistic scientist would induce from observation of nature. The aim of these laws was to be able to repeat the phenomena described, and exploit their consequences, and on the other hand to contribute to the creation of autonomous disciplines, in which each law was coordinated with others in an apparently logical construction that replaced the extemporaneous and contradictory sequence of acquisitions on the basis of which those fields of knowledge had been effectively formed.[7] Although the entire "Tendency" prefers to refer back to De Saussure,[8] the architect who comes to mind is Eugène Emmanuel Viollet-le-Duc, and in particular the complexity and precision of rules that he assembled in order to demonstrate how Gothic architecture was governed by invariable and rationally recognizable laws, as if a sort of internal logic could be reconstructed for each building.[9] All this served to confirm the reproducibility and relevance to the present day of French architecture in the Middle Ages, and to relinquish the theme as a parameter in the observation of architecture. In other words every gap between old and new, between existing and projected buildings, was cancelled out.

In the same way, typology, concentrating on the only elements that are apparently stable in time, apart from the causes that underlie its constancy or repetition, moves away from the city, the object of its scrutiny. As one proceeds with generalizations, the link with the existing becomes increasingly frail and imprecise, references become blurred, and the search for invariants is revealed to be a "poetical" choice that takes only a few morphological data from what has been constructed.

No wonder that one comes across projects which, starting out from typological premises, are only able to get a grip on the most formally peremptory parts of the buildings to which they apply; the parts which, incidentally, can best be fitted into the styles and categories of the most old-fashioned history of architecture: mediaeval castle, Greek theatre, Baroque villa . . . On these bases, the architect makes his additions and eliminations to transform the building into a museum of itself, and to create a bigger museum, on the scale of the city, to make it more comprehensible. In other words, more explicitly didactic, an illustration from a handbook of the history of architecture. This retreat in the discipline is certainly the fruit of discomfort with an acute and critical attitude towards reality, a reaction to the unseemly demands for intensive exploitation of every bit of the existing fabric. What it does not grasp is that the real challenge is to bring alive the buildings of the past, instead of just holding them up for contemplation. Despite all the subtlety and sensitivity of the solutions proposed, despite their deep roots in contemporary culture, this attitude – to the extent that it selects exemplary and didactic "monuments" – merely follows the lead of the restorers of the last century. These were all intent on constructing – from Viollet-le-Duc's Pierrefonds to Beltrami's Castello Sforzesco – gigantic justifications for their own theories of architecture, their own visions of the city and of social equilibria. At the same time, to the degree in which it gives preference to the formal datum, it ends up travelling down the same road as the most tired neo-idealism, resolving architecture, as work of art, in its figurative image.[10]

But buildings are a reality that cannot be reduced to mere architecture, i.e. to that set of techniques which governs their design and their realization in accordance with it. In the first place they are a means of making a profit, and this, though not this alone, can be seen from their plans and elevations.[11]

Buildings, unlike the project, are worked material. The quality of this, and the way in which it is worked, are in part elements of the design, and are in any case an essential factor in evaluating a building. Plaster coating is a fundamental characteristic of John Nash's buildings,[12] and it would be pointless to discuss many Russian country houses from the neoclassical era without taking account of their wooden structure. It is enough to open the first 18th-century guide or travel diary that comes to hand to perceive a sensitivity and a wonder, now lost, for complexity of execution and rarity of material. ". . . Till now you will have seen little represented the marvel of this edifice wholly built of very fine solid marble . . ."[13] wrote Carlo Torre of the Milan Cathedral, long before pointing out, of course, that "Gothic is its architecture, or German . . ." It is not rare for monolithic columns of marble to form part of later buildings. A unitary idea – the project – where present, no longer kindles interest in individual parts of exceptional quality, which cannot be brought down to that possible unitary idea. The marble facing of the Cremona cathedral – which can be attributed more to a habit of

building than to a design – or the fact that the pillars are still swathed with tapestries – a fact that has nothing to do with the architecture, but which affects it greatly – are essential elements of the building's identity. Worked material tells us about the building's yard, about the working conditions in which the building was constructed. For over a century a work has been judged by the extent to which it is the most coherent possible outcome of the corresponding process of construction. In an ancient mosaic or in a Baroque or even just 19th-century limewash, the marks of the different days on which it was applied are certainly not regarded as an imperfection. Appreciating a glossy plaster also means appreciating the sureness and the sense of proportion of the gestures that characterize its execution.

Material deteriorates and is transformed. ". . . It is in the golden patina of time that we must seek the real light, colour and value of architecture . . .," wrote John Ruskin,[14] emphasizing the "changing fate" of every building as distinct from its design. He also showed, starting out on the basis of the picturesque, of a culture that had been forming for over a century even then, how decay and even ruin have their own precise aesthetic relevance. But, leaving aside Ruskin's glorification of the ruin, which may be deplored but not ignored, it cannot be forgotten that over at least the last fifty years history has raised material remains to the level of sources, especially when they are large and widespread. Eliminating a building or even part of it means wiping out that page from the story of society which is carried by the material itself. Perhaps the writer is conditioned by his own curriculum of studies, in which a historian – in the strictest sense of the word – exerted an influence that was unrivalled by any architect, but he cannot help seeing even in spaces and their subsequent transformations a splendid, irreplaceable book in which to read the changes in customs and social balances. So that rather than their design, it is just what they tell us in their material and their form of the men who have lived in them that justifies the decision to go on living in them and the determination to preserve them. And I think that the feeling of emptiness conveyed by many recent works of architecture that are crammed with citations is due to the fact that they are used without knowing what ways of life and human relationships they hold, without taking account of the ambiguous capacity for evocation that architectural solutions, types of lay-out or finishings bring with them. What we end up with is a sad repetition of the fable of the crow who dressed up in the feathers of a peacock.

Faced with these difficulties in theory, what comes back to the fore-front is a question that has been systematically evaded for many years, but which is fundamental to the relations between old and new: when and why is it appropriate, or even necessary, to replace something? This is generally answered by asserting the superhistorical necessity of change, change that like snow or rain goes hand in hand with the destiny of mankind. The substitutions of past centuries are invoked, centuries in which the only attitude to the legacy of previous ages was cannibalism. But such appeals merely draw attention to the vast expanses uncharted by historiographers of architecture who, wholly taken up with forms, forget that they conceal patient efforts at maintenance. Given their technical means, this maintenance often took the form of faithful reproduction. The speed and the manner in which the existing is being replaced today have undergone a profound change. It is not possible to compare the Milan of today with building activities, however lively, in the Milan of the early 19th century, where, according to the account by Carlo Cattaneo, not a single road could be found in which at least one house had not been rebuilt. The rapid growth in population and the increasing commercial importance of some routes led – even before the "Cinque giornate" revolt – to blanket destruction in order to make intensive use of valuable areas. Nevertheless, the limited resources of the population, almost half of which was composed of occasional workers,[15] meant that alterations usually involved intensive exploitation of building material. Every wall, beam or fixture that offered a minimum guarantee of soundness and durability was reused, even as mere makeshift. Urban growth did not obliterate the body of the existing city.

Today, on the contrary, buildings are replaced without any heed being paid to their quality or possible further duration. Contractors and even the work force have got out of the habit of repairing or adapting, tending instead to make room for products that appear to provide the required services with little need for maintenance, and with particularly rapid rates of deterioration.

In Milan, the iron and aluminium fixtures of the fifties have been disappearing for some years now. The victims are famous ones: from the houses of Asnago and Vander in Via Larga to Gio Ponti's second Montecatini building. In the gamut of means chosen by architects, these elements are given a decisive role in defining facades: replacing them means redesigning the front of the building to a considerable extent. Leaving aside any judgement about the quality of this redesign, such a procedure either attests to the rapid deterioration of finishings that are widely adopted nowadays or can only be explained from the point of view of mere consumption. The only logic that can be found in such treatment of existing buildings is that of a sector of today's system of production.

So to check on the need for substitution, by looking at the soundness of building materials and their ability to resist atmospheric agents or support a load, for the architect means defending his own possibility of influencing social relations, and not being relegated to a mere draughtsman of ideologies.

The material, whose toughness needs to be verified, as a basic resource, becomes the frame of reference, the fixed context in which the project is set.

Faced with the continual destruction of resources and memories that, day by day, is wiping out our cities, the first parameter on which a project should be evaluated is its ability to respect and use existing resources without straining them. "The architect has not been born who, in order to give vent to an idea, needs the compass of half a mile and a fortune of thirty-two million . . ."[16] Carlo Cattaneo's words are still acutely relevant today. Yet what we are seeing is the daily destruction of materials and artifacts which are no longer available to the architect, whose cost is so great that it is no longer possible to provide them. To take up, for example, an 18th-century brick floor, once considered a sign of poverty, but whose surface, reinforced by innumerable layers of wax and polished by use, is infinitely more dignified and durable than the glazed tiles which take its place, merely to install wiring and plumbing beneath the floor, is nothing but technical incompetence. It is a sign of the incapacity to grasp and to handle the complexity of a building.

After the materials, one thinks of the time it took for a solution to be thought up, tried out and put into effect, of the infinite series of trials and improvements that the tempo and techniques of building made it possible to introduce in any work. Nowadays working conditions are such that it is sometimes necessary to go without even samples. From a strictly disciplinary point of view, avoiding replacements as far as possible means gaining precious time for those new interventions that are actually necessary, time that can be devoted to the growing complexity of requirements and details. On the urban scale, a quick stroll through any large city is enough to pick out innumerable opportunities, of small or great significance, to make its dreary vistas more bearable and decent. In individual buildings, once the commonplaces are over and done with, the long list of decay which comprises everything which does not fit with the most up-to-date standards, from floors that are not perfectly level to plastering that bears the mark of frequent repairs, along with such things as casings and their fastenings, the scope for design remains vast. It is necessary to find ways in which the deterioration of individual parts of the construction can be arrested, ways which in any case involve modifying the appearance and composition of materials. It is necessary to replace irreparably damaged components, or those elements that have been lost, where their absence makes preservation or use impossible – from a collapsed roof to a missing window or door. And finally it is necessary to add what was never there but which has become indispensable, like electric lighting or heating. But, like the building trade, architects also seem to have lost the ability to repair. Repairing means adding on without eliminating, increasing the complexity and density of the construction, just as a layer of stucco or plaster finish for frescoes was added to many German or Austrian Gothic churches in the 18th century. In these cases, the additional thickness recreates a unitary image for the building, one which is a viable alternative to the previous one. Yet there is a forgotten tradition of additions as minute as they were significant; not many people remember that when Etienne Louis Boullée was working on the boiseries and rocaille of the Hotel d'Evreux, the modern Elysée, he knew how to limit himself to supplementing the decoration of a mirror, or the trabeation of a transom.[17] All the more reason that today, when existing structures are recognized as resources and testimonies of the past, attention should be turned to the detail, to a section of plaster, a fixture, a floor . . . The building is a stratification and a palimpsest, in which the requirements of use and the effects of deterioration are laid down at differing rates. The project is built up out of distinct parts, those which are new of necessity and those which already exist. It is not a unitary design that brings them together, but the attempt to attain a level of quality in keeping with what is already there.

To preserve without distortion involves an awareness of and commitment to techniques that have very little to do with generic finishings and the widespread practice of mediocre mimicry. Windows and shutters that resemble antique ones, but are machine made, with badly-finished outlines. New renderings of spurious mortar covered with plastic paints. These are just the commonplaces of the lowest level of routine building restoration, whether publicly or privately financed. The failure of the project, or its success, is measured against the whole, and therefore against what already exists. So there is no sense in forcing opportunities, even if one is tempted to do so by the expectations or the public and or public bodies. A lift alongside a protected building is either a concealed, and often crude concrete structure, or it seems to require more zeal than Charles Garnier had to put into the grand staircase of the Opéra. The covering of a central-heating system may involve an iconographic and iconological display not inferior to the marble structure supporting the Holy Shroud in Turin. The undigested quotation will then reveal its true dimension in the wretched materials out of which it is made.

Granting equal dignity to the project for the preservation and maintenance of what exists and to its restoration brings down the artificial conflict involved in making additions recognizable as such: they cease to be the objective and go back to being the result of a work that responds, with a maximum of propriety and richness of intention, to a requirement that is determined at a given time. In the same way, every distinction between "advanced" and "traditional" techniques disappears. There are only suitable techniques, whether of recent or less recent origin. Modernity cannot be restricted to the use of products of the chemical industry: good design is certainly not based on the quantity of plexiglas domes, reinforced concrete vaults or epoxy resins employed. This is even more true when these means are used to recreate a lost image. An object or commodity cannot substitute for the intentions and the culture of its user. On the contrary, the appeal to traditional techniques often does not even have the support of the Encyclopédie. And yet the impoverishment of the builder's yard – even the ambiguous one of reconstruction that so rarely has any perverse, and therefore stimulating, coherence and culture – makes the recovery of a lost variety of techniques all the more urgent.

At other times, the need to adapt buildings to new requirements of comfort, or to changes in society (from the break-up of family groups to growth of the tertiary sector), is invoked as a justification for large-scale demolitions. But such interventions conceal a more basic attempt to impose patterns of living. They involve the use of products with which public opinion has been taught to connect the satisfaction of certain demands – completely ignoring how they fit in with specific cases. Hence the response consists of objects, and above all words, but not services. To go back to services means to "design for use." It is a question of use, not function. There is no sense in looking for or proposing to create in the spaces of existing building, at least in what was constructed up until the end of the last century, the indifference of form, spaces that are flexible and mutable to the extent that they lose specific connotations. Nor can one find rigid spaces that answer to an exact requirement, unable to adapt to any change in use. Indeed the buildings of the past, which reinstate modes of behaviour that have long been forgotten, testify to the limits and relative nature of those in existence, demonstrating the possibility of alternatives. One thinks of an apartment in a *hôtel particulier*, or private house, of the 17th or 18th century. The rooms, their ordered sequence in the suite, the light and the positioning of windows, their relationship with the doors, their dimensions and proportions, the thickness of the walls, the material, the importance of certain features – mouldings, casings, fireplaces, the shape of the vaults. These are all the means of expression for a culture and an organization of existence, the trace of a dignity of living that has been lost and of an equilibrium which was translated into dimensions and became through them a form of well-being. In their place, perhaps there are other services, another comfort, but the old settings remain a silent, subtle criticism of vaguely defined and proportioned spaces; spaces which are mere volumes, not coordinated, for example, with the sequence of apertures in the facade, which is how modern building transcribes the sense of living, inhabiting and having fun. The buildings of the past, in their totally paid for spaciousness, in their costly materials prepared for dominant groups that vanished long ago, or in the infinite inventiveness of poverty, present an exceptional opportunity for experimentation with alternative patterns of living. At least, for those who believe that in buildings and in the way they are designed and constructed, the relationship with those who build them and those who will use them is the main objective, an objective for which even the forms are instruments.

NOTES

1 Obviously, I am alluding to Gustavo Giovannoni's article "Vecchie città ed edilizia nuova," in *La Nuova Antologia*, July 1913, and to his book with the same title (Rome 1931), to the numerous articles by Ernesto Nathan Rogers, including "Le preesistenze ambientali e i temi pratici contemporanei" in *Casabella-Continuità*, 1955, no. 204, pp. 3 et seq, "Dibattito sugli inserimenti nelle preesistenze ambientali," in *Casabella-Continuità*, 157, 211, pp. 3 et seq. and "Dibattito sui inserimenti nelle preesistenze ambientali" in *Architettura-Cronache e storia*, 22, 1957, p. 225, and of course to Aldo Rossi, *L'architettura della città*, Padua 1966.

2 I refer to the "charter of restoration" approved by the IV Congress of Italian Architects and Engineers held in Rome in 1893, and now published, along with other material, in *Restauro*, no. 10, 1978, pp. 12, 13 and discussed in paragraph 2.

3 Cf. F. Dal Co, G. Mazzariol, M. Tafuri, *Carlo Scarpa, l'opera completa*, Milan 1984, section 102, p. 114, with bibliography, and Giorgio Vigni, "Ricordo di un lavoro con Scarpa," in *Carlo Scarpa – il progetto di Santa Caterina a Treviso*, Treviso 1984, pp. 34 et seq. Marisa Dalai Emiliani in "Musei della ricostruzione in Italia, fra disfatta e rivincita della storia" in *Carlo Scarpa a Castelvecchio*, Milan 1982, pp. 149–170, while presenting a very clear picture of the limits of post-war museography, emphasizes the more progressive role played by Scarpa within that picture; a role, however, which the edges of that picture would not surpass.

4 On the Palazzo Bianco cf. in particular Caterina Marcenaro's introduction to the Provisional Catalogue of the Palazzo Bianco Gallery, Genoa 1950.

5 I am thinking of the debate between Roberto Gabetti, Aimaro Oreglia d'Isola and Ernesto Nathan Rogers, for which cf. *Controspazio*, 1978.

6 I refer in particular to law 258/78 of the Emilia Romagna Region.

7 For the science of constructions, cf. for example, Edoardo Benvenuto's explanatory text *La scienza delle costruzioni e il suo sviluppo storico*, Florence 1981.

8 I am thinking of Aldo Rossi, *op. cit.*, Introduction, in the Milan 1978 edition, p. 14: "The points laid down by De Saussure for the development of linguistics could be transposed as a scheme for the development of urban science . . .".

9 Cf. G. Germann, "Viollet-le-Duc téoricien et professeur," in *Viollet-le-Duc, centenaire de sa mort à Lausanne*, pp. 9–19. The links between the Tendency and the theories of Viollet-le-Duc

have already been pointed out by Geert Bekaert in his "Introduction à l'edition de 1977" of the *Entetiens sur l'architecture*. As far back as 1966, Hubert Damisch had brought up the subject of a connection between Viollet-le-Duc's theory and structuralism in his introduction to *L'Architecture raisonée*.

10 See, by way of an example, R. Bonelli's entry on Restoration in the *Enciclopedia Universale dell'Arte*, Rome 1963. Architectural restoration which sees "in the artistic value, and therefore in the figurative aspects, the actual value of the work . . .".

11 I am thinking of Ennio Poleggi's studies on Genoa, i.e. of fundamental contributions to the more recent spectrum of the history of architecture in Italy.

12 Even his contemporaries were convinced of this, as is demonstrated by the ironic nursery-rhyme quoted by Steen Eiler Rasmussen in *London: the unique city*, London 1931, MIT Press 1967.

13 C. Torre, *Il ritratto di Milano*, Milano 1674, p. 206.

14 J. Ruskin. *The Seven Lamps of Architecture*, London 1849, "The Lamp of Memory," X. I quote from the New York edition, 1981, on p. 177.

15 Giovanni Salari, *Statistica della Regia città e provincia di Milano*, Milan 1840.

16 C. Cattaneo, "Sul progetto di una piazza del Duomo di Milano," in *Politecnico*, 1839, vol. 1, part III, pp. 237–52, in the edition of *Scritti letterari, artistici, linguistici e vari, raccolti e ordinati da Agostino Beltrami*, vol 2, Florence 1948, p. 26.

17 Cf. J. M. Pérouse de Montclos, *Etienne Louis Boullée . . .*, Paris 1969, pp. 99 et seq.

44
The Field of Study

James Strike

Source: *Architecture in Conservation: Managing Development at Historic Sites.*
Routledge, 1994, pp. 7–18

The following is a review of the evolution of attitudes towards conservation; it places particular emphasis on the ideas and opinions about the art of architecture within the field of conservation. It must be stressed that the study of conservation as a specific discipline is a relatively new subject; its origins stem from the birth of history as a separate subject, whence came the study of architectural and social history. The following observations are listed chronologically to trace this process of change.

It was common practice during the early centuries for building materials, especially stone, to be salvaged from disused buildings and redundant fortifications to construct new projects. The Anglo-Saxons and the Norman invaders made good use of the Roman sites as sources of building materials: where, for example, are the stones taken from London's Roman wall?[1] This is not to say that there was no duty of care by monarch or Church, but that the concern at that time was not to conserve buildings as a means of preserving history, but to conserve and embellish them as symbols of wealth, or to sanctify and glorify places of religious importance. Examples of deliberate demolition are commonplace, the destruction went on for centuries. What happened to the home of the Lancastrian monarchs at Richmond, Surrey?[2] Or to the fine ashlar taken as late as the 1830s from the buildings of the Blackfriars in Gloucester.[3]

Examples of new architecture constructed at historic sites during the medieval period are plentiful. The evidence is seen primarily in our cathedrals and large fortified houses. At Winchester in the fourteenth century, for example, Bishops Edington and William of Wykeham completely modernised the nave: the Norman structure was remodelled into the contemporary style of late Gothic.[4]

And at Gloucester Cathedral, a delicate and tenuous perpendicular Lady Chapel was built, uncompromisingly, up to the solid Norman east end.[5]

The dissolution of the monasteries between 1535 and 1539 contributed, unwittingly, to the germination of architectural conservation. The closure of 850 monastic houses engendered a feeling of loss, and thus a wish to restore, or at least to record, the past. (It also provided the sites which were to stimulate the interest in picturesque ruins during the eighteenth century.)

The conservation lobby was further strengthened by destruction of valuable buildings during Cromwell's Commonwealth of the 1650s. The Puritans sent their Commissioners on a punitive removal of religious images and 'superstitious' decorations from important churches and houses.

Little was written on the history of buildings prior to the seventeenth century. One of the earliest architectural texts to take a historical view about buildings of a previous age was Sir William Dugdale's *The History of St Paul's Cathedral in London from its Foundation until these Times*, 1658.[6]

The buildings of the Renaissance period created a number of architectural clashes with the new fashionable classical designs placed alongside, and even in front of, the embedded Gothic. Whatever discussion took place about the pros and cons of this new juxtaposition of new and old, the examples are so numerous that it must be assumed that there was little in the way of opposition or control against it. Inigo Jones's Banqueting Hall (1619–22) for example, must have been seen as aggressively modern and dominating against the rambling collection of its surrounding medieval structures;[7] and there is an assuredness in his new classical Renaissance portico for the west end of the old Gothic St Paul's Cathedral (1633–5).[8]

History was not as sacrosanct in the seventeenth century as it is today. A false ceiling was installed beneath the Gothic vaults of St Stephen's Chapel in the Palace of Westminster to accommodate the Houses of Parliament, and in 1706 Sir Christopher

Wren added oak panelling to the converted chapel which concealed the faded frescoes of the saints.[9]

The historian David Watkin,[10] in *The Rise of Architectural History* (Watkin 1980), points out that the history of art and architecture first became an academic discipline in Germany in the eighteenth century. This was long before similar developments in any other country in Europe. Notable publications include Fischer von Erlach, *A Plan of Civil and Historical Architecture, in the Representation of the Most Noted Buildings of Foreign Nations, both Ancient and Modern*, 1721, (translated into English 1730), and the influential text by J. J. Winckelmann *The History of Ancient Art*, 1764 (published in Boston 1880).[11]

The Society of Antiquaries of London received their royal charter in 1751. This group of eminent and learned persons (which had been in existence since the 1580s) established a reputation as the custodian of ancient monuments and as a pressure group to prevent the demolition of medieval remains.[12]

By the mid-eighteenth century, views about the past had moved towards the 'picturesque', that is, an enjoyment of history based not on a sense of reason or research, but on the impact of the 'picture image' on the eye; a visual and immediate stimulant.[13] These views had been nurtured through the paintings of such artists as Claude Lorraine and Salvator Rosa, and influenced by the aesthetic writing of Edmund Burke, whose text of 1757, *A Philosophical Enquiry into the Origin of our Ideas of the Sublime and Beautiful*, proposed the idea that views seen by the eye were communicated not with the conscious mind, but through subconscious instincts, thus 'begetting passions'.[14] This passion was for 'nature'. M. W. Thompson in *Ruins, Their Preservation and Display*, sums this up:

> Religious attitudes towards ruins were greatly eased by the intrusion of the eighteenth-century belief in nature; giving God a place off-stage as it were. There was, in the contemplation of nature, a solace to be derived from a ruin.[15]

The impact of this eighteenth-century view of the past is seen through prints and paintings of the period. Contemporary drawings show an emotive idea of nature represented by untamed ivy and overgrown ruins shrouded in mystery and moonlight. A watercolour painted by James Lambert in 1785, of Bayham Abbey, Sussex, shows how contrived was the romance: the overgrown ruins of the Abbey were created by selective removal and buttressing to form a picturesque prospect from the house built on the far side of the lake.[16] It is clear that there was no desire for conservation as we know it today. The aim was not to preserve the past, but to use it as a theatrical effect to excite the visitor. The Rev. William Gilpin, travelling in 1770, observed of Tintern Abbey:

> Though the parts are beautiful, the whole is ill-shaped. No ruins of the tower are left, which might give form and contrast to the walls and buttresses, and other inferior parts. Instead of this, a number of gable-ends hurt the eye with their regularity, and disgust it by the vulgarity of their shape. A mallet judiciously used (but who durst use it?) might be of service in fracturing some of them.[17]

The second half of the eighteenth century seems strange in retrospect: it looked both back into history and forwards to the future. It looked backwards through the Gothic revival, where, for example, Horace Walpole developed Strawberry Hill with a desire for the monastic 'in memory of Eloisa's cloister', a tower which 'erects its battlements bravely', a 'little parlour' based on the sixteenth-century tomb of Ruthall, Bishop of Durham, the staircase with panelling modelled on Prince Arthur's early sixteenth-century tomb in Winchester Cathedral, and balusters copied from the library of Rouen Cathedral.[18] It looked forward through a fascination in the scientific experiments which were moving more into the public domain.

By the beginning of the nineteenth century, the nature of criticism and imagination is represented by the 'Gothic novel'. There was a strange interweaving of interests between the new sciences and the darkness of the past; a fascination with historicism and a fictitious fear of science epitomised by Mary Shelley's novel *Frankenstein* of 1816.[19]

More medieval architecture was lost during the Gothic revival by over-conjectural 'restoration' than by demolition. Jane Fawcett explores this in *The Future of the Past* (Fawcett 1976), and attributes the loss to over-zealousness and over-confidence. The Gothic style was seen as the correct architectural expression for devout religious conviction actively fostered through the zeal of the Oxford Movement[20] and the 'Ecclesiologists'.[21] This single-mindedness gave architects little regard for accuracy of the past; their aim was to correct the mistakes of their forefathers and to regularise all the decay, patina and muddle that had built up through the previous layers of history (see section 4.4, 'Layers of history'). Many interiors, numerous churches, and several of the cathedrals were 'restored' according to current ideology rather than historical research. Examples include the Norman west end tower of Canterbury Cathedral which was rebuilt in 1834 to match its Gothic twin; symmetry was gained at the expense of Lanfranc's robust tower. Similarly, the west end of St Alban's Abbey, which was completely remodelled by Lord Grimthorpe into the Gothic style between 1879 and 1895.[22]

There was a reaction against this conjectural restoration. Pugin visited Hereford Cathedral in 1833 and was horrified at Wyatt's 'vile and rascally work' to the west end, and by the 'Saxon ornaments imitated in plaster in the most wretched style, a plain ceiling in the nave, and the Lady Chapel filled with bookcases with the end towards the church plastered up'.[23] Ruskin was equally single-minded in his criticism of alterations around the country.

In 1877 William Morris founded the Society for the Protection of Ancient Buildings. Its *Manifesto* indicates the nature of their criticism:

> [ancient buildings] have become the subject of one of the most interesting of studies, and of an enthusiasm, religious, historical, artistic, which is one of the undoubted gains of our time; yet we think that if the present treatment of them be continued, our descendants will find them useless for study and chilling to enthusiasm.

Morris goes on to say that any restoration which has to be made should be:

> wrought in the unmistakable fashion of the time. . . . The results [being] a building in which the many changes, though harsh and visible enough, were, by their very contrast, interesting and instructive and could by no possibility mislead.

The text portrays a rosy view of history in the wish to preserve the 'living spirit' and 'the appearance of antiquity' in the 'partly-perished work of the ancient craftsmaster'. The idea of cleaning the whole building would have been resisted:

> the whole surface of the building is necessarily tampered with . . . the reckless stripping of buildings . . . [the surface] made neat and smooth by the tricky hand of some unoriginal and thoughtless hack of today.

The Victorian 'spirit of the age' was steeped in the past. They considered 'the past' to be worthy, and a suitable model for the present. They saw the various historical styles as representing chivalry, honour, or rectitude.[24] There was rivalry between the styles: Gothic revival, Greek revival, and later all sorts of historical and colonial interests such as Egyptian and Indian revivals. The intense competition to design the new buildings for Downing College, Cambridge reads, in Cinza Sicca's *Committed to Classicism* (Sicca 1987), like an Anthony Trollope novel. There were collegiate rows and parliamentary questions before William Wilkins's Greek revival scheme was selected.

The Ancient Monuments Protection Act came into force in Britain in 1882. This was the first time the government had taken a positive role in the protection of historic sites, albeit rather tentatively due to the lobby of protest against interference with private property. The Act scheduled as few as sixty-eight prehistoric earthworks, burial mounds, and stone circles. Little did they realise that this would lead within a hundred years to the present schedule of 13,000 ancient monuments and the listing of 440,000 historic buildings. (For those unfamiliar with the system in Britain, ancient monuments are *scheduled* and historic buildings are *listed* under separate Acts.)

By the end of the century, the ancient monuments of most of Europe were covered by protective legislation of varying degrees of authority, and the USA enacted its first Federal Antiquities Law in 1906.[25]

The First World War (1914–18) upset the social balance. It took away many young men, servants became scarce, and the class structures were eroded. The days of the serviced country estate were over and the rich industrialists gave up building historic, look-alike country houses: this is the time of Isabel Colegate's novel *The Shooting Party* (Colegate 1980). Emancipation[26] eroded the upper classes' privileged enjoyment of history and the lower class became less a victim of their past.

Care of the government stock of archaeological sites, historic buildings, and medieval ruins in England was carried out by the Office of Public Buildings and Works. Their approach during the interwar period was one of tidiness and straight lines. Preservation consisted of taking out the undergrowth and the ivy, removing loose stones, repointing and capping the walls, and providing close-cut grass with neat edges. The guide books were of a standard academic format full of historical detail.

It was not until 1932 that any protection was given to historic buildings in Britain through the first of the Town and Country Planning Acts.

Buildings of the Modern Movement first appeared in Germany at the beginning of the nineteenth century: albeit, the roots of the movement had begun earlier in England through the Industrial Revolution and the industrial mills, and through experiments in concrete in both England and France.[27] Buildings of the Modern Movement arrived in Britain and the USA during the 1920s and 1930s: they set out to be totally non-historical and as such they were seen as a threat to history.

The Second World War (1939–45) shattered the historic core of many cities – Warsaw, Berlin, Dresden, and in Britain, Coventry and Portsmouth. Thousands of historic buildings were destroyed or damaged. Limited resources at the end of the war went to survival and economic recovery; restoration and conservation were low priorities. Requirements of the war effort also moved construction techniques further into industrialisation and this was used after 1945 for mass housing such as the prefab scheme[28] and later for tower blocks.[29] The spirit of the age after the war was for a better future based on industrial progress. Social beliefs and aesthetic judgements were based on a need for space, health, and education, rather than on cultural heritage. The early industrial mills, for example, which we now regard as heritage buildings, were considered as an architectural legacy of worn-out and inefficient production and as places of social exploitation.

Restoration of one particular building after the war needs to be looked at in detail as it represents one of the earliest uses of modern design for conservation project. The Alt Pinakothek in Munich, 1826–36, was designed by Leo von Klenze as part of Ludwig I of Bavaria's dream to turn Munich into the Venice of the North. The centre of this long neo-classical building was torn open by a bomb during the war and something had to be done so that the priceless contents could be returned from their safe-keeping in the countryside. The architect Hans Döllgast saw this as an opportunity to test the philosophy of the Modern Movement. He had trained under Peter Behrens, one of the founders of the movement, and had been appointed as Professor at the Munich Technische Hochschule just before the war.[30] His scheme, prepared in 1952, for the restoration of the Pinakothek was not only modern but also managed to reflect the rhythm and basic shapes of

the original building. The slender 250mm steel columns which were used to replace the 19-metre high brick piers destroyed from the elevation made use of the latest technology developed in the munitions factories. The new sections of roof were formed in the new building material of aluminium. Döllgast inserted two straight staircases into the missing parts of the south loggia to form improved circulation around the museum. Although his scheme to enclose these with a modern glass wall was later rejected in favour of brick, the foyer space today still has a powerful and modern feel. Bernhard Blauel gives a full account of the story in *Hans Döllgast 1891–1974*.[31] He refers to Döllgast's conviction that 'the building had a history, and the scar from the bomb was part of that history to hide it seemed absurd'. Blauel comments that the scheme represents one of the first examples of the bold yet sensitive approach similar to that now used by Carlo Scarpa at Castelvecchio, Verona,[32] and by Foster at the Royal Academy, London. It must be pointed out that Döllgast was able to convince the authorities on the grounds of cost and time, and that although his approach was common to the ethos of the Modern Movement, it had not yet become part of the *Zeitgeist*, His work was a lonely example; such is the nature of change.

Returning now to the chronological listing, many areas of close-knit terrace houses were demolished in the 1960s under the name of slum clearance, particularly in those historic cities that expanded out of the Industrial Revolution. There were, of course, dwellings which were beyond restoration or unsuitable for upgrading to a reasonable standard of facilities. None the less, the rules of classification for a slum became progressively more rigorous as the spirit of industrialisation demanded more sites to be cleared for concrete town centres and rows of tower blocks.

The thrust for the future was influenced during the 1960s by a push for material gain. Architecture and planning were fuelled by profit. Decisions were justified and veiled behind social progress and aims for a better future; history got in the way of progress and 1968 saw the demolition of the greatest number of listed buildings recorded in one year.

English Heritage was set up under the 1983 National Heritage Act. This brought together various government departments that had been dealing with conservation. Lord Montagu of Beaulieu, its first Chairman, recalls that historic monuments were at that time still:

forbidding places for the visitor. They were indeed well cared for, but the visitor faced a rather daunting custodian dressed like a prison warder, complete with jangling keys, whose main job seemed to be to tell them to keep off the grass.[33]

In 1988 the 'thirty-year rule' was adopted in England by which modern buildings thirty years old could be protected under the Planning Acts. Eighteen buildings, including the Royal Festival Hall[34] and the large concrete spans of Stockwell Bus Garage,[35] were covered.

This then is the history which leads us up to today's attitudes. It is salutary to see current conservation practice as part of this continuous process of change.

Conservation is now an international concern, issues are international news. ICCROM (The International Centre for the Study of the Preservation and the Restoration of Cultural Property) was founded by UNESCO in 1959, and ICOMOS (The International Council on Monuments and Sites) set their Conservation Charter in 1966.

National preservation groups are also joining internationally, notably DOCOMOMO (The International Working Party for the Documentation and Conservation of Buildings, Sites and Neighbourhoods of the Modern Movement), which held its first international conference at Eindhoven in 1990.

It is interesting to observe that, in spite of this increase in international debate, there are still differences of emphasis within the various countries; national characteristics still influence conservation practice.

Central Europe has a strong commitment towards rebuilding history, the response to extensive destruction during the Second World War has been to replicate many of the lost national monuments and city centres. Compare, for example, the rebuilding of Dresden against the new town schemes for Coventry and Portsmouth.

Another variant is seen in France, where building important projects in the heart of historic areas is used as a political gesture. Successive Presidents have commissioned 'des grands projets', almost vying with one another: the Centre National d'Art et de Culture in Les Halles; the National Opera House facing on to Place de la Bastille; and the vast structure of the Arche de la Défense, placed proudly on the important historical axis from the Palais du Louvre, Champs-Elysées, and Arc de Triomphe.

Pursuing the political dimension. It is interesting to observe how the Georgian houses of Dublin are now seen more as part of the valuable Irish inheritance rather than a sign of their colonialist past: the elegant houses in such areas as Henrietta Street are being taken up by Dubliners and carefully restored. The Ministry of Works in Ireland is also benefiting from politics through grants from the European Commission to provide new facilities at some of their more important historical sites: at Dublin Castle, for example, where an international conference centre has been unobtrusively inserted, and in Phoenix Park, where a new interpretation centre has been placed with confidence alongside Ashtown Castle.

There is an air of confidence in Italy. Here, however, interest in new architecture at historic sites is about the spirit of modernity in design; they enjoy the aesthetic tension between modern detailing placed against historic fabric. Architects such as Carlo Scarpa at Castelvecchio, and Guido Canali at Palazzo della Pilotta are willing, and permitted, to experiment. There is an immediacy and exuberance in their work. Italians accept this approach as commonplace; they have hosted the world-renowned Architectural Biennale in Venice since the epoch-making exhibition of 1981, 'The Presence of the Past'.

And finally, the reticence of the English. Nikolaus Pevsner in *The Englishness of English Art*[36] explores, through English architectural history, the English sense of detachment, distrust of the extreme, a wish for moderation and reasonableness, a holding back (Pevsner 1956, Chapter 3). The trio of famous English architects – Foster, Rogers, and Stirling – received acclaim for their work abroad before recognition at home. Stirling believes that distrust of modern design in Britain has 'set the cause of good architecture back in favour of a "Georgian" revival'.[37] His extension of the Tate Gallery, London, to form the Clore Gallery, met with a mixed reaction. For many it had a European edge to it: it was too stark, too blatant, too un-English.

NOTES

1 Built c.200AD. Over 3 kilometres in length and 6 metres in height. Built of Kentish ragstone facing with rubble infill and regular courses of flat brick.
2 Excavations around Richmond Green are beginning to disclose the extent of the buildings.
3 Particularly from the west range refectory which was remodelled into a terrace of houses.

4 See John Harvey, *The Mediaeval Architect*, London, Wayland, 1972, p. 82.

5 1457–99.

6 See David Watkin, *The Rise of Architechtural History*, London, Architectural Press, 1980, p. 49.

7 Peter Davey, 'Without pastiche', in *Architectural Review*, December 1990.

8 Harris, Orgel, and Strong, *The King's Arcadia*, London, Arts Council, 1973, p. 142.

9 James Pope-Hennessy, *The Houses of Parliament*, London, Batsford, 1953, p. 20.

10 Fellow of Peterhouse College, and University of Cambridge Lecturer in History and Art.

11 Watkin, op. cit., p.1.

12 Jane Fawcett (ed.) *The Future of the Past*, London, Thames & Hudson, 1976, p. 14.

13 Adrian Forty, 'The lure of the picturesque', in *Architecture Today*, September 1990, p. 44.

14 Christopher Hussey, *The Picturesque, Studies in a Point of View*, London, Frank Cass, 1927, p. 12.

15 M. W. Thompson, *Ruins, their Preservation and Display*, London, Colonnade Books/British Museum Publications, 1981, p. 14.

16 Glyn Coppack, *Abbeys and Priories*, London, Batsford, 1990, p. 18.

17 Quoted in Christopher Hussey, op. cit., p. 194. First published William Gilpin, *Observations on the River Wye, and Several Parts of South Wales, Relative Chiefly to Picturesque Beauty; Made in the Summer of the Year 1770*, London, R. Blamire, 1782, p. 32.

18 Mordaunt Crook, 'Strawberry Hill revisited', from *Country Life*, June 7–14–21, 1973.

19 See Muriel Spark, *Mary Shelley*, London, Constable, 1988.

20 Begun in 1833 under J. H. Newman and John Keble.

21 *Ecclesiologist* was the journal of the Cambridge Camden Movement. The name is used here in a general sense to include those Victorian architects whose work was influenced by High Church and obedience to past styles (e.g. Butterworth and Ruskin).

22 Gerald Cobb, *The English Cathedrals, the Forgotten Centuries*, London, Thames & Hudson, 1980, p. 14.

23 Jane Fawcett, op. cit., p. 77; B. Ferry, *Recollections of a Welby Pugin*, London, 1861, pp. 80–1.

24 See Richard Jenkins, *Dignity and Decadence*, San Francisco, HarperCollins, 1991, which deals with the nineteenth-century obsession for a classical inheritance.

25 Henry Cleere (ed.), *Archaeological Heritage Management*, London, Unwin Hyman, 1989, p. 1.

26 Together with women's suffrage, which began in 1866, leading to equal voting rights in 1928 (1920 in the USA).

27 See James Strike, *Construction into Design*, Oxford, Butterworth, 1991.

28 Ibid., p. 152.

29 Ibid., p. 155.

30 Döllgast had been teaching at Technische Hochschule since 1929.

31 Catalogue produced by *Architecture Today* for the exhibition of Döllgast's work, held at the Architectural Foundation, London, October 1991.

32 See Richard Murphy, *Carlo Scarpa and the Castelvecchio*, Oxford, Butterworth, 1990.

33 Speech for presentation of the Annual Report 1991.

34 1948–51, Robert Matthew and Leslie Martin. River front remodelled, Hubert Bennett, 1962.

35 1954, Adie Button and Partners.

36 Based on his Reith Lectures, 1955.

37 Kenneth Powell, 'A prophet without honour', in the *Daily Telegraph*, 9 November 1991. See also Sir James Stirling, obituary, *The Times*, 27 June 1992.

Bibliography

Alfoldy, S. and Helland, J. *Craft, Space and Interior Design, 1855–2005*. Ashgate. 2008. ISBN-13 978-0754657064

Atlee, James, Le Feuvre, Lisa, Matta-Clark, Gordon. *The Space Between*. Nazraeli Press. 2003. ISBN 1-59005-049-5

Bachelard, Gaston. *The Poetics of Space*. Beacon Press. ISBN-13 978-0807064733

Benjamin, W. *The Arcades Project*. Belknap/Harvard. 1999

Brooker, G. and Stone, S. *Rereadings: Interior Architecture and the Design Principles of Remodelling Existing Buildings*. RIBA-Enterprises. 2004. ISBN 859461328

Brooker, G. and Stone, S. *What is Interior Design?* Rotovision Publishers. 2010. ISBN 978-2888930174

Brooker, G. and Stone, S. *Form and Structure*. AVA Publications. 2007. ISBN-13 978-2940373406

Brooker, G. and Stone, S. *Context and Environment: Site and Ideas*. AVA Publications. 2008. ISBN 978-2940373710

Brooker, G. and Stone, S. *Elements and Objects – Occupying Space*. AVA Publications. 2009. ISBN 978-2940411108

Boyer, M. Christine. *The City of Collective Memory. Its Historical Imagery and Architectural Entertainments*. MIT Press. 1994. ISBN 0-262-52211-X

Buzas, Stefan and Carmel-Arthur, Judith. *Carlo Scarpa, Museo Cannoviano, Possagno*. Edition Axel Menges. 2002. ISBN 3-930698-22-6

Catacuzino, Sherban. *Re/Architecture – Old Buildings New Uses*. Thames and Hudson. 1989. ISBN 0-500341087

Coates, M., Brooker, G. and Stone, S. *The Visual Dictionary of Interior Architecture*. AVA Publications. 2008. ISBN 978-2940373802

Colomina, Beatriz. *Privacy and Publicity – Modern Architecture as Mass Media*. MIT Press. 1996. ISBN 0-262-53139-9

Colomina, Beatriz. *Sexuality and Space*. Princeton Architectural Press; and *Townscape*. Gordon Cullen. Architectural Press. 1961

Cramer, J. and Breitling, S. *Architecture in Existing Fabric: Planning, Design and Building*. Birkhauser. 2007. ISBN 978-3764377526

Curtis, William. *Modern Architecture since 1900*. Phaidon (3rd edn). 1996. ISBN 07148-35242

Dal Co, Francesco and Mazzariol, Giuseppe. *Carlo Scarpa: The Complete Works*. Electa Editrice/Rizzolli. 1984. ISBN 0-8478-0686-3

Diller, Liz and Scofidio, Ric. *Flesh – Architectural Probes*. Triangle Architectural Publishing. 1994. ISBN 1-87125-040-0

Edwards, C. *Interior Design: A Critical Introduction*. Berg. 2010. ISBN-13 978-1847883124

Evans, Robin. *Translation from Drawing to Building and Other Essays*. Architectural Association: London. 1997. ISBN 1-870890-68

Ferguson, Russell. *Robert Irwin*. Rizzoli. 1993. ISBN 0-8478-1770-9

Gregotti, Vittorio. *Inside Architecture*. MIT Press. 1996. ISBN 0-262-57115-3

Harvey, David. *The Condition of Postmodernity*. Blackwell. 1990. ISBN 0-631-162294-1

Holl, S. *Anchoring*. Princeton Architectural Press. 1999

Hollis, E. *The Secret Lives of Buildings: From the Parthenon to the Vegas Strip in Thirteen Stories*. Portobello Books. 2010. ISBN 978-1846271281

Hollis, E., Milligan, A., Plunkett, D., Gigli, J. and Hay, F. (Eds). *Thinking Inside the Box: A Reader in Interiors for the 21st Century*. Middlesex University Press. ISBN 978-1904750222

Hudson, Jennifer. *Interior Architecture: From Brief to Build*. Laurence King. 2010. ISBN-13 978-1856696975

Hudson, Jennifer. *Interior Architecture Now!* Laurence King. 2007. ISBN-13 978-1856695206

Kurtich, John and Eakin, Garret. *Interior Architecture*. Van Nostrand Reinhold. 1993. ISBN 0-442-24669-2

Lefebvre, H. *The Production of Space*. Wiley-Blackwell. 1991. ISBN-13 978-0631181774

Littlefield, David and Lewis, S. *Architectural Voices – Listening to Old Buildings*. Wiley. 2008. ISBN 978-0470016732

Los, Sergio. *Carlo Scarpa: An Architectural Guide*. Arsenale Editrice srl. 1995. ISBN 88-7743-144-X

Marot, S. *Sub-Urbanism and the Art of Memory*. AA Publications. 2003. ISBN 1-902902-26-2

Massey, A. *Interior Design since 1900*. Thames and Hudson. 2008. ISBN-13 978-0500203972

Mastropietro, Mario. (Ed). *Restoration and Beyond – Architecture from Conservation to Conversion. Projects and Works by Andrea Bruno (1960–1995)*. Edizioni Lybra Immagine. 1996

McKellar, S. and Sparke, P. (Eds). *Interior Design and Identity*. Manchester University Press. 2004. ISBN 0-7910-67289-4

Myzelev, A. and Potvin, J. *Fashion, Interior Design and the Contours of Modern Identity*. Ashgate. 2010. ISBN-13 978-0754669159

Nesbitt, Kate. (Ed). *Theorizing a New Agenda for Architecture: An Anthology of Architectural Theory 1965–1995*. Princeton Architectural Press. 1996. ISBN 1-56898-054-X

Olsberg, Nicholas. *Carlo Scarpa: Intervening with History*. Canadian Centre for Architecture and the Monacelli Press to accompany the exhibition. 1999. ISBN 0-920785-61-1 (cca). ISBN 1-58093-035-2 (monacelli)

Parissien, S. *Interiors: The Home since 1700*. Laurence King. ISBN-13 978-1856695381

Pile, John. *A History of Interior Design*. Laurence King. 2009. ISBN-13 978-1856695961

Plunkett, Drew. *Drawing for Interior Design*. Laurence King. 2009. ISBN-13 978-1856696227

Praz, M. *An Illustrated History of Interior Decoration: From Pompeii to Art Nouveau*. Thames and Hudson. 1982. ISBN-13 978-0500233580

Ranalli, George. *George Ranalli*. Princeton Architectural Press. 1988. ISBN 0-910413-42-8

Rendell, Jane. *Site-Writing: The Architecture of Art Criticism*. 2010. ISBN-13 978-1845119997

Rice, Charles. *The Emergence of the Interior*. Routledge. 2006. ISBN-13 978-0415384681

Risselada, Max. (Ed). *Raumplan versus Plan Libre*. Rizzoli. 1988. ISBN 0-8478-1000-3

Robert, Philippe. *Adaptations: New Uses for Old Buildings*. Princeton Architectural Press. 1989. ISBN 0-910413-73-8

Rossi, A. *The Architecture of the City*. MIT Press. 1982

Rowe, Colin and Koetter, Fred. *Collage City*. MIT Press. 1978. ISBN 0-262-18086-3

Ruskin, J. *The Seven Lamps of Architecture*. George Allen

Schittich, Christian. (Ed). *In Detail: Interior Spaces: Space, Light, Materials*. Birkhauser in co-operation with *Detail Magazine*. Published 2002. ISBN 3-7643-6630-3

Schittich, Christian. (Ed). *In Detail: Building in Existing Fabric: Refurbishment, Extensions, New Designs*. Birkhauser. 2003. ISBN 978-3762536024

Scott, F. *On Altering Architecture*. Routledge. 2007. ISBN-10 978-0415317528

Spankie, R. *Drawing out the Interior*. AVA Publishing. 2009. 978-2940373888

Sparke, P., Massey, A., Keeble, T. and Martin, B. *Designing the Modern Interior: From the Victorians to Today*. Berg. 2009. ISBN-13 978-1847882882

Stiles, Kristine and Selz, Peter. *Theories and Documents of Contemporary Art*. University of California Press. 1996. ISBN 0-520-20253-8

Strike, J. *Architecture in Conservation*. Routledge

Taylor, M. and Preston, J. *Intimus: Interior Design Theory Reader*. Wiley-Academy. 2006. ISBN-10 0470015713

Thornton, P. *Authentic Décor: The Domestic Interior 1620–1920*. Weidenfeld and Nicolson. 1993. ISBN 0-297-83239-5

Trocme, S. *Influential Interiors*. Mitchel Beazley. 1999. ISBN 1-84000-101-1

Various Contributors. *Old and New Architecture: Design Relationship*. The Preservation Press. 1980. ISBN 0-89133-076-3

Index